FAILURE AND NERVE
IN THE ACADEMIC STUDY OF RELIGION

FAILURE AND NERVE
IN THE ACADEMIC STUDY OF RELIGION

Essays in Honor of Donald Wiebe

Edited by
William E. Arnal,
Willi Braun and
Russell T. McCutcheon

Routledge
Taylor & Francis Group

LONDON AND NEW YORK

First Published 2012 by Equinox Publishing Ltd, an imprint of Acumen

Published 2014 by Routledge
2 Park Square, Milton Park, Abingdon, Oxon OX14 4RN
711 Third Avenue, New York, NY 10017, USA

First issued in paperback 2017

Routledge is an imprint of the Taylor and Francis Group, an informa business

Notices
Practitioners and researchers must always rely on their own experience and knowledge in evaluating and using any information, methods, compounds, or experiments described herein. In using such information or methods they should be mindful of their own safety and the safety of others, including parties for whom they have a professional responsibility.

To the fullest extent of the law, neither the Publisher nor the authors, contributors, or editors, assume any liability for any injury and/or damage to persons or property as a matter of products liability, negligence or otherwise, or from any use or operation of any methods, products, instructions, or ideas contained in the material herein.

ISBN 13: 978-1-138-11020-5 (pbk)
ISBN 13: 978-1-84553-898-9 (hbk)

British Library Cataloguing-in-Publication Data
A catalogue record for this book is available from the British Library.

Library of Congress Cataloging-in-Publication Data

Failure and nerve in the academic study of religion : essays in honor of Donald Wiebe / edited by William E. Arnal, Willi Braun, and Russell T. McCutcheon.
    p. cm.
Includes bibliographical references and index.
ISBN 978-1-84553-898-9 (hardcover)
1. Religion--Study and teaching. 2. Religion--Hermeneutics. 3. Wiebe, Donald, 1943- I. Wiebe, Donald, 1943- II. Arnal, William E. (William Edward), 1967- III. Braun, Willi, 1954- IV. McCutcheon, Russell T., 1961-
 BL41.F35 2012
 200.71--dc23
                           2012021686

Typeset by Forthcoming Publications Ltd

CONTENTS

Preface   vii
Acknowledgments   x
Contributors   xi

The Nerve of Donald Wiebe   1
   Luther H. Martin

The Failure of Nerve in the Academic Study of Religion   6
   Donald Wiebe

General Failures

Catching Up with Marx: Truth, Myth, and the Niceties of "Belief"   34
   Matthew Day

Fixed Geomorphologies and the Shifting Sands of Time   50
   Darlene M. Juschka

A Critical History of Religion as a Psychological Phenomenon   62
   Janet Klippenstein

Everything Old Is New Again   78
   Russell T. McCutcheon

Revisiting the Confessional: Donald Wiebe's "Small 'c'
Confessional," Its Historical Entailments and Linguistic
Entanglements   95
   Johannes C. Wolfart

Special Failures

Failures (of Nerve?) in the Study of Islamic Origins   112
  Herbert Berg

The Failure of Islamic Studies Post-9/11: A Contextualization
and Analysis   129
  Aaron W. Hughes

Religious Studies that *Really* Schmecks: Introducing Food to
the Academic Study of Religion   147
  Michel Desjardins

Cultural Anthropology and Corinthian Food Fights: Structure and
History in the Lord's Dinner   157
  John W. Parrish

The Identity of Q in the First Century: Reproducing a Theological
Narrative   177
  Sarah E. Rollens

The Failure of Nerve to Recognize Violence in Early Christianity:
The Case of the Parable of the Assassin   192
  T. Nicholas Schonhoffer[†]

Redescribing Iconoclasm: Holey Frescoes and Identity Formation   218
  Vaia Touna

In Lieu of Conclusion

The Irony of Religion   230
  William Arnal and Willi Braun

Index of Authors   239

PREFACE

> A sower went out to sow. And as he sowed, some seed fell along the path, and the birds came and devoured it... And other seeds fell into good soil and brought forth grain, growing up and increasing and yielding thirtyfold and sixtyfold and a hundredfold. (Mark 4:3–4, 8)

Using Donald Wiebe's programmatic 1984 essay as its organizational center, this collection of new essays further documents, refines, and examines his thesis that the academic study of religion suffers from a failure of intellectual nerve. When judged by the efforts of those who are today commonly recognized to be the late nineteenth-century founders of the field, this failure comprises an unwillingness to continue to distinguish sharply comparative religion, as pursued in the modern research university, from confessional, even broadly humanistic, studies that ought to be carried out only in denominationally affiliated institutions. In further documenting this problem—over twenty-five years after Wiebe first diagnosed it and now doing so at a far wider variety of sites across the field—the contributors press Wiebe's original case considerably further, both in terms of adding new evidence to the argument and greater nuance to its force. The contributors to this volume therefore all share the view that conceptualizing religion as an element of the mundane world of human doings is the first requirement of a public inquiry into the history and function of religion. Additionally, they are all in agreement that this requirement has consistently not been met.

Although those who are interested in pursuing a rigorously historical study of religion may lament that such an intellectual failure continues, in bringing together scholars writing not only from across the field but, more importantly perhaps, from different career stages, we are hopeful that this volume will reanimate this debate while also introducing new readers to Wiebe's dogged pursuit of a study of religion free from ahistorical assumptions and motives—whether concerning God, the Sacred, Mystery, Meaning, or some sort of enduring and timeless Human Nature. That not all of the contributors agree completely with Wiebe when it comes to documenting and diagnosing these failures—or, more accurately, that some are not convinced that it is sufficient simply to define the issue as theology versus a truly scientific study of religion—is, we think, an indication that his argument has legs, as they say.

The collection opens with a chapter by Luther H. Martin, Wiebe's longtime friend and collaborator; Martin's essay, followed by a reprint of Wiebe's own 1984 essay, "The Failure of Nerve in the Academic Study of Religion," set the stage for the chapters that follow. They provide both Wiebe's initial assessment of disciplinary failures and an insight into the author who penned the spirited critique with which the contributors were all invited to work—not simply reply to or to apply Wiebe's essay, but to work with it, develop it, press it and, if needed, refine it and move beyond it. The chapters that follow do this at two sites; adopting a division common throughout the history of the field (e.g., as seen in the works of phenomenologists and an earlier generation of comparativists), there are those authors who document failures at a general or methodological level, on the one hand, and then there are those who focus instead on failures in tradition- or data-specific sites. The collection then closes with a proposal for how to correct the field's recurring failures.

Whether trained by him at the University of Toronto or representatives of the succeeding generation who were either schooled by Wiebe's own students or who work in a tradition indebted to Wiebe's own efforts (e.g., our inclusion of the previous and the newly appointed editor of *Method & Theory in the Study of Religion*, a peer review periodical founded in 1989 by graduate students at the University of Toronto and, in part, inspired by Wiebe's critique of the field), the contributors each occupy a place in a critical school of thought in which Wiebe has played a significant role for the past thirty or so years. If we were less timid we might brand it the Toronto School of Thought, in honor of Wiebe's longtime home institution, the place where the editors all carried out their own doctoral studies in the late 1980s and early 1990s—during which time Wiebe played a key leadership role in determining what constituted legitimate graduate education in the study of religion. But significant differences of opinion among those who worked at what was then called the Centre for Religious Studies—differences still in evidence in what is now known as the Graduate Centre for the Study of Religion—concerning how the study of religion ought to proceed would make such a label overly ambitious. In fact, Wiebe has himself documented, in *The Politics of Religious Studies* (1999: Chapter 13), the various failures of nerve that have haunted this particular program over the years. The phrase "Toronto School of Thought" is therefore too ambiguous to do much good in providing a framework around which to organize this volume's chapters.

Although Wiebe's criticisms might be judged by some to be impudent, we believe that it is just this sort of nerve that is needed continually to draw our colleagues' collective attention to the mundane but nonetheless fascinating products of mundane but nonetheless fascinating human beings, rather than focusing on such things as texts, practices, and institutions as if they somehow floated free of their authors and the always messy historical, social, and political situations from which they arose. Documenting and correcting the failures of one's peers therefore takes nerve and that, we have concluded, is what unites this volume's authors. That representatives of succeeding generations of scholars are up to the challenge is, we hope, a tribute to what Don, as a teacher, a scholar, and a good friend, has consistently sowed in our academic field.

Acknowledgments

We would like to thank Ryan Olfert, a former graduate student at the University of Alberta, and now studying at the University of Toronto, for his help in preparing this manuscript, and also Ian Brown, then a graduate student at the University of Regina and now also at the University of Toronto, for helping to prepare Donald Wiebe's own essay for publication. We would also like to thank the Canadian journal, *Studies in Religion / Sciences Religieuses* (*SR*), for kindly permitting the reprint of Wiebe's essay, which originally appeared in *SR* 13 (1984): 401–22. We are also grateful to Janet Joyce and Val Hall, of Equinox Publishing, for their interest in the volume as well as their assistance to help keep it a secret despite their own interests in advertising it early. We also wish to thank Luther Martin who, when learning of Don's suspicion that a volume entitled *Failure and Nerve in the Academic Study of Religion* was in the works, was able to keep him off the scent by criticizing the audaciousness of the editors' for only slightly adapting (i.e., stealing) the title from one of Don's own essays, for a book of their own, without even consulting or including him. That Don's own essay is indeed included in the volume, and that all three editors have consulted Don on too many past occasions to count, suggests just what a good storyteller Luther is.

CONTRIBUTORS

William Arnal, University of Regina

Herbert Berg, University of North Carolina at Wilmington

Willi Braun, University of Alberta

Matthew Day, Florida State University

Michel Desjardins, Wilfrid Laurier University

Aaron W. Hughes, State University of New York, at Buffalo

Darlene M. Juschka, University of Regina

Janet Klippenstein, University of Alberta

Luther H. Martin, University of Vermont

Russell T. McCutcheon, University of Alabama

John W. Parrish, Brown University

Sarah E. Rollens, University of Toronto

T. Nicholas Schonhoffer[†], University of Toronto

Vaia Touna, University of Alberta

Donald Wiebe, Trinity College, University of Toronto

Johannes C. Wolfart, Carleton University

[T]heology, when it commits itself to the existence of the Ultimate, constitutes a form of religious thought that can only "infect" the academic study of religion and not complement it.

—Donald Wiebe (1984: 421)

THE NERVE OF DONALD WIEBE

Luther H. Martin

Nihil agit qui diffidentem verbis solatur suis:
Is est amicus, qui in re dubia re juvat, ubi re est opus.
                                        —Plautus, *Epidicus* 1.2.9

I am privileged to count Don Wiebe as one of my closest friends as well as a professional colleague and collaborator. For at least the past twenty years, we have read and criticized virtually everything the other has written (although Don rarely accepts my brilliant suggestions for his rewrites), he is a prolific author and editor (he checks with me regularly to ensure that the number of his publications continues to exceed mine), we recommend new theoretical and empirical studies to one another (Don is an avid reader; some would say promiscuously so), we have collaborated on writing articles, on founding professional societies, on organizing conferences; we have traveled together to, or met in, distant places in attempts to foster the study of religion, we have given lectures at our respective institutions, we have been to one another's home for food and drink (and, yes, Don does *occasionally* enjoy a gin and tonic [though he continues to prefer his diet soda]). My own professional life has benefited immeasurably from our collaborations (although I must acknowledge that, at times, Don's incessant arguments do push things a bit far. Perhaps our living 800 miles apart has helped; as his Mennonite forebears have it: *'Ne Hakj tweschen Frind bewoaht 'ne jreene Frintschoft*[1]).

I first met Don in 1975 at the XIIIth Congress of the International Association for the History of Religion (IAHR) at the University of Lancaster, where he had completed his PhD dissertation the previous year with Ninian Smart. Tom Lawson (E. Thomas Lawson) and I were also young scholars in the field and already interested in problems of theory and method in the study of religion (though, it must be admitted that, at the time, I was reading

---

1. Translation: "A hedge between friends preserves a green friendship."

the works of Carl Jung and Tom was excited about Black Elk). At a time when *sui generis* views and hermeneutical interpretations of religion dominated, Tom and I were immediately attracted to Don's presentation, "Is a Science of Religion Possible?" ([1978], based on his Lancaster dissertation "Science, Religion and Rationality: Questions of Method in Science and Theology"). As anyone who knows the three of us might imagine, we spent the remainder of the Congress in one another's company "frankly discussing" (i.e., arguing) about the study of religion. Don has since confided that when he returned to Canada, he told his wife, Gloria, that he had met two scholars in Lancaster who—though very interesting—he sincerely hoped he would never encounter again. That, however, was not to be.

Apart from meeting *en passant* at meetings of the American Academy of Religion (AAR), the next significant meeting of Don, Tom and I was in 1985 at the XVth Congress of the IAHR in Sydney, Australia, where, against Tom's and my advice, Don gave a paper that we thought was somewhat less impressive than his Lancaster presentation. Nevertheless, the three of us collaborated at that time to found the North American Association for the Study of Religion (NAASR), in order

> to encourage the historical, comparative, structural, theoretical, and cognitive approaches to the study of religion among North American scholars; to represent North American scholars of religion at the international level; and to sustain communication between North American scholars and their international colleagues engaged in the study of religion.

The founding of NAASR represented a response to the question raised by Don a decade earlier, about the possibility for a scientific study of religion; the three of us thought there was. At the same time, the AAR, founded as the professional society for scholars of religion in American colleges and universities, had begun to move in quite another, explicitly non-scientific, direction: sections devoted to the "academic study of religion," to "theory and method in the study of religion," even to "comparative religion," disappeared from the program of its annual meeting and overtly religious groups and organizations were invited to join. This anti-theoretical direction of the AAR was emphasized by its formal rejection of NAASR's application to become a "related society." This rebuff was motivated by fears among members of the AAR Executive Committee about the theoretical and scientific direction in the field of religious studies represented by our nascent group. (These fears were reported to us over a number of years by a member of that Committee.) The emphasis on theory and method in the study of religion represented by NAASR, began, however, to gain national and then international significance with the founding and increasing success of NAASR's journal *Method & Theory in the Study of Religion* (*MTSR*)—a journal initially founded by graduate students at the University of Toronto.

Over the years, Don has been an active participate in NAASR and in the IAHR, and has held leadership roles in both. His longtime service on the NAASR Advisory Committee, his organization and direction of the XIVth Quinquennial Congress of the IAHR at Winnipeg in 1980 and especially his role as Director of the XXth Congress of the IAHR at Toronto in 2010 represent highpoints of this participation. Despite the (expected) displeasure of some at the academic and scientific nature of the program in Toronto, a majority of participants in this latter Congress acknowledged and appreciated that this was perhaps the most intellectually honest conference in the study of religion they had ever attended. Don's contributions to the IAHR and to international scholarship generally were recognized by the Executive Committee of the IAHR when he was honored at the Toronto Congress with "Lifetime Honorary Membership" in the IAHR.

The possibility of a scientific study of religion in the context of modern university education and research, and its clear demarcation from religious and theological pursuits, has, of course, been the central theme of Don's work since his presentation at Lancaster in 1975—although his emphasis has shifted from this first presentation, when he was still under the influence of his Mennonite background, to one of his most cited articles (and the inspiration for the theme of this volume), "The Failure of Nerve in the Academic Study of Religion" (1984) to his monograph *The Irony of Theology* (1991). Although Don's intellectual commitment to a science of religion has remained constant, *Irony* completed his personal journey from passionate advocate for Mennonite Brethren religiosity, through a period of "methodological" atheism in the study of religion (a perspective he rightly continues to advocate for all academic work), to his present (though personal) stance of non-theism. Don speaks of an on-going nagging presentiment in this direction that he could no longer deny after thinking through and completing this monograph. As he concluded this study:

> to assume that we must find a new interpretation of science or religion that
> entails their compatibility and complementarity is unnecessary, unless, of
> course, our central concern is really a "theological" one. (1991: 227)

Don's early query about the possibility of a science of religion was no longer a question for him; it had become his intellectual and academic commitment. This commitment has most recently taken institutional form with his founding in Toronto of the Institute for the Advanced Study of Religion (IASR), the formal organization that actually organized and hosted the Toronto Congress of the IAHR.

Don's dogged commitment to scientific method, that is, to a dispassionate, intersubjective and critical pursuit of knowledge, has earned him a reputation of being something of a cantankerous provocateur—which, of course, he is. He talks about his pleasure at "rattling the cages" of entrenched interests. I recall one instance already in 1990 when Don presented quite a nice paper at a regional meeting of the AAR. When he completed his presentation, everyone in attendance expressed their agreement with and appreciation of the arguments he had presented. Unable to bear such acceptance, Don immediately added unnecessarily immoderate comments to his presentation that infuriated all. He then smiled with satisfaction and was happy. Nevertheless, Don delights in exposing hypocrisy in academia, whether inconsistent arguments in published articles or in papers presented at meetings of professional societies (a role for which he actually prepares in advance) or whether hypocritical applications for funding to support naturalistic "scientific research" from religiously interested sources (with, of course, their incumbent strings attached). Don has worked tirelessly to advance a truly scientific study of religion not only through his insightful philosophical "exposés" and sharp—sometimes unforgiving—critiques of what he calls "covert" theological agendas underlying and informing avowedly scientific research but through an unstinting contribution of his own time and resources to advance intellectual debate in this area. Though the establishment of a truly scientific study of religion faces enormous odds with virtually no prospect in sight for its general success, Don soldiers on in what many consider a Quixotic quest.

Don's sense of integrity is manifest not only in his approach to the study of religion but in his participation in institutional politics as well, especially in defending the underdog against bureaucratic heavy-handedness. Despite the sometimes unpopular nature of a cause, Don will take on all comers—from individual administrators to entire institutions—if he believes that principles of fairness or due process have been compromised—employing tactics which he delightedly refers to as "academic guerrilla warfare." But, as the old Latin playwright Plautus observed already in the second century B.C.E., "he does nothing who seeks to console a desponding person with words; a friend is one who aids with deeds at a critical time where deeds are called for." And Don's words have always been backed by his deeds.

When Don thinks he is right—which he often is—he will employ his formidable philosophical, rhetorical and political skills to buttress his currently favored position. And, if he turns out to be wrong—which he just as often is—he will acknowledge this as well (…sometimes). While Don is parochially viewed by some as a petty irritant in the field, he is internationally viewed by many more—by colleagues, by students, by those who have only read his articles—as an intellectual mentor and model for their own attempts to pursue a truly scientific study of religion. I have, over the years, come to have the utmost respect for Don's principled stands, rare in the pragmatic politics of university life and, perhaps, even more rare in light of the quotidian pressures of our intellectual pursuits. Although our field of study continues to falter as a scientific undertaking, it is nevertheless stronger and possesses greater integrity as an academic pursuit in the "modern research university" because of Don's tireless efforts on its behalf.

References

Wiebe, Donald. 1978. "Is a Science of Religion Possible?" *Studies in Religion*: 7: 5–17.
———. 1984. "The Failure of Nerve in the Academic Study of Religion." *Studies in Religion* 13: 401–22.
———. 1991. *The Irony of Theology and the Nature of Religious Thought*. Montreal and Kingston: McGill-Queen's University Press.

THE FAILURE OF NERVE
IN THE ACADEMIC STUDY OF RELIGION*

Donald Wiebe

1.

My concern in this essay is with the relationship of theology to the study of religion, and, more particularly, to the academic study of religion. I shall not, however, focus attention here on such legitimate concerns that theology may have with the results of academic research on religion (e.g., Drummond 1975; Gualtieri 1972; and Wiebe 1978), or with historical or institutional questions concerning the two communities of scholars (e.g., Edsman 1974; Pannenberg 1976; Sharpe 1975, 1983; and Hebblethwaite 1980: Chapter 2), nor with the fact that, as an element of the overall configuration of religion, theology is, obviously, a focus of interest and concern to the academic student of religion (e.g., Smart 1973: Chapter 4; Werblowsky 1959, 1975). It is, rather, the methodological problems implicit in that relationship that interest me, although putting the matter this way makes barely visible the burden of my argument. Stated bluntly, it seems to me that raising the question of theology's relationship to the academic study of religion on the methodological level jeopardizes the very existence of such an academic study for it opens to debate once again who or what it is that ought to set the

* This essay is a revised version of a paper prepared for the Eastern International Regional Meeting of the American Academy of Religion held at McMaster University in the spring of 1984. I wish to thank the participants, especially Mr. Lorne Dawson, for their helpful comments and criticisms. I am also grateful to Peter Slater whose criticisms of an early draft of this paper were of great assistance in its revision. [Ed. note: apart from changing the citation style and addressing some general stylistic issues, this chapter reproduces the 1984 original of this essay; for ease of reference the pagination to that published version appears in brackets throughout this chapter. All quotations of this essay in subsequent chapters in this book will refer to the original pagination followed by a bracketed reference to the essay's pagination in this volume. This essay also appears in Donald Wiebe's *The Politics of Religious Studies: The Continuing Conflict with Theology in the Academy*, 141–62. New York: St. Martin's Press, 1999.]

agenda for, and therefore to control, such a study; is it the scholar-scientist or the scholar-devotee, the church or the academy, the procedures of science or the (supposed) transcendent subject-matter of that science, etc.?

I shall show here that the study of religion gained a political identity within the academic community (i.e., the scholarly-scientific community), precisely by distinguishing itself from theology. I shall also show that there is a vigorous new call for an explicit role for theology in "religious **[402]** studies"—for an "interpenetration" of the two (for the use of such imagery see, amongst others, Drummond 1975 and Kitagawa 1971). And I shall argue that, even though it has always remained under pressure from a hidden (although invariably unconscious) theological agenda of many of its practitioners, it is the present call for re-establishing an explicit role for theology within its boundaries that constitutes a rejection of the scientific/ academic goals it originally espoused and, therefore, constitutes a massive "failure of nerve" by the academic community in religious studies.[1]

2.

Some clarification of the meaning of the concept of "theology" must precede the development of the argument of this paper. This is especially so in light of criticism of the ambiguity of my use of that term in earlier discussions,[2]

1. The phrase, "failure of nerve," which carries the thesis of this paper, is borrowed from Gilbert Murray and is used essentially in the same sense he gave it in his *Five Stages of Greek Religion* (1955). Murray used that phrase to characterize the shift from the confidence in human effort and trust in the enlightened mind since the emergence of philosophy with the Presocratics to the rise of asceticism and mysticism after Plato and Aristotle (see also Hook 1961). Other scholars, unfortunately, have used the phrase in quite a different way and even to the point of reversing its original intent (e.g., Raschke 1983; Sharpe 1971; and especially McClelland 1983). The Enlightenment, as I point out below, is the soil out of which the academic study of religion emerges. If Peter Gay's interpretation of that development as the re-establishing of the derailed Presocratic Enlightenment is anywhere near the truth (1966: xi, 44, 72–127), the use of Murray's phrase in this essay is particularly apposite.

2. See Mostert 1976. In hope of avoiding unnecessary confusion I point out here that the concept "theology" is used in a less specific sense than it is employed by theologians and that, therefore, its rejection here as part of religious studies ought not, in itself, to be taken as an argument for the rejection of theology per se. As used here—and generally in the methodological literature pertaining to religious studies—it symbolizes religious mentation whether in the narrative pattern of thought of the naïve devotee or of the discursive structure of the reflective and systematic thought of the intellectually more sophisticated devotee. Only "theoretical theology" will be used with a sense of "religious neutrality" but, as will become clear, there is a question as to whether it constitutes a distinct mode of thought (a discipline) since its supposed task is indistinguishable from that of the philosophy of religion.

and misinterpretations of earlier statements of my position that would place me inside the "theological camp."[3] Furthermore, the claim by Charles **[403]** Davis (1975) that the conflict between theology and religious studies is due to a failure of the antagonists to recognize a radical shift of meaning in the use of the concept with the mediaeval philosophers, especially with and after Thomas Aquinas, suggests that the argument to be taken up here is based simply on ignorance of the historical facts.[4]

In trying to account for the history of "God-talk" ("god-talk") and talk about God (the gods), or any other functionally equivalent Ultimate, I find it helpful to distinguish "confessional theology" from "non-confessional theology." The basis of the distinction is, essentially, a presuppositional one. Confessional theologies presume the *existence* of some kind of Ultimate, Transmundane Reality whereas non-confessional theologies recognize the cultural *reality* of "the gods" (i.e., some Transcendent Reality) and attempt rationally to account for it but without presuming that such an account is possible only on the supposition that "the Ultimate" *exists*.[5] Such a "theoretical theology" or theology proper, therefore, in attempting to provide a rational account of the reality of the gods leaves open the possibility for a reductionistic account.[6] As a truly scientific enterprise, theology must hold God (the Ultimate) as problematic, as I shall argue again later in this paper.[7]

I point out, furthermore, that not all confessional theologies are of the same order. I distinguish, for example, small "c" *confessional theology* from capital "C" *Confessional Theology*—the latter being the general sense commonly used to refer to the exclusivist theologies of particular creeds and

3.   This especially by Phillip B. Riley, "Theology and/or Religious Studies: A Case Study of *Studies in Religion / Sciences Religieuses*, 1971–1981," a paper presented at the 1983 meeting of the Canadian Society for the Study of Religion. A new version of that paper appeared in *Studies in Religion* (1984) and revises that judgment somewhat.

4.   I would, if time permitted, dispute this claim. I agree with Davis that theoretical theology emerges in the Middle Ages, but I would argue that he himself has not seen the full significance of that development. It seems to me that Bernard of Clairvaux saw the significance of the "new theology" of Peter Abelard, and others, more clearly than does Davis. A descriptive account of that conflict can be found in Leclercq 1961, and a persuasive alternative interpretation of its import can be found in Nelson 1981. The two kinds of theology, I would maintain, have the same tensions between them as are to be found between the religious and scientific communities in recent Western history. I hope to take up this whole problem, in a book to be entitled *The Irony of Theology* in the near future. [Ed. note: See Wiebe 1991.]

5.   On the distinction between the reality and existence of the Focus of the devotee's attention, see Smart 1973.

6.   The type of theology I have in mind here is that to be found, for example, in thinkers like Ludwig Feuerbach, or, more recently, the Christian atheism of the 1960s.

7.   This is done, for example, by Pannenberg (1976).

confessions in the history of Western religious thought.[8] Small "c" confessional theology, however, is used to cover *even* the more general acknowledgment or affirmation of the ontic reality (existence) of the [404] "Focus" of religion—that is, the independent existence of some Ultimate or other which religious discourse expresses or to which it refers.

Such distinctions, I suggest, will help students of religion to recognize that there is a radical difference between persons who acknowledge both the existence and the claim of a transcendent and sacred reality on their lives and those who do not—even when that claim is not tied to a particular historical and exclusivist understanding of revelation or something of the sort. That non-specific and non-exclusivistic "confession" I take here to be "confession" nonetheless, despite its lack of specificity.

To clarify further the notion of theology as it is used in this essay I shall respond, briefly, to Charles Davis's claim that a properly critical theology, which emerged with mediaeval Christendom, is wholly compatible with religious studies. Even for Davis there is a "theology" from which the academic study of religion is rightly separated, namely, that theology which is nothing more than an elaboration of a particular religious tradition or faith and that, therefore, merely presupposes and reconfirms it. This corresponds to what I have referred to above as Confessional theology and is rejected by Davis in favor of a critical or theoretical theology. The distinction between a naive and critical theology is not, however, clearly drawn and his conception of critical or theoretical theology will be seen to differ vastly from mine and to show much more the character of small "c" confessional theology as I have described it above.

Confusion is generated in Davis's discussion of this matter by several apparent reversals of meaning in his use of theological terminology. This occurs, for example, when he compares and contrasts concepts of "theology as a whole," "the properly theological," and the various theologies—historical, systematic, theoretical, foundational, Confessional, etc. At one point Davis insists that "Confessional theology" is not really theology at all (Davis 1975: 212). And his claim that systematic theology is concerned essentially with the ordered exposition of the doctrines of a particular tradition which rests on revelation and authority (1975: 212) seems contradicted by his further claim that the science of religion is simply a more advanced stage of systematic theology and not something essentially different (1975: 219)

8. It might be argued that a further distinction within capital "C" confessional theology is also necessary in order to account for the differences between the main Confessional churches of the Reformation and the groups of the left-wing or radical reformation that explicitly distinguished themselves from the mainstream and did not consider themselves Confessional in that sense. This is not, however, a problem that need be settled here. (I wish to thank Thomas Yoder Neufeld for drawing this point to my attention.)

while still maintaining that he has kept the term theology simply to refer to "reflection" upon religion and *not* for the process of expression and communication belonging to religion as such (1975: 220).

His claim to be using "theology" in a non-partisan and critical fashion is further undermined in his assumption that "the religious," whether it be experience, expression, or activity, is sufficiently different from other social phenomena for it to become the object of a distinct and special science.[9] The assumption excludes, a priori, reductionistic explanations of **[405]** religion on the rather tautologous grounds that "Religious phenomena...call for a direct investigation to analyze their common elements..." (Davis 1975: 214). This is "reinforced" later in the essay by the old claim that "the science of religion is an empirical enquiry distinguished from sociology and psychology by its primary concern with religious data as religious" (1975: 219). All of this amounts, of course, to the uncritical assumption that since theology, as "rational discourse about God," exists, then God too must exist—which is a patent *non sequitur*. That assumption, I suggest in light of philosophical discussion of this matter,[10] constitutes acceptance of what might be called "the presumption of theism" and makes of Davis a small "c" confessional theologian.[11]

To conclude: it is not theology of the theoretical kind that does not refuse to countenance the Ultimate as problematic, with which I take issue here, for such a theology, as "a rational account" of God or the gods, leaves open the possibility of an account that could be reductionistic. All uncritical thinking about God or the gods that rests on revelation and authority or on the "presumption of theism," and that, therefore, refuses to countenance the possible non-existence of God or the gods, is "confessional theology." Such theology constitutes a species of what I prefer to think of as "religious thought" which operates entirely within the framework of general religious assumptions, or within a particular religious tradition and is, therefore, incompatible with what will be referred to below as the basic minimum presuppositions for the academic study of religion.

9.   Similar arguments can be found in, amongst others, Streng 1970 and Klostermaier 1977.

10.   On this topic see Flew 1972. (The response to this essay by D. Evans and Flew's reply do not affect the substance of this article.)

11.   Davis's argument here might, on first sight, seem to find support in the attempt by R. Morgan and Michael Pye to "refit" Ernst Troeltsch. Troeltsch maintained that the positivist/materialist method of study was unacceptable in this field because it, in an a priori fashion, precludes the possibility that religion is veridical rather than illusory. A closer reading of Troeltsch, and the commentaries by Morgan and Pye, however, reveals rather Troeltsch's methodological idealism to be guilty of that misdemeanor. Space does not permit elaboration of that critique here. See the essays by Troeltsch and the Morgan and Pye commentaries in *Ernst Troeltsch: Writings on Theology and Religion* (1977).

3.

The scholarly study of religion as something other than a religious exercise[12] has a very long history; it, by far, antedates the institutionalized and academically legitimated study of religion that emerged in the last quarter of the nineteenth century.[13] And it is important to see that its acceptance in **[406]** the academic domain was not occasioned by a natural and spontaneous recognition either of its academic style or significance. Rather, it came about as a result of a quest for such recognition that required establishing the "scientific objectivity of religious studies"—a quest that, as has often been pointed out, is the product of the Enlightenment. This in turn required giving up the theological interests and Confessional stance that had characterized much of that study in the past.[14] Indeed, in some countries, although not all, the new study replaced the theological faculty altogether—France is a case in point (Sharpe 1975). In this sense Neusner (1977b) is right to suggest that the "new" academic student of religion attempted to overcome an unwanted past, although I think his further claim that s/he actually succeeded in the attempt is inflated. Wach (1951, 1958) and Kitagawa (1958) similarly talk of the study of religion being emancipated from a theological agenda whereas Friedrichs (1974) talks of the "detheologizing" of the subject. The study of religion it was hoped, therefore, would be neutral, objective, and scientific. This meant adopting a notion of a universally applicable mode of inquiry, implying that religion and the religions were to be studied in exactly the

12.   The scholarly study of religion has, in all major "world religions," always been a religious exercise and still is. On this score see, for example, Klostermaier 1978. On the suggestion that the academic study of religion substitute as a religious exercise, see Goodenough 1959. For a pejorative view of the same notion see section 5 below.

13.   The best source available for details on this development is Sharpe 1975; however, see also Jastrow 1981 and de Vries 1967.

14.   See, for example, Dawson's "Natural Theology and the Scientific Study of Religion" (in Dawson 1960) or Ogden 1978. It might be argued that the early practitioners of the new style of religious studies wished only to liberate that study from direct ecclesiastical control and therefore were ready "to give up," so to speak, only capital "C" Confessional theology, while still seeking to integrate that new study with their small "c" confessional stances. Even a superficial reading of the methodological literature of the period, however, will show the *intent* of the rejection of "Confessional theology" to be much more radical than that. Its intent was to allow the students of religion to prescind having to settle the "apparently unresolvable" ontological and metaphysical questions that preclude any "convergence of opinion/belief" even on the level of "confessional theology." Nevertheless, it is true, as I point out in section 4 below, that much of the work of these early practitioners in this field could, quite appropriately, be described as a species of "confessional theology." However, "doing theology" is not only *not* their conscious intention but rather, when noticed as being unintentionally present, is taken to be a contamination of their study.

same way as any other social phenomenon. The scholar *qua* scholar, therefore, was to eliminate her/his religious commitments from her/his studies. Its several concerns included: (1) the morphology of religion involving primarily a description of rites, rituals, beliefs, practices, art, and architecture, etc., of the various historical religions; (2) the "facts" of religious development; (3) the "parallels" amongst the various traditions; and, later, (4) the phenomenology of religious meaning and the structure of religions. The study, then, was primarily empirical, heavily centered on philological and historical concerns resulting in the production of scholarly **[407]** monographs, and, later, general handbooks, comparative analyses, and interpretive studies.

The institutionalization of this new study was not only to be found in the universities; an international association (The International Association for the History of Religions) was eventually formed in the 1950s—although International Congresses had been held from 1900 on. Under the pressure of various religious sentiments, especially as the Association expanded membership to include religious scholars from the far East (Sharpe 1975: Chapter 6), theological and religious matters began to appear on the agenda of its Congresses. This led to a reformulation of the scientific goals and intentions of the new study (*Religionswissenschaft*) by R. J. Zwi Werblowsky to which many members of the Association appended their names (Werblowsky 1960).[15] That five-point statement of "the basic minimum presuppositions" for the pursuit of historical and comparative studies of religion was reproduced in *Numen*, the official publication of the IAHR (as summarized by Schimmel 1960). A summary of that statement here will provide a kind of benchmark for the "retreat to theology" which I shall attempt to document below: (1) "Comparative religion"/*Religionswissenschaft* is a well-organized scientific discipline; (2) *Religionswissenschaft* is a branch of the humanities, but as such

> it is an anthropological discipline, studying the religious phenomenon as a creation, feature and aspect of human culture. The common ground on which students of religion *qua* students of religion meet is the realization that the awareness of the numinous or the experience of transcendence (where these happen to exist in religions) are—whatever else they may be—undoubtedly empirical facts of human existence and history, to be studied like all human facts, by appropriate method. (Schimmel 1960)

(3) *Religionswissenschaft* rejects the claim that religion is a *sui generis* phenomenon with its implicit claim that it can only be understood if seen, ultimately, to be a realization of transcendent truth; (4) that though the study

---

15. It is important to note here that Eliade and Kitagawa signed this positivist-sounding statement despite their sympathies lying elsewhere, as I point out below. See, on this point, Sharpe 1975: Chapter 6.

of religion may first arise out of non-academic motivation, it needs no such external justification; and (5) the Association must keep itself free of all ideological commitments (see also Werblowsky 1956, 1959, 1975).

This program, drafted by Werblowsky, was not, however, a Comtean *ersatz* religion as some critics are ready, it seems, to charge (e.g., Davis 1981). Werblowsky's review of Joachim Wach's "theological" approach to the study of religion leaves no doubt about that: "Of course historical analysis can never yield the norms without which life is not worth living…but, then, nobody [408] ever supposed historical analysis to do just that. There is, after all, a world of difference between study and living, between studying history and making it" (1959: 354).

4.

Religious studies, it is obvious, gained the academic legitimation it sought. But, I shall argue, it failed to live up to the commitments it had given the academic community to pursue its agenda in a religiously non-partisan fashion. Sharpe (1975: Chapter 6) points out, for example, that in the early days of the "discipline"[16] religious studies was still considered to be religious instruction even if not on the narrow scale found in theological faculties—an impression that was bolstered by the close association of some of its leading practitioners (e.g., F. Max Müller), with movements like the World Parliament of Religions held in Chicago in the 1890s. And Kitagawa has noted, in a review of the subject in the USA, that although its early formation followed European "scientific" lines, it lost out to the pressures of conservatism and orthodoxy (Kitagawa 1959, 1983; see also Jastrow 1981). Further suspicion is cast upon the discipline by the fact that the majority of those attached to the field hail from a religious background and entered the discipline, or so it would appear, with a theological agenda (see, for example, Oxtoby 1968 and Drobin 1982). And this is further compounded by the complaint, often voiced by Bleeker (1961, 1975), and still heard today, that the IAHR was not (and is not) able to attract the social scientists interested in the study of religious phenomena into the Association. As Oxtoby put it, religious studies was off limits to science "as being not scientific enough" (1968: 591).

I do not mean to suggest here, however, that scholars were being consciously duplicitous—indeed, they quite self-consciously "bracketed" their own *particular* religious beliefs and sentiments deriving from their specific

---

16. I put scare quotes around the word discipline because I use it as a word of convenience and do not assume that the academic study of religion is a discipline. See my own "Is a Science of Religion Possible?" (1978) and *Religion and Truth: Towards an Alternative Paradigm for the Study of Religion* (1981).

historical forms of religion and made this "bracketing" a general **[409]** requirement of their discipline. Thus emerged the general methodological agreement, a purely conventionalist stratagem and a good one at that, that the truth-question not be raised in religious studies. The academic study of religion was to forego the philosophical/metaphysical task of determining the truth or falsity of the various historical religious traditions which had thus far been an unsuccessful and divisive theological exercise. It is not that those who adopted the *epoché* denigrated that metaphysical exercise or denied its value in other contexts but just that, for the sake of achieving a short-range goal of a convergence of scholarly opinion on more general religious matters with other researchers from a wide range of competing metaphysical/theological frameworks, they agreed to restrict their concerns to less speculative, more positive matters where all could agree on the criteria of assessment to be applied to the claims.

The *epoché*, it is true therefore, freed the student and the study of religion from ecclesiastical control or domination, although there was still a certain amount of theological suspicion that attached itself to those so engaged (Oxtoby 1968: 591). However, there are several methodological corollaries implied in the *epoché* that suggest that such a study of religion, even though free from a certain ecclesiastical and therefore Confessional theological domination, is yet heavily influenced by a religious/theological commitment. The most important corollary, as I have referred to it elsewhere, is the "descriptivist doctrine," especially when it is held in connection with the widely held belief that such a study constitutes a new discipline, namely, that of the "science of religion" (Wiebe 1978). Stated negatively, the corollary implicit in the *epoché* requires that the study of religion must remain free of theory and forego explaining the religious phenomenon under consideration. To explain, it was argued, is to assume either that the phenomenon is, in some sense, illusory or veridical, and that is to invoke the very category of truth that the *epoché* banished in its attempt to achieve a neutrality that could ground an academic study of religion. However, the enterprise, if it is to be scientific (i.e., nomothetic and not merely ideographic [see Wiebe 1975 and 1983]), must necessarily move beyond description to explanation and theory. This can be done without entering the metaphysical/theological fray and so, without contravening the conventionalist stratagem of the *epoché*, by means of a comparative analysis of the cognitive components (both substantive and methodological) of the religious tradition concerned with that of the cognitive universe of the investigator. If the "cognitive worlds" clash, the student of religion is licensed, so to speak, to seek for alternative accounts of the religious phenomenon in terms of factors, elements, or aspects of human existence that are not in themselves religious. And it is this possible reductionist accounting for religion that the "descriptivist doctrine" is meant to preclude. "To explain" is "to explain away" and that, it appears, must be avoided at all costs. But to avoid that possibility altogether is to assume that it can never be "explained away." That a priori exclusion, I **[410]** suggest, however, indicates a religious/theological bias, for it presumes an ontic reality for religion that it may not really have.

The first corollary is complemented by the doctrine of "the autonomy of religion." Although quite obviously circular, it is argued that since the *discipline* of religious studies exists it must have a peculiar subject-matter not amenable to other kinds of analyses. Consequently, it is insisted, religion must be treated "on its own terms" for it is a *sui generis* phenomenon. To see it as anything other than "religious" is not "taking religion seriously" (amongst others, see especially Bleeker 1954, 1963, and 1971).

Taken together, the *epoché* and its corollaries imply that "religious studies" is a true science with a methodology peculiar to itself—distinct from theology/religion on the one hand and the physical and social sciences on the other. I have shown elsewhere (Wiebe 1978), however, that this "argument" is incoherent because it is based on mutually exclusive sets of assumptions and, furthermore, fails to delineate, in any clear or precise way, a methodology peculiar to itself.

My arguments on this score have been harshly criticized as gross distortions of the original intent of the founding fathers of this "new" science and of their successors (Widengren 1983). It has been claimed that the science is not restricted to the descriptive level but rather that it goes beyond that ideographic level to understanding. Widengren chooses as exemplar of such an approach the work of Bleeker who goes beyond mere "fact gathering" in his study of religion to phenomenological understanding (Bleeker 1954: 147–50; 1971: 18–19). I do not deny that Bleeker does in fact wish to transcend the purely fact-gathering stage, as do most of his colleagues, but wish only to point up the problematic character of that particular way of doing so. The understanding that Bleeker seeks, that is, quite obviously accepts a priori, is the validity of the devotee's position, for the *epoché* and bracketing are still very much in effect in this exercise. The devotee's position—that is, the self-understanding of the devotee—is the norm of this supra-descriptive task. This principle was accepted early on in "science of religion" circles, as can be seen, for example, in F. M. Müller's adoption of "comparative theology" as an element of such a science. The student, he insists, must deal with the facts as s/he finds them so that "if people regard their religion as revealed, it is to them a revealed religion and has to be treated as such by every impartial historian."[17] **[411]**

---

17. Müller 1893: lecture 4. Apart from Bleeker, see also Kristensen 1960; Smith 1959, 1963, and 1984 (the Presidential Address to the American Academy of Religion, Dallas, TX, November 1983).

It is not to be doubted that such understanding as phenomenology seeks to attain goes beyond the descriptive historical and philological fact-gathering referred to above. The question that needs to be raised, however, is whether it is still description, although at a deeper level, or whether it goes beyond the ideographic level to a truly nomothetic understanding of religion. If it is the latter, however, its *epoché* in fact amounts to an a priori acceptance of some ontic religious reality even though it persistently refuses to commit itself publicly, or even privately, to any particular historical manifestation of that reality. It is logically impossible, consequently, for a reductionist account to provide any understanding of religion, which means that religion—any and every religion—puts persons in contact with what is ultimately real, true, and good. *Understanding* automatically precludes any more basic causal explanation. Where causal explanations are applicable they are of limited value and one must seek and understand *beyond* explanation.[18] Such an "understanding," I maintain, constitutes a non-specific theology in that it assumes the ontic reality of the religious phenomenon but is not aligned with any particular historical religious tradition's view of that reality, at least at the level of explicit consciousness (Oxtoby 1968). It rests, quite uncritically, on the assumption of the (cognitive and metaphysical) validity of "religion in general."[19]

5.

What I hope to show in this section of the paper is that the hidden theological agenda present in religious studies has now, so to speak, come out of the closet. I do not wish here to assess why that is the case—what soil it is that gives root to these explicit attacks on the scientific study of religion.[20] **[412]**

---

18.   The concept of understanding used in this fashion has an existentialist/religious connotation in that it suggests that it constitutes not simply knowledge about religion but perception of a reality that goes beyond knowledge and, therefore, constitutes a kind of knowledge that goes beyond ordinary knowledge. That, surely, makes the concept somewhat suspicious and certainly places it in need of further analysis. This is not a task that can be taken up here. On this matter consult Waardenburg 1973.

19.   This constitutes, I think, a kind of "theology of humanism" and, therefore, an implicit religion. It is clearly on display in, for example, Blumental 1977: 23–39.

20.   Some discussion of such issues can be found in Kegley 1978 and Kaufman 1983. The image of "attack" regarding the opposition to a scientific study of religion is quite appropriate given the level of hostility expressed by a number of authors. Much of the literature degenerates into invective and is hardly worth analysis, but it does indicate the vehemence that lies behind the *reaction* to which I have referred as "a failure of nerve" and the extent of the fear generated by the Enlightenment that the academic life might be alien to the intellectual life of faith, or that it might transcend it. Amongst others see

Neusner's suggestion, just a few short years ago (1977a), that the academic study of religion in America and Canada has developed a set of norms that exclude religiosity in the classroom and that a study characterized by detachment and objectivity has, therefore, been established seems to me a fairytale and shows a simple blindness to the literature as the discussion to follow will show. Furthermore, the evidence, in terms of what goes on in our departments of religious studies and in our other academic institutions simply will not support his claim, but documentation of this will have to be left for another paper.[21]

Space, quite obviously, will not permit a detailed analysis of all the positions and arguments against what has been referred to above as a "detheologized" academic study of religion. This treatment, therefore, is not exhaustive and I shall attempt here to delineate only the major kinds of stances taken. Furthermore, I am not even wholly sure that the two major types of argument and their subdivisions that I shall set out here are clearly distinguishable from each other, nor that they are but seldom found in pure and pristine form in the authors they will be referred to. However, the typology offered here will be of some assistance in coming to terms with a large and growing body of literature and the overview that will be provided will at least indicate the disturbing trend in religious studies that would jettison the gains it has inherited from and since the Enlightenment.

The more common type of argument to be found in this literature, I think, is best designated the "complementarity thesis." The claim usually put forward is not that religious studies is useless or inhibitive in our search for understanding religious phenomena but simply that it is, in and of itself, inadequate. The "heart of religion," that is, is simply not perceived if it is treated "in purely informative, descriptive, scientific terms" (Kegley 1978: 280). "One must go *beyond* the historical and socio-scientific approach that adheres simply to [413] empirical methods of data collection and description or even explanation" (Mostert 1976: 8, 9), or, as one might put it, the proper

Ladner 1972; Novak 1972a: 65–78; 1972b; Burrell 1983; and Marty 1983. Others guilty of the same tack, such as Robert Bellah or W. C. Smith, are discussed below.

21.   I have in mind here the development in Canadian universities, for example, of rather close, official ties to church-related colleges characterized predominantly by their "advocacy learning" environment. See, on this score, Neufeldt 1983. It is also important to note that some Canadian universities have funded appointments financed by religious groups in the community since such a procedure contributes to a blurring of the distinction between religion and the study of religion. This type of activity has received some attention with respect to "study conferences" underwritten by the Unification Church in a recent "Symposium on Scholarship and Sponsorship," including I. L. Horowitz, B. R. Wilson, J. A. Beckford, E. Barker, T. Robbins, and R. Wallis, in *Sociological Analysis* 44 (1983).

study of religion "entails more than employing the intellectual instruments of criticism and analysis to investigate various forms of faith and belief" (Ladner 1972: 216). This is something that has been forgotten, so it is argued, in the shallowness fostered by an expansion of religious studies in the recent past which has erroneously led us to believe "that we are finally getting our intellectual foot in the academic door of secular education" (1972: 212).

Bernard E. Meland, in an early essay in this genre, raises serious questions about the assumption that the student of religion need only be concerned with "objective methods" (Meland 1961). According to Meland, the student of religion must somehow be different than the regular historian or the run-of-the-mill social scientist. The student of religion "is not *just* a historian or a scientist in the sense that defines the anthropologist or social scientist. He is a student of religions in a specific and specialized sense," involving "deeper" dimensions of religion (1961: 269–70; my emphasis). And Kees Bolle, although he admits that the study of religion, historically for example, is an enterprise that has its own validity and that emphasis on its use in the early days assisted the establishment of university centers and departments for such study of religion, denies that it *alone* will "make our field accepta-ble in a modern academic framework" (Bolle 1967: 98). Indeed, he argues that, without complement, it would bring the discipline to an end: "Religious phenomena, [he writes], are never *just* intellectual propositions or *just* indi-vidual affairs. Hence neither can the manner in which religious phenomena are approached have its center in logical investigation and a resulting syn-thesis of general laws *alone*, even if the individual following this method is a master in the fields of logic and anthropology" (1967: 100; my emphasis).

Such complementarity as here described might best be characterized as "incremental complementarity." It is unidirectional, so to speak, with the academic study of religion being "increased" by theology as, say, physics is exceeded by chemistry. Theology, that is, is an entirely different way of knowing than the knowing of science which increases our information or the structured pattern of information. As one exponent of the position puts it, the student of religion cannot remain detached in an information gathering exercise but must rather share in the religious experience of the devotee. And he maintains that "this…is not a call for indoctrination but for the wooing of the spirit" (Kegley 1978: 280; see also Holley 1978). It is true, however, that Kegley sees not a merely **[414]** unilinear kind of comple-mentarity but rather a "mutual benefitting" between theology and religious studies: "Theology without serious religious studies tends to pious arro-gance; religious studies without theology tends to parasitical aloofness. In a dialectical encounter, both may thrive" (Kegley 1978: 282).

A similar "mutual complementarity" thesis is to be found in Drummond: "If theologians need the history of religions to give fullbodiedness and contemporary relevance to their own work, the historians of religion need theology in order to come to grips with that which they are really supposed to deal—the central elements of the religious life of humankind" (1975: 403). And J. P. Mostert insists that "it rests with theology to illuminate its [i.e., religion's] ultimate depth dimension" (1976: 12), as do Meland and Bolle (e.g., 1967: 116) and others, although the last mentioned at least calls for a "deprovincializing of Christian theology" in the process.[22]

"Incremental complementarity," however, does not exhaust the type; there is also the response that might well be referred to as "incorporative complementarity." This position stands halfway between the simple "complementarity thesis" and the "identity thesis" which I shall discuss below. It does not fully insist on the distinction between religious studies and theology but rather points to the subordination of the former to the latter. The position seems to be well expressed by Jeffner in the conclusion to his paper on "Religion and Understanding":

> [R]eligion can be seen as a kind of understanding and explanation of a part of reality. Such religious understanding is parallel to other kinds of understanding, e.g., the scientific one. But religious understanding aims at an understanding of our total situation, in other words an all-inclusive understanding. The religious all-inclusive understanding need not be opposed to a scientific understanding of a part of reality, but it is opposed to a scientific world view and a scientific all-inclusive understanding. (1981: 225)[23]

Science, then, has its place, but it is subordinate; it can only make its contribution within a wider frame of reference. Theologians taking up this stance, therefore, usually "hybridize" disciplines and tend to talk of "religio-sciences" such as "religio-sociology," or "religio-ecology," or "religio-history," etc. (Wiebe 1983). As Kitagawa, himself an exemplar of this class, puts it regarding Joachim Wach's work, there is an attempt to "combine the insights and methods of *Religionswissenschaft*, philosophy of religion, and theology" (Kitagawa 1958: xxxviii). As one sees in Wach's writings and activities, this implies that although one does not, as a student of religion, wish to give up the ideal of objectivity, one comes to recognize that such objectivity has *strict limits* within a broader version in which "neutrality" is not possible. "What is required," he writes, "is not indifference, as positivism in its heydey be-[415] lieved…but rather engagement of

22. Bolle, that is, seems to be asking for "Confessional theology" to be replaced by "confessional theology."

23. This paper is one of several contributions to a European Conference on the Philosophy of Religion included in this number of the journal that are relevant to this topic.

feeling, interest, *metexis*, or participation" (Wach 1951: 9). And to settle for less is to adopt a form of scientism (Wach 1951, 1954, 1967). Kitagawa follows Wach faithfully in this matter, invoking the use of such, apparently new, disciplines as religio-sociology and religio-science in an effort to show the "syntheses" of disciplines and the "interpenetration" of disciplines for which Wach sought (Kitagawa 1971, 1975).

But Wach and Kitagawa are not the only representatives of this position. Indeed, as Kitagawa points out, this line of thought goes back to Wach's Marburg teachers including F. Heiler and Rudolph Otto. He argues that Wach, in effect, redefined the task of religious studies in relation to theology "following the example of Rudolph Otto" (Kitagawa 1975: 49). "What Wach envisages," he writes, "is the interpenetration between constructive theology, which is informed and purified by careful studies of history of religions, and history of religions, itself liberated from the 'narrowly defined' scientific approach to the study of religion" (1975: 52). Other scholars in this tradition, it seems to me, include, *inter alia*, Paul Tillich (1963, 1966; see also Burkle 1981), Mircea Eliade (1969), and his many "disciples" (e.g., Girardot and Rickets 1982). What one finds to be common to all, however, is what Kitagawa found to be essential to Wach's efforts to penetrate deeply into the nature of religion, namely, "the recognition of the objective character of ultimate reality" (1971: 46). That notion is usually tied up with the concept of *meaning* which involves, it would appear, a perception of a "something" that transcends (even where the imagery is that of depth rather than height) what is easily obtained outwardly or externally by the sciences.[24] The sciences, including the scientific study of religion, therefore, are subordinated to the religious vision. Science, that is, cannot ultimately comprehend religion; it remains, in Wach's words, "one of the inexplicable mysteries which have accompanied the ascent of man" (Wach 1944: 307).

[416] This sense of Mystery, I maintain, is essentially a religious quality of mind—a general confessional stance. And I would argue that it is a state of mind characteristic of all those proposed methods for the study of religion that subordinate the "outsider," detached, scientific approach to religion to the "insider" approach. An increasing number of essays supporting an insider approach to the study of religion are still being published but there is neither time nor space to analyse them here.[25]

---

24. The concept of meaning is both complex and ambiguous and requires a good deal of further clarification if it is to be a helpful interpretive category for the student of religion. Even bibliographical orientation would take more space than can be allowed here and must, therefore, be left for another paper.

25. Amongst others, see: Streng 1970, 1974; Reat 1983; Vernoff 1963; Martin 1975; and Blumental 1977. There are several essays by Neusner that seem to support this kind of position but do so ambiguously. Because of that ambiguity I reserve discussion of his

The final type of argument for a re-theologized religious studies to be found in the literature is but a mutation of the preceding form. I refer to it here as the "identity thesis" for it amounts to the claim that upon final analysis of the nature and task of theology and religious studies they will in fact be found to be essentially the same enterprise. This position has been set out on an elaborate scale by Pannenberg (1976) within the framework of a defense of theology as a science and therefore as an academic discipline. He admits that theology can, as a first approximation, be described as the "science of Christianity," but if Christianity is seen as only one religion amongst many others in the context of the history of religions, it should rather be placed under the general heading of the science of religion (1976: 256). That kind of unity that "reduces" theology to a sub-discipline, however, he rejects. He argues that theology does justice to Christianity only as a science of "God," where that term stands for "reality-as-a-whole" but does admit that an "anthropological turn" has taken place in theology that makes the concept problematic and theology itself, therefore, problematic. He then seems, however, to attempt to ground that hypothetical theology in the science of religion (1976: 346), whose thematic, as he puts it, is "the communication of divine reality experienced in them" (1976: 365). This then amounts to a **[417]** critical theology of religions "in virtue of its attempt to examine the specifically religious theme of religious traditions and ways of life, the divine reality which appeared in them, and not some other psychological or sociological aspect" (1976: 365–66). Theology, therefore, seems to be the science of religion when that task is being properly carried out. In an earlier essay he put forward an identical characterization of theology and the science of religion, but there he admitted that the exercise is not only or simply historical but rather a kind of "religious-historical" research and therefore a religious exercise (1971: 116).

position for another context. Further studies, moreover, seem to be in preparation for publication. The *Journal of the American Academy of Religion*, I understand, is soon to publish papers on this topic by J. Neusner, W. May, J. Cahill, W. Capps, and L. J. O'Connell (see O'Connell 1984). O'Connell's article appeared after this paper was written and so no account of it has been taken into consideration here although the paper is wholly in "the failure of nerve" stream as I have developed above. O'Connell does, however, refer to the forthcoming articles which he prepared for the *Journal of the American Academy of Religion* (1984: 146). W. Nicholls's recent paper to the Canadian Society for the Study of Religion annual meeting of this year in Guelph, entitled "Spirituality and Criticism in the Hermeneutics of Religion," and Jack Wiggins's presentation of a paper on "Theology and Religious Studies" at this year's Eastern International Regional Meeting of the American Academy of Religion at McMaster University are also likely to see publication in the near future.

Pannenberg's kind of stance is also taken up by a number of other scholars. An almost identical, although much briefer statement is presented, for example, by Hebblethwaite (1980: Chapter 2). Carl-Martin Edsman has pointed out, as well, that religious studies when placed in faculties of theology, as it has often been, have not fared badly, and he maintains that those who call for a separation of the two disciplines are ignorant propagandists unaware of the strictly scientific scholarship in both fields (1974: 70). Galloway also maintains that it is in the human quest for truth that we see "the *unity* and integrity of our disciplines" (1975: 165). And Paul Wiebe, although disclaiming any connection with the systematic theologies taught at seminaries, maintains that religious studies is a constructive science, not merely self-reflective and historical, and therefore indistinguishable from theology (P. Wiebe 1975: 18, 23). As he puts it: "the creation of norms is the final good of religious studies. This is to say that the real impetus behind the investigation of religion is not a mere intellectual or aesthetic curiosity, but is a desire for existential truth" (1975: 23). This position, of course, makes it obvious that the so-called academic discipline is also at the same time a religious activity. This is certainly reminiscent of Paul Tillich's view of the history of religion as but a form of theology that is in the process of transformation into what he calls the religion of the concrete spirit.

Charles Davis similarly maintains that once one recognizes theoretical theology for what it really is (and has been since at least the Middle Ages), the modern development of the science of religion will be seen to be in continuity with that dynamic thrust (Davis 1975: 207).[26] He does, on one level, insist that to study religion is not itself a religious exercise (1975: 207) but still maintains that theology cannot simply be seen as **[418]** a datum but must be on the same level as the science of religion (1975: 208). Consequently he talks of a convergence of the two disciplines, for each has as its primary concern religious data as religious (1975: 219), even though this seems to conflict with his earlier disclaimer about the religiosity of that study. He concludes, therefore, that "the science of religion is…a more advanced stage of systematic theology, [and] not an essentially different enterprise" (1975: 219).

There is a rude twist on the identity thesis that is often to be found in the literature. It is often claimed, that is, that the so-called academic study of religion is itself a religion and therefore simply a rival religious faith to the established religious traditions. This was the burden, for example, of W. C. Smith's 1983 presidential address to the American Academy of Religion (Smith 1984). It is, of course, the bulk of Smith's methodological message to the community of academic students of religion. Since I have discussed

---

26.   See also Baum et al., "Responses to Charles Davis," in the same issue of *Studies in Religion* (1975).

his position on a variety of occasions I shall say no more here.[27] The most vocal exponent of this thesis, in my opinion, however, is Bellah. He readily admits that he has no anxiety about blurring the boundary line between religion and the teaching of religion—of infecting, so to speak, the study with its own subject matter (1970b: 4). Indeed, he insists that this cannot be done since "whatever fundamental stance one takes in teaching about religion is in itself a religious position" (1970b: 4), although he does elsewhere (Bellah 1970a: 95) refer to it as implicitly religious. In the latter article he refers to his position as one of "symbolic realism" which is both academically sound, according to him, and self-consciously religious. Indeed, he maintains that it "is the *only* adequate basis for the social scientific study of religion" (1970a: 93; my emphasis).[28]

Paul Ingram captures the sentiments of Bellah well in his methodological statement against the "cartesian methodology" that is "basically a technology for manipulating "religious data" into precise intelligible patterns that can be understood by anyone who followed the same technical procedures" (Ingram 1976: 392). Rather than attempting to seize the truth about religion the students must be seized by truth and insight in spite of the methodologies they may hold (1976: 394). And Walter Capps also talks about the need to fight **[419]** against "the monopolozing compact between the Enlightenment and religious studies" (1978: 104). Religious studies, that is, must involve itself, as does theology, in the process of the formation of the truth (1978: 105). This, then, is the dominant "story" one hears from an ever-expanding circle of spokespersons for religious studies.

6.

Although lengthy, this review is neither an exhaustive (even including materials consulted for this paper but not cited) nor at all a detailed account of the bewildering variety of arguments that call for a return to theology in religious studies; a turn to religion and the Supermundane, to Ultimate Reality and the Truth. But the account does document the claim that the objective, detached, and scientific study of religion that was so eagerly sought for in the heady days of the late nineteenth century is now past. We have here a return to religion under the pressure, it would seem, of the breakdown of our culture (Altizer 1961: 172–74), but, I would argue, it is not religion from which we have wandered. To believe that we are returning to our origins, so to speak, is sheer illusion. The "limitations" of the classroom in our bid to understand religion (Neusner 1977a) have not so much led to a misunderstanding of religion, I would suggest, as they have fostered the creation of

27. See here especially Wiebe 1979 and Wiebe, Slater, and Horvath 1981.
28. For similar statements see also Bellah 1972 and 1978.

what Robert Michaelson has called a "classroom religion" (1972).[29] Bellah's symbolic realism is, I think, an example of precisely that, but it is arguable as to whether, with respect to the religious traditions originally studied by the academic community, such an interpretation is not itself reductionistic. Bellah's attempt to save religion from the students of religion, I am afraid, is about as effective as Durkheim's attempt to rescue the reality of religion from its "demise" at the hands of the intellectualist (largely British) anthropologists. But this argument cannot be taken up here.[30]

Before leaving this matter, however, I should like to focus special attention on my own academic community in Canada which I think is aptly described as having "lost its nerve" in this enterprise—if it ever had it—as is obvious in the work of Davis discussed above. In a more recent essay on theology and religious studies he categorically insists that a scientific study of religion is simply *not* compatible with a complete refusal of religious faith (Davis 1981: 13). That mind-set, moreover, shows itself in a much broader fashion as **[420]** well in Davis's work as editor of the Canadian journal *Studies in Religion*. The conclusions drawn by Riley after a close content analysis of the journal in the first ten years of its existence is that the journal has been devoted to "collaboration between theologians and religionists" (Riley 1984).[31] Indeed, he suggests—I think correctly so—that this is the distinctive contribution of the journal and, I would maintain, with only slight qualification, that the societies of which the journal is the official publication are quite happy with the ideological direction it has taken.

The editorial policy of Davis, moreover, continues a long tradition. In this regard it is interesting to note that, in some sense, *SR* is a continuation of the old *Canadian Journal of Theology*. That journal, experiencing financial difficulties and being unable to secure Canada Council funding because of its "religious character," signed away its existence to the new religious studies periodical that was able to secure such government funding. In return, however, the *Canadian Journal of Theology* group received assurance from William Nicholls, the first editor of *SR*, that the new journal would not abandon its theological readership. That was a promise that has been kept faithfully.[32]

---

29. A slightly different view can be found in McClelland 1972.

30. See here, for example, Aron's parallel critique of Durkheim (1967: 56).

31. Riley here expresses that judgment in agreement with and in the words of Charles Davis.

32. In fairness it must be noted that clarification of this whole matter is needed since Professor Nicholls has recently informed me that the theological turn taken by *Studies in Religion* was not an intentional policy of his or the result of any promise freely given by him. Whether his disappointment and mine with that "theological turn" converge or not is something we need to explore further.

This is not, of course, the only indication of the character of religious studies in Canada. The influence of W. C. Smith on the Canadian scene is almost all-pervasive and it is most certainly an influence favoring the "re-theologizing" of religious studies. Riley, in his look at *SR*, claims that Smith's "work and influence perhaps more than that of any individual, permeates the pages of *SR*,"[33] and the claim applies equally well, I think, to his influence on religious studies in general in this country and elsewhere,[34] although space does not permit substantiating that claim here. Other events in the emergence and operation of departments for the study of religion in Canada that I have already adverted to[35] would also support the claim made here.

[421]

7.

It was with some surprise that I found myself taken to be an exponent of the very position I have argued against here.[36] In my discussion of the possibility of a science of religion, it is true, I did admit that religious studies might well contain theological elements (Wiebe 1978). The "theology" I had in mind was one of scientific character in that, as I thought it possible, it could accept the demands of intellectual honesty in the sense of abandoning any absolute/ultimate commitments, leaving itself open to radical change, including abandonment of its position.[37] In this sense, which unfortunately I did not clearly explain, theology (philosophical, theoretical, or scientific), as "the rationale of God or the gods" countenances the possibility of reduction- ism, although it does not, quite obviously, necessitate it. It is for this reason that I found it reasonable to talk of the possibility of the study of religion proceeding from the point of view of the "critical participant" (or "detached devotee") while yet refusing to recognize an "autonomous discipline" that presupposes the "autonomy of the subject matter" of the discipline, that is, God, the gods, the Transcendent, the Ultimate Reality, etc. The a priori acceptance of (or belief in) the reality and existence of the Ultimate is, on

33. This judgment appears in the earlier version of his paper presented to the Canadian Society for the Study of Religion in 1983 (see n. 5 above).

34. In support of this claim see, for example, Gaultieri 1969 and 1981. Gaultieri is himself a good example of the results of that influence; see, for example, 1968, 1972, and 1979. There are a number of other influential Canadian scholars who show a similar influence, but to whose work I cannot even advert here, and still others who argue a similar case quite independently. It seems to me that they, jointly, dominate the Canadian scene.

35. See n. 23 above.

36. See n. 5 above.

37. I expressed that understanding of theology earlier in Wiebe 1973.

the other hand, a species of religious thinking and, if it is to be called theology at all, ought to be referred to as "confessional theology." And it is this kind of theologizing that I have been arguing is incompatible with religious studies since it, in fact, constitutes the subject matter of that study. As I have pointed out in my discussion of Davis and others above, to accept without question, as a condition of the Study, the existence of an Ultimate Reality, is to espouse and promote confessional theology, even if it is of a more ecumenical variety than in the past. Consequently, to avoid any further ambiguity, I reiterate here that theology, when it commits itself to the existence of the Ultimate, constitutes a form of religious thought that can only "infect" the academic study of religion and not complement it.[38]

Confusion on this matter was also created here by my failure to point out clearly that the "critical insider" and "sympathetic outsider" converge, and ought to do so, only on the descriptive level but need not necessarily do so on the explanatory/theoretical level of that study.[39] The confusions are **[422]** due, it appears to me now, to my earlier and predominant (Christian) apologetic concerns.[40] In my essay on the role of explanation in the study of religion (Wiebe 1975), however, even though showing some sympathy for the argument of the "insiders," I expressed "nagging doubts" about the matter but did not pursue this issue further at the time.

In this paper I have taken that matter up again and, I think, with a little more clarity. I have shown that the explicit agenda adopted by the "founders" of religious studies as an academic (university) concern committed the enterprise to an objective, detached, scientific understanding of religion wholly uninfected by any sentiment of religiosity. I also pointed out that the actual practice of that study was (and still is) dominated by a hidden theological agenda but that the *epoché* invoked by its practitioners provided, nevertheless, the ground for, and beginning of, a new tradition of thought on matters religious. And, finally, I have shown that the crypto-theological

---

38. Burkert expresses this conflict between religion and the study of religion most succinctly in his translated *Homo Necans* (1983), which is worth repetition here: "The language that has proved the most generally understood and cross-cultural is that of secularized scholarship. Its practice today is determined by science in its broadest sense, its system of rules by the laws of logic. It may, of course, seem the most questionable endeavor of all to try to translate religious phenomena into this language; by its self-conception, a religion must deny that such explanations are possible. However, scholarship is free to study even the rejection of knowledge and repudiation of independent thought, for scholarship, in attempting to understand the world, has the broader perspective here and cannot abstain from analyzing the worldwide fact of religion. This is not a hopeless undertaking. *However, a discussion of religion must then be anything but religious*" (xxi; my emphasis).

39. See section 4 of this paper.

40. This was the primary focus of my doctoral work at the University of Lancaster.

agenda informing, even if only subconsciously, that study is being brought out of the closet and proclaimed as the only proper method for the study of religion. That step, I have argued here, wipes out the tentative move towards the development of a scientific study of religion heralded in the *epoché* of the first generation of *Religionswissenschaftler* and, therefore, constitutes a failure of nerve in the academic study of religion.

References

Altizer, Thomas J. J. 1961. *Oriental Mysticism and Biblical Eschatology*. Philadelphia: Westminster Press.

Aron, Raymond. 1967. *Main Currents in Sociological Thought*, vol. 2. London: Penguin Books.

Baum, Gregory et al. 1975. "Responses to Charles Davis." *Studies in Religion* 4: 222–36.

Bellah, Robert N. 1970a. "Christianity and Symbolic Realism," *Journal for the Scientific Study of Religion* 9: 89–96.

———. 1970b. "Confessions of a Former Establishment Fundamentalist." *Council for the Study of Religion Bulletin* 1/3: 3–6.

———. 1972. "Religion in the University: Changing Consciousness, Changing Structures." In Claude Welch, ed., *Religion in the Undergraduate Curriculum*, 16–21. Washington: Association of American Colleges.

———. 1978. "Religious Studies as 'New Religion'." In J. Needleman and G. Baker, eds, *Understanding the New Religions*, 106–12. New York: Seabury Press.

Bleeker, C. Jouco. 1954. "The Relation of the History of Religions to Kindred Religious Sciences, Particularly Theology, Sociology of Religion, Psychology of Religion and Phenomenology of Religion." *Numen* 1: 142–52.

———. 1961. "The Future Task of the History of Religions." *Internationaler Kongress für Religionsgeschichte*, 229–40. Marburg: N. G. Elwert.

———. 1963. "The Phenomenological Method." In C. J. Bleeker, ed., *The Sacred Bridge*, 1–15. Leiden: Brill.

———. 1971. "Comparing the Religio-Historical and the Theological Method." *Numen* 18: 9–29.

———. 1975. "The History of Religions: 1950–1975. The Organized Study of the History of Religions During a Quarter of a Century." Lancaster, UK: University of Lancaster. (Pamphlet published on the occasion of the XIIIth Congress of the International Association for the History of Religion.)

Blumental, David R. 1977. "Judaic Studies: An Exercise in the Humanities." *Response at the Inauguration of the Jay and Leslie Cohen Chair of Judaic Studies*, 23–39. Atlanta, GA: Emory University Press.

Bolle, Kees W. 1967. "History of Religions with a Hermeneutic Oriented Toward Christian Theology?" In Joseph Kitagawa, Mircea Eliade, and Charles H. Long, eds, *The History of Religions: Essays on the Problem of Understanding*, 89–118. Chicago: University of Chicago Press.

Burkert, Walter. 1983. *Homo Necans: The Anthropology of Ancient Greek Sacrificial Ritual and Myth*. Los Angeles: University of California Press.

Burkle, Howard R. 1981. "Tillich's 'Dynamic-Typological' Approach to the History of Religions." *Journal of the American Academy of Religion* 49: 175–85.

Burrell, David. 1983. "Faith and Religious Convictions: Studies in Comparative Epistemology." *The Journal of Religion* 63: 64–73.

Capps, Walter H. 1978. "The Interpenetration of New Religions and Religious Studies." In J. Needleman and G. Baker, eds, *Understanding the New Religions*, 101–5. New York: Seabury Press.

Davis, Charles. 1975. "The Reconvergence of Theology and Religious Studies." *Studies in Religion* 4: 205–21.

———. 1981. "Theology and Religious Studies." *Scottish Journal of Religious Studies* 2: 11–20.

Dawson, Christopher. 1960. *Religion and Culture*. New York: Meridian Books.

Drobin, Kaj Ulf. 1982. "Psychology, Philosophy, Theology, Epistemology: Some Reflections." In Nils G. Holm, ed., *Religious Ecstasy*, 263–74. Stockholm: University of Stockholm Press.

Drummond, Richard H. 1975. "Christian Theology and the History of Religions." *Journal of Ecumenical Studies* 12: 389–405.

Edsman, Carl-Martin. 1974. "Theology or Religious Studies?" *Religion* 4: 59–74.

Eliade, Mircea. 1969. *The Quest: History and Meaning of Religion*. Chicago: University of Chicago Press.

Flew, Anthony. 1972. "The Presumption of Atheism." *Canadian Journal of Philosophy* 2: 29–46.

Friedrichs, Robert W. 1974. "Social Research and Theology: End of Detente?" *Review of Religious Research* 15: 113–27.

Galloway, A. D. 1975. "Theology and Religious Studies: The Unity of our Discipline." *Religious Studies* 11: 157–65.

Gay, Peter. 1966. *The Enlightenment: An Interpretation: The Rise of Modern Paganism*. New York: Random House.

Girardot Norman J. and M. L. Ricketts, eds. 1982. *Imagination and Meaning: The Scholarly and Literary Worlds of Mircea Eliade*. New York: Seabury Press.

Goodenough, E. R. 1959. *"Religionswissenschaft."* *Numen* 6: 77–95.

Gualtieri, Antonio R. 1968. "Descriptive and Evaluative Formulae for Comparative Religion." *Theological Studies* 2: 52–71.

———. 1969. "Faith, Tradition and Transcendence: A Study of Wilfred Cantwell Smith." *Canadian Journal of Theology* 15: 102–11.

———. 1972. "Confessional Theology in the Context of the History of Religions." *Studies in Religion* 2: 347–60.

———. 1979. "Normative and Descriptive in the Study of Religion." *Journal of Dharma* 4: 8–21.

———. 1981. "'Faith, Belief and Transcendence' According to Wilfred Cantwell Smith." *Journal of Dharma* 6: 239–52.

Hebblethwaite, Brian. 1980. *The Problem of Theology*. Cambridge: Cambridge University Press.

Holley, Raymond. 1978. *Religious Education and Religious Understanding*. London: Routledge & Kegan Paul.

Hook, Sydney. 1961. *The Quest for Being*. New York: St. Martin's Press.

Ingram, Paul O. 1976. "Method in the History of Religion." *Theology Today* 32: 382–94.

Jastrow Jr., Morris. 1981. *The Study of Religion*. Chico, CA: Scholars Press.

Jeffner, Anders. 1981. "Religion and Understanding." *Religious Studies* 17: 217–25.

Kaufman, Gordon. D. 1983. "Nuclear Eschatology and the Study of Religion." *Journal of the American Academy of Religion* 51: 3–14.

Kegley, Charles W. 1978. "Theology and Religious Studies: Friends or Enemies?" *Theology Today* 35: 273–84.

Kitagawa, Joseph M. 1958. "Introduction: The Life and Thought of Joachim Wach." In Joachim Wach, *The Comparative Study of Religion*, xiii–xlviii. New York: Columbia University Press.

———. 1959. "The History of Religions in America." In Mircea Eliade and Joseph Kitagawa, eds, *The History of Religions: Essays in Methodology*, 1–30. Chicago: University of Chicago Press.

———. 1971. "*Verstehen* and *Erlosung*: Some Remarks on Joachim Wach's Work." *History of Religions* 11: 31–53.

———. 1975. "Theology and the Science of Religion." *Anglican Theological Review* 29: 33–52.

———. 1983. "Humanistic and Theological History of Religions with Special Reference to the North American Scene." In Peter Slater and Donald Wiebe, eds, *Traditions in Contact and Change: Selected Proceedings of the XIV Congress of the International Association for the History of Religions*, 553–64. Waterloo, ON: Wilfrid Laurier University Press.

Klostermaier, Klaus K. 1977. "From Phenomenology to Metascience: Reflections on the Study of Religions." *Studies in Religion* 6: 551–64.

———. 1978. "The Religion of Study." *Religious Traditions* 1: 56–66.

Kristensen, William Brede. 1960. *The Meaning of Religion*. The Hague: Mouton.

Ladner, Benjamin. 1972. "Religious Studies in the University: A Critical Reappraisal." *Journal of the American Academy of Religion* 40: 207–18.

Leclercq, Jean. 1961. *The Love of Learning and the Desire for God*. New York: New American Library.

Martin, J. Arthur. 1975. "What Do We Do When We Study Religion?" *Religious Studies* 11: 407–11.

Marty, Martin. 1983. "Seminary/Academy: Beyond the Tensions." *The Christian Century* (February): 84.

McClelland, J. C. 1972. "The Teacher of Religion: Professor or Guru?" *Studies in Religion* 2: 226–34.

———. 1983. "Alice in Academia: Religious Studies in the Academic Setting." Lecture at Victoria College, Toronto, November 28. Unpublished.

Meland, Bernard E. 1961. "Theology and the Historian of Religion." *The Journal of Religion* 41: 263–76.

Michaelson, Robert. 1972. "The Engaged Observer: Portrait of a Professor of Religion." *Journal of the American Academy of Religion* 40: 417–24.

Morgan, Robert and Michael Pye (eds and trans). 1977. *Ernst Troeltsch: Writings on Theology and Religion*. London: Duckworth.

Mostert, J. P. 1976. "Complimentarity Approaches in the Study of Religion." Inaugural Lecture at the University of Zululand. Unpublished.

Müller, Friedrich Max. 1893. *Introduction to the Science of Religion*. London: Longmans, Green.

Murray, Gilbert. 1955. *Five Stages of Greek Religion*. New York: Doubleday.

Nelson, Benjamin. 1981. *On The Roads to Modernity: Conscience, Science, and Civilization*. Ed. T. E. Huff. Totowa, NJ: Rowan & Littlefield.

Neufeldt, Ronald W. 1983. *Religious Studies in Alberta: A State-of-the-Art Review.* Waterloo, ON: Wilfrid Laurier University Press.

Neusner, Jacob. 1977a. "Being Jewish and Studying About Judaism." *Address at the Inauguration of the Jay and Leslie Cohen Chair of Judaic Studies*, 1–22. Atlanta, GA: Emory University Press.

———. 1977b. "Religious Studies: The Next Vocation." *Council on the Study of Religion Bulletin* 8/5: 117–20.

Novak, Michael. 1972a. *Ascent of the Mountain, Flight of the Dove: An Introduction to Religious Studies.* New York: Harper & Row.

———. 1972b. "The Identity Crisis of Us All: Response to Professor Crouter." *Journal of the American Academy of Religion* 40: 65–78.

O'Connell, L. J. 1984. "Religious Studies, Theology, and the Undergraduate Curriculum." *Council on the Study of Religion Bulletin* 15/5: 143–46.

Ogden, Shubert M. 1978. "Theology and Religious Studies: Their Difference and the Difference it Makes." *Journal of the American Academy of Religion* 46: 3–17.

Oxtoby, Willard G. 1968. "Religionswissenschaft Revisited." In Jacob Neusner, ed., *Religions in Antiquity: Essays in Memory of Erwin Ramsdell Goodenough*, 590–608. Leiden: Brill.

Pannenberg, Wolfhart. 1971. "Toward a Theology of the History of Religions." In W. Pannenberg, *Basic Questions in Theology*, vol. 2, 65–118. London: SCM.

———. 1976. *Theology and the Philosophy of Science.* London: Darton, Longman & Todd.

Raschke, Carl A. 1983. "The Future of Religious Studies: Moving Beyond the Mandate of the 1960s." *Council on the Study of Religion Bulletin* 14/5: 146–48.

Reat, Noble Ross. 1983. "Insiders and Outsiders in the Study of Religious Traditions." *Journal of the American Academy of Religion* 61: 457–76

Riley, Phillip B. 1984. "Theology and/or Religious Studies: A Case Study of *Studies in Religion/Sciences religieuses*, 1971–1981." *Studies in Religion* 13: 423–44.

Schimmel, Anne Marie. 1960. "Summary of the Discussion." *Numen* 7 (1960): 235–39.

Sharpe, Eric J. 1971. "Some Problems of Method in the Study of Religion." *Religion* 1: 1–14.

———. 1975. *Comparative Religion: A History.* London: Duckworth.

———. 1983. *Understanding Religion.* London: Duckworth.

Smart, Ninian. 1973. *The Phenomenon of Religion.* London: Macmillan.

Smith, Wilfred Cantwell. 1959. "Comparative Religion: Whither and Why?" In Mircea Eliade and Joseph Kitagawa, eds, *The History of Religions: Essays in Methodology*, 31–58. Chicago: University of Chicago Press.

———. 1963. *The Meaning and End of Religion.* New York: Macmillan.

———. 1984. "The Modern West in the History of Religions." *Journal of the American Academy of Religion* 52: 3–18.

Streng, Frederick J. 1970. "The Objective Study of Religion and the Unique Quality of Religiousness." *Religious Studies* 6: 209–19.

———. 1974. "Religious Studies: Processes of Transformation." In Anne Carr, ed., *Academic Study of Religion: 1974 Proceedings.* Chico, CA: Scholars Press.

Tillich, Paul. 1963. *Christianity and the Encounter of World Religions.* New York: Columbia University Press.

————. 1966. "The Significance of the History of Religions for the Systematic Theologian." In Paul Tillich, *The Future of Religions*, 80–94. Ed. Jerald C. Brauer. New York: Harper & Row.

Vernoff, C. 1963. "Naming the Game: A Question of the Field." *Council on the Study of Religion Bulletin* 14/4: 109–11.

de Vries, Jan 1967. *The Study of Religion: A Historical Approach.* New York: Harcourt, Brace & World.

Waardenburg, Jacques. 1973. "Introduction: View of a Hundred Years' Study of Religion." In Jacques Waardenburg, ed., *Classical Approaches to the Study of Religion*, vol. 1, 3–78. The Hague: Mouton.

Wach, Joachim. 1944. *Sociology of Religion.* Chicago: University of Chicago Press.

————. 1951. *Types of Religious Experience: Christian and Non-Christian.* Chicago: University of Chicago Press.

————. 1954. "General Revelation and the Religions of the World." *The Journal of Bible and Religion* 22: 83–93.

————. 1958. *The Comparative Study of Religion.* New York: Columbia University Press.

————. 1967. "Introduction: The Meaning and Task of the History of Religions (*Religionswissenschaft*)." In Joseph Kitagawa, Mircea Eliade, and Charles H. Long, eds, *The History of Religions: Essays on the Problem of Understanding*, 1–19. Chicago: University of Chicago Press.

Werblowsky, R. J. Zwi. 1956. "Revelation, Natural Theology, and Comparative Religion." *Hibbert Journal* 55: 278–84.

————. 1959. "The Comparative Study of Religions: A Review Essay." *Judaism* 8: 352–60.

————. 1960. "Marburg—and After." *Numen* 7: 205–20.

————. 1975. "On Studying Comparative Religion." *Religious Studies* 11: 145–56.

Widengren, Geo. 1983. "Pettazzoni's *Untersuchungen um Problem des Hochgottglaubens: Erinnerungen und Betrachtungen.*" *Studi Storico-Religiosi* 7: 29–53.

Wiebe, Donald. 1973. " 'Comprehensively Critical Rationalism' and Commitment." *Philosophical Studies* 21: 186–201.

————. 1975. "Explanation and the Scientific Study of Religion." *Religion* 5: 33–52.

————. 1978. "Is a Science of Religion Possible?" *Studies in Religion* 7: 5–17.

————. 1979. "The Role of Belief in the Study of Religion: A Response to W. C. Smith." *Numen* 26: 234–49.

————. 1981. *Religion and Truth: Towards an Alternative Paradigm for the Study of Religion.* The Hague: Mouton.

————. 1983. "Theory in the Study of Religion." *Religion* 13: 283–309.

————. 1991. *The Irony of Theology and the Nature of Religious Thought.* Montreal and Kingston: McGill-Queen's Press.

Wiebe, Donald, Peter Slater, and T. Horvath. 1981. "Three Responses to *Faith and Belief*: A Review Article." *Studies in Religion* 10: 113–26.

Wiebe, Paul G. 1975. "The Place of Theology in Religious Studies." In Anne Carr and Nicholas Piediscalzi, eds, *The Academic Study of Religion: 1975.* Chico, CA: Scholars Press.

GENERAL FAILURES

CATCHING UP WITH MARX:
TRUTH, MYTH, AND THE NICETIES OF "BELIEF"

Matthew Day

If there is anything that unites the hopelessly disjointed field of religious studies, it is the methodological practice of suspending or "bracketing" the epistemic desire to evaluate a given community's claims about the world. According to Jacques Waardenburg, for example, "the study of religion modestly puts the question of the ultimate truth of these religions between brackets (*epoché*)" (2000: 107). Nevertheless, Don Wiebe has argued for nearly thirty years that the academic study of religion must abandon its strategic hedging about such matters and confront the question of truth headon. His conviction is that a genuinely "critical" or "scientific" study of religion—a distinction that he never *quite* makes clear—is impossible so long as we shy away from asking: *Is any of the stuff that these people say true?* Wiebe insists that until we stop bracketing this frankly philosophical issue, scholars of religion will be damned to a dismal choice between flaccid reportage and covert apologetics. As he makes the case in *Religion and Truth*: "The scientific study of religion insofar as it seeks an explanation of the phenomena it scrutinizes, far from resting on the distinction between 'the truth about religion' and 'the truth of religion,' precludes it" (1981: 3). One might say that Wiebe has been proposing a sort of professional methodological addendum to Alexander Kinglake's cheeky suggestion that plaques with the legend *Important If True* should be posted over the door of every church, synagogue, mosque and temple.

In what follows, I want to suggest that attending to "the truth of religion" is largely irrelevant for any academic study of religion worth having. Even if every public assertion that a given community made about itself and the world was a calculated lie, *it should make no difference at all* for what we do. As a matter of fact, worries about the truth or meaning of cosmological claims tend to be *counter-productive* inasmuch as they take for granted the utter peculiarity of having any such "beliefs" at all.

1. The True Science of False Beliefs

Over the past quarter-century, countless scholars have been seized by a genealogical imperative to demonstrate how even ostensibly timeless truths have awkwardly contingent pasts. A whole generation of theorists has set out to follow the historiographical path cleared by Michel Foucault and Friedrich Nietzsche—or, at the very least, Foucault's idiosyncratic reading of Nietzsche—and thereby reveal how things like *race* or *sexuality* are discursive "inventions" rather than natural kinds (e.g., Lott 1999; Dreger 2000). Given this Nietzschean pedigree, it was only a matter of time before *religion* became the object of genealogical scrutiny. After all, here was a feature of human life that seemed no less immutable, eternal, or necessary than gravity. It is now a fixture of contemporary scholarly *doxa* to argue that the category of *religion* emerged from a particular time, and a particular place, and for quite specific reasons. Painted in broad strokes, the genealogical consensus is that *religion* first emerged in late sixteenth- or early seventeenth-century Europe. One of the fossilized traces used to date this appearance is the way in which the category universalized the local, Protestant practice of using explicit theological doctrines as markers of communal membership. Religion, to put it bluntly, was all about what individuals believed (e.g., Harrison 1990; Schopen 1991; King 1999; Smith 2004; Fitzgerald 2007).

In many ways, the desire to articulate a naturalistic account of "religion" was a less-than-surprising by-product of the category's formation. Given that it is a generic category which includes some only by excluding others, the boundary question of "Is this a religion?" was as inevitable and intractable as the boundary question that preoccupies most North American teenagers: "Is this cool?" Yet, it is crucial to note that early modern, natural histories of religion were really only interested in explaining *false religion* (Day 2010a). Religious delusions, lies, and errors merited the naturalists' attention, while religious truth—which typically meant some version of abstract and idealized Protestantism—was self-explanatory. As a case in point, this formula underwrites Hume's project in *Natural History of Religion*. That is to say, it is only against the backdrop of "the primary principles of genuine theism and religion," about which "no rational enquirer can, after serious reflection, suspend his belief a moment," that *superstition* and *idolatry* exist as objects of naturalistic curiosity (Hume 2007: 124). Thus, the work of natural explanation was dependent upon a prior epistemic judgment that distinguished between true religion and false religion. Or, to slightly modify Wiebe's distinction, the *truth of (true) religion* was the original precondition for the early modern interest in the *truth about (false) religion*.

Beginning in the nineteenth century, however, we begin to find a variety of theorists attempting to identify *the truth about (false) religion* without the conceptual backdrop provided by *the truth of (true) religion*. Epistemic evaluation and naturalistic explanation remained intimately linked. Now, however, *false religion*'s Doppelgänger was *true science*. Thus, Marx reduced "religion" to ideological false consciousness and appealed to the positive science of political economy to account for an upside-down portrait of reality. Although Durkheim worked hard to treat "religion" as something more than a mish-mash of hallucinations, at the end of the day he invoked the positive science of sociology to demonstrate how religion was at best only *metaphorically* or "practically" true. Unencumbered by the confessional horizon that had first motivated seventeenth- and eighteenth-century writers, the classically modern theories of "religion" were committed to finding naturalistic explanations for objectively false beliefs. In fact, there is a sense in which a figure like Durkheim took religion's obvious epistemic failings as the *reductio ad absurdum* of any intellectualist explanation. He was only too happy to concede that "no matter how religions are explained, they have certainly erred about the true nature of things" (Durkheim 1995: 80), because this opened the door for his sociological adventures.

For most of the twentieth century, various schools of broadly hermeneutical and phenomenological analyses seized the academic spotlight by denouncing anything that betrayed any hint of nineteenth-century positivism. By the early 1970s, Clifford Geertz was summarizing much of what had already happened in the human sciences when he suggested that these fields are principally interested in "constructing a reading of what happens" (2000: 18). The semiotic turn in anthropological and sociological theorizing virtually guaranteed that *religion* would be conceptualized, more often than not, as meaningful symbolic systems to be decoded rather than sets of empirical claims to be adjudicated. Imagined as a cultural system, religion became a text to be read. Nevertheless, some version of the old model—one might even call it a latter-day Tylorian "survival"—can still be found today. For example, it is a prior act of (negative) epistemic judgment regarding "religious concepts" which supplies the object for cognitive theorists to provide a (positive) naturalistic explanation. "Apparently irrational cultural beliefs are quite remarkable," Dan Sperber notes in *Explaining Culture*: "they do not appear irrational by departing slightly from common sense, or by timidly going beyond what the evidence allows. They appear, rather, like downright provocations against common-sense rationality" (1996: 73). Considered in this way, theories of cultural transmission, cognitive relevance, intuitive knowledge, or agency-detection bias are needed to explain why unreason is so damn stubborn when confronted with the truth (Guthrie 1995; Boyer 2002; Whitehouse 2004). Indeed, we even have theories about why religious people do not *really* believe the things they say they believe (Sloan 2004)! The point worth noticing in all of this is that there is a barely concealed question that unites seventeenth-century natural historians of religion and firmly anti-hermeneutical, "scientific" theorists today: Why is it that people continue to hold this particular class of clearly false beliefs?

2. Taking Science Seriously: Epistemic Duties and Explanatory Progress in the Study of Religion

One of Wiebe's favorite targets is the family of hermeneutical or "non-cognitivist" theorists that dominated the twentieth-century study of religion. In other words, the sorts of scholars who, like Geertz, prefer to talk about *meaning* rather than *truth*. Because of this, Wiebe's ultimate target has always been the hoary contrast between *interpretation* and *explanation* that we inherited from the nineteenth century. Painted in broad strokes, this distinction structured a division of labor between the *Natur-* and the *Geistes-wissenschaften*. The natural sciences were there to explain Nature's mean-ingless, deterministic regularity through universal laws. The human ("spirit") sciences were there to examine the creative, meaning-generating freedom of human beings in contingent historical and cultural contexts. In this way, the difference between *interpreting* and *explaining* was informed by the Kantian intuition that while bodies operate along the principles of *phenomenal determinism*, our moral judgments operate along the principles of *noumenal freedom*. At the end of the day, the distinction between interpretation and explanation was part of a normative philosophical vocabulary.

This bit of intellectual history is worth knowing if only because Wiebe's chief complaint about non-cognitive accounts of religion is that they are invariably and ineluctably apologetic exercises. Once religion is made a non-cognitive activity, it can be protected from the inroads of scientific progress. This portrait of religion has emerged, he writes,

> largely as a response to pressures of science understood as the paradigm of knowledge-gaining procedures (where, of course, it has been assumed that "religious truth" is propositional truth). The reasons for its emergence are obvious: if religion were non-cognitive such pressures would immediately dissolve; conflict between religion and science would no longer be possible and constant retrenchment of the religious believer in the face of an ever-advancing scientific system would cease. (1981: 85)

When seen in this light, there is a straight line that unites Friedrich Schleier-macher's *absolute Abhängigkeit* (absolute dependence), Rudolph Otto's *mysterium tremendum et fascinosum*, Clifford Geertz's *webs of significance*, and Steven Jay Gould's *non-overlapping magisteria*. In each case, the hope is that if we are willing to agree that "science" and "religion" ask different questions and provide different answers, then we can finally achieve a perfect world where—like Garrison Keillor's Lake Woebegone—"all the women are strong, all the men are good looking, and all the children are above average." Nevertheless, while these sorts of non-cognitive accounts may be diplomatically useful, Wiebe has consistently argued that scholars of religion accept them at their own peril. More damning still, he charges that insulating religion from the ravages of hard-nosed explanation represents nothing less than a crypto-theological agenda and a collective failure of nerve. The decision to *understand* rather than *explain* religion, he writes, "amounts to a non-specific theology, for it assumes the ontological reality of the religious phenomenon without consciously espousing any particular historical tradition's view of that reality" (Wiebe 1999: 148). The only way out of this predicament is to gird up the loins of our minds and start explaining—which is where that jammy "truth question" enters the story.

According to Wiebe, it is impossible to explain religion without treating it as a "cognitive enterprise." His justification for this premise is relatively straightforward: what is distinctive about a specific religion, or religion in general, is the distinctiveness of its propositional claims about the nature of reality. "The study of the various religious traditions shows them to be very much concerned with a knowledge of the world, both mundane and super-mundane," he judges. "To ignore this primary cognitive interest is simply not acceptable—it is to overlook one of the key elements of several major religious traditions" (1994: 68). To be sure, religion is not *only* a matter of belief. Nevertheless, he assures us that every non-cognitive feature of religion—whether we describe it as part of a *Lebensform* or *Weltanschauung*—"if it is not entirely arbitrary and irrational, involves, if even only implicitly, the acceptance of a specific view of the nature and meaning of the universe" (1981: 139–40). Here's the rub. If the scholar's job is to go beyond interpretation and *explain* a religious claim, judgment, or belief, not only must we account for why someone endorses a specific propositional content; we must also establish whether this propositional content is true or false. Why? Because Wiebe is convinced that the task of explaining why someone holds a true belief is quite distinct from the business of explaining why someone holds a false belief. In a passage worth quoting at some length, we are told:

> Religion as projection or illusion will elicit a very different kind of explana-
> tion than religion as a partially justified "vision" (explanation?, theory?) of
> reality (or of meaning of the universe, etc.). One need only compare here the
> theories of Freud and Durkheim, for example, with those of say, Christian
> fundamentalists, or in a vastly different tradition, with an Eliade, to see the
> point. To explain religion, then, one assumes (either explicitly and with some
> supportive evidence, or implicitly and naively) that religion is either (a) a set
> of unfounded and superstitious beliefs and hence false and so in need of
> explanation as to how and why they persist, etc.; or (b) a set of propositions

that are true or at least worthy of rational acceptance in that they themselves explain, make sense of, states of affairs around us and of elements of life's experience, etc. It would seem, therefore, that the critical study of religion is concerned, and primarily so, with the question of the truth or falsity of religion. (1981: 159)

Thus, the very thing that makes the "critical" explanation of religion possible—namely, the methodological commitment to treat it as a cognitively significant enterprise—also makes the epistemological evaluation of religion's propositional claims necessary. You cannot have one without the other. This is why Wiebe maintains that non-cognitive theorists of religion, despite their best intentions, are guilty of protecting or insulating their subjects from epistemic harm. As a result, one cannot grouse about those of our colleagues who view the academic study of religion itself as "religio-cultural quest" and then strike an indifferent attitude about the truth. The homely distinction between the "truth about religion" and the "truth of religion," it turns out, was just another trick up the crypto-theologian's sleeve.

3. Academic Theorizing without a Warrant

Unfortunately, from where I stand much of what Wiebe has to say about the ineluctable relationship between the *truth about religion* and the *truth of religion* falls somewhere in-between really, really odd and just plain wrong. Yet, rather than dutifully trotting out a series well-measured criticisms, I want to offer a kind of existence proof for something that he believes is impossible: an explanatory model that takes no notice of the "truth question" but remains sternly non-apologetic nonetheless. Let me begin with a story that Bruce Lincoln has used to good effect in the past.

The scene is Swaziland, sometime in the mid-1930s. British colonial administrators are eager to build a new landing strip and have identified a field that suits their needs adjacent to a school. The Swazi ruler King Sobhuza has even given the British his consent. The local Swazi homesteads are not as enthusiastic, however. Some are unclear why the ambition to build a landing strip cannot be achieved with something the Europeans already have: their own land. Others want to know how they, rather than the British, will benefit from this project. The king's counselors devise a solution. The colonial authorities are informed that the Swazi rank and file will welcome the landing strip on one condition: the British must not disturb in any way a massive tree which sits in middle of the field. That tree is sacred. It is where King Mbandzeni, the last independent ruler of the Swazi, met with his councilors to discuss urgent matters of state. If they harm that tree, the British will have a real problem on their hands. Wary of provoking an uprising, the British begin looking for other construction sites.

Were the Swazi telling the truth or were they talking about an imaginary past? Some of them apparently believed that this tale was true. Others thought it was a complete lie, a shrewd way of playing on British prejudice regarding "the Natives" and their superstitions. According to Lincoln, however, if we bother to ask whether the claims about King Mbandzeni and the Sacred Tree are illusory or veridical we have taken our eyes off the ball. *It simply doesn't matter if this story is true, false, or an outright lie.* In his estimation,

> whatever its source and prior status may have been, once this account had been re-collected by Sobhuza's councilors, they went on to claim an authoritative status for it, asserting that it exerted continuing demands and obligations on actors in the present moment. (1989: 28)

Simply put, it is not the propositional content of the mythmaking which allows us to explain this particular standoff between the British and the Swazi. For example, the British might have agreed amongst themselves that the Swazi were lying through their teeth about the tree's historical signifi-cance and *still* have abandoned their plans to build an airstrip on the original site. Why? Because they could have easily recognized that the battle over the tree was a proxy war between the Occupier and the Occupied. For this reason, the relevant claim is not the explicit propositional content that *King Mbandzeni once sat under this Sacred Tree.* Rather, it is the implicit warn-ing that *the colonial governors are going to have trouble on their hands if they cut that tree down.* It is the unspoken threat, and not the myth, which must be credible.

I have introduced this borrowed anecdote about the Swazi because it highlights what I see as the fundamental tension between *the desire to explain* and *the obligation to evaluate* in the academic study of religion. Here is a clear case where an interest in truth gets in the way of explanation; epistemic reflection on the credibility of the Swazi myth's propositional content only serves to muddy the waters. If we boil this local lesson down to a general theoretical principle, it becomes the rule of thumb that in this all-too-human life what matters is the public deployment of a claim—who is authorized to speak, who is authorized to listen, which idiom is recognized, etc.—and not the claim itself. As Talal Asad judged more than thirty years ago:

> epistemological questions about the ultimate origin or the final guarantee of social concepts and forms of knowledge (so beloved by anthropologists) are really quite irrelevant to this kind of problem. They cannot tell us anything about the reasons why different kinds of ideological positions come to be held in social life, or about the ideological force or effectiveness of particular political arrangements. (1979: 612)

It strikes me as worth noting, for example, that it was King Sobhuza's coun-cilors and not an angry mob who presented this claim to the British authori-ties. The right speakers were speaking through the right channels. In this way, the propositional content of a "religious belief" ends up being a bit like the Kantian *Ding an sich*: "it appeared to be so much, indeed everything, and is actually empty, that is to say empty of significance" (Nietzsche 1986: 16).

It goes without saying—or, at least, it *should* go without saying—that whether a particular someone is prepared to make a specific something public at a given moment depends upon a great deal more than the principles of "rational-critical exchange" (Habermas 1991). For example, where manual and domestic laborers freely confess their inability to make sense of abstract art, members of the bourgeoisie typically adopt the redoubtable strategy of knowing silence. They may be no less confused than the laborers, but they nod their heads and squint their eyes instead of admitting that *they just don't get it*. The anxious bourgeoisie "at least know that they have to refuse—or at least conceal—the naïve expectation of expressiveness that is betrayed by the concern to 'understand'" (Bourdieu 1984: 43). Alternatively, the confession that something *makes no sense* can be a damning criticism if it comes out of the right mouth. Roland Barthes observed that whenever cultural critics publicize their inability to comprehend something—such as the "fashionable nonsense" of postmodernism (e.g., Sokal and Bricmont 1999)—what they are really saying is "I don't understand, therefore you are idiots" (1957: 35).

The point that I am driving at here is that the epistemic trait of being *true* or *false* cannot explain why a claim is made or not made, credible or dubious, heard or ignored. Rather than asking whether the members of a community are making objectively true or false claims about the world, our time is better spent examining how a variety of discursive genres participate within local regimes of truth that are themselves *neither true nor false* (Foucault 1994: 119). More to the point, however, the *authority* that a body of knowledge enjoys at a given time or place cannot be reduced to the veridical or illusory nature of specific propositions. "Authority is a social category and only we can exert it," David Bloor observes in *Knowledge and Social Imagery*. "We endeavor to transmit it to our settled opinions and assump-tions. Nature has power over us, but only we have authority" (1991: 41). From this vantage point, the crucial question is not whether someone is telling the truth. What matters is whether anyone is listening.

4. Medieval Heretics and the Belief Industry

Thus far, my modest goal has been teasing apart the two things that Wiebe insists must go together if the academic study of religion is to divest itself of its crypto-theological baggage. By my reckoning, the epistemic evalua-tion of propositional content is more or less irrelevant for grasping the innumerable contests that constitute collective life. Indeed, there seem to be points where such concerns actually hamstring the critical project of explaining why some people act and speak as they do. However, rather than ending on this sour note, I would like to close by offering a productive way forward with respect to cosmological credos.

The recognition that *religion* represents a sharply rhetorical and strategically idealized form of Protestant Christianity has yielded mixed results. Some have concluded—and I should confess that I am one of them—that it is best to move along and begin reimagining what this corner of the academy might look like without the category's dubious comforts (Day 2010b). Many more are convinced that the category can and must be salvaged, and that the key is to divest *religion* of its keen interest in belief. "In contrast to the Protestant-based paradigms in which precedence is given to belief, theology and doctrine," for example, Barbara Holderage has suggested that "Hinduisms and Judaisms provide alternative paradigms of religious tradition, in which priority is given to issues of practice, observance, and law" (2000: 86). The problem with this particular reclamation strategy is that it tends merely to repackage the old hermeneutical and phenomenological fascination with *experience* and *meaning*. As a case in point, Robert Orsi has praised the theoretical turn towards *lived religion* because it attends to the familiar sites of prosaic existence: the house, the pub, the street corner, and the gym. In other words, it embraces those "places where humans make something of the worlds they have found themselves thrown into, and, in turn, it is in these subtle, intimate, quotidian actions on the world that meanings are made, known, and verified" (1997: 7). No matter how hard I try, I am unable to see how this amounts to a theoretical difference that makes a substantive difference.

From where I stand, the important move is not saving *religion* from the ravages of *belief* but the other way round. The way forward is to preserve *belief* while abandoning *religion*. Both the brusque scientists and doting hermeneutists make the mistake of taking for granted that individuals and communities have cosmological, metaphysical, or ontological "beliefs" to examine in the first place. The questions "Are these beliefs true?" and "Are these beliefs meaningful?" only seem to obscure what I consider to be a far more intriguing question: "How do individuals and communities come to have shared, articulated cosmological beliefs?" The peculiar fact that people have *any articulated beliefs at all* about the nature of reality, the origins of the world, or the meaning of life is what needs to be explained. What are the conditions, strategies, and practices that give rise to social actors with beliefs? Couched in these terms, this has a vaguely Foucauldian ring to it (Asad 1993; Foucault 2010). Yet, my interest in the specific modes of labor and production associated with cosmological beliefs owes more to Marx than Foucault.

In the first volume of *Capital*, Marx claimed to have dissolved the mysteries surrounding commodities by distinguishing between their use-values and their exchange- or money-values. Commodities are more than mere instruments because they are objects of utility and depositories of value at the same time. That is to say, by virtue of being things that are bought, sold, or traded in the marketplace at quantifiable units, commodities have an "objective" value that is distinct from their ability to answer specific human needs. Marx was convinced that this transcendent realm of exchange-values pointed towards—as through a glass darkly—the type, degree, and amount of human labor and social relations required to produce the commodity form. From this vantage point,

> The mysterious character of the commodity-form consists therefore simply in the fact that the commodity reflects the social characteristics of men's own labour as objective characteristics of the products of labour themselves, as the socio-natural properties of these things. Hence it also reflects the social relations of the producers to the sum total of labour as social relation between objects, a relation which exists apart from and outside the producers. Through this substitution, the products of labour become commodities, sensuous things which are at the same time suprasensible or social. (Marx 1976: 164–65)

The only alternative to worshiping the commodity-form as an inherently valuable "fetish" was viewing them as the concrete materializations and abstract expressions of the vast social networks of human labor that produced them. "We may twist and turn a commodity as we wish," Marx advises, "let us remember that commodities possess an objective character as values only in so far as they are all expressions of an identical social substance, human labour, and that their objective character as values is therefore purely social" (1976: 138–39).

When situated against this theoretical backdrop, the epistemic evaluation and hermeneutical elaboration of the mundane "trade" in cosmological beliefs are both guilty of focusing almost exclusively on their "use-values." The hoary questions about the truth and meaning of "religious thought" are, at the end of the day, questions about the explanatory, functional, pragmatic or representational value of certain kinds of beliefs. Unfortunately, the current crop of cognitive theorizing about religion continues this long-term "fetishism" regarding cosmological beliefs. How else should we describe those bids to explain why some ideas are more likely to be transmitted from one generation to another by appealing to the "modestly counter-intuitive" *properties of the ideas themselves*? As ridiculously *passé* as it might sound, it is time for a Marxist revolution in the academic study of religion. The unfulfilled promise of our field is an explanatory account of the social relations and material practices that manufacture "beliefs." To get a sense for what this might look like, consider a chapter from the history of European Christianity.

Beginning in the late twelfth century, Innocent III introduced a series of papal decretals designed to standardize and enhance the strategies for handling ecclesiastical misfits. The new legal procedure or "process for inquiry" (*processus per inquisitionem*) fleshed out in these documents was eventually codified at the Fourth Lateran Council. By the early thirteenth century, canon law dictated that in cases where accusations from "prudent and upright persons" about clerical misdeeds reached a Church superior, it became his responsibility to "inquire into the truth of such reports." Thus, the method of *inquisitio* replaced the juridical model of *accusatio*, insofar as ecclesiastical judges rather than wronged plaintiffs were able to initiate a judicial investigation and file official charges against the accused. Canon Eight ("On Inquests") identified the fundamental guidelines that all judicial inquiries must follow:

> He about whom inquiry is to be made must be present, unless he absents himself through stubbornness; and the matter to be investigated must be made known to him, that he may have opportunity to defend himself. Not only the testimony of the witnesses but also their names must be made known to him, that he may be aware who testified against him and what was their testimony; and finally, legitimate exceptions and replications must be admitted, lest by the suppression of names and by the exclusion of exceptions the boldness of the defamer and the false witness be encouraged.

This may look like nothing more than a modest dose of ecclesiastical housekeeping. Nevertheless, its long-term significance can hardly be overstated. When read alongside the strategies for combating and punishing heresy articulated in Canon Three ("On Heresy"), the faint outlines of countless inquisitorial tribunals come into focus.

The word *inquisition* calls forth phantasmagorical images of gloomy underground prisons stocked with macabre contraptions for extracting heretical confession. These chilling associations may draw attention to the distinctive ferocity of the fifteenth-century Spanish Inquisition, but they are especially out of place here. To put it as plainly as possible, frightening tales of a single, systematic, and terrifying enterprise called *the Medieval Inquisition* are historical fantasies. There was no centralized, permanent institution responsible for rooting out heresy. There was no Dostoevskyean Grand Inquisitor that commanded a vast anti-heretical army. There was, instead, a single legal method (*inquisitio*) and three judicial fields of application: *inquisitio generalis* (general inquisition on the basic charges); *inquisitio specifialis* (inquisition into specific illegal acts); and *inquisitio heretice pravitatis* (inquisition into heretical depravity).

From the perspective of the religion category, the discoveries that inquisitors made during an *inquisitio heretice pravitatis* are sometimes extremely puzzling. For example, if asked how long they had followed Cathar teaching, inquisitorial subjects would provide oddly specific answers like *since a year before the last grape harvest until the day I was accused of heresy* or *from the time I first heard them until I made confession today* (Arnold 2001: 162). How should we make sense of "beliefs" that can be picked up or put down as precisely and effortlessly as a bag of groceries? Rather than viewing these statements as acts of rational self-preservation, we should instead notice the ways in which medieval "belief" designated a *social status* rather than an *epistemic commitment*: *to believe* meant something like *to associate with, to show allegiance to*, or *to participate in* a specific community. This much may be gathered from the way in which two pairs of medieval distinctions between heresy and orthodoxy mirrored one another.

The ecclesiastical statutes ratified at the councils of Narbonne (1227) and Toulouse (1229) carefully distinguish between heretics (*heretici*), believers (*credentes*), supporters (*fautores*), defenders (*defensores*), and those who offer refuge (*receptatores*) to such unseemly characters. There was a finely tuned calculus for measuring the degrees of guilt for each crime and applying distinct penalties for each transgression. Because of the way in which the category of religion assumes that individuals have "beliefs," the fundamental point of contrast between the Cathar *heretici* and the Cathar *credentes* can be tricky to tease out. After all, how can one explain how *being a heretic* is not the same thing as *being a heretical believer*? A local distinction made by the Cathars themselves between *perfecti* and *credentes* provides an important clue (Given 1997). The *perfecti* were fully initiated members who participated in ritual life, lived in single-sex communities, observed various ascetic regimes, and—until it made them easy targets for inquisitorial tribunals— wore distinctive black mantles. The *credentes* were those who associated with the *perfecti* but did not share their ritual, monastic, and ascetic practices. Anne Brenon (1998) has suggested that the purification ritual of the *consolamentum* represents a kind of second baptism and, as a result, should be viewed as the *sine qua non* for joining the ranks of the Cathar *perfecti*. Because of the austere demands that came with accepting the *consolamentum*, many *credentes* would make arrangements to perform the ritual on their deathbeds and enter heaven as a fully credentialed *perfectus* or *hereticus*, depending on your point of view.

Gradually, however, the *inquisitio heretice pravitatis* begins to drift away from a singular interest in discovering what heretics are *doing* to what they are *thinking*. Regarding the thirteenth-century inquisitorial campaign against the Cathars in the south of France, for example, John Arnold has written:

> To describe the evidence in broad terms, the earliest depositions are indeed
> concerned primarily with acts, whereas by the 1270s one finds quite long
> descriptions of belief and some discussion as to why people believed the
> things they did, while the [Jacques] Fournier registers, from the early
> fourteenth century, famously supply much greater detail from their deponents,
> including a lot of material on belief. (2001: 98)

Through the various acts of confession, penance, and punishment, beliefs
were deliberately provoked, methodically collected, systematically cata-
logued, and then bureaucratically pinned to individual subjects. The hero of
Carlo Ginsberg's *The Cheese and the Worms* provides us with a poignant
case study of this historical dynamic. Domenico Scandella—everyone just
called him "Menocchio"—was a sixteenth-century Italian miller in the town
of Montereale and an object of inquisitorial attention. Accused of being a
heretic in September, 1583, he was arrested on 4 February, 1584, and
detained in the prison of the Holy Office in Concordia. He endured extensive
interrogations on 7, 16, 22 February; 8 March; 28 April; and 1, 12 May.
Prompted again and again by his interrogators to address cosmological,
christological, ecclesiological, and soteriological matters, Menocchio eventually began to talk. He accused the Church of living off the misery of the
poor; judged that marriage was a human rather than divine institution;
condemned extreme unction as a waste of time; and speculated that angels
were "produced by nature from the most perfect substance of the world, just
as worms are produced by cheese" (Ginzberg 1980: 55). By the time he was
through, Menocchio had said enough to be found guilty of formal heresy. On
17 May he was condemned to publicly abjure his heretical statements, wear
a penitential garment until his death, and perform an extensive list of salu-
tary penances. Menocchio spent the rest of his life in prison at his family's
expense.

I have highlighted this grim tale because it suggests that the means for
producing knowledge about an individual's beliefs, and the mechanisms for
making judgments regarding the legitimacy of those beliefs, emerge from a
historically specific network of social relations. The inquisitorial judges,
techniques, spaces, and penalties represent something more substantial than
the mere "context" of medieval Christian beliefs. They are, in fact, crucial
elements of the medieval belief industry. That is to say, inquisitors began
expecting their subjects to have "beliefs" about God, christology, creation,
salvation, and the sacraments that could be explicitly articulated, bureaucratically collected, and systematically punished. Instead of describing the
Inquisition as the dogged pursuit of heretical "beliefs," it seems more
accurate to think of the social relations, human labor, and material practices
surrounding the *inquisitio* as the historical means for producing them.

Marx concluded that the commodity form was "a very strange thing, abounding in metaphysical subtleties and theological niceties" (1976: 163). That is to say, commodities replaced the material world of social relations and human activity with a fantastic world where intrinsically valuable things mysteriously appear and demand our reverence. For this reason, he proposed that the theoretical strategies called upon to assemble a materialist account of religion could be used to cut through this economic puzzle as well. To make sense of commodities, he judged,

> we must take flight into the misty realm of religion. There the products of the human brain appear as autonomous figures endowed with a life of their own, which enter into relations both with each other and the human race. So it is in the world of commodities with the products of men's hands. (Marx 1976: 165)

A growing number of economists, geographers, and historical sociologists have concluded that Marx, more than any other "classical" theorist, gives them the tools they need to make sense of the systemic crises of late capitalism. Perhaps it is time for the academic study of religion to catch up with Marx as well.

References

Arnold, John. 2001. *Inquisition and Power: Catharism and the Confessing Subject in Medieval Languedoc*. Philadelphia: University of Pennsylvania Press.

Asad, Talal. 1979. "Anthropology and the Analysis of Ideology." *Man* 14: 609–21, 624–27.

———. 1993. *Genealogies of Religion: Discipline and Reasons of Power in Christianity and Islam*. Baltimore: Johns Hopkins University Press.

Barthes, Roland. 1957. *Mythologies*. New York: Farrar, Strauss & Giroux.

Bloor, David. 1991. *Knowledge and Social Imagery*. 2nd ed. Chicago: University of Chicago Press.

Bourdieu, Pierre. 1984. *Distinction*. Trans. Richard Nice. Cambridge: Harvard University Press.

Boyer, Pascal. 2002. *Religion Explained: The Evolutionary Origins of Religious Thought*. New York: Basic Books.

Brenon, Anne. 1998. "The Voice of the Good Women: An Essay on the Pastoral and Sacerdotal Role of Women in the Cathar Church." In Beverly Mayne Kienzle and Pamela J. Walker, eds, *Women Preachers and Prophets through Two Millennia of Christianity*, 114–32. Berkeley: University of California Press.

Day, Matthew. 2010a. "The Sacred Contagion: John Trenchard, Natural History, and the Effluvial Politics of Religion." *History of Religions* 50: 144–61.

———. 2010b. "How to Keep It Real." *Method & Theory in the Study of Religion* 22: 272–82.

Dreger, Alice. 2000. *Hermaphrodites and the Medical Invention of Sex*. Cambridge: Harvard University Press.

Durkheim, Emile. [1912] 1995. *The Elementary Forms of Religious Life.* Trans. Karen Fields. New York: Free Press.

Fitzgerald, Timothy. 2007. *Discourse on Civility and Barbarity: A Critical History of Religion and Related Categories.* New York: Oxford University Press.

Foucault, Michel. 1994. *Power: Essential Works of Foucault, 1954–1984*, vol. 2. Ed. James D. Faubion. New York: Free Press.

———. 2010. *The Birth of Biopolitics: Lectures at the Collège de France, 1978–1979.* Trans. Graham Burchell. New York: Palgrave/Macmillan.

Geertz, Clifford. 2000. *Interpretation of Cultures: Selected Essays.* 2nd ed. New York: Basic Books.

Ginzberg, Carlos. [1976] 1980. *The Cheese and the Worms: The Cosmos of a Sixteenth Century Miller.* Baltimore: Johns Hopkins University Press.

Given, Thomas. 1997. *Inquisition and Medieval Society: Power, Discipline, and Resistance in Languedoc.* Ithaca, NY: Cornell University Press.

Guthrie, Stewart. 1995. *Faces in the Clouds: A New Theory of Religion.* New York: Columbia University Press.

Habermas, Jürgen. 1991. *The Structural Transformation of the Public Sphere.* Trans. Thomas Burger. Cambridge: MIT Press.

Harrison, Peter. 1990. *Religion and the Religions in the English Enlightenment.* Cambridge: Cambridge University Press.

Holderage, Barbara. 2000. "What's Beyond the Post? Comparative Analysis as Critical Method." In Kimberly Patton and Benjamin Ray, eds, *A Magic Still Dwells: Comparative Religion in the Postmodern Age*, 77–91. Berkeley: University of California Press.

Hume, David. [1779] 2007. *Dialogues Concerning Natural Religion: And Other Writings.* Cambridge: Cambridge University Press.

King, Richard. 1999. *Orientalism and Religion: Postcolonial Theory, India and the "Mystic East."* New York: Routledge.

Lincoln, Bruce. 1989. *Discourse and the Construction of Society: Comparative Studies of Myth, Ritual, and Classification.* New York: Oxford University Press.

Lott, Tommy. 1999. *The Invention of Race: Black Culture and the Politics of Representation.* Malden, MA: Blackwell.

Marx, Karl. [1867] 1976. *Capital*, vol. 1. Trans. Ben Fowkes. London: Penguin.

Nietzsche, Friedrich. [1878] 1986. *Human, All-Too-Human: A Book for Free Spirits.* Trans. R. J. Hollingdale. New York: Cambridge University Press.

Orsi, Robert. 1997. "Everyday Miracles: The Study of Lived Religion." In David D. Hal, ed., *Lived Religion in America: Toward a History of Practice*, 3–21. Princeton: Princeton University Press.

Schopen, Gregory. 1991. "Archaeology and Protestant Presuppositions in the Study of Indian Buddhism." *History of Religions* 31: 1–23.

Sloan, Jason. 2004. *Theological Incorrectness: Why Religious People Believe What They Shouldn't.* New York: Oxford University Press.

Smith, Jonathan Z. 2004. "Religion, Religions, Religious." In Jonathan Z. Smith, *Relating Religion: Essays in the Study of Religion*, 179–96. Chicago: University of Chicago Press.

Sokal, Alan and Jean Bricmont. 1999. *Fashionable Nonsense: Postmodern Intellectuals' Abuse of Science.* New York: MacMillan.

Sperber, Dan. 1996. *Explaining Culture: A Naturalistic Approach.* Malden, MA: Blackwell.

Waardenburg, Jacques. 2000. *Muslims and Others: Relations in Context.* Berlin: W. de Gruyter.

Whitehouse, Harvey. 2004. *Modes of Religiosity: A Cognitive Theory of Religious Transmission.* Walnut Creek, CA: AltaMira.

Wiebe, Donald. 1981. *Religion and Truth: Towards an Alternative Paradigm for the Study of Religion.* The Hague: Mouton.

———. 1994. *Beyond Legitimation: Essays on the Problem of Religious Knowledge.* New York: St. Martin's Press.

———. 1999. *The Politics of Religious Studies.* New York: St. Martin's Press.

Fixed Geomorphologies and the Shifting Sands of Time

Darlene M. Juschka

1. Introduction

Much of Donald Wiebe's work has challenged the shape and orientation of the field of Religious Studies. This has meant a herculean effort on his part to push the field more in alignment with a scientific study of religion. Like Wiebe, I too, as a poststructural feminist, have made efforts to shape the field, asking questions and providing analyses that veer from the mainstream. And, like Wiebe, I too have run into the field's failure of nerve to push beyond the status quo: unfamiliar theoretical premises and tools of analysis are often met with suspicion and rejection. In this chapter I will discuss my own efforts to bring a feminist and semiotic analysis to the field. To do this I will provide a context for the development of my own work, speak to the theoretical orientation I adopt and the kind of insights I think such an orientation provides, and lastly address change, resistance, and more change in the study of the systems of belief and practice otherwise known as "religion."

2. What's in a Name?

Tradition, as Raymond Williams writes, is an active force in any social body, a force that is "the most powerful practical means of incorporation" (1977: 115). Tradition can also refer to traditional understanding, so that, for example, in the study of religion, there has been a *modus operandi* whereby "religion" is understood to be a thing in the world, an object with fixed and distinct parameters, and although evincing variation based on geographical location, a universal phenomenon. Now whether you make this universal phenomenon *sui generis* in the human species, e.g., cognitively, psychologically, theologically, or as an essential piece of human organizational interaction, e.g., behaviorally or biologically, both positions assume from the outset that there is a singular phenomenon that can be defined as "religion"; and this assumption is a primary means by which a traditional understanding of "religion" is maintained in the field. Jonathan Z. Smith (2004), Russell McCutcheon (1997), and William Arnal (2000) have each in their own way challenged the taken-for-granted, traditional understanding and use of the term/concept "religion." As Smith has cogently demonstrated in his article "Religion, Religions, Religious":

> "Religion" is not a native term; it is a term created by scholars for their intellectual purposes and therefore is theirs to define. It is a second-order, generic concept that plays the same role in establishing a disciplinary horizon that a concept such as "language" plays in linguistics or "culture" plays in anthropology. (2004: 193–94)

Smith's understanding of "religion" resists the view that there is a thing out there in the world that is found, named, and described as a species of religion. Religion cannot be found out there; rather, "it" is defined in a particular way and then data are gathered and analyzed/interpreted according to the operative definition. If the operative definition, however, is that religion is a thing, a *sui generis* phenomenon, then that is how it will be understood. If one resists the old phenomenological definition of "religion," and resists even using the term "religion" in light of its association with that definition, one's discourse can be marginalized and may not make sense to those who assume a normative view of the category of religion. By contrast, Don Wiebe laments our field's "failure of nerve," not because religion is treated like a phenomenon, but rather because the phenomenon is not engaged scientifically and is instead inflected by theological commitments. Although I do not share Wiebe's definition of "religion," nor adhere to his scientific methodology, I do share his frustration with the narrow parameters of the field wherein discursive framings of systems of belief and practice must of necessity reproduce the status quo or gain no hearing. I do not believe that I would call the refusal of the field to engage seriously a scientific and/or academic methodology a failure of nerve as Wiebe suggests. Instead, I would suggest—with reference to my own efforts to bring a feminist and semiotic analysis to our inquiries—that the field itself tends toward conservatism; and linked to this conservatism, or emerging from it, is a traditional definition and engagement with the systems of belief and practice otherwise known as "religion."[1]

---

1. A traditional definition of religion takes religion to be a distinct, self-contained, and universal phenomenon, a thing in the world that is manifested in a multitude of ways, and/or an innate and inherent human orientation that manifests itself in a plethora of beliefs and practices.

3. My Context

I first entered the field of Religious Studies when I did a qualifying year in Religion and Culture at Wilfrid Laurier University in order to enter their Master of Arts program. I worked with some truly insightful people, each of whom approached the area in a different way, but who in general understood religion to be a more or less self-evident entity to be studied. Implied by this approach, however, was also data for "religion" as social phenomena shaped by numerous forces: ideological, psychological, sociological, anthropological, philosophical, and theological; and manifested in multitudinous ways: orally, textually, ritually, symbolically, materially, politically, economically, and, of course, ideologically. As a student also interested in feminism, this kind of decentering of "religion" as a fixed and static object was the first step on a path that would lead me to my current theoretical location, feminist poststructuralism, and my current methodologies of semiotic and discursive analyses.

My PhD, done at the Centre for the Study of Religion at the University of Toronto, allowed me to work with professors such as Donald Wiebe, who furthered my theoretical understanding, and pressed me to ask about the category of religion and its history. Although certainly Wiebe did not challenge the use of the term "religion," he did challenge how we thought about it and argued that a theological orientation was fine for god-talk but had nothing to do with the academic study of religion. As Russell McCutcheon later argued, a theological orientation positioned the scholar of religion as a "caretaker" and not a "critic" (2001).

McCutcheon and I were fellow students at the Centre and I was lucky enough to work on the journal *Method & Theory in the Study of Religion* with him, Ann Baronowski, Willi Braun, and Arthur McCalla over a period of four years. To my ongoing pleasure, the journal continues to thrive and is now published by Brill. Working with the graduate students and the professors at the Centre for the Study of Religion, my interest in ritual and mythology was deepened. During my Master's I worked with Ronald Grimes and previously had done an undergraduate degree in Classics at the University of Waterloo, which had whet my appetite for myth. Added to these were an interest in feminist and Marxian theories, fostered during my PhD by feminist peers and professors. As I developed a dissertation examining the reconceptualization of symbol, myth, and ritual from feminist theological perspectives and practices (Christian in the main), the theorists I studied made apparent the social and historical nature of myth, symbol, and ritual, and the ideological implications of each. Feminists such as Mieke Bal (1987, 1988), Nancy Jay (1992), and Susan Sered (1994) have been very astute in demonstrating the androcentrism and misogyny central to, and deployed by and through, symbol, myth, and ritual.

As my understanding of myth, ritual, and symbol began to shift and I began to work with them as social constructs, emergent from and necessarily bound and shaped within a social and historical context, each with their own hegemonic and normative views, accepted, taken for granted, resisted, revamped, and so forth, I realized that if these fundamental kernels that gave credence to the existence of something called "religion" were concepts shaped and reshaped in and through discourses, then certainly "religion" was equally a concept shaped and reshaped in and through discourse. Bruce Lincoln's text *Discourse and the Construction of Society* (1989) as well as other poststructural thinkers such as Chris Weedon (2001) were imminently helpful for my work in the study of religion. Approaching systems of belief and practice this way allowed me to understand better how, for example, gender/sex ideology is enfleshed and made "real."

4. Feminisms and Semiotics—Studying Systems of Belief and Practice

4.1. The Category Gender/Sex

Gender and sex, two tightly interrelated social categories that have been biologized and metaphysicalized through systems of belief and practice (among other discursive frames such as medicine, science, philosophy, anthropology) are central to understanding how we conceptualize and construct such systems. On the level of ritual, for example, gender and sex are brought into existence continually and repetitiously through rites of passage related to birth, puberty, marriage, and death. In the instance of sign-symbol (see "Semiotics," below), gender and sex are continuously and repeatedly produced and reproduced in the figuring of deities such as Gaia in Wicca, Jesus in Christianities and in the sign-symbols of the feminine *yoni* and masculine *lingam* of India. In the conceptualized domain of the biological, ritual manufactures gender/sex ideologies that are significant to the production of the female, male, and interstitial (trans- or asexual), the latter mediating between the former binary. In the conceptualized domain of the metaphysical, sign-symbol fashions gender/sex ideologies that are a significant means to the production of the feminine, masculine, and androgynous, the latter again acting as a mediating term between the former binary of feminine and masculine.

Ritual and sign-symbol, along with myth contextualized in the social domain, are hard-working ideological apparatuses used in most (if not all) social formations for multiple purposes, not least of which are status, identity, and boundaries in a variety of manifestations. If status, identity, and boundaries are among their central effects then they are significant to the shaping and reshaping of systems of belief and practice, and therefore important to include in one's analysis. Examining the mythological corpora of systems of belief and practice makes very apparent the centrality of status, as is seen, e.g., when the brother of Moses, Aaron, and Aaron's sons, all male, are marked by deity as priestly in the book of Exodus (28:1). Miriam, however, the sister of Moses and Aaron, also named as a prophet like her brothers (Exod. 15:20–21), was not as lucky as her brothers, and instead was afflicted by deity with a leprous disease for seven days. She had the effrontery to challenge (with Aaron) the authority of Moses (Num. 12). Status (priest) and gender/sex (rewarding of male/masculine and punishment of the female/feminine) *intersect* and signify as central to normative relations in the system of belief and practice, marking those who carry authority and directly commune with deity, and those who do not. Played out over thousands of years, systems of belief and practice, such as the majority of Judaisms, have drawn on this mythological corpus (among others) to exclude those humans marked as female/feminine from positions of governance within their institutions. Women within Judaisms, however, participating in second-wave feminism (mid-1950s to the present), have made efforts to read the texts, images, and rites related to their system of belief and practice in multiple and different ways. They have also sought to ensure that their religious institutions included women in roles of governance. Their efforts have been to redescribe and sign anew their systems of belief and practice, and although they have had some success, the adherence of many to gender/sex ideologies, understood as integral to existence, has frustrated their resignifications: gender/sex ideology matters in central and important ways to systems of belief and practice.

4.2. And Then Some Semiotics

The structural unit of language that interested Ferdinand de Saussure (1966) was of course the linguistic sign. The sign is a linguistic device by which humans shape, signify, and communicate existence. Thomas Sebeok, an American semiotician, comments:

> the derivation of language out of any animal communication systems is an exercise in total futility, because language did not evolve to subserve humanity's communicative exigencies. It evolved…as an exceedingly sophisticated modelling device…in *Homo habilis*. (1994: 114)

The significant point here is that language (the verbal signs of semiotics as differentiated from the nonverbal signs) is a modeling device or a means by which humans corporately and individually code and decode existence. Signs are understood to shape, signify, and communicate human existence; an existence that is socially and historically contextualized.

Operating within this framework, one is able to explicate how the sign functions, its shifting meanings, and how it operates in terms of human social systems. A sign is the unit that models, shapes, and communicates meaning.

Under the deft hand of theorists like Roland Barthes (1968, 1972) semiotics or semiology would continue to move toward an idea of language as a modeling device—one whose modeling and communicative functions exist in a dialectical tension, each forging and reforging the other (Weedon 2001). The models by which meaning is constructed are derived from, and produced within, social bodies, by their members who are themselves shaped by historical and social concerns. Humans develop models by which to encode and comprehend existence. Models allow us to make sense and shape the world(s) in which we live.

For the majority of poststructuralists, then, a common factor in the formation of social organization, social meaning, representation, power, and subjectivity is language. Language is that which constructs, mediates, and communicates the understanding of self, world, and existence. But more than this, language is a primary place where social organization and its dissemination and contestation are enacted. Chris Weedon argues that "language is not the expression of a unique individuality; it constructs the individual's subjectivity in ways which are socially specific" (2001: 21; cf. Althusser 1995). Language divides up the world and gives the world meaning; it is the basis of our categories. So, for example, the categories of femininity and masculinity mean differently depending on social, cultural, and historical location; they can even differ within one specific social body depending on their intersection with other categories such as systems of belief and practice, race, class, ethnicity, and so forth. For example, a brief semiotic analysis of the signification of the feminine as a fertile site of evil played out in Medieval and early modern Europe (and colonies), and the liminal feminine as the potential site of chaos played out in neocolonial Rajasthan reveal the interplay of ritual, gender/sex, and colonialism.

5. Expiatory and Alimentary Sacrifices: Consuming the Female/Feminine[2]

The European witch haunted the imagination of Europe, and tract after tract was written for the purposes of identifying and dealing with her, the most famous being the *Malleus Malificarum* (Institoris and Sprenger 2006), written by two Dominican monks in the late fifteenth century. The witch was perceived as a threat to society, Christian society, and was dealt with in courts filled with professional men: university professors, physicians, churchmen, monks, priests, and, of course, professional witch hunters. No woman was safe from the witchcraft charge, be she a child or elderly. The

---

2. I am indebted to Pompa Banerjee (2003) for the idea of comparing European early modern witchcraft burnings and the practice of *sati*.

female, as the misbegotten male, derived from Adam's crooked rib, and in a state of flux due to her menstrual cycle, was weaker than the male and subject to excess, particularly sexual excess. It was the natural lust of the female (of any age) that made her an easy prey for the devil. Institoris and Sprenger wrote in the *Malleus Maleficarum* that:

> As a result of them [carnal desires of the body] countless injuries happen to human life, so that we can justly say with Cato Uticensis that if the world could exist without women, we would interact with the gods. For if the evil of women did not in fact exist—not to mention their acts of sorcery—the world would remain unburdened of countless dangers. (2006: 120–21)

An awful mixture of sexuality, violence, and terror was a significant aspect of the mainstream gender/sex ideologies. The unrestrained female/ feminine was perceived as the repository and initiator of sinful and/or uncontrolled sexuality evoking a general superstitious terror that often underlaid the numerous acts of violence against those marked as female and/or feminine.[3] The witch was voluptuous, seductive, and under the control of no man. The female/feminine not properly bound within patriarchal relations was perceived as a threat to masculine hegemony.

To cordon this threat and purify contaminated social bodies, then, ritual was used in the form of torture, theatrical public trials, and the sacrificial burning, hanging, or drowning of the witch (Juschka 2009). These ritual actions carry symbolic weight and were instrumental in shaping gender/sex ideology (even as the ritual is shaped by gender/sex concerns) separating as they do kinds of people within the social body, in this instance those marked as female and those as male. But equally, the ritual also establishes a hierarchy and separation of men: priests, churchmen, university men, and physicians are distinguished from other men: peasants, burghers, artisans, actors, traders, and so forth. The former were those who were often, but not always, judges, while the latter were often spectators and at times even victims. Sign-symbols, however, are polysemic (Turner 1967), and even as these symbolic ritual acts speak the truth of gender/sex ideology and hierarchical relations, they also speak to expiatory sacrifice,[4] ensuring that the perceived evil understood to have contaminated the social body is purged from it by pain, suffering, and finally by the application of purifying elements: fire, water, or wood (hanging).

In another context, India, the immolation of the "widow," another imagined female/feminine figure no longer properly contained within patriarchal

---

3. For an extended discussion on this gender/sex ideology see Juschka 2009.

4. I draw on the work of Nancy Jay (1992) for the concepts of expiatory and alimentary sacrifices. The first is a sacrifice of separation and the second a sacrifice of communion. Often ritual sacrifice can include both.

relations, also speaks of hierarchy, but instead of being an expiation to purify the social body, she is an alimentary sacrifice who secures its boundaries. Called *sati*, this ritual sacrifice entails the immolation (self or otherwise) of a woman on the pyre of her dead husband. In the rite of *sati* we see an event, a spectacle—for this event takes place in the public arena—that gathers its viewers and participants (all except the *sati* herself) together as a community.

The ritual of *sati* is diverse and signifies gender in multiple ways due to shifting geographical and historical contexts. Its first "epidemic" in the modern period was in Bengal under British colonial rule in the nineteenth century, while its second "epidemic" appears within the frame of neocolonialism in Rajasthan. Under British rule the practice of *sati* was viewed by the British and Christian missionaries as a barbaric practice, one that affronted the civility and Christianity of the colonizers. British missionary women carried differing cultural mores into India and when they encountered the social practices of child brides, women in seclusion, widows driven out of communities, these women (and their male associates who had not really cared until it was pointed out to them) began to take up the cause of the oppressed "Hindu woman." They began to interfere actively in family relations and as the colonizers, even if female, their voices were stronger than the male Indian voices. Their interference was understood as a threat to systems of belief and practice in India and a surge of resistance to colonialism, purporting to hold to the "fundamentals" of Hinduism (not without contestations from other Hindus) arose in the broader cultural arena (Hawley 1994; Mani 1998; Sen 2001).

So too in the modern era of neocolonialism, feminisms have arisen around the globe in the last four decades of the twentieth century. Indian feminists, found on all parts of the subcontinent (home grown, although linked globally to other feminist organizations), have called for a halt to the practices of bride burning, widow burning, child brides, and have challenged the economic, educational, and social inequities experienced by those marked as female and feminine in India. In Rajasthan, a border country between Islamic Pakistan and Hindu India (borders mark the periphery between a "them" and an "us") there has been an increase in the practice of *sati* in recent decades. According to statistics from 1998, there had been twenty-eight instances of *sati* in Rajasthan since India's independence in 1947 (Mani 1998). The threat of a "them" who alters who "we" are, and the emergence of feminisms in India, with feminism seen as a Western phenomenon, may have fuelled the desire to adhere to the fundamentals of identity materialized in the act of *sati*.

5.1. The Practice of *Sati*

The practice of *sati* is a public event, and often there are spectators in the hundreds or even thousands. In the instance of the very publicized Roop Kanwar case from 1987, there were apparently thousands of spectators, and at the following *chunari* celebration, held twelve or thirteen days afterward in Deorala (district of Sikar), hundreds of thousands of mostly young Rajasthani men were in attendance. The *chunari* rite consists of burning a scarf of the young woman, in a flame, a flame supposedly derived from the funeral pyre on which her life was ended. This scarf, then, is released/ burned in the "spectral" flame at the cremation site as a final act to honor the physical remains of the *sati*. The *chunari* site then became a pilgrimage site honoring not only the *sati*, Roop Kanwar, but incorporating her memory into a mythic narrative connecting her to the Great Mother Sati (*mahasati*), to the goddess Sita, the first *sati*, and the many in between who have committed themselves or were committed to the funeral flames (Mani 1998; Hawley 1994; *Trial by Fire: A Report on Roop Kanwar's Death*, 1987).

Examining the ritual of *sati* and its culminating rite the *chunari* (its location now a pilgrimage site) makes apparent how ritual establishes identity. The rite of *sati* marks the *sati* herself as operating within the system of belief and practice, and all those in attendance in support of the *sati* are equally located within the system of belief and practice. The identity, taken up by the *sati* and shared with her spectators, has metaphysical ramifications: she evokes the mythic death of Sita who burned up in a yogic rage; she evokes the ritualistic, or the actions which are understood to link deities with humans; and she evokes the symbolic, in that the *sati* symbolizes pure and proper womanhood and authentic Hindu belief.

5.2. Gender/Sex Ideology of *Sati*

Those who were present and supported the sacrifice of Roop Kanwar in 1987 share an identity which they conceived as authentically Hindu. As a sacrifice, she brought the people together in communion around the site of her immolation, marking, for them at least (a great many other Hindus contested this marker of identity), authentic Hindu identity. She is the sacrifice that they will all share in, through (1) sight (in Hinduism *darshana* or seeing of the deity is an experience of epiphany—a visitation of deity; equally, seeing [*darshana*] the *sati*, is an experience of epiphany); (2) practice; (3) consumption (the purchasing of pictures, pieces of wood from the funeral pyre, articles that belonged to the young woman—souvenirs of her death that are now marked as icons); and (4) a shared identity that locates them within their conceptualization of a so-called authentic Hinduism through the act of pilgrimage to the site of the immolation. In all these acts, the burning of Roop Kanwar as *sati* established affinity[5] among one

5. I am drawing upon Bruce Lincoln (1989) for the concept of affinity and estrangement in the construction of social boundaries.

group—authentic Hindus—and estrangement from all those others whose discursive framing of Hinduism challenged the act of *sati* as definitive of Hinduism. The female/feminine that is not properly controlled by the male/masculine—in this instance the widow and fathers respectively—is perceived as a threat to those who would see themselves as authentic Hindus.

Specifically, then, in terms of gender/sex ideology, the act of *sati* is an encoded discourse defining and then affirming the proper Hindu wife. On the level of the mythic, Sita, the ideal of Hindu womanhood, is read to have committed *sati* because her spouse Shiva was insulted by her father. Therefore, the ideal woman sacrifices herself for her husband. The ideal woman is wife/mother and those women who are daughter/widow are in a liminal state and so represent the Outsider Within. On the level of the ritual, in this political-social location, the act of *sati* communicates that the female/feminine exists only in relation to the male/masculine and that without him she has no reason for existence. The *sati*, then, is the sacrifice that ritually marks gender/sex ideology wherein her uterus, the womb, is at the disposal of men (it is only men who enact the rite of *sati*): she is, after all, the most precious gift.[6] Symbolically, the necessary order of nature is reasserted with the feminine acting as the catalyst for masculine power. The Rajasthani have reasserted the order of their universe by asserting masculine control of feminine power and so order (masculine) in control of chaos (feminine); that "Hindu" (read Rajasthani) women are the commodities of men that ensure subsequent patrilineal generations, and finally, that the female is different from the male, that her power and essence are marked by the uterus, and its disposal is determined not by women but by the men of the group.

6. Conclusion

To my mind, attention to gender/sex ideology (among other ideologies) and to the semiological deployment of this ideology provides an interesting and fruitful analysis of systems of belief and practice. It provides insight into how contestation within systems of belief and practice is coded, how interpretation of myth and the use of ritual and sign-symbol are the means by which such struggles are evinced. Furthermore, treating "religion" as if it is a primary and not a secondary category means that in both instances of the sacrifices referred to above, the religious studies scholar would be forced to either accept the wholesale slaughter of witches as normative and logical or as nefarious and insane; as either right or wrong. Equally so with *sati*, so that

---

6.   See Gayle Rubin's article (1975), drawing upon Claude Lévi-Strauss (1969), for an analysis of the oppression and exploitation of the female based on control of the womb.

in this "disputation" the religious studies scholar would be positioned as naming one group as authentically Hindu and the other as inauthentic, or even misguided. There could be no analysis but only sides to choose.

My own work, like Donald Wiebe's, tends not to be a part of mainstream academic work in the study of religion. And like Wiebe I have at times been frustrated, exasperated, and disappointed. As a poststructuralist feminist, however, I argue that there can be no certain truth for all times and all places: humans are socially and historically bound and so too all their constructions and creations. If, then, I do not claim the position of truth, I must work to convince others of the validity of my work and of the lenses I develop and use for analyzing systems of belief and practice. How this work of convincing takes place is of course through teaching, research, and writing, and ongoing conversations. I am in dialogue with my colleagues and it seems to me that this is the only way to meet resistance and to effect change. Wiebe, of course, has always taken the path of dialogue. There have been those who have agreed, those who have not, and those who are still not quite certain or only agree in part. In all this, however, Wiebe's argument concerning the need for a scientific study of religion has not been ignored. And it is this, I think, that marks Wiebe's success and the success of his lens for studying systems of belief and practice. If indeed there had been a failure of nerve, I would not be writing about it now.

References

Althusser, Louis. 1995. "Ideology and Ideological State Apparatuses (Notes Toward an Investigation)." In Slavoj Žižek, ed., *Mapping Ideology*, 100–140. London and New York: Verso.

Arnal, William E. 2000. "Definition." In Willi Braun and Russell T. McCutcheon, eds, *Guide to the Study of Religion*, 21–34. London and New York: Cassell.

Bal, Mieke. 1987. *Lethal Love: Feminist Literary Readings of Biblical Love Stories*. Indiana Studies in Biblical Literature. Bloomington: Indiana University Press.

———. 1988. *Death and Dissymmetry: The Politics of Coherence in the Book of Judges*. Chicago Studies in the History of Judaism. Chicago: University of Chicago Press.

Banerjee, Pompa. 2003. *Burning Women: Widows, Witches, and Early Modern European Travelers in India*. New York: Palgrave Macmillan.

Barthes, Roland. 1968. *Elements of Semiology*. Trans. A. Lavers and C. Smith. New York: Farrar, Straus & Giroux, Hill & Wang.

———. 1972. *Mythologies*. Ed. and trans. Annette Lavers. New York: Farrar, Straus & Giroux, Hill & Wang.

Hawley, John S., ed. 1994. *The Blessing and the Curse: The Burning of Wives in India*. New York: Oxford University Press.

Institoris, Heinrich and Jacob Sprenger. 2006. *Malleus Maleficarum: The English Translation*, vol. 2. Ed. and trans. Christopher S. Mackay. Cambridge: Cambridge University Press.

Jay, Nancy. 1992. *Throughout Your Generations Forever: Sacrifice, Religion, and Paternity*. Chicago: University of Chicago Press.

Juschka, Darlene. M. 2009. *Political Bodies/Body Politic: The Semiotics of Gender*. London: Equinox.

Lévi-Strauss, Claude. 1969. *The Elementary Structures of Kinship*. Trans. James Harle Bell, John Richard von Sturmer, and Rodney Needham. Boston: Beacon Press.

Lincoln, Bruce. 1989. *Discourse and the Construction of Society: Comparative Studies of Myth, Ritual and Classification*. New York and Oxford: Oxford University Press.

Mani, Lata. 1998. *Contentious Traditions: The Debate on Sati in Colonial India*. Berkeley: University of California Press.

McCutcheon, Russell T. 1997. *Manufacturing Religion: The Discourse on* sui generis *Religion and the Politics of Nostalgia*. New York: Oxford University Press.

———. 2001. *Critics not Caretakers: Redescribing the Public Study of Religion*. Albany: SUNY Press.

Rubin, Gayle. 1975. "The Traffic in Women: Notes on the 'Political Economy' of Sex." In Rayna R. Reiter, ed., *Toward an Anthropology of Women*, 157–210. New York and London: Monthly Review Press.

Saussure, Ferdinand de. 1966. *Course in General Linguistics*. Eds Charles Bally and Albert Sechehaye, in collaboration with Albert Reidlinger. Trans. W. Baskin. New York: McGraw-Hill.

Sebeok, Thomas A. 1994. *Signs: An Introduction to Semiotics*. Toronto and Buffalo: University of Toronto Press.

Sen, Mala. 2001. *Death by Fire: Sati, Dowry Death and Female Infanticide in Modern India*. London: Weidenfeld & Nicolson.

Sered, Susan S. 1994. *Priestess, Mother, Sacred Sister: Religions Dominated by Women*. New York: Oxford University Press.

Smith, Jonathan Z. 2004. *Relating Religion: Essays in the Study of Religion*. Chicago and London: University of Chicago Press.

Trial by Fire: A Report on Roop Kanwar's Death. 1987. Bombay: Women and Media Committee, Bombay Union of Journalists.

Turner, Victor. 1967. *The Forest of Symbols: Aspects of Ndembu Ritual*. Ithaca: Cornell University Press.

Weedon, Chris. 2001. *Feminist Practice and Poststructuralist Theory*. 2nd ed. Oxford: Blackwell.

Williams, Raymond. 1977. *Marxism and Literature*. Oxford: Oxford University Press.

A CRITICAL HISTORY OF RELIGION
AS A PSYCHOLOGICAL PHENOMENON

Janet Klippenstein

One of the major themes running through Donald Wiebe's work is the argument that the academic study of religion should be a scientific endeavor. In fact, he argues that the academic study of religion has from its inception been a scientific endeavor, even if more current scholarship may indicate otherwise (Wiebe 1984: 419 [23–24]). The objective, scientific agendas of founding figures such as F. Max Müller (Wiebe 1999a) and Cornelus Petrus Tiele (Wiebe 1999b) distinguished Religious Studies from theological and confessional pursuits and ushered it into Western university curricula in the mid-nineteenth century (Wiebe 1984: 405–406 [11–12]; 1999c: 280). Since these early developments, however, scholars of religion have failed to pursue the project of explaining religion by using repeatable, reliable, and objective methodologies and have instead turned to the pursuit of under-standing religion in a non-reductionist manner. With this famous "failure of nerve" (Wiebe 1984) among contemporary scholars, problematic and unnecessary theological and confessional concerns have been integrated into the study of religion. Hence, Wiebe advocates for a return to the (original) scientific emphasis in the study of religion.

Psychology, firmly rooted in the social sciences, is one of the key disci-plines involved in the science of religion, and it has been for quite some time. Most of the "founding figures" of psychology have published works on religion (e.g., Coe 1917; Hall 1917; James 1902; Leuba 1912; Starbuck 1911; Wundt 1905). Despite getting little attention in Religious Studies or in broader psychological circles (Beit-Hallahmi 1974; Paloutzian 1996; Palout-zian and Park 2005a; Wulff 1998), the psychology of religion has been a rather prolific sub-discipline of Psychology since these early figures as well. For example, in 1976 the American Psychological Association established division 36, which in 1993 was named "Psychology of Religion." In addi-tion to the *Journal for the Scientific Study of Religion*, which has been publishing psychological and sociological studies of religion since 1949, the

International Journal for the Psychology of Religion and the *Journal for the Psychology of Religion* have been publishing articles on religion and psychology since 1991 and 1992, respectively (see Belzen 1999 for a more detailed history).

While the psychology of religion may get limited attention, the cognitive science of religion has enjoyed increasing visibility[1] within Religious Studies. Scholars such as Pascal Boyer (1994), Harvey Whitehouse (2000), Justin Barrett (2004), and E. Robert McCauley and Thomas Lawson (McCauley and Lawson 2002) have applied cognitive and evolutionary theories of more general human capacities like language, memory, attribution, and agency detection to questions related to religious behaviors like ritual and belief in deities. There may be some debate about the relationship between the psychology of religion and the cognitive science of religion,[2] but the existence of both indicates that there is considerable variation with respect to how psychological theories and methods are and can be applied to behaviors deemed religious. Underlying all of this variety is the assumption that there is something psychological about religion and that therefore psychologists have something to contribute to our understanding of it. Further, because Psychology is part of the social sciences, psychologists have something to contribute to the scientific—as opposed to confessional or theological—understanding of religion.

That there is something psychological about religion may seem like a very common-sense assertion, something not worth discussing in much detail. Since individuals participate in religion, then of course there will be psychological components to religious participation, such as beliefs, emotions,

---

1. Consider, for example, the wealth of new publications related to the cognitive science of religion (CSR), such as the exchanges between Edward Slingerland (2008a, 2008b, 2008c) and Francisca Cho and Richard K. Squier (2008a, 2008b, 2008c) in the *Journal for the American Academy of Religion* and the November 2008 issue of the *Council of Societies for the Study of Religion Bulletin* dedicated to CSR. Ann Taves has also recently published a book in which she applies research from CSR to the study of religious experience (Taves 2009).

2. While CSR and the psychology of religion are both part of the broader field of Psychology, there appears to be little interaction between the sub-fields. As I just mentioned, those scholars working within the cognitive science of religion tend to rely little on the scholarship produced by those working within the psychology of religion, instead preferring to utilize theories related to broad human capabilities (see Belzen 2005a: 828). Likewise, psychology of religion publications make few references to cognitive scientists of religion. One exception is Park and Paloutzian's edited volume, *Handbook of the Psychology of Religion and Spirituality* (2005b), which could indicate a coming change in the field. Elizabeth Weiss Ozorak suggests that such a change would be welcome, as it would save psychologists of religion from "toiling in obscurity" (Ozorak 2005: 216), seeing as they are hardly prominent in either Religious Studies or Psychology more generally.

thoughts, and experiences, as well as less conscious processes like memory and perception, all of which we can study using a variety of psychological methods. Still, the relationship between religion and psychology is more complicated than the relationship between an object of study and the scientific means of studying it. One, psychology and psychological concepts and discourses have become a prominent part of many forms of contemporary religiosity as well. As one example, individuals who describe themselves as "spiritual but not religious" tend to see their "spirituality" as free from the practical and dogmatic restrictions of specific religions, and choose beliefs and practices from a variety of traditions and cultures. The criterion for these choices is often that they "feel right" or "work" for the individuals in the pursuit of some form of self-improvement, self-fulfillment, self-realization, enlightenment, etc. (Carrette and King 2005; Heelas and Woodhead 2005; Roof 1999). When discussing their choices and goals, "spiritual but not religious" individuals tend to make copious use of psychological discourses (e.g., emotions, experience, thoughts, something "feeling right," etc.) (Heelas and Woodhead 2005: 3–4). In other words, one of the scientific disciplines used to study what we call religion is, in many cases, integrated into the practices and productions that we study, suggesting a fuzzy delineation between the object of study and our methods for studying it.

Two, the relationship between religion and psychology or the psychological is complicated because neither of the concepts in the relationship is self-evident or unproblematic. As has become very clear in the last two decades of Religious Studies scholarship, the concept of religion—and all of the practices and human productions that we associate with it—is not a natural one (see, for example, Fitzgerald 2000; King 1999; Masuzawa 1993, 2005; McCutcheon 1997). Religion as a taxonomic category or distinct object of scholarly (and other forms of) concern has its own particular history, one that is intertwined with not only Religious Studies and the theories and methodologies we use within the discipline, but also with broader social movements like colonialism and imperialism. Likewise, the existence of the psychological, which can be isolated and studied using a variety of methodologies and theories, is itself a historical emergence that is not tied solely to the emergence of Psychology as a university discipline.

Incidentally, Religious Studies and Psychology share a similar history. Max Müller took his chair in comparative philology at Oxford in 1868 (Masuzawa 2005: 212), and the first *Religionswissenschaft* departments were established at the Universities of Amsterdam, Groningen, Leiden (where C. P. Tiele was a professor), and Utrecht in 1877 with the Dutch Universities Act (Masuzawa 2005: 107–20; Smith 1982: 102–103). Just two years after the Dutch Universities Act, Wilhelm Wundt, generally considered the founder of experimental psychology, established his lab in Leipzig in 1879

(Danziger 1990: 17). So both Religious Studies and Psychology emerged as modern university disciplines in the same period, suggesting a similar heritage, at least as far as the disciplines are concerned.

Of course, while the disciplinary history of both Religious Studies and Psychology is useful for those interested in understanding better the two fields, it does not address all of the questions that arise (or at least should arise) when it comes to considering religion as a psychological phenomenon. While religion as an object of study is certainly tied to the emergence of the discipline dedicated to its scientific study, as discussed above religion is also tied to political and economic practices like imperialism and colonialism. Likewise, the notion of individuals in possession of a psychological life open to examination is tied to the emergence of Psychology as a discipline, but it is also tied to other political and economic developments as well. For example, as I will discuss in more detail shortly, Kurt Danziger links the emergence of the modern psychological subject to philosophical antecedents like the Cartesian distinction between mind and body (Danziger 1990: 21). Nikolas Rose and Jeremy Carrette connect the atomized individual of psychological study to the political and economic structure of the liberal nation state (Carrette 2008; Rose 1985, 1990, 1996). The relationship that modern individuals—scholars included—tend to see between religion and the psychological is not solely explained by the disciplines devoted to their study and their respective histories. There are broader historical and cultural influences at work, and they warrant consideration.

When I say that the emergence of religion, the psychological, and their relationship warrant consideration, what I am suggesting is that a critical history of the concepts and their associated disciplines could prove insightful for those scholars who are interested in better understanding their field and the concepts that they work with. As Nikolas Rose puts it when describing his critical history of psychology, this approach is "one that helps think about the nature and limits of our present, about the conditions under which that which we take for the truth and reality has been established" (Rose 1996: 18). Rose is referring specifically to the "truth and reality" (1996: 18) of humans as psychological beings equipped with an inner life that is both internal or private and open to examination and interpretation through a variety of methods (psychoanalysis, social psychological experiments, etc.), but in the case of this essay a critical history would involve attending to the conditions under which the "truth" of religion as a personal or psychological phenomenon has been established.

Such a foray into ostensibly postmodern territory is not intended to discredit science, to declare the non-existence of the mind, brain, or religion, or to call for a retreat from scientific inquiry in order to allow theological and confessional agendas to take precedence in the study of religion. Rather than negating or discrediting the scientific study of religion, I suggest that a critical historical examination of the concepts that such a study relies on broadens the scope of scholarly inquiry to include the rich historical, cultural, political, and economic context in which science is practiced. The nerve that scholars should have to study religion scientifically can be extended—and should be extended, I contend—to examining the conditions in which the theories, methods, and concepts that they utilize are possible. Just as a better understanding of the history of Religious Studies can help students and scholars grasp better their field and its goals (Wiebe 1999b: 32), so too can a better understanding of the historical developments of the concepts and scholarly practices that we rely on and often take for granted help us to develop a better sense of our field and the context in which it exists, and to develop more insightful theories and methods for studying the behaviors we tend to call religious.

Rather than try to trace the entire history of religion, the psychological, Religious Studies, and Psychology—which would be a rather daunting task—what I would like to do here to support my argument for the value of a critical history of the key concepts in our field is to look at one point at which the histories and contexts of all of these concepts and disciplines intersect. One of the most important sites of this kind of intersection is the modern subject, imbued with an inner life of thoughts, desires, beliefs, and experiences (see Henking 2001: 66, 71 for a similar argument). There are several scholars who have attempted to assess critically religion and psychology as intersecting disciplines and objects of knowledge, and who have touched on the centrality of the individual or subject as well. Tim Murphy, for example, spends a good deal of time in his book *Representing Religion* critiquing the assumptions that inform what in an earlier article he calls "mentalist" explanations of religion (Murphy 2003: 49), which treat individual consciousness—often the purview of psychology—as the starting point of analysis and explanation (Murphy 2007: 15). He lists several examples of such theories of religion, including work by Pascal Boyer, Stewart Guthrie, and Stark and Bainbridge (2007: 15), and he even devotes a chapter of his book to a critique of William James, focusing on his individualist analysis (2007: 38–53). Murphy's issue with mentalist theories of religion is that they take as unquestioned certain historically specific concepts, such as the Cartesian distinction between subject and object, mind and world, and interior and exterior (2007: 14). The cognizing individual is prioritized over the social structure in which that individual was constituted, with very little thought to how or why this is possible. To combat this Murphy develops a semiotic theory of religion that does not rely on the subject at all (Murphy 2007).

Similarly, Jeremy Carrette also finds the assumption that religion is a psychological phenomenon problematic. He argues that a critical assessment of the intersection of psychology and religion should focus on the historical conditions that brought religion and psychology together, the nature of psychological discourses and how they shape individual experience, the problematic individual/social and mind/body binaries that inform psychological theories, and the technologies that contribute to the psychologization of religion (Carrette 2001: 120). In his later work, Carrette integrates a concern with economic development and a critical history of psychology, connecting the psychology of religion (in its various guises, from psychotherapy to the cognitive science of religion) to the constructed individual–social divide and post-WWII economic structures (in other words, the free-market individual living with the neo-liberal state), and argues that the knowledge produced by scholars reinforces this same structure (Carrette 2008).

To return to the more localized context of the emergence of *Religionswissenschaft* and Psychology, Kurt Danziger, a historian of psychology, discusses the philosophical and scholarly developments that made Wundt's lab and his introspective methods possible. Wundt's methodology involved individuals monitoring and reporting on their own physiological states, and Danziger argues that introspection as a general possibility can be traced to the seventeenth-century Cartesian distinction between the mind and body (Danziger 1990: 21),[3] the same distinction that Murphy discusses with reference to mentalist theories of religion (Murphy 2007: 15). What Danziger argues Cartesian philosophy lacked until the nineteenth century, however, was a systematic methodology for investigating the mind. With the advent of the positive sciences in Europe in the nineteenth century, coupled with liberal individualist ideology (similar to, though slightly earlier than Carrette's arguments remarked above), Danziger argues that Wundt was not only able to presume the existence of the mind that one can "objectively" observe and describe, but also to devise a method of introspection based on the physical

---

3.   Like many cultural psychologists, Danziger's analysis of Wundt's lab is, in part, an attempt to reclaim and valorize earlier, more culturally-embedded forms of psychology (for another example, attempting to reclaim folk psychology, see Bruner 1990). This same nostalgia can been seen in those scholars who aim to rehabilitate the psychology of religion by returning to a more cultural psychological analysis, an approach they typically develop through reaffirming the value and importance of William James's (Belzen 2005b; Wulff 2005: 50) and Wilhelm Wundt's work (Belzen 2005a), as well as the work of classic phenomenologists of religion (Belzen 2005b: 61). While these analyses of cultural psychology more generally (see Shweder 1990 for an overview) do an excellent job of challenging contemporary psychological methods and theories, either "rehabilitating" a long-forgotten theorist or developing a new, more culturally embedded approach to psychology and the mind, they do not address how scholars—and everyone else, for that matter—are able to discuss such a thing as the mind or its analysis in the first place, nor how religion relates to the mind and its study.

sciences and the experimental method developed in physiology in Europe between 1830 and 1860 (Danziger 1990: 18–27).

Nikolas Rose expands considerably on Danziger's claim that Wundt's lab was possible because of liberal individualist ideology. In several books (1985, 1990, 1996), Rose has discussed what he calls the "psy complex"—the conglomeration of psychology, psychiatry, psychoanalysis, and psycho-therapy—and its role in the modern liberal democratic state. Since liberal government is based on a balance between respect for the autonomy of the family, the market, and the free citizen on the one hand, and the need for public order on the other hand, Rose argues that the psy disciplines provide a way of managing individuals at their most individual and inner levels for the sake of public order (Rose 1996: 69).

This type of management has roughly two related forms that together comprise what Michel Foucault calls "government" (1988: 19). In one, individuals recognize themselves as having inner lives, and apply psycho-logical technologies to themselves and make a variety of choices about their lives in order to shape a self that is both personally fulfilling (according to various objectives) and beneficial to their families, communities, and nation (Rose 1996: 78). In fact, individuals are not only free to choose, but they *have* to choose (their food, their home, their wardrobe, their career, their relationships, their religion, and so on), and choose correctly in order to fulfill themselves and satisfy their responsibilities to others (Rose 1996: 16, 78). In the other form of management, agents of the psy complex, such as parents, priests, doctors, and police officers, apply psychological techniques to individuals throughout their lives not in order to control them—which would restrict choice—but in order to *normalize* those who have made "inappropriate" or "wrong" choices and are therefore unable to fulfill themselves or their responsibilities to others (Rose 1985: 3–6).

The relationship between the individual "obliged to be free," as Rose puts it (1996: 17), and the impetus to normalization is also observable in some analyses of religion. For example, William Arnal links the emergence of religion as an object of scientific knowledge to the modern liberal nation state. He claims that the assumption that religion is generally defined in terms of beliefs about supernatural entities functions to render potentially conflicting group allegiances a matter of personal choice, thus making them largely inconsequential to general public order.[4] Further, the fact that religion

---

4. Arnal also notes that religious institutions are in this characterization of religion an "almost anti-liberal in-between land," existing betwixt the self-regulated individual and the (non-coercive) modern state. Any persistent social or collective utopian or absolute claims that a religious institution may make are, by rendering religion personal, private, and individual, domesticated, since with this particular configuration any collective claim can be explained as a violation of religion's "true" purpose (i.e., personal, private belief)

as a personal choice is related to the supernatural means that individual choices related to religion are, quite literally, immaterial (Arnal 2000: 31–33; 2001).[5] Talal Asad makes similar arguments in his analysis of the simultaneous emergence of religion and the secular as universal concepts in the middle of the nineteenth century. He contends that both religion and the secular emerged in the midst of social reforms that articulated the relationship between state law (being secular) and personal morality (being religious) or, in other words, the relationship between society and the individual in possession of subjective rights and moral agency (Asad 2003: 24).

If religion is, as Arnal and Asad argue, all about individual choice in the modern liberal nation, and the psy complex is, as Rose argues, an integral apparatus of the modern liberal nation and a key set of technologies related to the normalization of individual choices, then I think this establishes a significant intersection between psychology and religion. Following their analyses, the modern subject is an individual with an inner life that is simultaneously private and available for monitoring and normalization. This individual is also capable of and responsible for any number of choices. Religion is one of these many choices, and primarily relates to the individual's inner beliefs and experiences which, while irrelevant to the functioning of the state, are still open to study and potential normalization should someone make an improper or disruptive choice.

Given this connection between religion and psychology, the fact that most of the first psychologists—that is, the first to try to study systematically the individual's inner states—examined religion is placed in a broader context. Early American psychologists like William James (1902), James Leuba (1912), G. Stanley Hall (1917), George Albert Coe (1917), and Edwin Diller Starbuck (1911) all focused on religion in their work and are also considered central figures in early Psychology and "founding fathers" of the psychology of religion (Wulff 1991: 9–14). Even Wilhelm Wundt wrote three volumes on myth and religion (Wundt 1905). These scholars did not just happen to develop spontaneously an interest in religion and then accidentally define religion primarily in terms of belief and experience (Taves 1999: 261–307). Rather, the application of psychological study to religion was supported and reinforced by discourses that expanded far beyond Psychology or the

---

and a form of social control, which the modern state denies explicitly in itself (Arnal 2001: 5).

5. Arnal's argument works well with Donald Lopez's analysis of belief in the study of religion, wherein he observes that the phrase "I believe…" is only sensible when there are people who are different from the speaker (i.e., they do not believe the same thing). He also argues that the phrase acts as an agonistic affirmation of something that cannot be verified with material evidence (Lopez 1998: 33), which also works with Arnal's statements regarding the modern concept of religion and belief in the supernatural.

university. Likewise, it is not mere coincidence that many of these early psychologists of religion were interested in "better" forms of religion, thus adding an element of normalization to their research. For example, Starbuck wrote on the process of conversion and religion's roots in order to "allow the religious educator cautiously to ease the individual's way through the stages of growth into religious maturity" (Wulff 1991: 10), thereby providing guidelines for what we could call normalization. Similarly, Leuba argued that science, such as psychology, was capable of developing modified forms of confession, prayer, art, and ritual that would circumvent what he saw as religion's potential evils (Wulff 1991: 11). The impetus to normalization is part of broader discourses that informed and were reinforced by this kind of research.

Many psychologists of religion, including early ones, also distinguish between favorable and unfavorable religion in relation to how private and individual it is, bringing in again Murphy's (2007: 14), Carrette's (2008), Danziger's (1990: 21), and Rose's (1996: 17) discussions of the individual-social divide and its relationship to psychology and religion. William James famously distinguishes between institutional forms of religion and "the feelings, acts, and experiences of individual men in their solitude, so far as they apprehend themselves to stand in relation to whatever they may consider the divine" (James 1902: 36), and clearly favors the latter form. One of the most famous research frameworks in the psychology of religion, Allport's intrinsic–extrinsic religious orientation model (Allport 1950), also distinguishes between inner, experiential motivations and external, self-serving, practical motivations for participating in a religion (see Hill 2005: 45). Both orientations imply a choice, in keeping with Arnal's and Rose's arguments above, and the degree to which scholars often measure the correlations between extrinsic and intrinsic motivation and traits like ethnocentrism (Dicker 1977; Ponton and Gorsuch 1988), authoritarianism (Kahoe 1974, 1977), and grade point average (Kahoe 1974) also indicates that psychologists often apply the model with normalizing implications. More contemporary examples of normalizing implications in the psychology of religion include Silberman's discussion of the correlations between religion and violence and terrorism (Silberman 2005), and Geyer and Baumeister's discussion of religion and self-control (Geyer and Baumeister 2005), wherein certain kinds of behavior are favored over others.

While he does not discuss normalization, Jeremy Carrette also contextualizes the cognitive science of religion (CSR), arguing that the scholarship fits well in the broader neo-liberal economic structure of Europe and North America and the circulation and commodification of knowledge within it (Carrette 2008: 165). While there is a wide variety of theories produced within the cognitive sciences, Carrette argues that CSR overwhelmingly focuses on codified theories of cognition, those theories which maintain a more static division between the mind/brain and the outside world. Rather than being a better or more insightful form of theory, Carrette argues that codified theories of cognition are more economically efficient within the structures in which they are produced. The knowledge produced by them is more amenable to models of control and calculation (Carrette 2008: 166), making them more likely to be widely transmitted within the knowledge economy (2008: 172). While Carrette does not discuss normalization, his arguments could be related to those of Rose in particular: if the models of thought that CSR promote are widely transmitted within a social system, this is because they contribute to economic models of efficiency. CSR could be seen as contributing to the broader psy complex, in which individual choices are normalized in the name of self-fulfillment (Rose 1985: 3–6), which can in many cases be defined in terms of efficiency (in a work setting, for example).

Based on Arnal's, Asad's, and Rose's arguments, it also seems hardly coincidental that contemporary psychologists are increasingly interested in applying religion or spirituality[6] to their research, especially when said research relates to therapeutic (i.e., normalizing) practices. For example, Belzen argues that the majority of current psychology publications that deal with religion connect it to general health-related concepts like "well-being, stress, adjustment, affective disorders, trauma and intervention, [and] addiction" (Belzen 2005a: 815),[7] all of which could be substituted by the concept of self-fulfillment that Rose discusses. The psychology of religion also has similar contemporary applications. Park and Paloutzian's 2005 textbook on the psychology of religion and spirituality includes chapters on health and religion (Oman and Thorensen 2005), mental health and religion (Miller and Kelley 2005), religion and coping (Pargament, Ano, and Wacholtz 2005), and the role that spirituality can play in helping individuals deal with changes

6. Spirituality is also becoming a more regular focus in the psychology of religion. Some scholars argue that spirituality is a more all-inclusive moniker for what psychologists of religion have been studying all along (belief, experience, etc.). Others treat spirituality as a new object of study at least partially distinguishable from religion, and thus in need of new methods and theories. See Zinnbauer and Pargament (2005) and Zinnbauer et al. (1997) for discussions on religion and spirituality within the context of psychology of religion.

7. Belzen laments this focus because it is not related to some "clearly religious phenomena like prayer, visions, stigmata, exorcism, celibacy, tantrism, faith healing, and so on" (Belzen 2005a: 815). I find his assumption that he can distinguish between "clearly" religious and non-religious phenomena highly problematic, for reasons that I hope are clear based on the problematizations of religion that I offer above. Still, his statement that contemporary psychology of religion research is increasingly related to what could be called roughly "self-management" or "self-optimizing" techniques is worth considering.

in the workplace (Giacolone, Jurkewicz, and Fry 2005). To return to "spiritual but not religious" identities and discourses, Jeremy Carrette and Richard King discuss the relationship between therapeutic psychological practices and spirituality (2005: 54–86), making explicit reference to Rose's analyses of psychology and the constitution of the modern subject (2005: 57).

One of Carrette and King's arguments regarding contemporary spirituality is that it is closely intertwined with psychology, just as I argued earlier. However, they depict the relationship between spirituality and psychology as almost parasitic. They discuss and critique the psychologization of religion, or psychology's "takeover" of religion, with contemporary spirituality being the byproduct of the takeover (2005: 65). As I argued above, however, both religion and psychology are constructions emerging in the modern period, and draw from and reinforce some of the same ideologies and assumptions, such as the subject with an inner life, making a model in which one concept parasitically "takes over" the other one problematic. Carrette and King's claim that modern spirituality is closely related to the connection between psychology and religion is, however, very apt. Scholars of contemporary spirituality regularly observe that the people they study often reference personal experience, belief, and choice when discussing their spirituality (see, for example, Heelas and Woodhead 2005; Roof 1999; Carrette and King 2005). These "inner features" highlighted in spirituality discourses are similar to the ones that Arnal remarks are a central feature of religion within the context of the modern nation state (Arnal 2001) and that Rose identifies as the central focus of psychological research (Rose 1985: 4). Further, the ways in which spiritual beliefs, experiences, choices, and their associated practices are aimed at self-improvement or self-transformation relate to Rose's arguments about technologies of the self and their role in normalization and government (Rose 1996).

One of the benefits of an examination of the context in which religion as a psychological phenomenon, Religious Studies, and Psychology are each possible is that more contemporary practices like those of people who identify themselves as "spiritual but not religious" fit into that context. Rather than being some oddity, "spiritual but not religious" practices, in particular their integration of psychological concepts and discourses, make quite a lot of sense when understood in terms of the conditions in which religion and the psychological relate to one another through the modern subject. Similarly, other examples of modern forms of religiosity that integrate psychological concepts into their practices also make sense. Rather than just being some form of misappropriation of science (e.g., Martin 2008: 97), groups or individuals who, say, make use of cognitive theory to explain or justify their practices also fit within this framework, and can be understood in terms of the conditions underlying the possibility of religion as a psychological phenomenon.

Another benefit of contextualizing the scientific study of religion and its objects of study is that it makes for a richer understanding of scientific practices and how they relate to religion. Just as theological applications of cognitive science and "spiritual but not religious" discourses are not inauthentic nonsense but rather practices that make sense within this broader critical history of the relationships between religion, the psychological, Psychology, and Religious Studies, so too is the scientific study of religion not invalidated but rather contextualized. Such contextualization, in my opinion, fits well with the call for scholars steadfastly to refuse non-reductionistic studies of religion. Studies of religion as *sui generis*—that is, religion as somehow removed or immune from social, political, economic, psychological, and historical analyses—constitute a loss of scholarly nerve. Likewise, scientific studies of religion that try to maintain some *sui generis* status—again, scholarship removed from contextual considerations—for the theories and methodologies we use lack scholarly nerve.

References

Allport, Gordon W. 1950. *The Individual and His Religion: A Psychological Interpretation*. New York: Macmillan.

Arnal, William. 2000. "Definition." In Willi Braun and Russell T. McCutcheon, eds, *Guide to the Study of Religion*, 21–34. London: Cassell.

———. 2001. "The Segregation of Social Desire: 'Religion' and Disney World." *Journal of the American Academy of Religion* 69: 1–19.

Asad, Talal. 2003. *Formations of the Secular: Christianity, Islam, Modernity*. Stanford: Stanford University Press.

Barrett, Justin L. 2004. *Why Would Anyone Believe in God?* Toronto: Altamira.

Beit-Hallahmi, Benjamin. 1974. "Psychology of Religion 1880–1930: The Rise and Fall of a Psychological Movement." *Journal of the History of the Behavioral Sciences* 10: 84–90.

Belzen, Jacob A. 1999. "The Cultural Psychological Approach to Religion: Contemporary Debates on the Object of the Discipline." *Theory & Psychology* 9: 229–55.

———. 2005a. "A Way Out of the Crisis? From *Völkerpsychologie* to Cultural Psychology of Religion." *Theory & Psychology* 15: 812–38.

———. 2005b. "The *Varieties*, the Principles, and the Psychology of Religion." In Jeremy Carrette, ed., *William James and the Varieties of Religious Experience*, 58–78. New York: Routledge.

Boyer, Pascal. 1994. *The Naturalness of Religious Ideas: A Cognitive Theory of Religion*. Berkeley: University of California Press.

Bruner, Jerome. 1990. *Acts of Meaning*. Cambridge, MA: Harvard University Press.

Carrette, Jeremy. 2001. "Post-Structuralism and the Psychology of Religion." In Diane Jonte-Pace and William Parsons, eds, *Religion and Psychology: Mapping the Terrain*, 110–26. New York: Routledge.

———. 2008. *Religion and Critical Psychology: Religious Experience in the Knowledge Economy*. New York: Routledge.

Carrette, Jeremy and Richard King. 2005. *Selling Spirituality: The Silent Takeover of Religion*. New York: Routledge.

Cho, Francisca and Richard K. Squier. 2008a. "Reductionism: Be Afraid, Be Very Afraid." *Journal of the American Academy of Religion* 76: 412–17.

———. 2008b. "'He Blinded Me with Science': Science Chauvinism in the Study of Religion." *Journal of the American Academy of Religion* 76: 420–48.

———. 2008c. "Reply to Slingerland." *Journal of the American Academy of Religion* 76: 455–56.

Coe, George Albert. 1917 [1969]. *A Social Theory of Religious Education*. New York: Arno.

Danziger, Kurt. 1990. *Constructing the Subject: Historical Origins of Psychological Research*. Cambridge: Cambridge University Press.

Dicker, H. I. 1977. "Extrinsic–Intrinsic Religious Orientation and Ethnocentrism in Charitable Volunteering (St. John's University, 1975)." *Dissertation Abstracts International* 37: 4214B. Ann Arbor, MI: University Microfilms International.

Fitzgerald, Timothy. 2000. *The Ideology of Religious Studies*. Oxford: Oxford University Press.

Foucault, Michel. 1988. "Technologies of the Self." In Luther H. Martin, Huck Gutman and Patrick H. Hutton, eds, *Technologies of the Self: A Seminar with Michel Foucault*, 16–49. Amherst, MA: University of Massachusetts Press.

Geyer, Anne L. and Roy F. Baumeister. 2005. "Religion, Morality, and Self Control: Values, Virtues, and Vices." In Raymond F. Paloutzian and Crystal L. Park, eds, *Handbook of the Psychology of Religion and Spirituality*, 412–32. New York: Guilford.

Giacolone, Robert A., Carole L. Jurkewicz and Louis W. Fry. 2005. "From Advocacy to Science: The Next Steps in Workplace Spirituality Research." In Raymond F. Paloutzian and Crystal L. Park, eds, *Handbook of the Psychology of Religion and Spirituality*, 515–28. New York: Guilford Press.

Hall, G. Stanley. 1917. *Jesus, the Christ, in the Light of Psychology*. 2 vols. Garden City, NY: Doubleday, Page & Company.

Heelas, Paul and Linda Woodhead, with Benjamin Seel, Bronislaw Szerszynski, and Karin Tusting. 2005. *The Spiritual Revolution: Why Religion Is Giving Way to Spirituality*. Malden, MA: Blackwell.

Henking, Susan E. 2001. "Does (the History of) Religion and Psychological Studies Have a Subject?" In Diane Jonte-Pace and William Parsons, eds, *Religion and Psychology: Mapping the Terrain*, 59–74. New York: Routledge.

Hill, Peter C. 2005. "Measurement in the Psychology of Religion and Spirituality: Current Status and Evaluation." In Raymond F. Paloutzian and Crystal L. Park, eds, *Handbook of the Psychology of Religion and Spirituality*, 43–61. New York: Guilford Press.

James, William. 1902 [1999]. *The Varieties of Religious Experience: A Study in Human Nature*. New York: The Modern Library.

Kahoe, Richard D. 1974. "Personality and Achievement Correlates of Intrinsic and Extrinsic Religious Orientations." *Journal of Personality and Social Psychology* 29: 812–18.

———. 1977. "Intrinsic Religion and Authoritarianism: A Differentiated Relationship." *Journal for the Scientific Study of Religion* 16: 179–83.

King, Richard. 1999. *Orientalism and Religion: Postcolonial Theory, India, and "The Mystic East."* New York: Routledge.

Leuba, James. 1969 [1912]. *A Psychological Study of Religion: Its Origin, Function, and Future.* New York: AMS.

Lopez, Donald S. 1998. "Belief." In Mark C. Taylor, ed., *Critical Terms for Religious Studies*, 21–35. Chicago: University of Chicago Press.

Martin, Luther H. 2008. "The Uses (and Abuses) of the Cognitive Sciences for the Study of Religion." *Council of Societies for the Study of Religion Bulletin* 37(4): 95–98.

Masuzawa, Tomoko. 1993. *In Search of Dreamtime: The Quest for the Origin of Religion.* Chicago: University of Chicago Press.

———. 2005. *The Invention of World Religions: Or, How European Universalism was Preserved in the Language of Pluralism.* Chicago: University of Chicago Press.

McCauley, Robert N. and E. Thomas Lawson. 2002. *Bringing Ritual to Mind: Psychological Foundations of Cultural Forms.* New York: Cambridge University Press.

McCutcheon, Russell T. 1997. *Manufacturing Religion: The Discourse on* Sui Generis *Religion and the Politics of Nostalgia.* Oxford: Oxford University Press.

Miller, Lisa and Brien S. Kelley. 2005. "Relationships of Religiousity and Spirituality with Mental Health and Psychopathology." In Raymond F. Paloutzian and Crystal L. Park, eds, *Handbook of the Psychology of Religion and Spirituality*, 460–78. New York: Guilford Press.

Murphy, Tim. 2003. "Elements of a Semiotic Theory of Religion." *Method & Theory in the Study of Religion* 15: 48–56.

———. 2007. *Representing Religion: Essays in History, Theory, and Crisis.* London: Equinox.

Oman, Doug and Carl E. Thorensen. 2005. "Do Religion and Spirituality Influence Health?" In Raymond F. Paloutzian and Crystal L. Park, eds, *Handbook of the Psychology of Religion and Spirituality*, 435–59. New York: Guilford Press.

Ozorak, Elizabeth Weiss. 2005. "Cognitive Approaches to Religion." In Raymond F. Paloutzian and Crystal L. Park, eds, *Handbook of the Psychology of Religion and Spirituality*, 216–34. New York: Guilford Press.

Paloutzian, Raymond F. 1996. *An Invitation to the Psychology of Religion.* 2nd ed. Boston: Allan & Bacon.

Paloutzian, Raymond F. and Crystal L. Park. 2005a. "Integrative Themes in the Current Science of the Psychology of Religion." In Raymond F. Paloutzian and Crystal L. Park, eds, *Handbook of the Psychology of Religion and Spirituality*, 3–20. New York: Guilford Press.

———. Paloutzian, Raymond F. and Crystal L. Park. 2005b. *Handbook of the Psychology of Religion and Spirituality*, 3–20. New York: Guilford Press.

Pargament, Kenneth I., Gene G. Ano, and Amy B. Wacholtz. 2005. "The Religious Dimension of Coping: Advances in Theory, Research, and Practice." In Raymond F. Paloutzian and Crystal L. Park, eds, *Handbook of the Psychology of Religion and Spirituality*, 479–95. New York: Guilford Press.

Ponton, Marcel O. and Richard L. Gorsuch. 1988. "Prejudice and Religion Revisited: A Cross-Cultural Investigation with a Venezuelan Sample." *Journal for the Scientific Study of Religion* 27: 260–71.

Roof, Wade Clark. 1999. *Spiritual Marketplace: Baby Boomers and the Remaking of American Religion.* Princeton: Princeton University Press.

Rose, Nikolas. 1985. *The Psychological Complex: Psychology, Politics and Society in England 1869–1939*. Boston: Routledge & Kegan Paul.

———. 1990. *Governing the Soul: The Shaping of the Private Self*. New York: Routledge.

———. 1996. *Inventing Ourselves: Psychology, Power, and Personhood*. New York: Cambridge University Press.

Shweder, Richard A. 1990. "Cultural Psychology: What Is It?" In James W. Stigler, Richard A. Shweder, and Gilbert Herdt, eds, *Cultural Psychology: Essays on Comparative Human Development*, 1–43. New York: Cambridge University Press.

Silberman, Israela. 2005. "Religion, Violence, Terrorism, and Peace: A Meaning-System Analysis." In Raymond F. Paloutzian and Crystal L. Park, eds, *Handbook of the Psychology of Religion and Spirituality*, 529–49. New York: Guilford.

Slingerland, Edward. 2008a. "Who's Afraid of Reductionism? The Study of Religion in the Age of Cognitive Science." *Journal of the American Academy of Religion* 76: 375–411.

———. 2008b. "Reply to Cho and Squier." *Journal of the American Academy of Religion* 76: 418–19.

———. 2008c. "Response to Cho and Squier." *Journal of the American Academy of Religion* 76: 449–54.

Smith, Jonathan Z. 1982. *Imagining Religion: From Babylon to Jonestown*. Chicago: University of Chicago Press.

Starbuck, Edwin Diller. 1911. *The Psychology of Religion: An Empirical Study of the Growth of Religious Consciousness*. New York: C. Scribner's Sons.

Taves, Ann. 1999. *Fits, Trances, and Visions: Experiencing Religion and Explaining Experience from Wesley to James*. Princeton: Princeton University Press.

———. 2009. *Religious Experience Reconsidered: A Building-Block Approach to the Study of Religion and Other Special Things*. Princeton: Princeton University Press.

Whitehouse, Harvey. 2000. *Arguments and Icons: Divergent Modes of Religiosity*. New York: Oxford University Press.

Wiebe, Donald. 1984. "The Failure of Nerve in the Academic Study of Religion." *Studies in Religion / Sciences Religieuses* 13: 401–22.

———. 1999a. "Religion and the Scientific Impulse in the Nineteenth Century: Friedrich Max Müller and the Birth of the Science of Religion." In *The Politics of Religious Studies*, 9–30. New York: St. Martin's Press.

———. 1999b. "Toward the Founding of a Science of Religion: The Contribution of C.P. Tiele." In *The Politics of Religious Studies*, 31–50. New York: St. Martin's Press.

———. 1999c. "Appropriating Religion: Understanding Religion as an Object of Science." In *The Politics of Religious Studies*, 279–95. New York: St. Martin's Press.

Wulff, David M. 1991. *Psychology of Religion: Classic and Contemporary Views*. Toronto: John Wiley & Sons.

———. 1998. "Rethinking the Rise and Fall of the Psychology of Religion." In A. L. Molendijk and P. Pels, eds, *Religion in the Making: The Emergence of the Sciences of Religion*, 181–202. Leiden: Brill.

———. 2005. "Listening to James a Century Later: The *Varieties* as a Resource for Renewing the Psychology of Religion." In Jeremy Carrette, ed., *William James and the Varieties of Religious Experience*, 47–57. New York: Routledge.

Wundt, Wilhelm M. 1905 [1920]. *Völkerpsychologie: Eine Untersuchung der Entwicklungsgesetze von Sprache, Mythus und Sitte.* Vols. 4–6: *Mythus und Religion.* Stuttgart: Kröner.

Zinnbauer, Brian J. and Kenneth I. Pargament. 2005. "Religiousness and Spirituality." In Raymond F. Paloutzian and Crystal L. Park, eds, *Handbook of the Psychology of Religion and Spirituality*, 21–42. New York: Guilford .

Zinnbauer, Brian J., Kenneth I. Pargament, Brenda Cole, Mark S. Rye, Eric M. Butter, Timothy G. Belavich, Kathleen M. Hipp, Allie B. Scott, and Jill L. Kadar. 1997. "Religion and Spirituality: Unfuzzying the Fuzzy." *Journal for the Scientific Study of Religion* 36: 549–64.

EVERYTHING OLD IS NEW AGAIN*

Russell T. McCutcheon

Preamble

Almost thirty years ago Don Wiebe published the hard-hitting essay that opens this volume. It is therefore more than just lamentable that today, preparing a chapter for a book that further documents the problems that he first identified a generation ago, it is rather easy to find a site within the academic study of religion where scholars continue to illustrate their failures of critical intelligence. For example, looking no further than a recent issue of the flagship journal for the study of religion in North America, *Journal of the American Academy of Religion*,[1] readers find an essay where it is argued that scholars of religion can be "critical caretakers" in pursuing "constructive engagement" intended to bring about peace and justice (Omer 2011). Borrowing from my own work the opposed terms critic and caretaker—terms that I had earlier taken as a gift from Burton Mack (Mack 2001; McCutcheon 2001)—the author proposes a synthesis (or in keeping with her article's theme, a hybridization) that transcends the dichotomy, arguing that

> [t]he problem with McCutcheon's approach is that it blocks the possibility of thinking constructively about alternative modes of socializing that both redress past injustices and ask how religion and theology...may fit into the refashioning of national boundaries... Hence, McCutcheon's critical approach is insufficient for thinking about transforming conflicts and underlying structures of injustice. (Omer 2011: 460)

As I see it, the problem here is not that my work "blocks the possibility of thinking constructively." Instead, because such constructive work, as I see, is not part of the scholar of religion's task, the problem is that this author

* An earlier version of this essay was published as McCutcheon 2010b.

1. Of note are Wiebe's own critiques of the American Academy of Religion as well as *JAAR*'s content, specifically the annual Addresses of the American Academy of Religion's President; for example, see Wiebe 1997 and 2004 (both of which also appear in Wiebe 1999). See also Wiebe 2006.

either fails to understand or to sanction the basic distinction between studying social processes and participating in them. Whether or not I wish to live in the world that her efforts might make possible, she confuses me for a colleague and thus my work for a model, rather than see me as someone who is interested in studying the sort of social work that her efforts accomplish. The problem, then, is in failing to understand that there is no reason why the tools that I use to do my work ought to be useful to her in doing hers.[2]

Although a deserving site for Wiebe's critique, an article such as Omer's—one that assumes as self-evident the meaning of (i.e., social interests that drive the use of) "justice," "human rights," or "peace" and, furthermore, one that sees the scholar of religion as occupying a special place from which she can help to correct the ills of the world—would make for far too easy a target. It is for this reason that, despite the unfortunate manner in which the theologically liberal scholarship that Wiebe rightly critiqued still dominates the field, I am interested instead in considering here the failures in a rather different branch of scholarship, one supposedly defined by a more rigorously scientific attitude and thus one assumed by its practitioners to have finally overcome the poor habits of both the theological and the humanistic study of religion. But, as we all know, old habits some-times die hard.

1.

The recent publication of Ann Taves's book, *Religious Experience Reconsidered* (2009), provides me with an opportunity to comment on the synthesis of two aspects of our field, one quite old and the other rather new. The first is the common practice—at least since the Pietist-affiliated writers first appeared on the scene, but perhaps going back even further—of using the category "religious experience" to name what was assumed to be the unseen yet uniform causal force that inspired the various empirical things that scholars of religion study (what amounts to the old essence/manifestation distinction); the second is the far more recent application to our field of findings from that collection of disciplines now known as the cognitive sciences—applied, at first, to those behavioral practices classed as ritual (e.g., Lawson and McCauley's agenda-setting work [1990, 2002]), but now used to explain the persistence (i.e., not necessarily the actual origins so

---

2. Of course, one of the larger problems is that this author's argument for "envisioning a distinct relevance to the academic study of religion" and a "uniquely religious studies approach" (from the abstract of the article [Omer 2011: 459]) fails to see her work as merely an update of Mircea Eliade's (by now well critiqued) New Humanism thesis, in which scholars of religion bring to the table important tools for realizing basic features of human nature.

much as the successful transmission) of certain sorts of beliefs (e.g., in gods, ancestors, the afterlife, etc.).[3] Finding these two seemingly contradictory research traditions in the same book—contradictory inasmuch as one assumes an irreducibly private sentiment residing outside the historical world while the other is concerned with explaining our object of study in a rigorously naturalistic manner—is a curious mix and thus something worth considering.[4]

This coupling of mundane theories with a unique datum is worth considering because, in my reading of cognitive scientists of religion, the provocative gains that they announce (i.e., to have finally explained religion [e.g., Boyer 2001]) strike me as being based on surprisingly conservative assumptions, all of which leads to familiar and, for me, disappointing conclusions. To begin to demonstrate this, consider a talk that I attended in the Spring of 2010 in my own Department, given by one of our former undergraduate students, now pursuing graduate work in the cognitive science of religion (or what practitioners refer to as CSR).[5] The work was concerned with testing the theory, associated first with Pascal Boyer and now with Justin Barrett (e.g., Gregory and Barrett 2009), that certain ideas, if they differ in some small regard, from what is assumed to be a trans-human stock of hardwired, intuitive knowledge, will be more likely to be remembered and thus hold a competitive advantage when it comes time to pass them along to the next generation. (The assumption being that the persistence and widespread nature of beliefs in beings just like you and I but who are also, for instance,

3. Perhaps the best single essay overview of this emergent subfield is to be found in Geertz 2004. Slone 2006 is also very helpful.

4. That Taves is hardly the only cognitively-inclined scholar to bring these two together (e.g., most recently, see McNamara 2009; see also the essays collected in Andresen 2001) needs to be said, of course.

5. As an aside, I admit that I am curious about the number of acronyms that appear in the writings of those who work in this field. Some common examples include: TAVS (threat–activation system), HADD (hyperactive agency detection device), VM (vestibular-motor experiences and sensations), and, of course, the widely cited TOM (theory of mind) and MCI (minimally counterintuitive concepts). While effectively distinguishing the initiated from the uninitiated, and thereby assisting to establish in-group/out-group identities, this shorthand seems to lend a degree of scientific complexity and thus legitimacy to this fairly new subfield. For while any intellectual pursuit has its own technical vocabulary that its practitioners repeatedly employ in their work and, furthermore, while all technical vocabularies are the tips of large bodies of organized sets of assumptions that scholars put into practice while carrying out their work (what we might loosely call theories), not every field relies to such an extent on abbreviations to do such heavy theoretical lifting—though perhaps there are some literary critics who, when speaking to peers whom they assume equally well understand the trouble of assuming that T (i.e., text) is a repository of an AIM (i.e., author's intended meaning), simply roll their eyes and say "AS IF" (i.e., always simplistic intentional fallacy).

immortal or immaterial, might be explained by means of this theory.) Apart from suggesting that minimally counterintuitive ideas seem no more catchy (to pick up on Dan Sperber's now widely used epidemiological metaphor [1996]) than other sorts of ideas, the student's presentation made evident the difficulty (some might say impossibility) of trying to study a presumably necessary, universal, and thus pre-social human trait by means of such historically shifting, cultural constructs as language (e.g., the just used computer-based metaphor "hardwired").[6]

Case in point: consider the minimally counterintuitive sentence, "A rock that is sick," that was part of the questionnaire (or what those in the field might call the stimulus) presented to a group of test subjects by the student, in hopes, I presume, that the odd meaning conveyed by such a sentence would be more memorable than the test's more mundane meanings and sentences (i.e., those that confirmed the folk epistemology of the test subjects, such as the seemingly uncontroversial "A girl that is wise"). What I found most interesting, however, was that the sick rock prompted one of the other students in attendance jokingly to agree that, yes indeed, the rock was cool.[7] My point in citing this presentation? Only if we assume what some would regard as a rather conservative or at least very traditional correspondence theory of meaning (i.e., that words gain their meaning by referring, in some sort of stable and direct relationship, with real things and their actual qualities) could we hope, presumably along with those presenting test subjects with such a stimulus, for "A rock that is sick" to elicit something like the following chain of premises and inferences in a hypothetical test subject's mind:

1. All empirical items can be divided between organic and inorganic;
2. All organic items can be further subdivided between animate and inanimate;
3. Poorly functioning animate organic items can be termed sick;
4. Only animate organic things can be sick;
5. All rocks are inorganic;
6. Therefore, rocks cannot be sick.

6. It is not difficult to imagine the hardware/software metaphor (used to distinguish biology from culture) sometime soon sounding just as dated to our ears as does Marx's architectural metaphor of base/superstructure. What both sets of metaphors share, of course, is the effort to identify the pre-linguistic and thus abiding real in distinction from the merely linguistic, the epiphenomenal.

7. Apart from what it identifies as the "old version" of the word (to signify illness), the online *Urban Dictionary* (http://www.urbandictionary.com) indicates that the word "sick" is now commonly used to signify the following partial list of synonyms: awesome, sweet, nasty, gross, amazing, tight, wicked, vomit, dope, crazy, disgusting, sex, rad, shit, puke, nice, hot, good, gnarly, bad, great, ugly, drunk, fuck, insane, awesome, gay, fresh, fly, phat, dirty, badass, ass, mad, chill, etc.

Only by assuming these premises to be intuitive and thus naturally linked could we attribute the ability to remember "A rock that is sick" to its supposed counter-intuitiveness. But the moment that we abandon the correspondence theory of meaning, the moment that we view language as a culturally relative and historically dynamic closed system in which each signifier is made meaningful by its arbitrary and infinitely variable relationship to all other signifiers within the system—such as coming to see "sick" as signifying "rad" or "wicked" or possibly associating "sick rock" with a genre of music that is sweet and tight—then the theorist is back to square one, having no idea why the memory of the rock stuck out[8]—if indeed it is even recalled with any more frequency than the other test sentences (which, according to my former student, it is not).[9] If, of course, you have not controlled for the almost infinite malleability of the medium through which you are trying to study hypothetically trans-cultural universals (and how, precisely, does one control for this?), and, instead, have drawn conclusions about the universal only because you have pursued such experiments within a socially, and thus semantically, homogenous audience (in which sick just means sick!), then your survey results will simply indicate the degree to which a collection of signifiers are used in the accustomed way within your test population and will *not* necessarily tell you anything about a basic feature of pre-social cognition or, for that matter, how the custom came about—an experimental design flaw akin to the once common ethnographic practice of drawing conclusions about an entire group after only interviewing its leaders.[10]

8.   Even if the minimally counterintuitive thesis held then I could easily imagine someone whom feminists might once have called a male chauvinist pig, remembering another of the test sentences, "A girl that is wise," for reasons unanticipated by a more politically liberal researcher (because, for our hypothetical chauvinist, female wisdom could very well be considered counterintuitive). The point? Stimuli designed to signify uncontroversial universal traits are, contrary to the apparent hopes of the researcher, deeply embedded in socially variable worlds.

9.   Given that some recent studies have not supported the prediction that minimally counterintuitive ideas are more memorable, we now find ourselves at an interesting moment where this new field in the study of religion will be challenged to live up to its scientific billing as being based on testability and falsifiability. Simply put, as elegant as this theory is, how long will people continue to use it despite evidence to the contrary?

10.   This, of course, amounts to the common critique of IQ and other standardized tests in which information that is culturally and generationally specific to the researcher is assumed to be universally shared among the test subjects. Playing an edition of a trivia board game that is either too old or too young for its players, or using a dated popular cultural references to illustrate a point while teaching college students illustrate the problem with making such an assumption.

2.

We thus come to a question that, despite how cognitivists proceed with their work, has hardly been settled: is language a neutral medium that conveys meanings about things that exist outside of language (such as about sick rocks or how human cognition works) or is language itself constitutive of the worlds in which we live (and in which we do our cogitating)? The point I wish to press is that one does not have to be a Derridean deconstructionist to be a little more cautious about deciding this issue than cognitivists have so far been. Eager to find the root of religion in the mind/brain—which, it appears, will then comprise the ultimate naturalistic reduction of religion— they have failed to ask questions concerning the apparent ease of moving from part to whole, from contingent to necessary, from history to ahistory, from local to universal, and from culture to nature. My concern is that scholars applying the findings from such fields as cognitive and evolutionary psychology to the study of religion have failed to investigate these sorts of questions—a failure that, in my estimation, undermines the identification of their work as rigorously historical and scientific.

This failure is perhaps most evident in how such work adopts a culturally and historically local nomenclature (i.e., the ability to judge that this is religion and that is not) and then dehistoricizes and normalizes this classifi- cation system inasmuch as the ability to be religious is then assumed to be a natural and thus universal/eternal part of the human mind/brain.[11] This naturalization of the category religion troubles me because we all know—or at least I thought we did—of the critiques of the category religion as it was once used (I think here of critiques of the notion of *sui generis* religion). We all know that none of its possible Latin precursors likely meant what we mean by religion today (or at least as we have commonly defined it for the past few hundred years). We also all know that both this and the previous sentence's first person plural pronoun is something that, for critically minded scholars, always needs attention, for it signifies a rather precise group, originating in that part of the world commonly known as Europe, whose members eventually perfected the use of the marker "religion" to name a seemingly distinct domain of diverse (though, to contemporary critics, not necessarily inherently related) items of human activity and production. The corollary to this should also be well known: people outside of Europe (and by this I mean a Europe of fairly recent memory) were not spontaneously organizing themselves and their world in terms of what was and what was not religion or religious[12]—not, that is, until imperialism's

11.   Case in point, consider Wiebe 2010 for a survey of a neuropsychological theory of religion drawing on ancient rock art.

12.   I add the adjective here because some scholars make much of its difference from the noun, inasmuch as the adjective supposedly names a deeply human and thus universal

advance guard (i.e., those who are still colloquially known as explorers, traders, and yes, missionaries[13]) arrived on distant shores and, quite understandably, tried to make sense of the strange by means of a classification system that divided up and thereby managed the so-called new world in a way that was entirely familiar to those arriving for the first time.

As I said, my hope is that it would be difficult to find a contemporary scholar in our field not familiar, at least to some extent, with the work done in this area over the last twenty or thirty years—work originally aimed at critiquing the notion of irreducible and thus unexplainable religion but which easily applies to all uses of the category (when the category is presumed to name a permanent trait of the human).[14] But despite this critical turn away from seeing our object of study as somehow being a special case, we now find a thriving naturalistic industry developing a *unique* theory to discover the *unique* place in the brain or in the genome or in a collection of cognitive processes where the *uniquely* religious resides. The once and still popular "religious experience" has, however, now been replaced by Taves with a seemingly more inclusive, preferred term, "special experiences"—or, to be more accurate, experiences considered or, as she writes, deemed, special. But what are the special experiences? To begin with, they are something other than ordinary experiences—they're "unusual sorts of

quality of people rather than the noun, which is thought to name only reified, impersonal institutions (one would be correct, I think, to hear echoes of Wilfred Cantwell Smith's critique of "religion" in this widely used distinction). I would argue that this is purely a rhetorical distinction, as if saying that something is political (the adjective) amounts to something other than asserting that politics (the noun) exists. That the plurals of the noun—i.e., religions or Christianities—are often favored over the singular is an equally suspect move, for it effectively bypasses the question of definition and instead simply asserts the existence of a plurality, as if this is an historically rigorous move. For example, speaking only of "birds" naturalizes the presumption (rather than defending it and elaborating on it) that the word/concept "bird," in distinction from, say, fish or plant, is useful. Settling the question of its utility takes argumentation rather than a more detailed study of the variety of birds.

13.   Another worthwhile study in failure of nerve would be to examine the manner in which scholars have uncritically adopted other participant or folk taxonomies and the interests that drive them, such as assuming that such a local, participant term as "missionary" is somehow a unique, apolitical social role and not simply an imperial social actor benefiting from the cover of a particular form of social rhetoric.

14.   Presumably it is because this was the focus of my first book, *Manufacturing Religion* (1997), that results in it, at least up to now, being cited in many works by cognitivist scholars of religion; such citations allow them to take as given that the notion of *sui generis* ought to be abandoned, thereby opening the door for their own explanatory work. That my subsequent work is rarely cited by these writers—work that has argued that *any* use of the category religion is a socio-political technique of management—is, perhaps, to be expected.

experiences" (2009: xv) and "singular experiences" (2009: 10). Despite the reconsidered nomenclature, the unusual experiences that Taves brings to her readers' attention are, of course, the usual suspects, for they still fall within a family resemblance domain familiar to anyone acquainted with the study of those experiences formerly known as religious, those that "people some-times ascribe the special characteristics to[,] things that we (as scholars) associate with terms such as 'religious,' magical,' 'mystical,' 'spiritual,' et cetera" (2009: 8). So, despite the change in name, it is not clear that the data has been all that reconsidered—we still end up finding people the world over who see "religion-like" things as like. The common (common to a particular us, that is) limits of the folk taxon "religion," naming a distinct domain, are here reproduced; once again, then, a local and therefore familiar folk discourse has simply been adopted by scholars and uncritically elevated to the analytic level, and then used by them as if it described actual states of affairs in the world that need to be explained.

For some time I have been perplexed by how willing many serious, supposedly scientific scholars are to adopt an untheorized folk taxon, as if a classification used by a group whom we *happen* to study (and, in many cases, of which we *happen* to be members ourselves) somehow corresponds to an actual aspect of reality that *ought* to be studied.[15] After all, all groups of humans have complex, local taxonomic systems that they use to signify, classify, and thereby sort their worlds, yet scholars do not necessarily conceive of each of them as universal properties of the human mind. To take but one, rather silly example, there is no academic study of nerds despite the fact that my niece and her friends once called themselves "math nerds," in contradistinction to those of their friends who were not. Or, closer to our academic home, and recalling Pascal Boyer's *The Naturalness of Religious Ideas* (1994), I wonder what scholars in North America would make of a book originating from, say, a contemporary Polynesian author that argued that mana was a *natural* part of the pan-human cognition and not simply a local term that is merely of ethnographic curiosity to non-Polynesians—a book that described and then explained the mana-like experiences that you and I have, despite our lacking the word in our own vocabulary.

This, of course, will strike most scholars as just silly, since we of course know that "their" concept of mana is but a curious, ethnographically local concept; yet scholars who are themselves no less immersed in an

---

15. Scholars of religion ought to be familiar with this. For instance, they are often frustrated by specialists in other fields (e.g., Political Scientists) who, when they venture to talk about religion, merely drag out what often amounts to a Sunday School level of expertise on the subject. This is the same frustration I am trying to identify but, this time, in the work of serious scholars of religion.

ethnographically local socio-semantic world routinely make claims such as the following, from the opening lines to a handbook's chapter on African religions:

> If there is wisdom in starting with first things first, then a philosophical discussion of African religions should start with an inquiry into the applicability of the concept of religion to African life and thought. Not only is the word "religion" not an African word…, it is doubtful whether there is a single-word or even periphrastic translation of the word in any African language. This does not mean, of course, that the phenomenon itself does not exist among Africans. One may have something without being given to talking about it. [John S.] Mbiti himself, for example, maintains in his *African Religions and Philosophy* that Africans are pre-eminently religious, not even knowing how to live without religion. (Wiredu 1997: 34)

This is a perplexing, and thus frustrating, paragraph, for the historical specificity that is offered in its opening sentences is quickly taken away by its close, in which the limitations of actual languages are overcome by the presumed presence of a cross-cultural universal that, despite being an element of language, somehow floats free of it—"One may have something without being given to talking about it." And voilà, via the correspondence theory of language (i.e., language is secondary and merely corresponds to prior, pre-linguistic, and thus real, things in the world) the old essence/manifestation distinction has returned to the field. Just how it is that the author knows us to have some thing even if we cannot quite put it into words is, predictably, simply asserted and not argued or defended. Substituting "taboo" or "dharma" for "religion" in this paragraph, and also "North American" for "African," makes evident just how intellectually troublesome this approach is. But why is this not apparent to scholars who pride themselves on their historical and scientific precision? Why is it that those of us who happen to originate from a cultural/historical context in which "religion" is used to name an aspect of the social world (and I do not just mean theologians or liberal humanists doing this work, as I might have earlier in my career, but also ardently reductionistic, naturalistic scholars[16]) continue to invest time in developing a theory of religion as if this word names a stable, cross-cultural reality that needs to be described and then demands explanation?

---

16. It must be said that the recently assembled neurobiological toolbox has been equally useful to members of all three of these groups—for entirely different purposes, of course. Tracing the role of the Templeton Foundation in making this work possible, for members of all three seemingly distinct groups, would be a project well worth tackling.

3.

To see some of the problems involved in such a research program consider the opening pages to his well received, *Modes of Religiosity* (2004), in which Harvey Whitehouse devotes an early section to "What Is Religion?"[17] After acknowledging that "[t]he everyday meaning of the word 'religion' is not all that easy to pin down" he argues that, despite "a range of exemplary features" often being called upon to name something as religious, "[n]one of these features is necessary for the attribution of the label, but almost any combination is sufficient" (2004: 1) He therefore concludes that this utterly vague and rather imprecise use of the folk term signals the need to develop a scientific approach to the topic. But it does not strike me as the task of scholarship to adopt and then systematize other people's folk taxons— because those folks just got it wrong or were sloppy, despite their having had a pretty good intuition into a cross-cultural universal. Of course, we might wish to theorize why some humans (hardly all) use "religion" to name aspects of their social world, thereby studying the various ways in which the taxon (and its wider discourse) is used, and the practical effects of these uses (which amounts to developing a theory as to why "religion," and not religion, is so catchy). But then we will no longer be studying religion, describing religions, or defining religion but, instead, studying social actors who use the term, regardless of its definition, and the work to which it gets put.

However, as with so many of the other scholars, Whitehouse's work is premised on the old troublesome folk notion of religion: belief in superhuman agents and the actions grouped around these beliefs. The trouble is this: some of the people whom we study say that superhuman agents exist, and that a collection of beliefs, behaviors, and institutions relevant to these agents are somehow set apart from other aspects of culture, making this set of items "religious." But many of the people we study do not talk, write, act, or organize in this way at all. Taking just some of our research subjects' word for this set-apartness and interconnection (a move that is likely linked to scholars feeling rather comfortable with a folk system in which they have themselves been reared), scholars then busily set about accounting for the existence of this coherent, distinct domain—after all, they develop theories of religion and are not content to understand the thing that some of their research subjects call religion to be sufficiently explained by a higher order theory of something else entirely, of which those things grouped together as religion are but ethnographically and historically local instances (that Bloch [2008] is pushing in this direction is, however, encouraging). What if, as suggested above, what attracted the scholarly imagination was not the

17. The example of Whitehouse's work relies on material from my own "Religion Before 'Religion'?" (2010a).

taken-for-granted distinctness of that grouping of things some know as religion (thus requiring a specific theory to account for its existence as a unique domain of human practice) but, instead, the practitioners' compulsion to represent certain features of their social world *as* essentially interconnected and thus distinct, unique, set-apart, and, with a nod to Taves, special? Then, we would work on developing not a theory of religion but, instead, a theory of "religion"—a theory of the process of specialization (which, unlike religion, may very well turn out to be among the cognitive processes Geertz refers to as "the most fundamental aspects of human cognition" [2004: 385]).[18] What's more, such an approach would simply be a component of a far wider theory of social classification/identity construction (in a word, a theory of signification, in the most general sense of the term). If *this* was our approach, then those who study the things their research subjects called religion would quickly understand themselves to part of a much larger study of how humans make and enforce meanings and identities in the world—the most supposedly mundane and ordinary no less central to such a study than any other, since the process of centralization itself is the object of study. This would be a truly cross-disciplinary project, one affording none of its contributors the pretense of having data that hold a special place. Moreover, it strikes me that only such an approach would be truly scientific—if by "scientific" we meant an approach that studies all emic reports equally and according to etic procedures and interests rather than one that elevates select emic terms or interests to etic status and thus legitimacy.

To rephrase: since we can trace the history of "religion" and "religious experience" as items of discourse—and by this I mean, for example, a genealogical study of the invention of religious experience as an agreed upon subset of the broader range of interior dispositions known as experiences—it is indeed odd to find naturalistic scholars so confident that they will find precisely where this local discursive construct resides in the brain of *all* human beings—past, present, and future. This I find puzzling, for it could be persuasively argued that the only reason scholars find religion everywhere in the world, and religious experience in everyone's heads, is because those very scholars approach the world—in fact, *make* their world— by using this term, defined broadly enough, so as always to find sufficient things that they can deem/group together as religion—suggesting to me that a theory of *deeming* (i.e., a theory of signification) and *grouping* (i.e., a theory of classification) are far more required than a theory of religion. For example, because so many scholars today understand "magic" or "cult" no longer to be analytically useful (inasmuch as they are either linked to bygone

18. Taira (2010) provides an excellent, recent example of what our work begins to look like when we make this switch to examining not religion but the discourse on religion.

concerns or troublesome politics), a theory concerning why they were ever used (or continue to be used by some) makes far more sense than trying to develop a new theory of magic or a better theory of cults. Although I have some differences of opinion with parts of his thesis (for example, see McCutcheon 2007a: 234–35; 2007b: 188 n. 12), this was what David Chidester so nicely did in his *Savage Systems* (1996): trace the history not of religion but, instead, of the deployment of consecutive (and, generally, ever-widening) definitions of religion, whereby an ever-greater number of things people did and said on the colonial frontier got to count *as* religious and therefore be treated in a certain manner.

4.

To come at the problem from another direction: just because we find people who self-identify as citizens all over the world does not mean that there is a necessary, evolutionary, cognitive basis to citizenship. The very precise mode of social membership signaled by the concept of citizen is only as recent (and as successful) as the rise (and the unchecked coercive power) of the nation-state—one of the many ways in which human beings have organized social life. Or, to call on a more timely and, for some, emotionally potent example, because we know that there is no agreed-upon definition of "terrorism" (the last time I checked the UN had no such definition, for one group's freedom fighter is likely its opponent's terrorist), it would be far from sensible to look for a gene or a cognitive trigger that makes one a terrorist. Or because legislatures all over the world define and then, when it suits the majority or the powerful (not necessarily overlapping groups!), redefine what gets to count as a crime, looking for a neurobiological basis for criminality would be downright silly. Right? But—and *this* is the interesting thing!—given how high the stakes are in normalizing and thereby regulating competing forms of human behavior, just such fields *do indeed exist*—fields of study that naturalize and, in doing so, substantialize what others would simply "deem" as culturally produced (and perhaps even class-relevant) concepts and identities.[19] But in the face of the almost infinitely variable ways in which those things we call terrorism or criminality get defined, nailing down a definition will, I conjecture, meet with as much success as the effort to ensure that we always mean just one thing by "sick."

But if our object of study, such as terrorism and crime, is a product of classification systems and choices driven by specific sets of social interests (i.e., making both terrorism and crime discursive objects and not natural

19. Murphy's (n.d.) attempt to provide a neurobiological approach to terrorism is questionable on many grounds but the growing field of biocriminology is being taken very seriously; for an overview, see Monaghan 2009.

facts), then it makes sense that one would have great difficulty discovering "in the bones" some trait that identified one as either a terrorist or a criminal. In support of this, consider one of the conclusions of the following 1999 report commissioned by the Federal Research Division of the US Library of Congress:

> In addition to having normal personalities and not being diagnosably mentally disturbed, a terrorist's other characteristics make him or her practically indistinguishable from normal people, at least in terms of outward appearance. (Hudson 1999: 61)

Indeed; for it would not be difficult to argue that what makes the so-called abnormal terrorist distinguishable from, say, the normal freedom fighter is (despite the above quote's insinuation of some invisible inner intention) the definition that is or is not applied to the act, not the inherent traits of the act or the social actor so named. Identity, I would therefore argue, is a social attribution, a choice and an act, and not an interior disposition that is first felt and then given an "outward appearance."

Of course, if one were seeking to authorize one among many definitions, one among many identities, and thereby legitimize the interests that it supported, then being able to lodge the product of that definition in the very fabric of some person's cognition and genes would be a pretty handy device. And, like controlling for all of the definitions of the signifier "sick," so as to normalize one and only one way of using the term, such scholars would likely have to develop ways to control the variability of social interests and language, so as to find a secure biological home for those otherwise immaterial discursive objects. Take, for example, this attempt to find a neurobiological basis to behavior understood as violent. But what counts as violence, you ask?

> For the purpose of this review, violent behavior is defined as overt and intentional physically aggressive behavior against another person. Examples include beating, kicking, choking, pushing, grabbing, throwing objects, using a weapon, threatening to use a weapon, and forcing sex. The definition does not include aggression against self. Violent crimes include murder, robbery, assault, and rape. In this review, I will not deal with organized state violence or ethnic warfare. (Volavka 1999; see also 2002: 2)

Although I would imagine violence could be defined as a far wider, and thus far more complex thing than simply intentional, individual aggression coupled with low self-control (curiously, professional football linebackers, boxers, and hunters escaped the scholar's net and why not include war, suicide, genocide, or police violence?), such a narrow definition *makes good analytical sense*, for it produces a nicely manageable discursive object that can be tackled and seemingly controlled with a small set of tools. What's more, the result of such work is an object that mirrors the taken-for-granted assumptions about the world that we had before embarking on the analysis. Authors count on readers not recognizing this oddly self-serving nature of their work, of course. For instance, only because they all know what counts as terrorism will most readers see no problem with a *New York Times* reviewer making the following claim, in a review on recent works on "the terrorist mind": "Despite the lack of a single terrorist profile, researchers have largely agreed on the risk factors for involvement" (Kershaw 2010). Translation? We don't really know what it is, but we nonetheless know how you become one. In this one sentence, moving as it does from indecision to utter conviction, we see how easily a discursive object can be treated as a stable fact.

5.

And this is the problem with the neurobiological approach—it takes what some of us understand to be a variable (i.e., historical, contingent, local, etc.) discursive object as a settled matter of eternal biological fact (i.e., ahistorical, necessary, universal, etc.), thereby interiorizing, medicalizing, and thus normalizing what, some of us would argue, is a contestable and always ongoing social, discursive event (i.e., not religion but, instead, the very act and implications of naming, treating, etc., this or that *as* religion[20]). This is a point nicely made by Jeff Ferrell, a professor of sociology at Texas Christian University and editor of the NYU Press series, Alternative Criminology. The discipline of Criminology's goal, as he understands it, has been to explain that what societies take to be criminal behavior is constructed out of historical and cultural forces. However, as he writes, the newly emerging sub-field of Biocriminology, by looking inside human bodies rather than at the inherent ambiguity of crime's social context, "strikes me as misguided at a minimum, if not morally and politically questionable" (cited in Monaghan 2009).

---

20.   Perhaps the parenthetical aside is too obvious a point but it is worth stressing; for while much of my own work has consistently been on the very fact that we think religion exists I nonetheless find responses to my work which assume I am talking about religion. For instance, most recently Omer fails to understand that, in the work of mine which she cites (2005; cited by Omer 2011: 470]), mentions of religion always refer to the socio-semantic (i.e., discursive) systems that enable one to think religion into existence rather than to actual things called religions (this latter being a product of the former). This category is so embedded in our way of seeing the world (i.e., distinguishing such things as good from bad, private from public, legitimate from illegitimate, authentic from inauthentic, and, ultimately, us from them) that some readers seem incapable of historicizing it.

And it is on this note that I return to the topic of a cognitive (or any other, for that matter) theory of either religion or religious experience: looking for the pan-human, pre-social constraints that make people religious is evidence of a failure far more general than simply infecting the field with theological assumptions, as Wiebe has argued (1984: 421 **[25–26]**). Instead, it marks a basic methodological failure to historicize thoroughly our object of study, for it amounts to taking but one local, recently developed folk classification system and universalizing it by finding it (or better put, by placing it into) all people's hearts and minds, as the old saying goes. In uncritically accepting and then using the category, and all that comes with it, such supposedly theoretical work is but a more nuanced application of the participant's own manner of seeing the world, indicating that we have yet to realize the dream for a scientific basis to the field. For we have yet to move beyond description to theory—theory not of religion but of "religion"!

That scholars' ability to find religion all over the world is a product of *our* folk classification system, and that *we* are very comfortable living in the world that its use helps to make possible, should not prevent us from recognizing this system's history, its utility, and also the limits of this way of grouping together and naming the items of the world. Failing to do so, and instead, naturalizing this item of discourse—whether we say we study religion, religions, or special, religion-like experiences—marks a failure of critical intelligence that allows that pesky old notion of *sui generis* religion to re-enter our field, this time through a new biological back door.

References

Andresen, Jensine, ed. 2001. *Religion in Mind: Cognitive Perspectives on Religious Belief, Ritual, and Experience.* Cambridge: Cambridge University Press.

Bloch, Maurice. 2008. "Why Religion Is Nothing Special but Is Central." *Philosophical Transactions of the Royal Society* 363: 2055–61.

Boyer, Pascal. 1994. *The Naturalness of Religious Ideas: A Cognitive Theory of Religion.* Berkeley: University of California Press.

———. 2001. *Religion Explained: The Evolutionary Origins of Religious Thought.* New York: Basic Books.

Chidester, David. 1996. *Savage Systems: Colonialism and Comparative Religion in Southern Africa.* Charlottesville: University Press of Virginia.

Geertz, Armin W. 2004. "Cognitive Approaches to the Study of Religion." In Peter Antes, Armin W. Geertz, and Randi R. Warne, eds, *New Approaches to the Study of Religion.* Vol. 2, *Textual, Comparative, Sociological, and Cognitive Approaches,* 347–99. Berlin and New York: W. de Gruyter.

Gregory, Justin P. and Justin L. Barrett. 2009. "Epistemology and Counterintuitiveness: Role and Relationship in Epidemiology of Cultural Representations." *Journal of Cognition and Culture* 9: 289–314.

Hudson, Rex A. 1999. "The Sociology and Psychology of Terrorism: Who Becomes a Terrorist and Why? A Report Prepared Under an Interagency Agreement by the Federal Research Division, Library of Congress, Washington DC." Online: http://www.loc.gov/rr/frd/pdf-files/Soc_Psych_of_Terrorism.pdf (accessed April 10, 2010).

Kershaw, Sarah. 2010. "The Terrorist Mind: An Update." *The New York Times* (New York Edition). January 10: WK1. Online: http://www.nytimes.com/2010/01/10/weekinreview/10kershaw.html (accessed April 15, 2010).

Lawson, E. Thomas and Robert N. McCauley. 1990. *Rethinking Religion: Connecting Cognition to Culture*. Cambridge: Cambridge University Press.

Mack, Burton. 2001. "Caretakers and Critics: On the Social Role of Scholars Who Study Religion." *Council of Societies for the Study of Religion Bulletin* 30: 32–38.

McCauley, Robert N. and E. Thomas Lawson. 2002. *Bringing Ritual to Mind: Psychological Foundations of Cultural Forms*. Cambridge: Cambridge University Press.

McCutcheon, Russell T. 1997. *Manufacturing Religion: The Discourse on Sui Generis Religion and the Politics of Nostalgia*. New York: Oxford University Press.

———. 2001. *Critics Not Caretakers: Redescribing the Public Study of Religion*. Albany, NY: State University of New York Press.

———. 2005. *The Domestication of Dissent, Or How to Live in a Less than Perfect Nation*. London: Equinox.

———. 2007a. "Africa on Our Minds." In Theodore Trost, ed., *The African Diaspora and the Study of Religion*, 229–37. New York: Palgrave Macmillan.

———. 2007b. "They Licked the Platter Clean: On the Co-Dependency of the Religious and the Secular." *Method & Theory in the Study of Religion* 19: 173–99.

———. 2010a. "Religion Before 'Religion'?" In Panayotis Pachis and Donald Wiebe, eds, *Chasing Down Religion: In the Sighs of History and the Cognitive Sciences*, 285–301. Thessaloniki, Greece: Barbounakis Publications.

———. 2010b. "Will Your Cognitive Anchor Hold in the Storms of Culture?" *Journal of the American Academy of Religion* 78/4: 1182–93.

McNamara, Patrick. 2009. *The Neuroscience of Religious Experience*. Cambridge: Cambridge University Press.

Monaghan, Peter. 2009. "Biocriminology." *The Chronicle of Higher Education* (April 17), 55/32: B4. Online: http://chronicle.com/article/Biocriminology/17685 (accessed April 7, 2010).

Murphy, Todd. n.d. "Neurobiology of Religious Terrorism." Online: http://www.shaktitechnology.com/terrorism.htm (accessed April 3, 2010).

Omer, Atalia. 2011. "Can a Critic Be a Caretaker too? Religion, Conflict, and Conflict Transformation." *Journal of the American Academy of Religion* 79: 459–96.

Slone, D. Jason, ed. 2006. *Religion and Cognition: A Reader*. London: Equinox.

Sperber, Dan. 1996. *Explaining Culture: A Naturalistic Approach*. Cambridge, MA: Blackwell.

Taira, Teemu. 2010. "Religion as a Discursive Technique: The Politics of Classifying Wicca." *Journal of Contemporary Religion* 25: 379–94.

Taves, Ann. 2009. *Religious Experience Reconsidered: A Building Block Approach to the Study of Religion and Other Special Things*. Princeton and Oxford: Princeton University Press.

Volavka, Jan. 1999. "The Neurobiology of Violence." *Journal of Neuropsychiatry and Clinical Neurosciences* 1: 307–14. Online: http://neuro.psychiatryonline.org/cgi/content/full/11/3/307 (accessed May 3, 2010).

———. 2002. *The Neurobiology of Violence*. 2nd ed. Washington, DC: American Psychiatric Publishing.

Whitehouse, Harvey. 2004. *Modes of Religiosity: A Cognitive Theory of Religious Transmission*. Walnut Creek, CA: AltaMira Press.

Wiebe, Donald. 1984. "The Failure of Nerve in the Academic Study of Religion." *Studies in Religion / Sciences religieuses* 13: 401–22.

———. 1997. "A Religious Agenda Continued: A Review of the Presidential Addresses to the AAR." *Method and Theory in the Study of Religion* 9: 353–75.

———. 1999. *The Politics of Religious Studies: The Continuing Conflict with Theology in the Academy*. New York: St. Martin's Press.

———. 2004. "Against Science in the Academic Study of Religion: On the Emergence and Development of the AAR." In Thomas Ryba, George D. Bond, and Herman Tull, eds, *The Comity and Grace of Method: Essays in Honor of Edmund Perry*, 58–83. Evanston: Northwestern University Press.

———. 2006. "An Eternal Return All Over Again: The Religious Conversation Endures: A Critical Assessment of Recent Presidential Addresses to the AAR." *Journal of the American Academy of Religion* 74: 674–96.

———. 2010. "Recovering 'Religious Experience' in the Explanation of Religion." In Panayotis Pachis and Donald Wiebe, eds, *Chasing Down Religion: In the Sights of History and the Cognitive Sciences: Essays in Honor of Luther H. Martin*, 511–30. Thessaloniki, Greece: Barbounakis Publications.

Wiredu, Kwasi. 1997. "African Religions from a Philosophical Point of View." In Philip L. Quinn and Charles Taliaferro, eds, *A Companion to Philosophy of Religion*, 34–42. Oxford: Blackwell.

REVISITING THE CONFESSIONAL:
DONALD WIEBE'S "SMALL 'C' CONFESSIONAL,"
ITS HISTORICAL ENTAILMENTS
AND LINGUISTIC ENTANGLEMENTS

Johannes C. Wolfart

1.

Sometime in the late 1980s, the academy as a whole entered a phase of intense self-scrutiny, occasioned by a combination of factors ranging from the end of the Cold War, to a radical shift in the way universities around the world were funded, to the conditions of the American culture wars, to various theorists' shrill insistence on something called "reflexivity." Remarkably, Religious Studies was at that time already well poised to join the orgy of self-criticism. One of the texts that prepared us so well for the emergence of the dedicated sub-discipline of Religious Studies commonly called "method and theory" was Don Wiebe's "The Failure of Nerve in the Academic Study of Religion," which appeared in 1984.

It was a full decade after the appearance of that article that I was appointed to my first full-time academic position in the Department and Centre for the Study of Religion at the University of Toronto. I had just completed a doctorate and a two-year postdoctoral fellowship in History (German Reformation), and was a neophyte in Religious Studies. So I read hundreds of articles and monographs in my first years as a bona fide "religionist." None impressed me as deeply as Wiebe's article. To this day, among the carefully cultivated rows in the maturing forest of methodologically and theoretically "informed" studies of religion—poststructuralist, postmodernist, postcolonialist, etc.—Wiebe's article still towers above and stands apart, an ancient tree affording unique orientation for those lost in the woods.

To put things another way: though it was probably not his intention, Wiebe's article is an open invitation to historians of early modern European religion to enter the method and theory debates. This is due to the seriousness and rigor with which Wiebe chose to address what he called "confessional" approaches to the academic study of religion. Indeed, one wonders why more historians have not engaged with Wiebe's conceptualization of the confessional, since something called "confessionalization" has been so central to their own debates over the last decades. My primary purpose in what follows below, therefore, is to initiate some conversation between what historians of early modernity mean by "confessional" and its cognates, and what religionists, many of them following Wiebe, are doing when they use term.

Certainly, the term "confessional" and its derivatives have acquired some currency in Religious Studies since the publication of Wiebe's article. For the most part, however, and despite Wiebe's efforts at clarification, the term appears to be deployed largely as a vague term of opprobrium, with a meaning corresponding, roughly, to "faith-based" and "insider," when these latter are used in a rhetorical context indicating disapproval. Furthermore, the field of Religious Studies appears to have remained relatively unaffected by extensive scholarly discussion among early modern historians of epoch-defining key terms like "confessional," "confessionalism," and "confessionalization." This is both odd and regrettable, since the particular conjunction of institutional and intellectual aspects central to historians' notions of confessionalism constitutes precisely the condition of ideological formation identified by Tim Fitzgerald as key to the "ideology of Religious Studies" (Fitzgerald 2000).

Thus, it is my secondary point that while it may be possible for Wiebe, and others, to identify and isolate methodologies and theories that are confessional in a number of strictly defined philosophical senses, they cannot themselves escape the burdens of our shared history in the West, burdens which include ongoing confessionalism as it is commonly understood by historians. This is because such confessionalism not only endures in language, and may thus be part of our discourse either congenitally, as it were, or by re-infection (to adapt a metaphor favored by Wiebe), but also because there are ideological functions that certain confessional practices, first and foremost among them the act of confessing itself, can perform.

2.

Historians' "confessionalization" may be described quite aptly as "that hardening of doctrinal differences in a divided Christendom that would haunt Europe for centuries" (Koerner 2004: 158). At another level, however, and especially historiographically, there is much more to the concept than that. Historians' accounts of the emergence of the subfield of "confessionalization" studies usually begin with the work of Ernst Walter Zeeden, who developed a model of confessional formation (*Konfessionsbildung*) in the 1950s.[1] Zeeden's understanding focused quite narrowly on the practice,

---

1. For recent overviews see Boettcher 2004; Lotz-Heumann 2008; see also http://www.h-net.org/~german/discuss/Confessionalization/Confess_index.htm.

which proliferated in the sixteenth century, of subscribing to so-called confessions, creedal statements far exceeding in elaboration (and hence in exclusivity) the creeds of early Christianity. Commonly these fairly extensive documents were circulated with the names of the signatories, the legal representatives of polities and churches, appended. Eventually, affirmations of elements of these documents were also integrated into liturgical practice in various ways. Well-known—at least to historians—examples of such statements include the Augsburg Confession, the *Confessio Tetrapolitana*, the Schleitheim Articles or the Westminster Articles, but there were many more. The point is this: for Zeeden, confession was roughly equivalent to "faith commitment" and the process he described corresponds closely to the production of what Wiebe identified as "capital 'C' confessional" (Wiebe 1984: 403 [8–9]).

In the 1970s and 1980s two more German historians, Heinz Schilling and Wolfgang Reinhard, noted that Zeeden had downplayed a good deal of what made such confessional practice specifically modern (especially in scale), and thus sought to extend and elaborate Zeeden's original concept. Moreover, for Schilling and Reinhard the effects of being confessionalized operated at a different level altogether from that imagined by Zeeden, at a deeper cultural and social level, where consciousness or volition of faith were or are not necessary. In this way the outcome of this model corresponds to what Wiebe described as "small 'c' confessional" (Wiebe 1984: 403 [8–9]).

Schilling and Reinhard are commonly credited with developing the basic model for what has become known as the confessionalization paradigm. According to Lotz-Heumann (2008) the Schilling–Reinhard model stresses four basic historical processes:
1. confessional homogenization and the Christianization of popular religion;
2. confession/church establishment and state formation as reciprocal processes;
3. confessional/church contribution to social disciplining;
4. confessionalization of cultural and political identities.

Furthermore, since in this model confessional valence or identity of individuals is not a matter of choice, Reinhard identified seven distinct mechanisms of confessionalization as an ideological process:
1. pursuit of doctrinal purity, especially via formal confessional statements;
2. testing the orthodoxy of key personnel and the thereby implied persecution of dissidents;
3. propaganda and censorship;
4. public education projects;

5. confessional discipline, via the processes of visitation and church discipline; expulsion of confessional minorities in incidents of "confessional cleansing";
6. cultivation of ritual practice that signaled confessional identity and demarcated confessional boundaries;
7. a confessional regulation of language. (Lotz-Heumann 2008: 141)[2]

It should be noted that Reinhard's formulation is simply a very succinct iteration of what most historians of early modern Europe now take for granted, and which has been described and narrated at great length in countless historical studies over the past decades. It is also important to note that the Schilling–Reinhard model did not so much supplant Zeeden's concept as augment it. Indeed, a third concept of what constitutes the "confessional" is currently emerging and it seems likely that all three will be able to coexist. Critics of the "etatist" model propounded by Heinz Schilling in particular have recently gained some attention for the concept of "confessional cultures" (*Konfessionskulturen*), a term usually credited to Thomas Kaufmann (for example, 1998 and 2006). Kaufmann's aim is to countermand the determinism of the older model in an attempt to address data that suggest considerable variability in the "strength" of early modern confessional identities. Moreover, it is now widely accepted that early modern religious communities without state affiliation or sponsorship were nevertheless perfectly capable of confessionalism. According to Lotz-Heumann (2008: 149), scholarly interest has focused especially on Jewish and Mennonite cases.[3]

Three further recent developments in the historical scholarship on confessionalism warrant final mention. First, while the model developed primarily in relation to the history of the German-speaking lands, its application has not been limited to the Holy Roman Empire. Recently, for example, models of confessionalization have also been used effectively by historians of situations as diverse as Ireland or France, or as a European paradigm (Lotz-Heumann 2000; Benedict 2002; Headley, Hillerbrand, and Papalas 2004). Second, scholars in adjacent historical disciplines, especially art historians and musicologists, have been making effective use of the concept (and one could imagine here yet another possible bridge to Religious Studies; for example, see Fisher 2004). And third, as one would expect in the case of an historical category, the general trend in usage has been away from the static implication of a structural model, towards a more dynamic concept, one

---

2. Lotz-Heumann observes that this last mechanism has been under-examined to date. It is, however, an important part of our discussion below.

3. In keeping with a long-standing German scholarly tradition, Lotz-Heumann actually identifies the confessional status of the historians she discusses, thereby indicating something of the ongoing effects of confessionalization in Germany!

which cannot only describe social or cultural relations, but can explain the changing nature of those relations over time.

All of which is to say that complex historical processes called "confessionalization" would now be central to any historian's understanding of how what Wiebe called "small 'c'" confessionalism came to be.[4] Such processes are postulated at both the macro-political level, especially in terms of the very close relation of confessional churches to various emerging state apparatuses (see especially, Schilling 1992), as well as at the micro-political level. In the latter case, recent scholarship has focused on the institutional development of confessional education in early modern universities, schools, and libraries, a dizzying variety of legal institutions, especially consistories (also known as "morals courts," a bland rendering of vernacular terms like *Zuchtherren*, "Discipline Lords"), the institutions of the family, as well as on the more obviously confessional institutions of ecclesiastical visitation and inquisition. The consequences of such developments amounted to nothing short of a socio-cultural revolution, one which established, by means of indoctrination, acculturation, social disciplining, repression, etc., much of what we understand to be "modern" and "Western" cultural norms or social ideologies (Strauss 1978; Ozment 1983; Hsia 1989; Roper 1989; Puff 2003; Lederer 2006). Indeed, the combined impact of macro-political church–state alliance and micro-political "social disciplining" so transformed European society that many historians, especially in Germany, have taken to calling the period beginning anywhere from the end of the first to the end of the third quarter of the sixteenth century "the age of confessionalism" or "confessional age" (Klueting 1989; Haag 1997; Nischan 1999).

Interestingly, while historians generally agree that the confessional age, like any epoch, was at least somewhat discrete, even some of the more conservative accounts set the later terminus well into the eighteenth century. For example, Reinhard's model postulates confessionalization as a process of the so-called *longue durée*, one which began in the 1520s and ended only with the infamous Salzburg expulsions of 1731–32 (Lotz-Heumann 2008: 142). Moreover, accounts of the end of the confessional age tend to focus on the grossest macro-politics, and especially on confessional warfare (which is presumed to have yielded to more rational and thoroughly modern warfare in the age of nationalism). There is rather less scholarship that emphasizes the conclusion or termination of confessional micro-politics as manifested in, say, the development of early modern family relations, or the modes of academic intelligence or discourse. Indeed, it is here that one sees continuity rather than discontinuity between early modernity and modernity. That is, unlike early modern armies, confessional concepts and

---

4. In addition to Lotz-Heumann 2008, Boettcher 2004, and Headley et al. 2004, see Harrington and Smith 1997.

categories—including, not incidentally, "religion" itself—and confessional rhetoric or polemic do not appear to have exhausted themselves.

Moreover, recent scholarship has questioned the degree to which confessional discourse can be taken as evidence of confessionalized personal identity *per se* (Greyerz et al. 2003). In other words, we now have a fairly good reason to see "small 'c' confessionalism" not just as a philosophical orientation, as Wiebe originally had it, but as an historical formation, and as an inescapable dimension of Fitzgerald's ideology of Religious Studies. While Fitzgerald emphasized colonial histories as factors in the production of that ideology, he did not preclude the possibility of other histories contributing to the ideological formation of Religious Studies. One obvious reason Fitzgerald emphasized colonialism and neglected—but did not preclude—confessionalism as the institutional basis for the ideology of Religious Studies is that he was primarily interested in Western scholarship on Indian and Japanese "religion," for which much of the groundwork was laid in the nineteenth century. He is worth quoting at some length to clarify the exact parameters of his argument:

> The construction of "religion" and "religions" as global, crosscultural [*sic*] objects of study has been part of a wider historical process of western imperialism, colonialism, and neocolonialism. Part of this process has been to establish an ideologically loaded distinction between the realm of religion and of non-religion or the secular. (Fitzgerald 2000: 8)

But at the same time, Fitzgerald was very careful not to claim too much for colonialism in this regard. Instead, he implied that there may be several sources of the ideology just described, "*including* the nineteenth-century period of European colonization" (2000: 4, my emphasis). Fitzgerald made no claims whatsoever on the early modern period, and certainly never excluded confessionalism from consideration. Thus one might reasonably restate Fitzgerald's thesis and simply substitute "confessionalism" for "colonialism." The result would be as follows:

> The construction of "religion" and "religions" as global, crosscultural objects of study has been part of a wider historical process of western imperialism, *confessionalism*, and *neoconfessionalism*. Part of this process has been to establish an ideologically loaded distinction between the realm of religion and of non-religion or the secular.

3.

All of which is to say that, while twenty-first-century scholars may not necessarily be "capital 'C' Confessional" in the sense that they subscribe to a sixteenth-century confessional document (though some still do), and while most academics now eschew overt and aggressive confessional conflict of the early modern variety, in other significant ways the academy as a whole remains "small 'c' confessional." And this is not just due to a "failure of nerve" on the part of Religionists, as Wiebe once argued. Rather, the scientific methods once so heralded by proponents of the "academic study of religion" simply cannot overcome or transcend our historical linguistic entanglements, no matter how much we would like them to. The same is of course of true of the more general cultural propensies, which such linguistic practices project, and which are maintained via certain institutional forms and habits. In the broadest sense our predicament is realized in the degree to which education, including post-secondary education, is still viewed as the appropriate place for the inculcation of moral virtue. This is just as the confessional-age inventors of our modern system of "public" (as opposed to strictly ecclesiastic) education would have imagined it. Indeed, their heritage as religio-political leader-educators is currently enjoying new vigor via the character of the "public intellectual."

In a more narrow sense, historical continuity of confessionalism is witnessed in both the form and the content of those academic conversations or debates by which scholars presume to produce knowledge as distinct from moral content. In some very significant ways—significant for Religious Studies, at least—these conversations still closely resemble the polemics and *Publizistik*, academic and otherwise, that was so integral to the confessional age proper (on which see especially Rein 2008). Moreover, the substitution of moral virtue and failing for intellectual merit and discredit remains very much part of the academy. Finally, the current vogue for "postmodern" reflexivity and "postcolonial" self-criticism may owe an historical debt to the complex dynamics of early modern conversion, a process in which the ritual confession of moral failing resulted not just in social prestige but in intellectual authority. This is a point to which this essay will return at its conclusion.

To watch some scholars in Religious Studies in action can remind one very much of the polemical exchanges that were so characteristic of the confessional age. The vigorous self-righteousness, the thinly disguised contempt for colleagues and the thereby apparently warranted attacks *ad hominem*, and even the occasional scatological outburst are all peculiarly familiar to the historian of the confessional age (on one aspect of the contemporary practice, see Strenski 2004). Of course, one might conclude that this is merely rhetorical affect, perhaps an incidental effect of the fact that so many of our colleagues are also preachers or former preachers in various traditions. But consideration of, say, the exchange once carried out between Conrad Cherry and D. G. Hart in the review pages (a review, a letter to the editor, a response to the letter to the editor!) of the *American Historical Review* would put paid to any notion of such hostility as, say, merely incidental incivility (Cherry 2001a, 2001b; Hart 2001).

More than that, though, one of the central features of the so-called *sui generis* debate and similar controversies in Religious Studies betrays the confessional roots of the enterprise, even if it does not actually display them for all to see. Instead of actually engaging in ideology critique, practitioners of Religious Studies still habitually suspect each other of hidden agendas and undisclosed, secret thoughts, as did their confessional-age forebears. The culture of the confessional age developed elaborate tropes around secrecy, identity concealment, undisclosed thoughts, un-forthright social transactions, and the like. One might say that the notion that people are not what they appear or purport to be, notwithstanding their own vigorous protestations, was a confessional-age commonplace. The "problem" of such duplicity, artificial though it may appear, nevertheless required a concrete "solution." Thus the presumed ubiquity of secret false beliefs was addressed institutionally in early modern Europe by hallmark confessional innovations such as auricular confession (Bossy 1975; Duggan 1984; Wolfart 1996; Rittgers 2004) and visitation (Zeeden and Lang 1984; Dixon 1996; Burnett 2000; Smith 2008), as well as by a revitalized inquisitorial tradition.

In light of this history, it is extremely telling that the absolutely central theme in much of the debate over the proper constitution of the discipline of Religious Studies over the last several decades has been fear and loathing of something called "crypto-theology." The term appears to have entered the discussion at the instigation of Donald Wiebe (1984; also personal communication of 01/2009). Significantly, in this seminal essay Wiebe also confessed his own past as a Christian apologist and conceded that his personal history may have been the source of some confusion on the part of his interlocutors (1984: 421–22 **[25–26]**). At the same time, however, Wiebe disallowed that his apologetic-confessional past was at all problematic, and certainly not on the scale of the theological "infection" he diagnosed in the work of others in the field. Nor did Wiebe concede that he might be subject to larger historical forces, including perhaps those originating in early modern confessionism. Instead, Wiebe took care to explain not only religion, but also crypto-theology itself, in thoroughly modern and scientific terms, using "unconscious" and "subconsciously" in his etiology of crypto-theology (1984: 402, 422 **[7, 27]**).

In a limited sense, then, Wiebe managed to establish a significant difference between his thought and that of more overtly confessional scholars, especially early modern ones, who were more likely, for example, to posit demonic possession rather than psychology as the hidden cause of disorder. But in another sense the distinction appears little more than the difference, albeit perhaps somewhat "shifted," between his "small 'c' confessional" and "capital 'C' Confessional."

Thus Wiebe was clearly participating on some level in "small 'c' confessional" practice, inasmuch has he was availing himself of historical confessional discourse. That is, not only does his "invention" of the key concept of crypto-theology turn out to have precedents (and significant ones at that!), but the mode of its deployment as a critical term also falls into a familiar pattern. Moreover, Wiebe continued to develop his accusations of crypto-theology and, in a move that may be read either as highly self-reflexive or simply as ironic, subsequently identified the defining indicator of crypto-theology. In considering a range of "founding fathers" of Religious Studies, Wiebe asserted that the presence of crypto-theology was evidenced, first and foremost, by the reliance of these authors on the "idealist distinction between appearance and reality" (1990: 20). But if crypto-theologians are those who construct critical arguments on the basis of this fundamental distinction between appearance and reality, does not any utterance of the accusation of crypto-theology automatically make the speaker a crypto-theologian? It would appear that, in this instance at the very least, Wiebe has availed himself of what is by his own definition a key piece of confessional discourse.

Indeed, the *Oxford English Dictionary* (s.v. crypto-) confirms one's suspicion that early modern confessional usage was the first of a long but not very distinguished line of all such "crypto-" formations. The real power of Wiebe's coinage, therefore, is that it resonates at some fundamental level with that most fearsome secret thinking known in the confessional age as "crypto-Calvinism," a term which apparently preceded all other "crypto-" formations in the English language. Even before the term had entered the English language, the representation, both in text and image, of crypto-Catholicism and crypto-Lutheranism was a commonplace of confessional polemic (Rein 2008: 30, 95). Of course it would be quite silly to conclude that Wiebe got his key idea straight from the sixteenth century. There are other, later usages, even more resonant, that may just as easily have been vectors. Thus terms like "crypto-Jew" (nineteenth century) and "crypto-Fascist" (twentieth century) are probably the most common today. Nevertheless, in addition to distant confessional origins, some such formulations maintained a specifically confessional character well into the nineteenth century. For example, on the eve of the *Kulturkampf* German scholar-polemicists used it both to describe a medieval movement in Thuringia and to slander the modern Jesuit order as "cryptoflagellants" (Largier 2007: 146–55, 232–35).[5]

---

5. Largier attributes the first use of the term "Cryptoflagellant" to Förstemann (1828), but also cites Fetzer (1834) which appears to be a more salacious work. I have not been able to consult a copy of this work, but it is conceivable that a copy exists in the Don Wiebe collection.

It is not the aim here to suggest contradiction or incoherence in Wiebe's concept of "crypto-theology." Nor is there much point in accusing Wiebe of "crypto-confessionalism" or in attempting to engage in an unsolicited game of "gotcha" (although by his own definition of "crypto-theology" he has presented a perfect instance of "what you say is what you are"). Rather, the purpose is a more general one: namely, to illuminate the role of historical confessional discourse in the formation of the ideology of Religious Studies, inasmuch as ideology, while it may be cast in institutional forms, which is to say material conditions or relations, can certainly also be preserved and transmitted in language. Furthermore, while some scholars clearly associate the "crypto-theology" concept with Wiebe's work in particular (Orye 2005), in other work the term has been taken up and generalized, presumably because it resonated or made intuitive sense, by which one really means that it was already ideologically available. Thus, for example, Tim Fitzgerald's (2000: 18) widely cited book used the variant "cryptotheologians" without attribution to Wiebe.

4.

By way of conclusion one might consider one final concept addressed in Wiebe's seminal essay, that of the *epoché*. By this he—and others—meant the "setting aside" or "bracketing" of one's personal religious convictions in the name of "objective" scholarship. Of course it was Wiebe's point that such a gesture was meaningless, since it did not preclude the operation of "small 'c' confessional theology." More than that, though, two decades on we can see that the attempt to rid Religious Studies of theological residue, especially by those who did not fully comprehend Wiebe's distinction between "Captital 'C'" and "small 'c'" confessional theology, has grossly distorted our field. This is so because instead of actually pursuing what Gregory Schopen (1991) once so memorably called the "protestant presup-positions" inherent in the comparative study of religion, Religious Studies departments have simply purged most of the study of Christianity. Thus, with the exception of a few well-established sub-fields—Christian Origins (sometimes under other names) and some contemporary Christian theology (again, often disguised as social or critical theory)—the academic study of Christianity became increasingly rare in the 1990s. This is especially true of the study of early modern Christianity, that field which would be best able to inform attempts at comprehending confessionalism.

To illustrate the situation one can turn (in somewhat Wiebean fashion) to such evidence as is contained in the structure of several prominent North American graduate programs in Religious Studies. As one would now expect, these tend to be focused on one or the other "end"—chronologically speaking—of Christian history. Thus they inevitably include a muscular program in New Testament Studies and Christian Origins and then, commonly, some emphasis on American religion (i.e., Christianity) or on something called "global" Christianity. It is quite transparently the case that the institutional shape of Religious Studies still assumes an avowedly protestant Christianity, one that is shaped like a dumbbell. At the same time, however, programs either assume or even preclude knowledge of the historical development of that protestant Christianity, especially on the part of future scholars in Religious Studies. For example, in Princeton's venerable Department of Religion, Christianity is studied historically either under the rubric "Religions of Late Antiquity" or as "Religion in America."[6] Similarly, Yale's Department of Religious Studies offers graduate studies in three areas of Christianity that one might consider historical: "American Religious History," "Ancient Christianity," and "New Testament."[7] On the face of it the situation is even more severe outside of post-Puritan New England, for example in Stanford University's Department of Religious Studies, where doctoral students can pursue research in four areas: "Buddhist Studies," "Islamic Studies," "Jewish Studies," and "Modern Western Religious Thought, Ethics and Philosophy." In fact, however, the Stanford website indicates faculty specializations which include "early modern European religious thought and the religious reforms of the sixteenth century that formed the immediate context for the development of modern worldviews and societies."[8]

Of course, not all neglect of early modern Christianity and its confessional legacy has been the result of facile attempts to purge theology from Religious Studies by simply scapegoating Christian studies. It would be misleading not to mention also the influence of critiques of the colonialist dimensions of the ideology of Religious Studies. It appears that by the later 1990s even those most astute at discerning the ideological sinews of Religious Studies had opted for a kind of learned obtuseness on this score. Thus even while scholars interested specifically in the historical development of the study of religion have recently refocused their attention from the eighteenth and nineteenth centuries to the sixteenth century, they have done so in a peculiarly distorting fashion. For example, following the lead of Samuel Preus (1987), Jonathan Z. Smith's very widely read essay "Religion, Religions,

6. Http://www.princeton.edu/religion/graduate/academic_fields/ (accessed November 2010). Ironically, the website adverts "Princeton University pioneered in developing the study of religion outside the context of theological seminaries and without formal tie to particular religious traditions."

7. Http://www.yale.edu/religiousstudies/fields.html (accessed November 2010).

8. Http://www.stanford.edu/dept/relstud/gradprogram.html (accessed November 2010).

Religious" (1998) located the beginnings of modern discourse on religion, and especially comparative discourse, in the work of a sixteenth-century European writer. But whereas Preus chose a figure and a text, Jean Bodin and his *Colloquium Heptaplomeres*, particularly well known for their engagement with the acute confessional conflict of their day, Smith chose a rather more obscure figure and text, Richard Eden's *Treatise of the New India*, which he read as an expression of an emerging colonial impulse. In an oft-quoted passage Smith more than implied a colonial context for the primary othering function of the concept religion:

> Religion is not a native category. It is not a first person term of self-characterization. It is a category imposed from the outside on some aspect of native culture. It is the other, in these instances colonialists, who are solely responsible for the content of the term. (Smith 1998: 269)[9]

While Smith did not explicitly preclude an "other" other than the colonialist one, his intentions are clear: to present sixteenth-century European discourse on religion as primarily if not exclusively colonialist.

On balance, one would have to say that Preus got it right and Smith got it wrong. Apart from the question of whether Smith got Eden himself right, there is the problem of the relative importance of colonialist thinking in the sixteenth century. Undoubtedly, as an immediate matter of life and death, confessionalism was a more pressing concern for most sixteenth-century Europeans than colonialism (and whether that had even changed by the nineteenth century must remain an open question here). Therefore, if modern European ideology was shaped first in the sixteenth century, to claim that such ideology contained primarily colonialist concepts of "the other" is to distort the past. What we do know is that early modern Europeans developed the concept of the other, along with co-operative practices such as discerning "our" religion from "their" religion, or distinguishing religion from "the secular." But they clearly did so in the context of infra-European encounters with an "other" that was (nearly) always a confessionalized other. Indeed, it

---

9.   The full title of Eden's work is "A treatyse of the new India, with other new founde landes and Islands, as well eastwarde as westwarde, as they are knowen and found in these oure dayes, after the description of Sebastian Munster in his boke of Universall Cosmographie: wherein the diligent reader may see the good successe and rewarde of noble and honeste enterpryses by the which not only worldly ryches are obtayned, but also God is glorified, & the Christian fayth enlarged. Translated out of Latin into Englishe. By Rycharde Eden" (from the British Library Copy, via Early English Books Online). Though Smith cites the British Library copy he does not cite the full title, nor does he tell his readers that Eden's work was actually a translation of the Cosmographia of Sebastian Münster. It is thus in fact the work of an author much more commonly considered a proto-confessional writer, but only by a very great leap of the imagination as a proto-colonialist. See also Burmeister 1969.

is likely that it was precisely their confessional sensitization that moved the earliest modern European ethnographers to include "religion" as a category of description. For example, Hans Staden's famous account, first published in 1557, of his time spent among the natives of Brazil is as much a confession of Staden's Calvinism and a testament to divine providence as it is a description of the Tupinambá and their culture, including their "idols" and "what they believe in" (Staden 2008: 57, 124). As the editors of a recent English translation make clear "the religious tensions and conflicts of Europe were transposed to Brazil where the native practice of ritual cannibalism became the colonial mirror of theological dispute over the meaning of the Christian Eucharist" (Staden 2008: xxxiii). The editors further remark that the German Staden was in no way peculiar in this regard, since exactly the same confessional concerns were also the starting point for the Frenchman Montaigne's famous essay of 1580, *de Canibales* (Staden 2008: xi).

Nevertheless, in a recent account of the "invention" of the World Religions paradigm Tomoko Masuzawa has asserted that "[i]t is uncontroversial enough to say that European modernity commenced, for whatever reasons, with a dramatic transformation of Europe's relation to the rest of the world" (2005: 180). While Masuzawa may be strictly correct that such a view of European modernity is currently uncontroversial, it is certainly not, as she implies, incontrovertible. While postcolonialism currently enjoys something approaching a hegemonic position in the academy, it is far from immune to criticism both ideological and historical. It may even be possible to combine the two critiques.

Which brings us to the question *not* of whether confessionalism has shaped modern ideology, including the ideology of Religious Studies (it has), *nor* whether confessionalism and its history have been neglected in attempts to account for the ideology of Religious Studies (it has). Instead, it raises the question of the ideological mechanisms of the ongoing denial of confessionalism, both historical and philosophical, in our discipline. In short: *cui bono?* Subject to such consideration Smith and Mazusawa emerge as first-rate mythographers, as opposed to historiographers, of Religious Studies. Yet, while they may thus be providing an essential service to the community of Religious Studies scholars, they have also complicated considerably the task of actually knowing our own history, and especially its confessional dimensions. Central to the myth they have helped create is a narrative account of the origin of the category for knowing our central object of study, religion, in the moment of colonial contact, ostensibly because colonial encounter produced the requisite confrontation with "the other." On this Masuzawa and Smith are quite straightforward. Furthermore, the myth relocates the site of the origins of Religious Studies, and indeed of modernity, from continental Europe to "the Atlantic World," a point presumably not entirely lost on their predominantly Anglo-American audiences.

And yet the strongest undisclosed mythological function of the colonial origins narrative for Religious Studies may once again be primarily confessional. Thus the purpose of identifying colonialism as the source of modernity, and the associated ability to deploy religion as a comparative category, is to unite us all in the recognition of when and where we went wrong, of how evil came into the academy, if not into the world. Thus, Timothy Burke, in a particularly insightful formulation, has observed that "[t]he original sin of modernity is seen as the expansion of the West; it is perceived as a kind of singularity that utterly destroyed or erased historical experience to that point" (Burke 2005).[10] It is in this very ordinary or common sense, then, that our field in particular remains in a mode that is confessional: in Religious Studies one today confesses the sin of colonialism quite eagerly, as a *peccadillo*, and as a distraction to conceal the *peccatum gravissimum* of confessionalism proper. Put another way, over the course of the last two decades Wiebe's "capital 'C' Confessionalism" appears to have been replaced by "capital 'C' Colonialism" as the thing everybody recognizes and disavows. All the while "small 'c' confessionalism" has remained unstudied, not so much disavowed as denied, enduring as something more than just our collective inheritance as moderns, but as the ideology of Religious Studies.

References

Benedict, Philip. 2002. "Confessionalization in France? Critical Reflections and New Evidence." In Raymond Mentzter and Andrew Spicer, eds, *Society and Culture in the Huguenot World 1559–1685*, 44–61. Cambridge: Cambridge University Press.

Boettcher, Susan. 2004. "Confessionalization: Reformation, Religion, Absolutism, and Modernity." *History Compass* 2: 1–10.

Bossy, John. 1975. "The Social History of Confession in the Age of the Reformation." *Transactions of the Royal Historical Society* 25: 21–38.

Burke, Timothy. 2005. "Off the Hook." *Easily Distracted*. Weblog. Online: http://www. swarthmore.edu/SocSci/tburke1/perma20205.html (accessed November 2010).

Burmeister, Karlheinz. 1969. *Sebastian Münster: Versuch eines biographischen Gesamt-bildes*. Baseler Beiträge zur Geschichtswissenschaft 91. Basel: Helbing & Lichtenhahn.

Burnett, Amy N. 2000. "Basel's Rural Pastors as Mediators of Confessional and Social Discipline." *Central European History* 31: 67–85.

Cherry, Conrad. 2001a. Review of *The University Gets Religion: Religious Studies in American Higher Education* by D. G. Hart. *American Historical Review* 106: 572–73.

———. 2001b. Reply to D. G. Hart, *American Historical Review* 106: 1539–40.

10.   Burke's immediate target was Ward Churchill, who emerged from very public disputes as spectacularly unconcerned with historical accuracy, but also gloriously untouchable in his moral conviction.

Dixon, C. Scott. 1996. *The Reformation and Rural Society: The Parishes of Brandenburg-Ansbach-Kulmbach, 1528–1603.* Cambridge: Cambridge University Press.

Duggan, Lawrence. 1984. "Fear and Confession on the Eve of the Reformation." *Archiv für Reformationsgeschichte* 75: 153–75.

Fetzer, Karl A. [Giovanni Frusta]. 1834. *Der Flagellantismus und die Jesuitenbeichte: Historisch-psychologische Geschichte der Geisselungsinstitute, Klosterzüchtigungen und Beichtstuhlverirrungen aller Zeiten.* Leipzig and Stuttgart: no publisher.

Fisher, Alexander J. 2004. *Music and Religious Identity in Counter-Reformation Augsburg, 1580–1630.* Aldershot: Ashgate.

Fitzgerald. Timothy. 2000. *The Ideology of Religious Studies.* Oxford and New York: Oxford University Press.

Förstemann, Ernst G. 1828. *Die Christlichen Geißlergesellschaften.* Halle: Renger.

Greyerz, Kaspar von, Michael Jakubowsky-Tiessen, Thomas Kaufmann, and Hartmut Lehmann, eds. 2003. *Interkonfessionalität—Transkonfessionalität—Binnenkonfessionelle Pluralität: Neue Forschungen zur Konfessionalisierungsthese.* Heidelberg: Gütersloh.

Haag, Norbert. 1997. "Zum Verhältnis von Religion und Politik im konfessionellen Zeitalter: system- und diskurstheoretische Überlegungen am Beispiel der Lutherischen Erneuerung in Württemberg und Hessen." *Archiv für Reformationsgeschichte / Archive for Reformation History* 88: 166–98.

Harrington, Joel and Helmut W. Smith. 1997. "Confessionalization, Community and Statebuilding in Germany, 1555–1870." *Journal of Modern History* 69: 77–101.

Hart, D. G. 2001. Letter to the Editor. *American Historical Review* 106: 1538–39.

Headley, John M., Hans J. Hillerbrand, and Anthony J. Papalas, eds. 2004. *Confessionalization in Europe, 1555–1700: Essays in Memory of Bodo Nischan.* Aldershot: Ashgate.

Hsia, R. Po-chia. 1989. *Social Discipline in the Reformation: Central Europe 1550–1750.* London: Routledge.

Kaufmann, Thomas. 1998. *Dreißigjähriger Krieg und Westfählischer Friede: Kirchengeschichtliche Studien zur lutherischen Konfessionskultur.* Tübingen: Mohr Siebeck.

———. 2006. *Konfession und Kultur: Lutherischer Protestantismus in der zweiten Hälfte des Reformationsjahrhunderts.* Tübingen: Mohr Siebeck.

Klueting, Harm. 1989. *Das konfessionnelle Zeitalter.* Stuttgart: Ulmer.

Koerner, Joseph Leo. 2004. *The Reformation of the Image.* Chicago: University of Chicago Press.

Largier, Niklaus. 2007. *In Praise of the Whip: A Cultural History of Arousal.* Trans. Graham Harman. Brooklyn, NY: Zone.

Lederer, David. 2006. *Madness, Religion and the State in Early Modern Europe: A Bavarian Beacon.* Cambridge: Cambridge University Press.

Lotz-Heumann, Ute. 2000. *Die doppelte Konfessionalisierung in Irland: Konflikt und Koexistenz im 16. und in der ersten Hälfte des 17. Jahrhunderts.* Tübingen: Mohr Siebeck.

———. 2008. "Confessionalization." In David M. Whitfort, ed., *Reformation and Early Modern Europe: A Guide to Research*, 136–57. Kirksville, MO: Truman State University Press.

Masuzawa, Tomoko. 2005. *The Invention of World Religions.* Chicago: University of Chicago Press.

Nischan, Bodo. 1999. *Lutherans and Calvinists in the Age of Confessionalism*. Aldershot: Ashgate.

Orye, Lieve. 2005. "Reappropriating 'Religion'? Constructively Reconceptualising (Human) Science and the Study of Religion." *Method & Theory in the Study of Religion* 17: 337–63.

Ozment, Steven E. 1983. *When Fathers Ruled: Family Life in Reformation Europe* Cambridge, MA: Harvard University Press.

Preus, J. Samuel. 1987. *Explaining Religion: Criticism and Theory from Bodin to Freud*. New Haven: Yale University Press.

Puff, Helmut. 2003. *Sodomy in Reformation Germany and Switzerland, 1400–1600*. Chicago: University of Chicago Press.

Rein, Nathan. 2008. *The Chancery of God: Protestant Print, Polemic and Propaganda Against the Empire, Magdeburg 1546–1551*. Aldershot: Ashgate.

Rittgers, Ronald K. 2004. *The Reformation of the Keys: Confession, Conscience, and Authority in Sixteenth-Century Germany*. Cambridge, MA: Harvard University Press.

Roper, Lyndal. 1989. *The Holy Household: Women and Morals in Reformation Augsburg*. Oxford: Clarendon Press.

Schilling, Heinz. 1992 [1988]. "Confessionalization in the Empire: Religious and Societal Change in Germany Between 1555 and 1620." In Heinz Schilling, ed., *Religion, Political Culture and the Emergence of Early Modern Society: Essays in German and Dutch History*, 205–45. Leiden: Brill.

Schopen, Gregory. 1991. "Archaeology and Protestant Presuppositions in the Study of Indian Buddhism." *History of Religions* 31: 1–23.

Smith, Jonathan Z. 1998. "Religion, Religions, Religious." In Mark C. Taylor, ed., *Critical Terms for Religious Studies*, 269–84. Chicago: University of Chicago Press.

Smith, William Bradford. 2008. *Reformation and the German Territorial State: Upper Franconia, 1300–1630*. Rochester, NY: Rochester University Press.

Staden, Hans. 2008. *Hans Staden's True History: An Account of Cannibal Captivity in Brazil*. Ed. and trans. Neil. L. Whitehead and Michael Harbsmeier. Durham, NC and London: Duke University Press.

Strauss, Gerald. 1978. *Luther's House of Learning: Indoctrination of the Young in the German Reformation*. Baltimore: Johns Hopkins University Press.

Strenski, Ivan. 2004. "Ad Hominem Reviews and Rejoinders: Their Uses and Abuses." *Method & Theory in the Study of Religion* 16: 367–85.

Wiebe, Donald. 1984. "The Failure of Nerve in the Academic Study of Religion." *Studies in Religion / Sciences Religieuses* 13: 401–22.

———. 1990. "Disciplinary Axioms, Boundary Conditions and the Academic Study of Religion: Comments on Pals and Dawson." *Religion* 20: 17–29.

Wolfart, Johannes C. 1996. "Why Was Private Confession So Contentious in Early Seventeenth-Century Lindau?" In B. Scribner and T. Johnson, eds, *Popular Religion in Germany and Central Europe, 1400–1800*, 140–65. London: Macmillan.

Zeeden, Ernst W. and Peter T. Lang. 1984. *Kirche und Visitation: Beiträge zur Erforschung des frühneuzeitlichen Visitationswesens in Europa*. Stuttgart: Klett-Cotta.

SPECIAL FAILURES

FAILURES (OF NERVE?)
IN THE STUDY OF ISLAMIC ORIGINS

Herbert Berg

I would like to ask a more specific question than the one asked by Don Wiebe (1984) at the beginning of his essay, "The Failure of Nerve in the Academic Study of Religion." Does Islamic theology jeopardize the existence of the academic study of Islam, and even more specifically, the study of Islamic origins? At first glance, this question will strike almost all scholars of Islam as odd at best. Many scholars of Islam are neither Muslims nor former Muslims. Therefore, few of these scholars feel bound by Muslim confessional claims, nor are they subject to a hegemonic Muslim culture that might circumscribe their inquiries. Were one to ask, as Wiebe does for the study of religion in general, whether the scholar-scientist or the scholar-devotee controls the agenda for such a study, the scholar of Islam would again see the question as odd. Obviously the scholar-devotees of al-Azhar in Egypt or of Qom in Iran do not control the study of Islamic origins in the West.

There seems little doubt that such questions are more apropos in the study of Christian origins in which Christian theology and Christian scholars are so pervasive. Many scholars of the historical Jesus seem bound by theological constraints or have theological agendas, such as creating an image of Jesus that would still allow Christians to be followers of Jesus (Mack 2003: 38; Berg and Rollens 2008: 279). Despite the divergent confessional and cultural influences on these two groups of scholars, the outcomes of Islamic origins and Christian origins scholarship do parallel each other in one noteworthy way: many, or even most, of these scholars imagine a Muhammad or a Jesus who either bears a remarkable resemblance to the Muhammad or the Jesus of their respective confessional tradition, or who is made religiously significant in some other (fashionable) way. The study of Islamic origins is often just as, if not more so, "descriptivist" (Wiebe 1984: 409 [14]) as the study of Christian origins. Thus, despite the ostensible freedom from theological commitments or constraints, some failure permits theological concerns to imbue the study of Islamic origins. But is it a failure of *nerve*?

1. The Origins of Islamic Studies

One must be careful not to overemphasize the parallels between the studies of Christian origins and Islamic origins. Wiebe (1984: 401 **[7]**) pointed out that the study of religion achieved its political identity within the academy by distinguishing itself from theology. It is more precise to say that the study of the religion of Christianity had to distinguish itself from Christian theology. In a similar fashion, Christian origins continues to distinguish itself from its past, which began with people such as Hermann Samuel Reimarus, whose (Deist) theology certainly guided his quest for the historical Jesus. The academic study of religion's concern for other religious traditions including Islam, by contrast, was one means of emphasizing the distinction between theology and what F. Max Müller (1899) called the Science of Religion or Comparative Religion. The study of Islam in the academy began well before the late nineteenth century, of course. Originally part of Oriental Studies (now more politically correctly named and divided into Middle East Studies and Asian Studies), it emerged out of the French and British colonial enterprise and the German philological tradition. In his book *Orientalism*, Edward Said (1978) argued that the study of Islam (both of the religion and of the civilization) implicitly justified and helped sustain European and later American imperial ambitions. Among the most obvious consequences of orientalism was to "other" the East; the West's essential identity included the characteristics of strength and rationality, the East's included weakness and inscrutability. One of many consequences of this dichotomization was that the so-called East and Muslims were not permitted to create their own narratives inasmuch as the West had constructed these identities.

Therefore, although the study of religion is a product of the Enlightenment and developed in the nineteenth century out of the discipline of theology and in opposition to it (Wiebe 1984: 406 **[11]**), the study of Islam emerged as a product of colonialism—and in the last quarter century at least—in opposition to it. With regard to religious studies having eschewed theology in favor of scholarship, Jacob Neusner states, "We took that road to overcome an unwanted past. I think we had no choice" (Neusner 1977: 117). The study of Islam also sought, and continues to seek, to overcome an unwanted past, but a different one. Its fear is not *theological* atavism,[1] but *orientalist* atavism.

---

1. Wiebe doubts if scholars of religion have successfully overcome that unwanted past as suggested by Neusner (Wiebe 1984: 406 **[11]**). Theology has crept back into the study of religion through postmodernism (Wiebe 2008: 470–73) by being "employed either as a rhetorical device to place some taste, preference, practice, belief, or self-representation beyond criticism" (Braun 2008: 489–90). The study of Islam has not yet been infected to the same degree by this form of postmodernism, I suspect, because of Muslim suspicion of postmodernism.

Regardless of whether one agrees or disagrees with Said's critique, one cannot deny his impact on the study of Islam. Most scholars of Islam have gone to great lengths to avoid the greater sins of the now pejorative term, orientalism. In particular, they avoid both negative essentializations and appropriating the voice of Muslims. There is no doubt that Said's critique has also had negative consequences for the study of Islam. Aaron Hughes points out, for example, that "the North American study of Islam has largely moved beyond the quest for origins and gravitated towards subjects such as Sufism (Islamic mysticism) or Islam in the modern world, especially the important need to counter and dismantle forms of Islamophobia" (Hughes 2008: 31). Despite describing myself as a "scholar of Islamic origins," I have argued (Berg and Rollens 2008: 281) that to fixate on origins is to accept a theological perspective on the religion, so I welcome the diversification of the study of Islam. However, the emphasis on Sufism allows scholars to focus on the "nice face of Islam," and fighting Islamophobia, while certainly valuable, can lead to the uncritical acceptance of Muslim points of view.

Ironically, some of these points of view encourage the positive essentialization of Muslims and the presumption of a continuous essence in Islam from its origins to the present. Thus Said's critique has given impetus to scholars of Islam to accept the validity of the devotee's position. This crypto-theological approach, however, has a long and respected pedigree in the study of religion and the study of Islam, which Said seems merely to have reinforced. Max Müller demanded, "If people regard their religion as revealed, it is to them a revealed religion and has to be treated as such by every impartial historian" (Müller 1899: 74). This sentiment pervaded the work of many prominent scholars of religion who focused on Islam, particularly Wilfred Cantwell Smith and Charles Adams. Both ultimately argued the scholar's responsibility to be sensitive to the believers' experience of Islam (Hughes 2008: 58–64, 74–79). In other words, the insider perspective seems to take precedence over any "reductionist" explanation. As Hughes (2008: 81–92) also points out, this trend is visible in the most popular textbooks on Islam, such as those by John Esposito and Frederick Denny, and even more so in the books of popular writers and apologists for "genuine" Islam (read: peaceful and spiritual Islam), such as Karen Armstrong.

No doubt Said's critique and Müller's dictum (via scholars such as Smith and Adams) have affected the contemporary study of Islam, but have they had an impact on the study of Islamic origins? None of them wrote much about Islamic origins, and scholars such as Esposito, Denny, and Armstrong fail to appear in the bibliographies of articles and books by scholars of Islamic origins. Therefore, one cannot simply assume that the crypto-theological methodologies of these scholars also explain the tendency of recent reconstructions of Islamic origins or of biographies of Muhammad by non-Muslims to closely resemble those by Muslims.

2. The Study of Islamic Origins

Some of the most prominent scholars of the Qur'an and its interpretation (for example, Theodor Nöldeke, Angelika Neuwirth, and John Wansbrough), of the Sīra (for example W. Montgomery Watt and Gregor Schoeler), of early Islamic history (for example, Hugh Kennedy, Patricia Crone, and Michael Cook), of the Sunna (for example, Ignaz Goldziher, G. H. A. Juynboll, and Harald Motzki), and of the formation of Islamic law (for example, Joseph Schacht and Norman Calder) are not Muslims. I suspect it would be impossible to construct a list of prominent scholars of Christian origins who are not Christians or who had not been Christians at one point in their life. I am thinking here of Dominic Crossan, James Robinson, Luke Timothy Johnson, Elisabeth Schüssler Fiorenza, and Bart Ehrman. Even more critical scholars such as John S. Kloppenborg, Burton Mack, Willi Braun, and William E. Arnal can hardly be said to be uninfluenced by Christianity in some significant way. As Wiebe points out about an earlier stage in religious studies, but which seems to apply now to the study of Christian origins, "the majority of those in the field hail from religious backgrounds and likely entered the discipline with theological baggage if not an agenda" (1999: 146). Baggage and agendas may also be present in the study of Islamic origins, but at first glance they must be of a very different variety.

Moreover, most scholars of Islamic origins are historians or philologists teaching in Departments of History, Middle East Studies, or Near Eastern Studies in the West. This academic geography matters, for they do not generally need to bracket out their personal beliefs to be critical nor do they feel the need to conform to or to reject a hegemonic Muslim belief system. And, being outside Departments of Religious Studies, they are also much less likely to have inherited from the study of religion the legacy of Müller, Smith, and Adams so evident in Esposito, Denny, and Armstrong.

The argument could be made, however, that since so many prominent scholars of early Islam are not Muslims, they need to bracket out their disbelief in Islam or at least their belief in traditions such as Christianity or Judaism. This criticism is an old one that has been made of early Western works on Islamic origins such as Abraham Geiger's *Was hat Mohammed aus dem Judenthume aufgenommen?* (1833), Hartwig Hirschfeld's *Jüdische Elemente im Koran* (1878), and Richard Bell's *The Origin of Islam in Its Christian Environment* (1926). Although it is hard to deny that some forms Judaism and Christianity played a role in the origin of Islam as these three scholars argued, it would be naïve to assume that Geiger, Hirschfeld, and Bell were not influenced by their respective confessional theological commitments.

It was in part to counteract such accusations that W. Montgomery Watt (1953) felt that "a historian of the mid-twentieth century, while not neglecting or belittling the religious and ideological aspects of the movement initiated by Muhammad, wants to ask many questions about the economic, social and political background" (1953: xi). Watt, however, was not simply advocating reductionist, material explanations in favor of the confessional ones of Geiger, Hirschfeld, and Bell, for he elaborated: "I do not, however, regard the adoption of a materialist outlook as implicit in historical impartiality, but write as a professing monotheist" (1953: xi). The use of the term "monotheist" (as opposed to "Christian") was obviously meant to appease Muslim readers. Later, in his forward for his revision of Richard Bell's *Introduction to the Qur'an*, Watt again deferred to Muslim sensibilities:

> It has become imperative for a Christian scholar not to offend Muslim readers gratuitously, but as far as possible to present his arguments in a form acceptable to them. Courtesy and an eirenic outlook certainly now demand that we should not speak of the Qur'ān as the product of Muhammad's conscious mind; but I hold that the same demand is also made by sound scholarship. (Watt and Bell 1970: vi)

Speaking of influences and development was permitted, though not on Muhammad, just influences on the Arabian environment and development of his community's outlook. "Muhammad [must be] regarded as a man who sincerely and in good faith proclaimed messages which he believed came to him from God" (Watt 1953: 18). Watt mirrored Müller's demand to accept at face value the claims made by adherents of a religion. The result of this attitude was a biography of Muhammad that took into account Meccan and Medinan economic, political, sociological, and religious settings. It also produced a biography that was almost identical to that of the Muslim tradition. Much the same was true for his account of the collection and canonization of the Qur'an. Watt was aware that Ignaz Goldziher's and Joseph Schacht's negative conclusions about the authenticity of the *hadith*s of the Sunna (which are critical to Islamic law) had implications for the *hadith*s of the historical tradition. Watt justified his wholesale acceptance of the latter: "In the legal sphere there may be some sheer invention of traditions…but in the historical sphere, in so far as the two may be separated, and apart from some exceptional cases, the nearest to such invention in the best early historians appears to be 'tendential shaping' of material" (Watt 1953: xiii). The distortions may have been introduced by later transmitters (such as ascribing motives to the participants), but the underlying events could be discerned by the critical scholar. In other words, he accepted as fact the basic claims of Islamic origins as presented by Muslim tradition.

Wiebe (1984) makes a distinction between confessional theology and non-confessional theology. The former comes in two forms. A capital "C" Confessional theology, using Islam as an example, would only be practiced by Muslims scholars who assumed the existence of Allah, most likely in a fairly exclusive manner. As noted already, this form of theology is all but absent from scholars of Islamic origins. Small "c" confessional theology is non-exclusive and ecumenical for it recognizes the existence of some Ultimate or Sacred of which Allah is but one expression (1984: 403–404 **[8–9]**). There are several scholars of Islam already mentioned in this paper who belong in this category, most notably Karen Armstrong. The smaller subset of scholars of Islamic origins, however, is also infected with small "c" confessional theology. Watt's use of "monotheist," however, indicates that his notion of the Ultimate and his ecumenism are more narrowly defined, embracing only the perceived overlap of the Jewish, Christian, and Islamic gods. According to Wiebe, non-confessional theology recognizes only the cultural reality of Allah, and is characteristic of the "revisionist" scholars of Islamic origins who burst on the scene in the mid-1970s.

Two of the most infamous of these non-confessional works are John Wansbrough's *Quranic Studies* (1977) and Patricia Crone and Michael Cook's *Hagarism* (1977). They, like Watt, are not scholars of religion, but historians and scholars of Semitic languages. Wansbrough pointed out that "the seventh-century Hijaz owes its historiographical existence almost entirely to the creative endeavor of Muslim and Orientalist scholarship" (1987: 9). All the information on Islamic origins comes from texts and compilations written by Muslims some two centuries later. Given that all we have is literature, the appropriate methodology for their study must be literary criticism. In so doing, Wansbrough first noted that the main themes of the Qur'an are clearly Judeo-Christian. After examining the structure of the Qur'ān, he suggested that the Qur'ān is not a product of "deliberate edition"; that is, the various traditional and more recent accounts of the canonization process are incorrect. He suggested instead that the Qur'ān is "the product of an organic development from originally independent traditions during a long period of transmission" (1977: 47). Wansbrough terms these independent pericopes, "prophetical *logia*," which were reports about direct utterances from Allah. He proposes that these *logia* originated as separate collections with communities "essentially sectarian but within the mainstream of oriental monotheism" (1977: 50), that is, within a Judeo-Christian sectarian milieu. Such a scenario would certainly explain why so much of the Qur'ān was not understood by early Muslims. If Wansbrough's hypothesis is correct, it would seem to break the connection between Muhammad and the Qur'ān that was so essential to the methodology of Watt. The "Arabian prophet," to use Wansbrough's term, had no connection to the contents of the Qur'ān for they originated in another milieu. However, that does not mean the connection is severed; rather, he has reversed the connection. Wansbrough suggests that the biography of Muhammad or *sīrah* (the "Muhammadan *evangelium*" as he calls it) represents a historicization of the *logia*. That is to say, the essentially anonymous material of the Qur'ān was linked to the independent Arabian prophet via narrative exegesis.

Crone and Cook (1977) examine early Islam by purposely setting aside Muslim sources since none of them are (or were at the time of their book's publication) demonstrably early. Therefore,

> it makes some sense to regard the tradition as without determinate historical content, and to insist that what purport to be accounts of religious events in the seventh century are utilisable only for the study of religious ideas in the eighth. (Crone 1977: 3)

Thus setting aside Muslim insider confessional claims, they instead employ the admittedly meager historical, archeological, and philological evidence from outside the Islamic tradition to reconstruct Islamic origins. Crone and Cook conclude that what became Islam began as an Arab (or Hagarene) form of Judaism. Muhammad is argued to have introduced the Jewish god to polytheistic Arabs, who for a time united with Jews to conquer the Holy Land from Christians. This exodus from Northern Arabia is the real *hijra* (not the emigration from Mecca to Medina). Islam formed as the Hagarenes, or Mahgraye (the Syriac term conveniently referring both to the *muhājirūn* and to the descendants of Hagar), sought to distinguish themselves from Jews and Christians, but they did so by adapting their myths and symbols— particularly via Samaritan calques. The Qur'ān is modeled on the Torah, Mecca on Jerusalem, and Muhammad on Moses. These conclusions by Crone and Cook are obviously ones that believing Muslims cannot accept.[2] The authors recognized this, even describing their book as "written by infidels for infidels" (Crone and Cook 1977: viii) with no Watt-like appeals to a shared monotheism.

In contrast to the Müllerian regard for Muslim sensibilities and sensitivities advocated by Watt, the blatant disregard for them by Wansbrough, Crone, and Cook did not go unchallenged. For example, R. B. Serjeant (1978: 76) criticized Wansbrough's *Quranic Studies* as "a thoroughly reactionary stand in reverting to the over-emphasis of the Hebrew element in Islam… [O]ne has the sense of a disguised polemic seeking to strip Islam and the Prophet of all but the minimum of originality." Asserting that the Qur'ān consisted "almost exclusively of elements adapted from the Judeo-Christian" ignored

> the vital Arabian element (about which he appears ill- or uninformed), but the Prophet himself and his followers deliberately drew upon these elements to carry refutation into the Jewish and Christian camps… The plain and uncontested evidence is that the Hijāz was its birthplace. (Serjeant 1978: 76)

---

2. However, it is claimed that both Crone and Cook have more recently retreated from their conclusions (Khan 2006).

The criticisms, therefore, are the same as those that had been leveled at Geiger, Hirschfeld, and Bell—though Wanbrough was not Jewish. Moreover, Serjeant demanded, it seems, at least some small "c" confessional theology from scholars of Islamic origins. Ironically, elsewhere Wansbrough is accused of having a theological background and of applying "the model of the historical criticism of the New Testament to the Qur'an" (Neuwirth 2003: 4–6). As for Cook and Crone, Serjeant berated them: "*Hagarism*, foaled in the same stable, though lacking the depth of Dr. Wansbrough's undisputed learning, is not only bitterly anti-Islamic in tone but anti-Arabian" (Serjeant 1978: 78). A similar charge is made by L. Ali Khan (2006): "Scholarly decency, however, demands that the authors officially repudiate a scandalous thesis, one in which they no longer believe and one that maligns the faith of more than a billion people." For both Serjeant and Khan, "reverence" is held to be a scholarly virtue and these revisionists are being scolded for not permitting those whom they study to define the terms in which they will be understood.[3] Descriptivism is virtuous, revisionism is not.

3. The Study of Islamic Origins Redux

In the several decades since Wansbrough's and Crone and Cook's first books, a new generation of scholars of Islamic origins has had to confront the scholarship of these revisionists. However, their scholarship too seems as schizophrenic as that of the earlier work. The dichotomy is still not one of the critical insider versus the sympathetic outsider (Wiebe 1984: 421 **[26]**). There are still relatively few Muslim insiders engaging in the study of Islamic origins. But there is no shortage of sympathetic outsiders, judging by the biographies of Muhammad that have appeared since the revisionists: Martin Lings (1987), Karen Armstrong (1992, 2006), F. E. Peters (1994), and Daniel Peterson (2007). All are even more descriptivist than Watt and conform to the basic narrative provided by Muslim tradition; the emphasis is not on explanation or even theory—at least Watt had that. Armstrong even seeks to make Muhammad a mystic and a political and social reformer who can be

---

3.   Reference is being made to two of Bruce Lincoln's "Theses on Method," number 5: "Reverence is a religious, and not a scholarly virtue. When good manners and good conscience cannot be reconciled, the demands of the latter ought to prevail [...]" and number 13: "When one permits those whom one studies to define the terms in which they will be understood, suspends one's interest in the temporal and contingent, or fails to distinguish between "truths," "truth-claims," and "regimes of truth," one has ceased to function as historian or scholar. In that moment, a variety of roles are available: some perfectly respectable (amanuensis, collector, friend and advocate), and some less appealing (cheerleader, voyeur, retailer of import goods). None, however, should be confused with scholarship" (Lincoln 1996: 226 and 227, respectively).

a model "for our time." Three more critically aware contributions to Islamic origins have recently been made by: Fred Donner (2010), Andreas Görke and Gregor Schoeler (2008), and Christoph Luxenberg (2007). The two most recent works are not confined by Müller's dictum or Said's critique. Nevertheless, their reconstructions are largely descriptivist. Luxenberg, by contrast, could be seen as revisionist, for his reconstruction certainly provokes the same reaction the earlier revisionists did. In examining them, I hope to show that the underlying approaches of earlier generations of scholars of Islamic origins survive, but the continuing "failures" are not ones of *nerve*.

Frederick Donner is a historian and currently the Professor of Near Eastern History at the University of Chicago. His recent book, *Muhammad and the Believers* (2010), makes claims that might seem reminiscent of those of Crone and Cook. He too thinks that *muhajirun* was one of the earliest self-designations employed by the movement that would develop into Islam and that Jews played an early significant role in that movement. However, it seems that Donner is largely making a terminological distinction. Instead of Muslims and Islam, he prefers to use Believer and Believers' movement. This so-called Believers' movement is, for him, a

> strongly monotheistic, intensely pietistic, and ecumenical or confessionally open religious movement that enjoined people who were not already monotheists to recognize God's oneness and enjoined all monotheists to live in strict observance of the law that God had repeatedly revealed to mankind—whether in the form of the Torah, the Gospels, or the Qur'an. (2010: 75)

Early textual evidence supports his claim that the term "believer" (i.e., *mu'min*) was preferred as a term of self-designation. One wonders if he could not have achieved the same results by using "early Muslim" or "proto-Muslim"—defined to be an ecumenical movement. More significantly, when it comes to describing the beliefs and practices of this movement, it becomes evident that neither radicalism nor revisionism is inherent in his neologisms. Donner presents something akin to the traditional five pillars and five principles of Islam. His chronology of events and revelations in the Qur'ān (into Meccan and Medinan surahs) is also traditional. So, while it may appear that Donner is being quite radical, accepting at least in part, various points made by Geiger, Hirschfeld, Bell, Wansbrough, Crone, and Cook, in reality his historical framework is far closer to that of Watt. And, if one scratches beneath the surface, one discovers that the theological frameworks of Watt and Donner bear some resemblance too.

Donner argues "that Islam began as a religious movement—not as a social, economic, or 'national' one; in particular, it embodied an intense concern for attaining personal salvation through religious behavior" (2010: xii). Elsewhere he reiterates that the Believers were "a movement rooted in religious faith" (2010: 219) and driven by a "religious motivation—the desire to extend the recognition of God's word" (2010: 197). Ironically, Donner dismisses early expansion of the Believers out of Arabia as an "Arab" movement. Arab identity is an effect, not a cause of the movement. He writes, "It usually represents the facile interpolation back into the seventh century C.E. of modern concepts of Arab nationalism that only came into existence in the late nineteenth century" (2010: 218). He is no doubt correct, but were one to substitute "religion" for "Arab nationalism" in the quotation, he would be critiquing his own goal, which is to highlight the *religious* causes of the movement.

Another of Müller's many dicta declared, "Where we see the reverence due to religion violated, we are bound to protest" (1899: 7). Müller no doubt meant "due to a specific religion" and Watt, we saw, took up this charge by largely accepting the traditional account of Islamic origins. Donner, however, seems to have a wider interpretation, that is, by treating the *religious* as equal or superior to, and independent of, the *social*, the *economic*, or the *political*. That is, he treats religion as abstract and universalized with an autonomous essence—a claim that Talal Asad (1993) has convincingly undermined. However, even if one does not accept Asad's critique of the modern category of "religion," among scholars of Islamic origins, Donner seems to exemplify Wiebe's statement:

> Where causal explanations are applicable they are of limited value and one must seek and understand *beyond* explanation. Such an "understanding," I maintain, constitutes a non-specific theology in that it assumes the ontic reality of the religious tradition's view of that reality, at least at the level of explicit consciousness. It rests, quite uncritically, on the assumption of the (cognitive and metaphysical) validity of "religion in general." (1984: 411 [16])

This non-specific theology is also evident when Donner argues that "the social dimensions of the message are undeniable and significant, but they are incidental to the central notions of the Qur'an, which are religious: Belief in the one God and righteous behavior as proof of obedience to God's will" (2010: 89). Donner recognizes the difficulty in trying to separate material, ideological, and religious motives (2010: 197), but for him they are separable. Thus, decontextualized belief is the efficient cause (and perhaps the final cause) of the movement that became Islam. Moreover, his use of the word "religious" highlights yet another issue. The emphasis on faith reflects a fairly narrow definition of religion, one which the essence of religion is the private, the interior experience—a notion of religion that traces back to the theologies of Friedrich Schleiermacher's "essential feeling" and even further to the Protestant Reformation's *sole fide*. Finally, Donner (2010) also repeatedly emphasizes that early believers were (monotheistically) ecumenical. Although upsetting to some Muslims no doubt, one might compare it to the claim that very early Christians saw themselves as Jews and shared their synagogues. That is to say, he takes for granted that Islam emerged in some sort of Judeo-Christian sectarian milieu. More importantly, one cannot help but notice that Donner's description of Muhammad and his Believers' movement (in other words, *original* Islam or ideal Islam) as ecumenical, neither anti-Jewish nor anti-Christian, and "not fanatical" (2010: 84), is remarkably compatible with our modern theology of religious pluralism (see, for example, McCutcheon 2005: 89). Thus, Donner, like Watt, has a small "c" confessional theology, albeit a modern, internal, and politically correct version of it.

Görke and Schoeler (2008) engage in a different kind of reconstruction: not of the origin of Islam but of the origin of its historical traditions. The fact that the extant literary sources for the life of Muhammad date from at least 150 years after the events they purport to describe led the aforementioned revisionist scholars to question their usefulness in reconstructing the historical Muhammad, forcing "research on Muhammad…to be restricted to the study of the Islamic self-image" (Görke and Schoeler 2008: 282). In their search for a middle ground between taking the received biography of Muhammad more or less at face value (as Watt did, for instance) and dismissing it entirely (as Wansbrough, Crone, and Cook did), Görke and Schoeler seek to reconstruct the original corpus of 'Urwa b. al-Zubayr (d. 713) out of the many thousands of traditions about Muhammad ascribed to him in later, extant works. 'Urwa is seen as the first collector and transmitter of such biographical material, and so they can claim that

> the material that can be securely ascribed to 'Urwa was collected some 30 to 60 years after Muhammad's death. It would therefore go back to eye-witnesses and to persons in very close contact to Muhammad. It may therefore be assumed that these reports reflect the general outline of the events correctly. (Görke and Schoeler 2008: 294)

Görke and Schoeler (2008: 290) determine that 'Urwa's corpus included the stories of Muhammad's first revelations, the reactions of the Meccans, the harassment of the Muslims, their flight to Abyssinia and later to Medina, and the military conflict with the Meccans up to the eventual success of Muhammad's mission (i.e., the conquest of Mecca). The more fantastic elements, such as Muhammad's night journey and ascension to heaven, the more problematic ones, such as the reference to the "Satanic verses," and the many conflicts with the Jews seem to be absent from the reconstructed corpus.

Görke and Schoeler (2008) do not seem motivated by theological concerns but historical ones, and have a (perhaps too sanguine) belief that they can reconstruct historical kernels. In an earlier work, Schoeler (1996) examined the reports about Muhammad's very first revelation and traced their transmission from the (probable) first reporter to their final redaction in extant works. He concluded that that story was very early, but the various motifs were likely combined in the first century A.H. and emerged within the Zubayrid family, of which 'Urwa was a part and which had a rival caliphate from 681 to 691. 'Urwa cleansed the report of its storyteller (*qāss*) elements, reworking it into *hadīth*-format. Schoeler (1996: 59–117) further suggested that the original report is that of the storyteller, 'Ubayd b. 'Umayr, who built the story out of various components while with the Zubayrid court. Significant changes were still introduced afterward; it was paraphrased, shortened, adorned, and rearranged. This conclusion about such a critical story is clearly at odds with how Muslims would present themselves, belying any conscious theological bias in Schoeler.

Even if one were to assume an *Urtext* could be reconstructed in this manner, there remains the problem of the nature of the *Urtext*. Does closing the gap (between extant texts and the events they purport to describe) from 200 years to less than 100 years, perhaps even as little as 20 years make that *Urtext* historical? Here, Christian origins tell a cautionary tale. Just two decades separate the historical Jesus from Paul's Christ, and Jesus the miracle worker in the Gospel of Mark from the Cosmic Lord in the Gospel of John. Speaking of the Gospel of Mark, which was written approximately four decades after Jesus, William Arnal states:

> The nature of the sources for Jesus exacerbates the situation. While the object of our supposedly "historical" inquiry keeps transforming into a theological entity in front of our very eyes, the main sources on which we base our reconstructions present him as a theological entity in the first place... In seeking to find the real, historical person behind these narratives, we are using these texts as sources for a figure that they themselves show no interest in at all. (2005: 75–76)

The study of Islamic origins and the study of the historical Muhammad, if based on Görke and Schoeler's *Urtext*, are forced to rely on material that would have been produced with a confessional theological perspective. In claiming their reconstruction as a historical text, they are reproducing, in a scholarly voice, the basic theological claims of the Muslim tradition's presentation of its origins. Thus, the failure of Görke and Schoeler appears to be the opposite of that of Donner. Crudely put, Donner overemphasizes religion and Görke and Schoeler neglect it. In fact, what they do is quite similar. Donner creates an artificial and mystifying boundary between the internal experiences of the Believers and the social, historical, economic, and political context in which they appeared. Görke and Schoeler create a boundary between a later context and the material ascribed to 'Urwa in which it was produced. For Donner, Görke, and Schoeler, "religion" is somehow independent of the social and cultural contexts.

What then of the recent infamous, revisionist conclusion that the Qur'ān is a corpus of Arabic translations and paraphrases of some Syriac original made by the so-called German (see below) scholar of Semitic languages publishing under the pseudonym of Christoph Luxenberg? Luxenberg (2007: 22–26) focused on passages that Western scholars deem to be obscure. First he consulted the *Tafsīr* (or commentary) on the Qur'ān by al-Tabarī (d. 923) and the *Lisān al-'Arab*, the lexicon of Ibn Manzūr (d. 1311), looking for the traditional explanations of the passages that might hint at an Aramaic reading. If none were found and the passage remained problematic, Luxenberg then searched for a Syro-Aramaic homonym that might better explain the passage. Again if unsuccessful, Luxenberg experimented with altering the diacritical points and vocalizations (since both were later additions to the Qur'ān) in hopes of discovering an Aramaic root. Finally, as a last resort, he translated the passage into Aramaic in order to find calques. It is a "very mechanistic, positivistic linguistic method" (Neuwirth 2003: 10), and obviously it presupposes what he hopes to show, that what became the Arabic Qur'ān was excerpted from a Syriac canonical and/or proto-scriptural *Urtext*. Moreover, Luxenberg (2007) suggests that an Aramaic–Arabic hybrid was spoken in Mecca, which was an Aramean settlement. Later Arabic-speaking exegetes and philologists had access only to the written Qur'ān whose hitherto defective script was standardized only in the second half of the eighth century. Consequently, the numerous misinterpretations and misreadings, as they read it in light of Arabic, were inevitable (Luxenberg 2007: 326–33).

There is little doubt that the methodology is problematic. Luxenberg's book has received considerable attention from the media and within the blogosphere, especially his argument that the virgins of paradise are in reality references to "white raisins" (e.g., Theil 2003). Some scholarly reviewers have not been as harsh as they were with Wansbrough, Crone, and Cook, focusing more on the methodological problems. Some point out that it stands in the same tradition as Geiger, Hirschfeld, Bell, Wansbrough, Crone, and Cook, i.e., scholars who "have endeavored to trace the content of the Qur'ān back to its Jewish or Christian sources" (Baasten 2004: 268). Others have been harsher. François de Blois (2003), after attacking the methodology and the conclusions, states, "It is a reading that is potentially attractive only in its novelty, or shall I say its perversity, not in that it sheds any light on the meaning of the book or on the history of Islam" (de Blois 2003: 96). He also points out that Luxenberg is not German, but Lebanese Christian. As it had been for Wansbrough, religious affiliation is used to critique revisionist scholars. I have very serious qualms about listing Luxenberg among Wansbrough, Crone, and Cook. However, reaction to his book is similar: "Luxenberg claims that the entire scholarly edifice of Islam, largely based on the reliability of oral tradition, is unfounded" (Neuwirth 2003: 9–10). Apparently, it suffices to point out that a scholar has deviated from the "historiographical existence" previously created by Muslim and Orientalist scholarship of which Wansbrough spoke. That Donner, Görke, and Schoeler are spared this criticism suggests that they have not deviated far from the descriptivist norm. In other words, scholars of Islamic origins are expected to accept (for the most part) the tradition as it presents itself.

4. Conclusions

I have tried to highlight that, despite the distance between the scholars of Islamic origins and the scholars of religion in terms of discipline and genealogy, the issues raised by Wiebe in "The Failure of Nerve in the Academic Study of Religion" (1984) are applicable to the former as well. It may be that scholars of early Islam, like scholars of Islam in general, fear being accused of reductionism and orientalism, particularly of appropriating the Muslim voice. However, the descriptivist tendency of scholars of Islamic origins seems more a product of a lack of interest in, or even ignorance of, theoretical concerns raised within the study of religion. The fact that most are not scholars of religion may help account for that failing.

The theological consequence of descriptivism is particularly evident in the issue of the origin of Islam's relationship to Judaism and Christianity. With Geiger, Hirschfeld, and Bell, then with Wansbrough, Crone, and Cook, and yet again with Luxenburg (and even somewhat with Watt and Donner), there have been repeated attempts to contextualize Islam within these other religious traditions. As G. R. Hawting has noted, "That Islam is a mono-theistic religion related to Judaism and Christianity is a generally accepted commonplace" (1997: 24). One need only consult the grouping of religions in every Western Religions or World Religions textbook. Hawting continues:

> However, although the interrelationship of the three monotheistic religions is generally accepted in principle, Islam has often continued, both at a scholarly and at the popular level, to be treated as something rather distinct from the other two, even when there is no discernible polemical motive for doing so... In its equation of the origins of Islam with the career of Muhammad and its detailed depiction of Muhammad's life in Mecca and Medina, Muslim tradition effectively dissociates Islam from the historical development of the monotheist stream of religion as a whole. Islam is shown to be the result of an act of divine revelation made to an Arab prophet who was born and lived most of his life in a town (Mecca) beyond the borders of the then monotheis-tic world. (Hawting 1997: 24)

Most of the aforementioned scholars recognize this charge, although Donner (like Geiger, Hirschfeld, Bell, and Watt before him) inserts Christians and/or Jews into Arabia, whereas Wansbrough and Luxenberg insert Muslims (or proto-Muslims) into a Christian and/or Jewish (or Judeo-Christian sectarian) milieu. Yet all but Donner and Watt stand condemned. Why? Whereas Hawting seems to assume that the motive must be polemical, I am suggesting that it is in part theological (or at least crypto-theological) and in part apologetical (in both senses of the word).

This is evident if one compares reactions to claims of Jewish influences on Muhammad versus Jewish influences on Jesus. One sees opposite reactions, though the motives are much the same. As Arnal points out (2005: 39–72), New Testament scholarship has had an anti-Jewish and anti-Semitic past, but the last few decades of scholarship have more than overcompensated for that past and the continued emphasis on the Jewishness of Jesus is a manufactured controversy. The "Jewish-Jesus non-debate" is a reflection of political, religious, and cultural identities of the scholars. In other words, scholars are attempting to distance the study of Jesus from theology in order to redeem Christianity from anti-Semitism, to legitimize contemporary traditionalist definitions of religion, especially Judaism and Christianity, and to resist "postmodern or globalizing homogenization and fragmentation precisely in their insistence on the coherence of 'Jewish' identity" (Arnal 2005: 72). Likewise, the fact that Islam originated in some Judeo-Christian (probably sectarian) milieu is, or should be, a non-debate. Scholars of Islam are trying to distance themselves from the accusation that "Islam is derivative" and particularly from "Islam is derivative of Judaism." Fear of the charge of orientalism, and perhaps also a fear of the charge of crypto-Zionism, seems to underlie this. It seeks to resist "postmodern or globalizing homogenization and fragmentation precisely in their insistence on the coherence of" "Muslim" identity that is rooted in Muhammad. It plays with cultural identity as Arnal suggests, but it is also a theological position; there is an essence in Islam which runs from Muhammad to the Muslims of today. The category of "Muslim identity" is a modern category and Muhammad is a screen on which these debates are projected. Most critically, maintaining that Islam or any other religious tradition, figure, text, etc. is *not* derivative of its social and cultural context is to make two closely related asseverations about the academic study of religion: (1) "religious" entities must be ring-fenced from critical analysis, and (2) religion is *sui generis*.

Wiebe's concern was the reversal of the tentative move toward the development of a scientific study of religion heralded by the first generation of *Religionswissenschafter*, which, "therefore, constitutes a failure of nerve in the academic study of religion" (Wiebe 1984: 422 **[27]**). The study of Islamic origins (if not the study of Islam) was in many ways independent of that first generation of scholars of religion—and subsequent ones as well. In that sense, the problems that I have highlighted are not failures of *nerve*. They are failures nonetheless. These four overlapping failures include a failure to understand the modern construction of "religion," a failure to accept the theological nature of the sources, a failure to avoid overcompensating for our orientalist past by describing that tradition as it presents itself, and a failure to shun a modern pluralist theological agenda. All these failures in the study of Islamic origins, however, could be characterized as products of various forms of (crypto-) theology, and so scholars of Islamic origins would do well to heed Wiebe's warning.

References

Armstrong, Karen. 1992. *Muhammad: A Biography of the Prophet*. San Francisco: HarperCollins.

———. 2006. *Muhammad: A Prophet for Our Time*. San Francisco: HarperCollins.

Arnal, William E. 2005. *The Symbolic Jesus: Historical Scholarship, Judaism and the Construction of Contemporary Identity*. London: Equinox.

Asad, Talal. 1993. *Genealogies of Religion: Discipline and Reasons of Power in Christianity and Islam*. Baltimore: Johns Hopkins University Press.

Baasten, Martin F. J. 2004. Review of *Die syro-aramäische Lesart des Koran: Ein Beitrag zur Entschlüsselung der Koransprache* by Christoph Luxenberg. *Aramaic Studies* 2: 268–72.

Bell, Richard. 1926. *The Origin of Islam in its Christian Environment: The Gunning Lectures, Edinburgh University 1925*. London: Macmillan & Co.

Berg, Herbert and Sarah E. Rollens. 2008. "The Historical Muhammad and the Historical Jesus: A Comparison of Scholarly Reinventions and Reinterpretations." *Studies in Religion / Sciences religieuses*, 32: 271–92.

de Blois, François. 2003. Review of *Die syro-aramäische Lesart des Koran: Ein Beitrag zur Entschlüsselung der Koransprache* by Christoph Luxenberg. *The Journal of Qur'anic Studies* 5: 92–97.

Braun, W. 2008. "Introducing Religion." In Willi Braun and Russell T. McCutcheon, eds, *Introducing Religion: Essays in Honor of Jonathan Z. Smith*, 480–98. London: Equinox.

Crone, Patricia and Michael Cook. 1977. *Hagarism: The Making of the Islamic World*. Cambridge: Cambridge University Press.

Donner, Fred M. 2010. *Muhammad and the Believers at the Origins of Islam*. Cambridge: Belknap.

Geiger, Abraham. 1833. *Was hat Mohammed aus dem Judenthume aufgenommen?* Bonn: F. Baaden.

Görke, Andreas and Gregor Schoeler. 2008. *Die Ältesten Berichte über Muhammads: Das Korpus 'Urwa ibn az-Zubair*. Studies in Late Antiquity and Early Islam, 24. Princeton: Darwing.

Hawting, G. R. 1997. "John Wansbrough, Islam, and Monotheism." *Method & Theory in the Study of Religion* 9: 23–38.

Hirschfeld, Hartwig. 1878. *Jüdische Elemente im Koran: Ein Beitrag zur Koránforshung*. Berlin: Im Selbstverlag.

Hughes, Aaron. W. 2008. *Situating Islam: The Past and Future of an Academic Discipline*. London: Equinox.

Khan, L. Ali. 2006. *Hagarism: The Story of a Book Written by Infidels for Infidels.*
    Online: http://baltimorechronicle.com/2006/042606AliKhan.shtml (accessed July
    19, 2010).
Lincoln, Bruce. 1996. "Theses on Method." *Method & Theory in the Study of Religion* 8:
    225–27.
Lings, Martin. 1987. *Muhammad: His Life Based on Earliest Sources.* New York: Inner
    Traditions International.
Luxenberg, Christoph. 2007 [2000]. *The Syro-Aramaic Reading of the Koran: A Contri-
    bution to the Decoding of the Language of the Koran.* Berlin: Verlag Hans Schiler.
Mack, Burton. 2003. "The Historical Jesus Hoopla." In *The Christian Myth: Origins,
    Logic, and Legacy*, 25–40. London: Continuum.
McCutcheon, Russell T. 2005. *Religion and the Domestication of Dissent: Or, How to
    Live in a Less than Perfect Nation.* London: Equinox.
Müller, F. Max. 1899 [1873]. *Introduction to the Science of Religion: Four Lectures
    Delivered at the Royal Institution in February and May, 1870.* London: Longmans,
    Green, & Co.
Neusner, Jacob. 1977. "Religious Studies: The Next Vocation." *Bulletin of the Council of
    Societies for the Study of Religion.* 8: 117, 119–20.
Neuwirth, Angelika. 2003. "Qur'an and History—A Disputed Relationship." *The Journal
    of Qur'anic Studies* 5: 1–18.
Peters, Francis Edward. 1994. *Muhammad and the Origins of Islam.* Albany: State
    University of New York Press.
Peterson, Daniel C. 2007. *Muhammad, Prophet of God.* Grand Rapids: Eerdmans.
Said, Edward. 1978. *Orientalism.* New York: Vintage.
Schoeler, Gregor. 1996. *Charakter und Authentie der muslimischen Überlieferung über
    das Leben Mohammeds.* Berlin: W. de Gruyter.
Serjeant, Robert B. 1978. Review of *Quranic Studies: Sources and Methods of Scriptural
    Interpretation* by John Wansbrough and *Hagarism: The Making of the Islamic World*
    by Patricia Crone and Michael Cook. *Journal of the Royal Asiatic Society* 1: 76–78.
Theil, Stefan. 2003. "Challenging the Qur'an." *Newsweek* 142/4: 51.
Wansbrough, John. 1977. *Quranic Studies: Sources and Methods of Scriptural
    Interpretation.* Oxford: Oxford University Press.
———. 1987. *Res ipsa loquitur: History and Mimesis.* Jerusalem: The Israel Academy of
    Sciences and Humanities.
Watt, W. Montgomery. 1953. *Muhammad at Mecca.* Oxford: Oxford University Press.
Watt, W. Montgomery and Richard Bell. 1970. *Introduction to the Qur'an.* Edinburgh:
    Edinburgh University Press.
Wiebe, Donald. 1984. "The Failure of Nerve in the Academic Study of Religion." *Studies
    in Religion / Sciences religieuses* 13: 401–22.
———. 1999. "The Failure of Nerve in the Academic Study of Religion." In Donald
    Wiebe, *The Politics of Religious Studies: The Continuing Conflict with Theology in
    the Academy*, 141–62. New York: St. Martin's.
———. 2008. "The Scientific Study of Religion." In Willi Braun and Russell T.
    McCutcheon, eds, *Introducing Religion: Essays in Honor of Jonathan Z. Smith*,
    467–79. London: Equinox.

THE FAILURE OF ISLAMIC STUDIES POST-9/11: A CONTEXTUALIZATION AND ANALYSIS

Aaron W. Hughes

In his "The Failure of Nerve in the Academic Study of Religion" (1984; republished 1999), Donald Wiebe correctly pointed to the categorical mistakes and conceptual failures that have plagued the academic study of religion. Whether in the grand comparative studies of yesteryear or increasingly in more focused sub-disciplinary treatments, the tendency is to privilege understanding and description at the expense of explanation and analysis. Although certainly Religious Studies, speaking generally, has yet to take Wiebe's assessment seriously, I focus here on what is, perhaps, the weakest and most apologetical link in its disciplinary chain: the academic study of Islam. This sub-discipline, especially in the years post–9/11, has gained considerable capital and the interest that goes along with it.

For Wiebe, Religious Studies—and, by extension, Islamic Studies—has given up any claims to scientific disciplinarity owing to its wholesale rejection of objectivity, disinterestedness, and reductionism. What we have, instead, is nothing short of confessionalism: an academic discipline that endorses and indeed even apologizes for the religious beliefs and practices of others. Although I disagree with Wiebe's dismissal of humanistic or, what he calls, "postmodern" theorizing of religion and his desire to replace such theorizing, especially in recent years, with a more cognitive "turn," I find myself indebted to Wiebe for his refusal to accept the status quo, his unwillingness to make the academic study of religion into a smorgasbord of world spirituality, and his fight for academic respectability. Because many of my conversation partners over the years have been Wiebe and his students, I had assumed his critique was *de rigueur*. Alas, I now realize what wishful and wistful thinking that was.

1. Defining the Problem

I have called attention to the study of Islam's failure of nerve in several recent publications (e.g., Hughes 2008, 2012), so rather than risk being labeled a one-trick pony let me here focus on some of the extra-disciplinary forces that have, in recent years, exacerbated this failure. My goal is neither to apologize for the products (i.e., the disciplinary discourses) of these forces nor to imply that they are somehow a, let alone the, natural reaction to them. On the contrary, I wish simply to draw attention to them and, in the process, showcase how the academic study of Islam is caught up in a host of geopolitical, media, and administrative forces that circumscribe it, pull it in certain directions (and not others), all of which contributes to the malaise of the current disciplinary moment. The location and articulation of such forces permit us to see more clearly the "confessionalism" inherent in the study of Islam. Moreover, it is my hope that an exposé of such forces will goad us to get up the "nerve" to develop more productive theoretical stances and methodological procedures to replace what currently passes for "theorizing" in the discipline.

Although it hardly needs saying, let me be clear that my goal here is less about what Islam actually says than about how others (e.g., neo-conservative pundits, liberal Muslims, conservative campus organizations) construct it, often in their own images. Such constructions, I wish to suggest, have worked to create a largely *responsive* scholarly discourse as professional Islamicists seek to respond to or reinforce the Islams imagined by these groups. Because of the tremendous repercussions this dialectic has on how scholars present this religion—that is, what they privilege and what they deny in classrooms, among their peers, and in the public arena—it becomes necessary to reflect upon how the discipline of Islamic Studies creates a set of authorized and authorizing discourses. What can and should be said of Islam? What topics are acceptable and what topics ought to be avoided?

Lest I am accused of creating a straw man here (as I customarily am)—choosing a few random scholars who I believe largely reflect my concerns and, in the process, ignoring the majority of Religious Studies scholars dealing with Islam—I do have a specific constituency in mind. So let me here plagiarize a paragraph I use whenever I write about such matters (see Hughes 2012):

> The scholars of Islam, I have in mind, are largely associated with the Study of Islam section at the AAR. These individuals have created a collective response to the events of 9/11—a response that is described on their website as the product of "the cooperation of over 50 professors of Islamic Studies and Middle Eastern Studies from the US and Canada. These scholars are members of the Study of Islam section at the American Academy of Religion, the largest international organization responsible for the academic study of

religion" (Safi 2001). They write that "as scholars of religious traditions, we observe that religious symbols are used for political motives all over the world in Hindu, Christian, Jewish, and Muslim traditions. However, we must critically distinguish between politically motivated deployment of religious symbols and the highest ideals that these traditions embody. Just as most would regard bombers of abortion clinics to be outside the pale of Christianity, so the actions of these terrorists should not be accepted as representing Islam in any way." (Safi 2001)

This statement by the Study of Islam section at the AAR says much about what these scholars imagine "real" Islam to be: peaceful, non-political, internal. Muslims who commit terror in the name of Islam misunderstand their own tradition and are motivated by political as opposed to spiritual gain. It is these "over 50 scholars"—and the graduate students they have trained in the meantime and who they continue to train—who are responsible for producing this response, and responses like them, that I have in mind when I talk about a largely "apologetical" discourse of Islam. Rather than critique them for this, as I have elsewhere, my goal here is to show how the discourses manufactured by these individuals emerged from and continues to be in conversation with a set of larger geo-political events. When I use the generic term "Islamicists," "scholars of Islam," or "professional Islamicists" below, then, I refer almost exclusively to this group.

2. Neo-Conservativism and the Construction of a Bellicose Islam

Critics of Islam in general and scholars of Islam in particular are manifold. They run the gamut from the so-called "Islamophobic" to constructive Muslim critiques of certain aspects of the tradition. Under this latter rubric I refer not to apologists such as Tariq Ramadan, but to neo-conservative-endorsed Muslim critics such as Irshad Manji (2003, 2005) and Stephen Schwartz (2006). What such critics often share is a mistrust of scholars of Islam, whom they often associate with liberal biases. Such biases, these critics contend, lead to anti-Israeli and anti-American sentiments. The conservative Campus Watch, an organization that seeks to monitor the activities and discourses produced by scholars of Islam and the Middle East, represents this tendency most succinctly. On their website, they claim: "...the professorate is almost monolithically leftist due to a systematic exclusion of those with conservative or even moderately liberal views. The result is that Middle East studies lack intellectual diversity" (Campus Watch 2011a).[1]

---

1. Organizations such as CampusWatch.com (run by Daniel Pipes), jihadwatch.com (run by the neo-conservative David Horowitz), and IslamicPluralism.com (run by

How do Islamicists respond to such attacks? The usual way is to deny the charges. Typical rebuttals include claims such as: Islam is not monolithic (although this is also what the critics say); and not all Muslims are potential terrorists (again, something with which the critics would agree). Where scholars of Islam differ from such critics, however, is in the association between religion and violence, as the above statement by the "over 50 scholars" attests. To articulate the impact that such (neo-) conservative scholars have on the academic study of Islam, let me now examine some of their more vociferous representatives.

2.1. Irshad Manji's Trouble with Islam

One of the most popular critics of a type of Islam (and, concomitantly, the spokesperson for another type) has been the Canadian Muslim journalist Irshad Manji. In light of the 9/11 attacks, Manji has called for an end to "Islam's totalitarianism, particularly the gross human rights violations against women and religious minorities" (2003: 3). Her book, *The Trouble With Islam Today: A Muslim's Call for Reform in Her Faith*,[2] has been translated into 30 languages and has received widespread media attention. She is also the creator of the Emmy-nominated PBS documentary, "Faith Without Fear," which chronicles her journey to reconcile Islam with human rights and freedom. This documentary (and other materials) may be found on her official YouTube channel, IrshadManjiTV.

Manji is a journalist by training and has no formal training in the academic study of Islam. Her website, however, presents her as a "scholar,"[3] and, based on the fact that many are supportive of her attempts to reform Islam from within, she has been appointed as the Director of the Moral Courage Project at New York University, which aims to develop leaders who will challenge so-called "political correctness," intellectual conformity, and self-censorship.

Because she offers a critique from within the tradition, some liberal Muslims—but more frequently neo-conservative commentators, such as Daniel Pipes—have labeled Manji as a visionary.[4] The tendency in Islamic

---

Stephen Schwartz) all claim expertise in identifying what the "true" Islam is, how others corrupt it, and how "liberal" forces seek to accommodate a loosely defined "Wahhabism" or "Salafism" in North America.

2. Originally entitled *The Trouble With Islam* (2003).

3. Although in 2008 she was awarded an honorary doctorate from the University of Puget Sound.

4. Manji draws criticism from liberal Muslim theological circles as well. Omid Safi, editor of *Progressive Muslims* (2003), for example, says of Manji: "all of us are working to identify, challenge, and resist problematic practices and interpretations in Islam and Muslim societies. That is fine, and necessary. However, I also believe that it is imperative

Studies circles, however, is to write her off as a gadfly, as someone who, lacking the requisite academic and historical skills, largely misunderstands the complexity of Islam. And because she is frequently endorsed by (neo-)conservative groups, scholars of Islam tend to see her as guilty by association. This dismissal comes at a cost, however, as Manji's critical voice has reached an audience far wider than anything produced by scholars. Moreover, others frequently cite her, including those mentioned below, as the moderate face of the tradition. Pipes, for example, argues that the views of those like Manji ought to be included in the highest level of government discussion, and taught in universities:

> Governments and leading institutions can do a lot. If you look at the situation today throughout the West including North America, you'll find that the Islamists, the radicals, are the ones invited into government circles who are generally in the media, are cited as authorities, who do the research in universities, who engage in discussions with the churches and so forth. It is important for all these institutions, governmental, academic, media and alike, to remove the recognition from the Islamists and give it to the moderate Muslims. (Pipes 2003a)

2.2. Stephen Schwartz and the Neo-Con Appropriation of Sufism

Another self-styled critic from within is also a journalist, this time the American Stephen Schwartz. Unlike Manji, who for the most part is either uninterested in or unaware of Sufism, Schwartz presents this tradition as the "moderate," "spiritual" (2008: 14) face of Islam, and the path towards, as the subtitle of one his books indicates, "global harmony." Schwartz is also the Executive Director of the Center for Islamic Pluralism (CIP), whose mandate, according to its website, is to:

- Foster, develop, defend, protect, and further mobilize moderate American Muslims in their progress toward integration as an equal and respected religious community in the American interfaith environment;
- Define the future of Islam in America as a community opposed to the politicization of our religion, its radicalization, and its marginalization, which has taken place because of the imposition on Muslims of attitudes opposed to American values, traditions, and policies;
- Educate the broader American public about the reality of moderate Islam and the threat to moderate Muslims and non-Muslim Americans represented by militant, political, radical, and adversarial tendencies. (CIP 2011)

for us as Muslims to identify areas in Islam that are deep reservoirs of wisdom and compassion for us. I don't see Irshad doing this. When one doesn't talk about what it is that keeps one a Muslim, spiritually nourished from the broad spectrum of the tradition, then it becomes very easy to side with the Muslim-bashers. Take a look at who sponsors most of Irshad's talks, and this point takes on even more urgency" (Safi 2005).

The rhetoric of this mandate creates a chasm between the "religious" or the "spiritual" (i.e., Sufism) forms of Islam on the one hand as opposed to the "political" or the "ideological" forms of the tradition on the other (e.g., that which is alternatively referred to as Wahhabism, Salafism, or jihadism, all of which Schwartz often lumps together under the omnibus term "Islamo-facism"). The result is, as several critics of Schwartz's 2008 *The Other Islam: Sufism and the Road to Global Harmony* have noted (see, for example, Geertz 2003), a Manichean approach to Islam, one wherein everything good apparently derives from Sufism and everything bad emerges from "Wahhabism."

There are, of course, problems with such a bifurcation, which neither time nor space allow me to develop here, suffice it to say that it largely ignores the various ways that one's commitment to Sufi doctrine is often a commitment over and above one's commitment to other forms of Islam (e.g., Sunni or Shiʿa). Moreover, in blaming Islam's ills on the Saudi-inspired and Saudi-supported Wahhabi movement, Schwartz ignores how certain threads of Shiʿism have been implicated in support of terrorism. In the conclusion to *The Other Islam*, he writes that it is Sufism that holds itself out as the threshold to "global harmony":

> I believe that the world needs Sufism. It is God's most deeply hidden treasure, *another Islam*, a miraculous sanctuary. One need not go all the way to Turkistan to find it, for it is present in the hearts of many who live throughout this world. Its gates are open; and in the world of Rumi it appeals to all believers: only come. (2008: 239; his italics)

In fact, so zealous is Schwartz in his desire to uphold his vision of Islam as the most authentic that one of the main tasks of the CIP, the organization that he runs, is to monitor and publicize the activities of those whom the organization regards as anathema to liberal Islam: the so-called Wahhabi movement. A quick perusal of the headlines on the CIP's website, for example, shows that they are not significantly different from various neo-con websites. Articles (as of February 10, 2010) include the following: "Is Uzbekistan a U.S. Ally?"; "Ayatollah's Leviathan"; "Kosovo Sees Continuing Infiltration by Islamicists."

Following the attacks of 9/11, Schwartz became a senior policy analyst, and the director of the Islam and Democracy program at the Foundation for the Defense of Democracies, a conservative think tank. His *An Activist's Guide to Arab and Muslim Campus and Community Organizations in North America* (unpublished), written under the name Suleyman Ahmad al-Kosovi, identifies numerous organizations that he describes as belonging to the "Wahhabi lobby" in the United States. These include, but are not limited to, the American-Arab Anti-Discrimination Committee, the Muslim Students' Association, the Council on American–Islamic Relations, the Muslim Public

Affairs Council, the American Muslim Council, and the Islamic Society of North America. After providing an indictment against these groups, Schwartz concludes that

> American Muslims must now take the initiative in finding a proper and legitimate place for the faith at the table of American religions. This means counteracting Islamophobic propaganda and prejudice. It also means protecting civil liberties. But above all, it means taking the microphone away from the Wahhabi lobby. To do that, new organizations must emerge. Shiʿa Muslims must organize civic groups that will introduce their concerns into discussion of such issues as the future of Iraq. Muslim students must create independent campus organizations that will allow real debate over their destiny as believers. America offers Muslims a place to develop faith and activism as nowhere else in the world. But this mission cannot be accomplished if American Islam remains the captive of extremists. The encouragement of such activism, and education of all campus and community groups in its tasks, has been the intent of this survey.[5]

Daniel Pipes, in an article entitled "Where are the Moderate Muslims?" appearing in the conservative *New York Post* (September 23, 2003) argues that individuals such as Manji and Schwartz are the necessary future of Islam and that academics and other organizations must pay closer attention to them:

- For them to be heard over the Islamist din requires help from the outside—celebration by governments, grants from foundations, recognition by the media, and *attention from the academy*.
- Those same institutions must shun the now-dominant militant Islamic establishment. Moderates have a chance to be heard when Islamists are repudiated.

Promoting anti-Islamists and weakening Islamists is crucial if a moderate and modern form of Islam is to emerge in the West. (Pipes 2003b)

2.3. Daniel Pipes's Criticism of the Academic Study of Islam

Daniel Pipes is the founder and director both of the Middle East Forum, a conservative think tank, and, as noted above, of Campus Watch, a controversial organization, whose goal, according to its website, is to address

> five problems [of Middle Eastern Studies]: analytical failures, the mixing of politics with scholarship, intolerance of alternative views, apologetics, and the abuse of power over students. Campus Watch fully respects the freedom

---

5. The whole treatise may be found online at http://www.discoverthenetworks. org/guides/Muslim%20Booklet.pdf (accessed June 2, 2011). It can also be accessed on the Frontpagemag.com website (http://archive.frontpagemag.com/readArticle.aspx? ARTID=18058; accessed June 2, 2011), that is run by the conservative writer and policy advocate David Horowitz, a website with links to, *inter alia*, jihadwatch.com.

of speech of those it debates while insisting on its own freedom to comment on their words and deeds. (Campus Watch 2011b)

To achieve its goals, Campus watch monitors what academics have to say about Islam and the Middle East. It is particularly critical of what it perceives to be the liberal and anti-Israeli biases of many scholars. According to its webpage, Campus Watch

- Gathers information on Middle East studies from public and private sources and makes this information available on its website, www.Campus-Watch.org.
- Produces analyses of institutions, individual scholars, topics, events, and trends.
- Makes its views known through the media—newspaper opeds, radio interviews, television interviews.
- Invites student complaints of abuse, investigates their claims, and (when warranted) makes these known. (Campus Watch 2011a)

Critics refer to this activity as a form of academic "McCarthyism" (Beinin 2002). Campus Watch replies, however, that its goal is not to police such discourses, but to insure that alternate viewpoints on the Middle East are heard and included.

Pipes is particularly fond of often citing the work of Martin Kramer, former director of the Moshe Dayan Center for Middle Eastern and African Studies at Tel Aviv University, and the author of the influential *Ivory Towers on Sand* (2001), published in the aftermath of the 9/11 attacks by the conservative Washington Institute for Near Eastern Policy. The book is perhaps better contextualized by its subtitle: *The Failure of Middle Eastern Studies in America*. This work amounts to a stinging indictment of the entire field of Islamic and Middle Eastern Studies, especially on the grounds that so-called experts do not engage objectively with the political situation of the contemporary Middle East. Kramer is particularly critical of what he perceives to be the harmful influence of Edward Said on the discipline. He writes, for example,

> *Orientalism* made it acceptable, even expected, for scholars to spell out their own political commitments as a preface to anything they wrote or did. More than that, it also enshrined an acceptable hierarchy of political commitments, with Palestine at the top, followed by the Arab nation and the Islamic world. They were the long-suffering victims of Western racism, American imperialism, and Israeli Zionists, the three legs of the Orientalist stool. (2001: 37)

This and related criticisms have led individuals such as Pipes to call for a "more balanced" treatment of the Middle East among scholars, by which he means, of course, one that is "less liberal" and "more conservative." As I have shown in a previous study (Hughes 2008: 99–105), criticisms by those such as Kramer and Pipes led, at least during the Bush administration, to the establishment of hearings in Washington to look into anti-American biases in higher education (read: modern Middle Eastern Studies).[6]

3. Local Pressures

Professional Islamicists, however, do not simply respond to these external forces. In this section, I shall focus attention on various local pressures that many scholars of Islam confront, and to which they respond. In this regard, I wish to focus on two such pressures. The first stems from Muslim groups on campus who are often not interested in—in fact, are often hostile to—the non-theological presentation of Islam. These groups, perhaps best symbolized by, but certainly not limited to, Muslim Students' Associations (MSAs), present themselves as the protector of "real" and "authentic" Islam on campus. The second pressure stems from the relatively new institutionally ascribed authority granted to the Islamicist, especially his or her perceived role in creating and disseminating a positive discourse on Islam that is meant to counteract discrimination against Muslims and Islam.[7]

3.1. Muslim Students' Association (MSA)
The MSA National functions as an umbrella organization for numerous affiliated chapters at various campuses throughout North America. The local chapters, however, are only loosely affiliated with the MSA National and, thus, may have policies and views not shared by one another or even with the National organization. This can create problems, as it is not uncommon for local MSA chapters to bring highly controversial speakers to campus,[8] although with or without the national organization's awareness it is difficult to ascertain. According to its constitution:

6.   See the comments in Lockman 2004, online at http://www.mafhoum.com/press6/179C36.htm (accessed June 2, 2011).

7.   I am here influenced by the discussion of authority in Lincoln 1994: 4–8.

8.   When I taught at the University of Calgary, for instance, the local MSA brought in a Hasidic Jewish speaker from the anti-Zionist movement called Neturei Carta. Guest speakers at other campuses include radical Muslim preachers (e.g., Muhammad al-Asi). An interesting article by David Horowitz, although not one that I necessarily endorse, explains the tensions between himself, a conservative commentator, and various MSAs, entitled "My Encounter With the Enemy in Milwaukee" (2008), may be found online at http://archive.frontpagemag.com/readArticle.aspx?ARTID=30832 (accessed June 2, 2011). This article is also posted on a site entitled "Muslims Against Sharia" (http://muslimsagainstsharia.blogspot.com/2008/05/my-encounter-with-enemy-in-milwaukee.html; accessed June 2, 2011).

> The aims and purposes of MSA shall be to serve the best interest of Islam and Muslims in the United States and Canada so as to enable them to practice Islam as a complete way of life. Towards this end, it shall, in cooperation with the Islamic Society of North America [ISNA]:
> - help Muslim student organisations carry out Islamic programs and projects;
> - assist Muslim students organising themselves for Islamic activities;
> - mobilise and coordinate the human and material resources of Muslim student organizations. (MSA National 2011)

As this makes clear, the MSA—both as a national organization and as regional chapters—perceives itself as the voice of Islam on campus. MSAs are actively involved in the debates on campus that revolve around the Israeli-Palestinian conflict, often joining forces with related and overlapping organizations such as the Arab Students Association or Palestinian Students Association.

Because of their conservative nature, MSAs are often critical of the "secular" tools and the pluralism inherent in the academic study of religion (including Islam). Shiʿism, Sufism, and Islamic philosophy, all become topics that threaten to undermine what they consider to be Islam's absolute monotheism. In my personal experience teaching Islamic Studies, there is always a representative—whether official or unofficial, I have never been able to ascertain—from the MSA who signs up for my classes, presumably with the aim of reporting back to someone, somewhere that Islam was being discussed "fairly" or "accurately." And, if it is not, their vocal nature in class insures that it is.

To try and rectify the situation, many MSAs often run classes on campus with titles such as "Introduction to Islam" or "Introduction to Arabic" that sound remarkably similar to academic classes taught in Religious Studies or language departments.[9] These classes are often geared towards non-Muslims and arguably, whatever else they might deliver, the ultimate goal of the courses with which I am familiar appears to be proselytization.[10] Although there is little likelihood that students mistake these MSA-sponsored courses

---

9.   Anecdotally, I once had a non-Muslim student who had taken such an introductory Arabic class from the MSA at the University of Calgary write a rudimentary pro-Hamas slogan in Arabic on my blackboard.

10.   Here it is worth noting that Islam is an extremely proselytizing religion. The MSA, for example, annually sponsors "Islamic Awareness Week" on many North American campuses. The goal of these events is not simply to dispel misconceptions about Islam, but to invite non-Muslims to consider converting to Islam. For example, an official poster at the University of Waterloo (http://uwmsa.com/main/index.php?option=com_content& view=article&id=276&Itemid=160; accessed June 2, 2011) challenges non-Muslims with the following questions: "Do you really know God? Do you really know his Message? Do you really know your purpose? Join us and sincerely search for the truth."

for academic offerings,[11] their existence, I maintain, contributes to the more general notion that the MSA has little regard for and is often openly hostile to the secular study of Islam.[12]

Conservative Muslims students are often very vocal in the Islamic Studies classroom. They tend to take exception to what they perceive to be the liberal presentation of Islam associated with Islamic Studies. This frequently creates a series of stubborn tensions within the classroom. Such tensions, moreover, frequently make it very difficult to nuance highly politicized topics such as Islam and violence, terrorism, women, and relations with other religions. In the face of the protests of conservative students, my impression is that scholars tend to forgo more complex accounts of Islam in favor of versions in which Islam is presented more monolithically and apologetically. For instance, the "real" Islam now endorses women's rights, rejects violence, and so on (which often ends up sounding remarkably similar to MSA presentations).

3.2. Administrative Pressures
Another reality of the modern university is that the scholar of Islam is supposed to represent Islam publically to students, colleagues, local church groups, the media, and so on. This can certainly put the scholar of Islam at cross-purposes with others who claim to speak for Islam on campus and in the community; however this is not my concern here. What is my concern is that, because the scholar is the *de facto* and institutionally sanctioned spokesperson for Islam on campus, there are certain aspects of the religion that s/he is expected to uphold (e.g., not all Muslims are terrorists; Islam is an inherently beautiful and peaceful religion; certain agents have hijacked it for political or ideological ends as opposed to religious ones) and not say (e.g., that terrorists can be and are Muslims; that such individuals uphold themselves and their version of Islam as the most authentic).

The result is that scholars of Islam, as part of their unofficial job description, are expected to apologize for Islam, to defend it on campus, in churches and synagogues, and in the media. All those in the previous section who

11. A related pressure, albeit one I cannot pursue here, is when the person teaching Islam in a university setting is the local cleric or a (Muslim) professor in another discipline. How this might bode when an academically trained professional Islamicist arrives on campus is difficult to say. Universities, for example, might not want to hire a professional Islamicist on a tenure-track line when they can get the local cleric to teach as an adjunct.

12. Anecdotally, I taught at the University of Calgary for roughly ten years, and not once was I approached by Muslim groups on campus (or off campus) for an opinion or to give an informal lecture to students. I was frequently approached, however, by Muslim students to inquire as to why I had never converted to Islam, even though I had devoted my life to studying it.

criticize this vision of a liberal, open-minded Islam actually contribute further to the discourses responsible for the formation of this Islam. My goal here is not to argue whether this is right or wrong. I do mention it, however, with the aim of showing how the scholarly presentation of Islam (at least among scholars of Islam within the AAR) is sustained and circumscribed by numerous constituencies.

To conclude the previous two sections, the end result of all these processes is that Islamic Studies scholars who want to take their role as a scholar seriously are caught between numerous subcultures. These include, but are not necessarily limited to, (a) orthodox Muslim students who reject the scholarly approach and who want only positive things said about Islam; (b) public discourse leaders (like Manji, Schwartz et al., but also mainstream Islamic agencies who have a strong tilt toward PR and advocacy) who favor an essentialized version of Islam as under siege from within by perversions of its pure, progressive, and peaceful nature, and who want the academy to back them up; (c) bona fide Islamophobes who cannot think of anything "fair and balanced" or positive to say about Islam and who feel any positive claims must be anti-Semitic, anti-Western, illiberal, or both; (d) students and colleagues who think all religions are basically good, and the same at heart; and finally, (e) policy makers who want to use a particular portrait of Islam, or Arabs, to justify one or another political decision.

4. Scholars of Islam and the Creation of a Liberal Islam

In the space that remains, let me briefly highlight how scholars of Islam have responded to some of the aforementioned critiques—although it is important to remember that these scholars rarely respond directly to such criticisms, rather they tend to refine their categories often by retreating to apologetical claims. In their recent *Rethinking Islamic Studies*—with the telling subtitle: *From Orientalism to Cosmopolitanism*—the editors, Carl W. Ernst and Richard C. Martin, seek to create new conceptual modeling for the field by encouraging "the development of a new subfield that is fully integrated with religious studies" (2010: 12).[13] The editors, and the individual authors,

---

13. So well connected are the editors in the AAR that at its 2010 annual meeting in Atlanta there was an all-day workshop devoted to their book. For $50, one could survey "the changes that have taken place in Islamic studies in the field of religious studies over the past few decades. At the same time, [the book] proposes new directions based on interdisciplinary connections to current debates in different fields of study. We believe this furnishes the occasion for a fruitful interaction with younger scholars in Islamic studies, who can benefit from the opportunity to discuss the theoretical implications of their research with colleagues in the field. Our goal for the workshop is not to replicate the volume, but to use it as a springboard for thinking about the agendas for research in

however, never define what they mean by terms such as "Orientalism," "Cosmopolitanism," or even "Religious Studies." Although they can be certain that "Orientalism remains for most scholars the bête noir in the expanding family of Islamic studies today" (2010: 4), they seem to include within this term any hermeneutic that takes a critical approach to Islam and the sources, thereby ignoring some important work, both in the past decade (e.g., Hawting 1999; Melchert 1997) and more recently (e.g., Donner 2010; Powers 2010) that deal with issues of identity and community formation.

By creating a "Post-Orientalist" Islamic Studies, the editors of *Rethinking Islamic Studies* largely seek to define an uncritical and apologetical approach to Islam, albeit one couched in jargon recognizable from the humanities and social sciences. Insider and outsider approaches pirouette and ultimately collapse on one another; the line separating critics and caretakers is all but erased. In their introduction, for example, the editors invoke the names of Talal Asad and Pierre Bourdieu, but neither the editors nor the individual authors engage with their thought. The editors write that Asad "argued force-fully that Muslim societies must be understood on their own terms and not a superimposed Western model" (Ernst and Martin 2010: 9). And that's it! No mention of critical category analysis, ideology, and power (except when it suits a Saidian agenda); only that Asad—sounding remarkably like W. C. Smith—says that Muslims must be understood on their own terms. The editors also name-drop Pierre Bourdieu, but none of the essays are interested in Islam as a social formation and what the repercussions of this might be.

The result is that none of the essays in the volume, which the editors describe as "a benchmark for the future development of Islamic Studies," take a critical approach to Islam. At least half of the essays are in fact theological or quasi-theological. The first essay, for example, is written by Vincent J. Cornell, a Muslim intellectual, who is described on the "Contributors" page as "a key participant in the Building Bridges Seminars hosted by the archbishop of Canterbury" (2010: 325). The goal of his essay, described by the editors "is to reflect on the 'epistemological crisis' of Muslim intellectuals who have not yet thoroughly analyzed the principles of Islamic tradition in terms relevant today" (Ernst and Martin 2010: 15). Another contributor, Omid Safi, someone I have been critical of in the past, throws all pretence to outsider claims aside (at least he is honest) when he writes that

> ...[this] is not merely an academic exercise. As someone who considers himself a participant-observer in both [Reform] movements, it seems to me that both progressive Islam and the Iranian reform movement presently have foundational shortcomings that have to be remedied before each can achieve its potential. (Safi 2010: 73)

Islamic studies in the next decade or so" (http://www.aarweb.org/publications/e-Bulletin/2010/2010–16MAR.html; accessed June 2, 2011).

Safi's goal here is provide a first-hand account of his role in the formation of a progressive Islam in North America, link it to what is going on in the Reform movement in Iran, and detail its shortcomings. This will enable him and like-minded colleagues to regenerate Islam for the present. All of these scholars who are engaged in this creation of a North American progressive Islam, as I have shown elsewhere (Hughes 2008: 105–13), are professors of Islam housed in departments of Religious Studies throughout America. And this, to me, is the real problem with the academic study of Islam today. Perhaps the goal of such scholar-theologians is noble, but certainly not academic, unless, of course, the study of religion becomes so "cosmopolitan" that it permits everything under its canopy.

Moving beyond this volume—which seems to be the mouthpiece of the apologetical study of Islam that occurs at Duke, UNC-Chapel Hill, and Emory—other scholars of Islam are interested in showing a liberal Western audience that Islamists and other conservative Muslims are the ones that undermine Islam. For example, Khaled Abou Fadl talks about "*the* Islamic civilizational experience with all its richness and diversity" that he deftly separates from fundamentalist attempts to "reduce Islam to a single dynamic" (2003: 43, my italics). But surely such fundamentalisms must also be part of Islam's "richness or diversity." Or Gwendolyn Zoharah Simmons writes: "we Muslims, feminists, and progressives…must fight to re-interpret the texts in keeping with the socio-historical context of our times" (2003: 243). But what does it mean to "re-interpret"? And who gets to decide what texts? Or Omid Safi, moving beyond the realm of scholarship, argues that it is necessary to re-invent Islam along liberal lines. In his *Progressive Muslims*, a collection of theological essays penned by academic scholars of Islam, he writes that

> being a progressive Muslim is the determination to hold Muslim societies accountable for justice and pluralism. It means openly and purposefully resisting, challenging, and overthrowing structures of tyranny and injustice in these societies. At a general level, it means contesting injustices of gender apartheid (practiced by groups such as the Taliban), as well as the persecution of religious and ethnic minorities (undertaken by Saddam Hussein against the Kurds, etc.). It means exposing the violations of human rights and freedoms of the speech, press, religion, and the right to dissent in Muslim countries such as Saudi Arabia, Turkey, Iran, Pakistan, Sudan, Egypt, and others. More specifically it means embracing and implementing a different vision of Islam than that offered by Wahhabi and neo-Wahhabi groups. (2003: 2)

Implicit in such liberal or progressive Muslim desiderata is the assumption that there exists an authentic Islam that is somehow compatible with the sentiments behind these critiques. According to the broader story being told here (and in the work of Irshad Manji, for example), the essential Islam of

Muhammad and the Qur'ān was subsequently co-opted by male, illiberal, and hegemonic elites. All those Islams—e.g., those practiced by the Taliban, Saddam Hussein, Wahhabi and neo-Wahhabi groups—are somehow inauthentic precisely because they stray from a pure, divine, and revealed original message.

All of the responses surveyed in this section can, I think, fairly easily and uncontroversially be labeled as apologetic and theological. My goal here is not to call these individuals to task for such apologetics, as I have done elsewhere (Hughes 2008, 2012), but rather to demonstrate that the regnant public discourses in Islamic Studies have emerged in large part as a response to the type of public, political, and academic pressures articulated in the previous sections. The public discourses created and disseminated by professional Islamicists, in other words, do not emerge ex nihilo, but are molded and shaped as Islamists react to a set of external and internal, global and local, pressures. The tendency among some Islamicists to create an Islam that is consistent with liberal democratic values and has no place for those who commit violence, or conversely, the tendency among critics to construct an Islam that is essentially oriented toward violence and totalitarianism says less about an authentic Islam than it does about those doing the constructing. Another problem is the fact that the tendency to be apologetical and theological as opposed to more critical and objective has, as mentioned, not only entered the classroom but also has begun to infiltrate the ways that scholars of Islam present their work in professional venues. A consideration of the 2009 program of the AAR, for example, has panels such as "Abdul Karim Soroush and Tariq Ramadan in Conversation." The abstract for this session indicates that the conversation

> is a much-awaited discussion among some of the leading Muslim intellectuals in the world today, organized around contentious issues of Islamic reform. Featured are Tariq Ramadan, the leading European Muslim intellectual, and the author of *Radical Reform: Islamic Ethics and Liberation*, as well as *What I Believe*, as well as Abdalkarim Soroush, the leading Iranian Muslim reformist, and the author of *Reason, Freedom, and Democracy in Islam.* The conversation is moderated by Omid Safi, a leading American Muslim intellectual and the author of *Memories of Muhammad*, and the Chair for the Study of Islam Section at the AAR. The issues debated will include dynamics of Islamic reform, citizenship, gender debates, Islam and democracy, and human rights. The session will also allow for a question and answer period. (AAR 2009)

This is not a scholarly presentation of Islamic data, but a "conversation" about what authentic Islamic consists of and where it is to be located. This annual meeting of the AAR also included panels on the Qur'ān with titles such as "Understanding the Qur'an" or "Interpretive Plurality in the Qur'an." Neither of these panels nor those who presumably present in them are interested in understanding the Qur'ān from what has now been pejoratively labeled as "Orientalist" approaches (e.g., archeology, source critical, redaction criticism); rather, they seem to be interested in the Qur'ān solely from confessional and descriptive approaches.

5. Conclusions

I have argued that the dominant public discourse currently among Islamicists who teach in Religious Studies departments in North America, has largely emerged as a *response* to global forces. The presentation of Islam as an inherently peaceful religion or the victim of people who pervert this religion for merely "political" purposes is precisely that: a presentation, one no less constructed by external social, political, and religious forces than xenophobic, mendacious negative portrayals.

Scholars of Islam, however, must take more seriously their commitments to academic and objective ends. This does not mean the simple invocation of scholars such as Asad or Bourdieu or familiar categories with little or no analysis. The goal of the scholarly study of Islam is not to defend Muslims at all costs, to couch this in the vague notion of "cosmopolitan" theory, or to be the purveyors of a selective discourse that privileges and denies certain aspects of the tradition in the name of inter-faith dialogue or of some form of liberal Protestant ecumenicism.

I would not want to argue that the events of September 11, 2001, completely changed the regnant discourse of Islam in Religious Studies circles. On the contrary 9/11 and subsequent events have only underscored or exacerbated this discourse. If such events had not happened, would the manufactured discourses have been different? I doubt it. However, what the above analysis has revealed is how the larger geopolitical world impinges upon the academy. No academic discourse, no matter how hard its proponents may try, can completely separate itself from the outside world.

References

Abou El Fadl, Khaled. 2003. "The Ugly Modern and the Modern Ugly: Reclaiming the Beautiful in Islam." In Omid Safi, ed., *Progressive Muslims: On Justice, Gender, and Pluralism*, 33–77. Oxford: Oneworld.

American Academy of Religion [AAR]. 2009. "AAR Online Program Book. November 5–10, 2009. Montréal, Québec." Online: http://www.aarweb.org/Meetings/ Annual_Meeting/Past_and_Future_Meetings/2009/default.asp?ANum=A8–311& DayTime=&KeyWord=&Submit=View+Program+Book#results (accessed June 2, 2011).

Beinin, Joel. 2002. "Who's Watching the Watchers?" *History News Network*. Online: http://hnn.us/articles/1001.html (accessed June 2, 2011).

Campus Watch. 2011a. "About Campus Watch." Online: http://www.campus-watch.org/about.php (accessed June 2, 2011).

———. 2011b. "Monitoring Middle East Studies on Campus." Online: http://www.campus-watch.org/ (accessed June 2, 2011).

Center for Islamic Pluralism [CIP]. 2011. "About Us." Online: www.islamicpluralism.org/about/ (accessed June 2, 2011).

Donner, Fred. 2010. *Muhammad and the Believers*. Cambridge, MA: Harvard University Press.

Ernst, Carl W. and Richard C. Martin, eds. 2010. *Rethinking Islamic Studies: From Orientalism to Cosmopolitanism*. Columbia: University of South Carolina Press.

Geertz, Clifford. 2003. "Which Way to Mecca? Part II." *New York Review of Books*, 50/11. Online: http://www.nybooks.com/articles/16419 (accessed June 2, 2011).

Hawting, G. R. 1999. *The Idea of Idolatry and the Emergence of Islam: From Polemics to History*. Cambridge: Cambridge University Press.

Horowitz, David. 2008. "My Encounter with the Enemy in Milwaukee." *FrontPage Magazine*, May 13, 2008. Online: http://archive.frontpagemag.com/readArticle.aspx?ARTID=30832 (accessed June 2, 2011).

Hughes, Aaron W. 2008. *Situating Islam: The Past and Present of an Academic Discipline*. London: Equinox.

———. 2012. "The Study of Islam Pre and Post 9/11: A Primer and a Provocation." *Method and Theory in the Study of Religion* 25.4-5.

Kramer, Martin S. 2001. *Ivory Towers on Sand: The Failure of Middle Eastern Studies in America*. Washington, DC: Washington Institute for Near Eastern Policy.

Lincoln, Bruce. 1994. *Authority: Construction and Corrosion*. Chicago: University of Chicago Press.

Lockman, Zachary. 2004. "Behind the Battles over Midle East Studies." *Interventions: Middle East Report Online*. Online: http://www.mafhoum.com/press6/179C36.htm (accessed June 2, 2011).

Manji, Irshad. 2003. *The Trouble With Islam: A Muslim's Call for Reform in Her Faith*. New York: St. Martin's Press.

———. 2005. *The Trouble With Islam Today: A Muslim's Call for Reform in Her Faith*. New York: St. Martin's Griffen.

Melchert, Christopher. 1997. *The Formation of the Sunni Schools of Law, 9th–10th Centuries*. Leiden: Brill.

MSA National. 2011. "Constitutions/Bylaws." *Msanational.org*. Online: http://www.msanational.org/about/constitution/ (accessed June 2, 2011).

Pipes, Daniel. 2003a. "A Muslim reformation?" Online: http://www.danielpipes.org/1270/a-muslim-reformation (accessed June 2, 2011).

———. 2003b. "Where are the Moderate Muslims?" *New York Post*, September 23. Online: http://www.danielpipes.org/1255/moderate-voices-of-islam (accessed June 2, 2011).

Powers, David S. 2010. *Muhammad Is the Not the Father of Any of Your Men: The Making of the Last Prophet*. Philadelphia: University of Pennsylvania Press.

Safi, Omid. 2001. "AAR Study of Islam Section's Response to the Tragedy of September 11th, 2001." Online: http://groups.colgate.edu/aarislam/response.htm (accessed April 17, 2012).

———, ed. 2003. *Progressive Muslims: On Justice, Gender, and Pluralism*. Oxford: Oneworld.

————. 2005. "Omid Safi on Irshad Manji." Online: http://hikm. wordpress.com/2005/
07/30/omid-safi-on-irshad-manji/ (accessed June 2, 2011).

————. 2010. "Between 'Ijtihad of the Presupposition' and Gender Equality: Cross-
Pollination between Progressive Islam and Iranian Reform." In Carl Ernst and
Richard Martin, eds, *Rethinking Islamic Studies: From Orientalism to Cosmopoli-
tanism*, 72–96 Columbia, SC: University of South Carolina Press.

Schwartz, Stephen. 2006. *Is It Good for the Jews? The Crisis of America's Jewish Lobby*.
New York: Doubleday.

————. 2008. *The Other Islam: Sufism and the Road to Global Harmony*. New York:
Doubleday.

————. unpublished. *An Activist's Guide to Arab and Muslim Campus and Community
Organizations in North America*. Online: http://www.discoverthenetworks.org/
guides/Muslim%20Booklet.pdf (accessed June 2, 2011).

Simmons, Gwendolyn Zoharah. 2003. "Are We Up to the Challenge? The Need for a
Radical Re-Ordering of the Islamic Discourses on Women." In Omid Safi, ed.,
Progressive Muslims: On Justice, Gender, and Pluralism, 235–48. Oxford:
Oneworld.

Wiebe, Donald. 1984. "The Failure of Nerve in the Academic Study of Religion." *Studies
in Religion / Sciences religieuses* 13: 401–22.

————. 1999. "The Failure of Nerve in the Academic Study of Religion." In Donald
Wiebe, *The Politics of Religious Studies: The Continuing Conflict with Theology in
the Academy*. New York: Palgrave.

RELIGIOUS STUDIES THAT *REALLY* SCHMECKS: INTRODUCING FOOD TO THE ACADEMIC STUDY OF RELIGION

Michel Desjardins

There is a measure of irony in what follows. In honoring a scholar who is renowned for his razor-sharp mind, his command of the literature, and the dispassionate nature of his prose, I am offering something here that is more personal and less rigorous. I suspect that Don Wiebe will not be surprised. We have known each other now for over a quarter century, and my predilections have not escaped him.

As readers of this volume well know, over the years Don has been interested more in *how* we study and teach about religion than in *what* we study. Study, if you will, Christian theology, he says, or Wiccan rituals, or Buddhist sacred texts, but conduct the research as an entomologist might study the mating practices of praying mantes: gather all the data, be in conversation with other researchers across the world, and publish the results in quality peer-reviewed sources. Other approaches to the study of religion, for example by insiders to further their own beliefs or conversely by outsiders to ridicule religion, have their place, but not in secular universities—and certainly not within the academic study of religion that ought to be dedicated to the scientific examination of religion as a fully human phenomenon.

Don has also insisted that researchers stay true to the discipline when they teach about religion and the study of religion in the classroom. His advice to his colleagues in that regard has been: do not impose your own confessional or religious orientation on students (do entomologists preach sexual morality when teaching about praying mantes?), do not waver when students kick against the goads, and do not confuse university teaching with religious formation or the promotion of religion. Since the vast majority of scholars of religion come to the discipline not simply because of an interest in understanding the religious nature of humans but because of deep-seated religious convictions, the challenge is how to deal with those convictions in ways that distort the data as little as possible. Rigor, detachment, and critical engagement: these have long been Don's guiding principles in his discourse on how to study religion.

The *how* and the *what*, of course, are linked. If we exegete Leviticus, Romans, or the Qur'an, or study Kierkegaard and Kant with the belief that their worldviews help us to make sense of religion, we will imagine and engage the study of religion differently than if we study cognitive theory, the role of women among Sikhs in Los Angeles, or the seventeenth-century Japanese poet Matsuo Basho. Our academic responsibilities, I should add, will also change if we decide from the outset that, despite appearances to the contrary, there is no such thing as "religion" outside an interpreter's imagination.

This chapter considers how our choice of *what* we study, when we study "religion," affects our notion of religion and especially the extent to which our beliefs and biases impact our research. Change the object of study, and you change the study of religion. Not only that, but I will suggest that our chances of moving the discipline toward Don's ideal increase when scholars turn their attention to some currently underrepresented aspects of religious life. More specifically, the worry that confessional or religious orientation will negatively impact the academic study of religion is lessened when the spotlight shifts from founders, sacred texts, and theology to everyday expressions of religion.

I would like to develop this point by comparing two quite different areas of research with which I am now acquainted: Christian origins, in which I trained in the 1970s and 1980s, and the role that food plays in contemporary religious people's lives, with which I have been engaged over the last six years. The first area, long embedded in the discipline, requires linguistic, textual, and historical-critical skills; the second, still in its infancy, is grounded in anthropological field studies and the comparative study of religion. I consider both these areas examples of broader approaches within the academic study of religion. Christian origins falls comfortably within other well-established textual, historical, and philosophical studies of religion, while food and religion can be situated within newer forms of the anthropology of religion. My comparison will be complemented by a nudge for researchers to devote more academic attention to topics like food and religion—Religious Studies that schmecks, if you will.[1]

Let me start by explaining why Christian origins has been foundational to the discipline and the study of food has not. This question takes us back to our roots, a place that Don has frequently explored.

---

1. This phrase is adapted from the title of Edna Staebler's many Mennonite country cookbooks, which are well known in my region.

Any reconstruction of origins is at least partly mythical. I am reminded of that with the institution in which I currently teach, which this academic year is celebrating its hundredth anniversary. What exactly does that anniversary reflect? In 1911 the Evangelical Lutheran Seminary of Canada opened its doors in Waterloo, and thirteen years later the Waterloo College of Arts was added to it; both in turn were subsumed under the umbrella of Waterloo Lutheran University in 1960—from which Don Wiebe, by the way, received his B.A. in "Pre-theology" in 1967. Then, in 1973, this first-edition WLU transformed itself into the second WLU, Wilfrid Laurier University, a publicly funded secular institution that over time has resembled its predecessor less and less. The two WLUs reflect their times and aspirations: the earlier university grounded its liberal arts education within a form of increasingly inclusive Protestant Christianity, while the current university, legitimated by government charter, has expanded its offerings to comprise areas of study like science and business that are more in keeping with the broader societal ethos.

Religious Studies has a similar mixed pedigree. Our discipline's origins can be seen to emerge from two distinct places and times, roughly a century apart: late nineteenth-century Europe and Britain, and late twentieth-century America.[2] Both these contexts have significantly shaped what we study and how we study it, including why almost all departments have positions in Christian origins, while none have positions in food and religion.

Regarding the first phase, the Müllers, Tylors, Frazers, and Tieles of that period generated their research, as we well know, in the midst of faculties of theology, heated discussions about evolution and the supremacy of Christianity, heightened interest in the Orient and indigenous peoples, and linguistic advances and textual discoveries that magnified the importance of textual study. It is no surprise, therefore, that the academic study of religion begins by giving pride of place to origins, liberal Christian views concerning interreligious understanding, sacred texts, and languages.

The second round of founders, which this time leads to significant changes in university culture, emerges in America shortly following the 1963 U.S. Abington School District vs. Schempp court ruling that disallowed the teaching *of* religion in schools (in this case, reading Bible verses in school), while at the same time allowing for teaching *about* religion in schools and universities—the court ruling going so far as to suggest that the study of comparative religions should be an integral component of a complete education. As a result, over the next decade Departments of Religious Studies emerged and mushroomed across North America. Almost all had a liberal,

---

2. Points of contact are Friedrich Max Müller's lectures to the Royal Society in 1870, published as *Introduction to the Science of Religion* (1873), and the 1963 U.S. Abington School District vs. Schempp court ruling.

Protestant Christian flavor, and an expanded seminary-type arrangement of streams that typically included Christian Thought, Biblical Studies, (Christian) Ethics, Philosophy and Psychology of Religion, Judaism, and sometimes one or two other traditions, while also providing courses in canonical languages.[3] Students were taught that religion mattered in a world perceived (by scholars, at least, with no small degree of projection) to be struggling to find meaning, that one had to be open to a diversity of religious expressions, and (sometimes explicitly, usually implicitly) that exclusivist religious ideologies were regressive forms of human thinking.[4]

These late nineteenth- and late twentieth-century ideological contexts had points of overlap. Most notably, in both cases a significant number of scholars were grounded in their Christian beliefs, including those individuals who eventually moved to the margins of Christianity and beyond. A quote from one of Don Wiebe's articles, though focused on C. P. Tiele, could apply to a wide range of founders in both contexts:

> even though such scholars hoped that the results of their scientific study of religion would be consistent with their Christian faith, they were nevertheless concerned to establish the study of religion as an autonomous academic discipline worthy of inclusion alongside the other sciences in the curriculum of the university. (Wiebe 1999: 32)

As times and contexts changed so too did theoretical frameworks. One need only read Tylor, Frazer, and Durkheim before turning to Boyer (2001), McCarthy Brown (1991), and Tweed (2006) to experience the epistemological shifts in the discipline. Or compare the European and British colonial attitudes about gathering data at the turn of the twentieth century with the work of W. C. Smith (1963), Said (1978), and Masuzawa (2005) to witness the shifts in the grounds of discourse over the course of a century. But Christian origins remained. Given these particular set of roots of the academic study of religion, it is not surprising that positions in Christian origins (earlier called New Testament) were built into the structure of the vast majority of Religious Studies departments in North America, and that most of them remain.

---

3. For an overview of departments of Religious Studies in Canada in 1972 see Charles P. Anderson, *Guide to Religious Studies in Canada* (1972). This guide (the first book published by the Corporation, with the help of Michel Campbell for French-language programs) includes broad coverage of the academic study of religion in Canada in the second decade of Religious Studies in Canada.

4. For an excellent snapshot of the goals of this discipline as conceived by scholars in that period, see the lead-off editorials by William Nicholls (1971) and Michel Campbell (1971) in the first issue of the journal *Studies in Religion / Sciences religieuses*. This journal replaced the *Canadian Journal of Theology*, which had served the Canadian academic community from 1955 through 1970.

How, then, is the academic study of religion configured for those who take up Christian origins, and what does the study of religion become when departments are staffed by individuals trained in this way? Let me start with a point that may seem obvious: Christian origins is focused on the past. This area of study could have been conceived in a way that included the interpretation of the Bible over the last 2000 years. But it was not. Given the Protestant roots to much of the research, this focus on the authority of the text itself is perhaps not surprising. As a result, the academic focus was placed on ancient languages and textual analysis, and contemporary lived religion was de-privileged as data or even as method for uncovering historical Christianity. Authority was displaced: the freedom gained by breaking away from the confines of modern Christian belief was counterbalanced by placing power instead in the hands and imaginations of a small group of biblical exegetes.

The focus on origins is sharpened by the search for the primary strata in the New Testament. Examining 1 Timothy and Ephesians, for example, is typically considered not as valuable as looking at Romans and 1 Corinthians because "Paul" is more important than "Deutero-Paul." It is also not enough to look at Matthew and Luke; one needs to return to Q, the imagined text they are thought to have shared—and the earliest stratum of Q if possible.

How does this matter? This type of scholarship not infrequently becomes a religious (or anti-religious) practice as much as an academic quest. There are significant exceptions, to be sure (including the research done by the editors of this book), but usually it is the Jesus of faith and the "correct" ideology that are sought. A second implication is that the scholar's imagined world of origins becomes as real, indeed more real, than the actual religious remains like the texts themselves.[5] We are talking about the construction of professionally crafted, imagined spaces.

Let me add another point: not all scholars of Christian origins are Christian, but the vast majority of them have been, and continue to be, practicing Christians for whom the New Testament has profound religious associations. Accordingly, interpretations in this area are frequently (if not

5. I think of J. Z. Smith who has stated in several places, including his 2010 American Academy of Religion (AAR) plenary in Atlanta, that he is actually not interested in studying religion "out there"; what interests him are ideas and theories about religion, which at times can be quite disconnected from real religious individuals. This attitude brings to mind the scene in the movie "The Last Temptation of Christ," where Paul, who is preaching a message about the resurrected Jesus, meets the actual Jesus who never died. Jesus calls Paul a liar for preaching this message; Paul's response: "Look around you. Look at all these people. Look at their faces. Do you see how unhappy they are, how much they're suffering? Their only hope is the resurrected Jesus. I don't care whether you're Jesus or not. The resurrected Jesus will save the world, and that's what matters."

always) driven by Christian sectarian ideology: Baptists find and create interpretations to support their orientation, as do Anglicans, Roman Catholics, Mennonites, and so forth.

We might again ask: how does *this* matter? One result is a restricted, at times deeply divided, cohort of scholars. I have long wished for a more diverse company of Christian origins scholars, who would then constitute a better auto-reflexive scholarly community. Moreover, a distinct type of scholarship develops when, on the one hand, scholars in an area like this are not all working within the confines of the academic study of religion, and, on the other, when a good number of those who do hold positions in secular colleges and universities are studying a text that is religiously significant to them. Indeed, the vast majority of scholars who work in Christian origins teach in sectarian Christian institutions, which often give priority to rather different principles and interpretive traditions. While the work of these scholars is academic, it certainly is more in keeping with the pre-1963 era of the study of religion. The result: Christian origins is an extraordinarily rich, imaginative, complex, and conflicted area of study.

Another implication of the Christian base of scholarship is that interpretations matter. They matter enormously, actually, since they have the possibility of significantly affecting a person's core beliefs and religious practice. Scholars are taught and frequently reminded to pay attention to the smallest of details: a verb tense, the context of a particular passage, a marginal biblical allusion. Michael Warner, in a different context, underlines this point in an article that begins in this way:

> I was a teenage Pentecostalist. Because that is so very far from what I am now—roughly, a queer atheist intellectual—people often think I should have an explanation, a story. Was I sick? Had I been drinking? How did I get here from there? (1997: 223)

Later in the article he goes on to say: "Being a literary critic is nice, I have to say, but for lip-whitening, vein-popping thrills it does not compete. Not even in the headier regions of Theory can we approximate that saturation of life by argument [based on biblical interpretation]" (1997: 226).[6] Yes indeed, and that is why becoming a member of the guild of biblical scholars requires a long and rigorous apprenticeship.

---

6. The close attention to details in this area of study is one reason, I believe, why some of the most creative theorists in Religious Studies (e.g., J. Z. Smith, W. Braun, W. Arnal) have been trained in Christian origins; another reason is that biblical scholars often enter the field with a set of presuppositions about the Bible, only to have their study disrupt and, at times, mangle those presuppositions. The result is the need to think carefully through broader questions about the academic study of religion.

Let me add one final point concerning the focus on origins: if origins and texts matter, and "the historical Jesus" matters most of all, justification for current religious ideology must be grounded in those early strata. Should Christians support free choice on abortion, or same-sex marriage, or participation in war, or women leadership in the community, or married priesthood? Answers to these questions depend to a considerable extent on how the texts are interpreted. This link between current religious ideology and textual analysis results in a pull in two opposite directions: careful, responsible scholarship of a kind that one rarely finds in other areas; and scholarship that is significantly driven by forced interpretations.[7] The "Theology" vs. "Religious Studies" debate cannot be avoided here.

What might we expect, then, in Departments of Religious Studies staffed by Christian origins scholars? Not surprisingly, we find many of these scholars to be superb and sensitive teachers, used to interacting with large numbers of very engaged students for whom these canonical texts carry significant weight for personal and religious reasons. We also find many to be what I might call good old-fashioned scholars, with enormous libraries, respect for scholarship, and finely honed interpretive skills. Most Christian origins scholars are also personally invested in what they teach, and they are keen to ensure that their students not only learn the art of biblical scholarship but are left with the "proper" interpretations of these texts—however that is understood by each scholar. Their confessional and ideological orientations, in other words, are in full bloom for those with eyes to see and ears to hear.

The intersection of food and religion offers a significantly different way of engaging the discipline. This area of study, I have discovered, is not as ideologically driven, it can be less engaged with questions raised by the religious leaders themselves, and it consults more closely with practitioners. It may not always have the rigor of well-established areas of study or the determination to move from description to explanation, but it opens up possibilities consistent with the goals of the founders of our discipline. Let me expand on these comments.

In talking with people about the role that food plays in their religious lives it does not take long to appreciate that, even on a personal level, the categories developed by scholars are fragile constructs. The comment "Jews eat

---

7. For an expansion on this point see Arnal: "in the case of 'biblical studies,' even conceived ideally, it is not entirely clear that we are dealing with a reasonable area of potentially dispassionate and productive scholarship, at least outside of the confines of a confessional Christian identity. Not only the origins but the bulk of biblical scholarship today remains fundamentally interpretive, and thus, far from raising the question of its own relevance, continues to assume a role as expounder of God's holy word, even if this role is not to be claimed explicitly" (2010: 571).

kosher food," for instance, would bring a loud chortle from most Jews, since the majority of them in North America rarely eat kosher. And in what category does one place the Indonesian Muslim leader who offers food to the sea goddess? Or the Catholic university students in my university who, after watching their Muslim classmates during Ramadan, revitalize their own Christian fasting tradition by taking on a 40-day Ramadan-type fast?

This type of evidence suggests that the data with which the scholar works constantly challenge standardized categories, including the coherence of religious traditions themselves. To be sure, such an appreciation of categories is (or should be) understood by all scholars of religion, but the functional rather than ontological nature of academic categories, such as Jew and Christian (and religion), is more quickly ignored in an established area of study like Christian origins, with its centuries-long academic tradition and its ongoing links with religious authority. When it comes to the study of food and religion, however, it is more difficult to ignore the fluidity and functionality of categories—and the role that the interpreter plays in determining and interpreting information.

The data for the study of religion and food also more easily lead to locations outside the Christian matrix of the discipline. If one starts by examining Hindus in India, research on daily religious life is quickly overwhelmed with food—food offerings at home and at the temple, food charity, food restrictions, and the list goes on. The same could be said of Orthodox Jews in different parts of the world. Were one to start with Protestant Christians in Boston, however, it would take longer to tease out the role of food in people's religious lives. Food is vital to religious life everywhere on this planet, but in some parts of the world and with some traditions only sight-, smell- and hearing-impaired researchers could ignore it. So how does this matter? If one wants to reduce the centrality of Christianity in the study of religion, one need only shift the gaze elsewhere: away from theology, away from philosophy and dogma, onto food...and dance, music, and clothing. Once the gaze shifts, so too do the questions.

The same applies to broadening the base of researchers. Most scholars who write about food and religion, not surprisingly perhaps, are Hindus and Jews. I might add that the discourse is also lighter, more playful, and more open to considering a variety of views. If we wish to add more voices to scholarship on religion, we are likely to have more success, I think, by changing the categories of study than by introducing affirmative action.

Similar points can be made about the role of women (and children). If we keep studying leaders, and writers of texts and rule books, we will find men, and more men. If we look for other ways in which religious life is nurtured—often in equally significant ways—women are everywhere; in fact, when looking at the vital role that food plays in people's religious lives the question sometimes becomes, where are the men? Women are minorities in only certain parts of religious life. By highlighting some aspects of religious life and not others in the academic study of religion we have reinforced the male religious leadership's notions of what matters in their community. Not surprisingly again there are far more women scholars, of various ethnicities, who write about food than there are who write about the Bible, or Christian philosophy and theology.

Research in this area also raises additional comparative observations. Qualitative data is more open to question by scholars, especially those doing quantitative research. There are good reasons for questioning the validity of qualitative studies, particularly since the nature of the data depends to a considerable extent on the questions asked, and the experience and expertise of the person doing the fieldwork. In the academic study of religion training in fieldwork is considerably less developed than the training students receive to interpret ancient texts. Moreover, basic data that are collected (transcripts and the like) are usually not available to other scholars, so it is practically impossible to verify if a researcher has made proper use of the data, let alone collected the material well. In the context where an afternoon conversation with someone over a coffee at Starbucks is considered "fieldwork," I frequently yearn for the hard-earned rigor of biblical scholarship. It must be noted, though, that research on food and religion certainly facilitates access to data that we could not even dream of obtaining from first-century documents.

How does this matter? Despite the inherent problems with qualitative analysis, properly conducted fieldwork brings researchers face to face with abundant lived religious experience, lessening the possibility that scholars will construct fantasy worlds to serve their personal and religious proclivities. Field researchers are forced to pay more attention to actual religious people. These people also care about the research, and are usually not threatened by it.

What we would also expect from departments staffed by scholars exploring food and religion is increased engagement with a wide range of research in the humanities and social sciences since this area adds more inter-disciplinarity to the standard multidisciplinary Religious Studies setting. We would also expect increased collaborative scholarship at our own institutions, helping to raise the legitimacy of our discipline.

This research would also not be as entangled with religious ideologies. To be sure, ideologies are always present in interpretations. The functionalist interpretations of a Marvin Harris (1974) are contentious,[8] one finds Hindu scholars making a case for the superiority of their tradition's dietary

8.   E.g., Jews and others prohibited the eating of pigs because the ecology changed, making the raising of these animals more resource intensive.

practices, and some scholars promote vegetarianism with a zeal that would make current Israeli settlers blush. But it would not be the academy if these differences of opinions were not voiced. The zeal that comes with the *religious* study of religion, however, dissipates when the religious stakes are not so high, when religious authority is not as threatened.

I would think, therefore, that as areas such as food and religion increasingly take their place in the academic study of religion, Don Wiebe will less frequently have to make his plea for the scientific examination of religion as a fully human phenomenon. That development comes with certain regrets. I will sorely miss the full-blown expressions of Don's prophetic spirit: staying unwaveringly firm to principles and speaking truth to power. Religious Studies that *really* schmecks can never do without these qualities.

References

Anderson, Charles P. 1972. *Guide to Religious Studies in Canada.* N.p.: Corporation for the Publication of Academic Studies in Religion in Canada.

Arnal, William. 2010. "What Branches Grow Out of this Stony Rubbish: Christian Origins and the Study of Religion." *Studies in Religion / Sciences religieuses* 39: 549–72.

Boyer, Pascal. 2001. *Religion Explained: The Evolutionary Origins of Religious Thought.* New York: Basic Books.

Cambell, Michel. 1971. "Editorial." *Studies in Religion / Sciences religieuses* 1: 3–5.

Harris, Marvin. 1974. *Cows, Pigs, Wars, and Witches: The Riddles of Culture.* New York: Random House.

Masuzawa, Tomoko. 2005. *The Invention of World Religions, Or, How European Universalism Was Preserved in the Language of Pluralism.* Chicago and London: University of Chicago Press.

McCarthy Brown, Karen. 1991. *Mama Lola: A Vodou Priestess in Brooklyn.* Berkeley: University of California Press.

Müller, Friedrich Max. 1873. *Introduction to the Science of Religion: Four Lectures Delivered at the Royal Institution, with Two Essays on False Analogies, and the Philosophy of Mythology.* London: Longmans, Green.

Nicholls, William. Date. "Editorial." *Studies in Religion / Sciences religieuses* 1: 1–3.

Said, Edward. 1978. *Orientalism.* New York: Pantheon.

Smith, Wilfred Cantwell Smith. 1963. *The Meaning and End of Religion.* New York: Mentor.

Tweed, Thomas. 2006. *Crossing and Dwelling: A Theory of Religion.* Cambridge, MA: Harvard University Press.

Warner, Michael. 1997. "Tongue Untied: Memoirs of a Pentecostal Boyhood." In Gary David Comstock and Susan E. Henking, eds., *Que(e)rying Religion: A Critical Anthology*, 223–31. New York: Continuum.

Wiebe, Donald. 1999. "Toward a Founding of a Science of Religion: The Contribution of C. P. Tiele." In *The Politics of Religious Studies: The Continuing Conflict with Theology in the Academy*, 31–50. New York: St. Martin's Press.

Cultural Anthropology and Corinthian Food Fights: Structure and History in the Lord's Dinner

John W. Parrish

> In all societies, both simple and complex, eating is the primary way of initiating and maintaining human relationships... Once the anthropologist finds out where, when, and with whom the food is eaten, just about everything else can be inferred about the relations among the society's members... To know what, where, how, when and with whom people eat is to know the character of their society. (Farb and Armelagos 1980: 4)

As we have known at least since Shklovsky, the task of "defamiliarization"—to make familiar what, at first glance, appears strange to us, and to make strange what we first thought familiar—is essential to the study of any human social formation (Shklovsky 1965; cited in Smith 2004a: 484). In the field of Christian Origins—the branch of the academy charged with the study of early Christian writings, and a field that, as Jonathan Z. Smith has pointed out, has remained overwhelmingly an affair of native exegesis—defamiliarization is especially imperative, since it is sometimes easy to forget that our data are unfamiliar. Though, in anthropological terms, a text like 1 Corinthians should appear no more familiar to the scholar than any ethnography of a nineteenth-century Fijian village, we scholars of Christian origins often allow the "self-evidence" of the Corinthian Christ group to stand unquestioned. We often assume we know why this association was formed, why it continued to meet, and what kind of problems it was experiencing. Upon reflection, however, this self-evidence cannot be allowed to stand.

If, as the above quote from Farb and Armelagos suggests, it is possible to know the character of a social formation from its eating practices, then we have every indication that the Corinthian Christ association was a strange formation indeed. If we were to attempt an historical ethnography of this group based on its eating practices, we would have several ethnographic markers to guide us. There are many references to meal practices in Paul's letter, and they tell us quite a bit about Paul's understanding of the group, not to mention the nature of the social formation itself. One of the most interesting references occurs while Paul is arguing against the consumption of "food sacrificed to idols" (*ton eidolothyton*; 1 Cor 8–10). He warns the Corinthians, "it is impossible to share the cup of Christ and the cup of demons" (1 Cor 10:21), with the obvious implication that he equates the taking of *ton eidolothyton* with demon worship—meaning that he thought some Corinthians were dining with demons!

This theological concern of Paul serves as an anthropological clue for us. It alerts us to the presence of at least two divergent forms of religiosity in the Corinthian formation. As Jonathan Z. Smith informs us, "demon worship" is rarely ever a first order term that one applies to one's own religiosity. It is almost always "a term of estrangement" that is applied to the religion of others. It "represents a reduction of their religiosity to the category of the false but not (it is essential to emphasize) to the category of the impotent" (Smith 1978b: 425). Paul is obviously afraid of the harm demons can cause, just as he considers it dangerous to partake of the Lord's Dinner in vain (1 Cor 11:27–30). Thus, when trying to dissuade certain Corinthians from participation in these meals, he appeals to demons in order to scare these Corinthians away.

Since Paul uses the category of "the demonic" in a regulatory manner, attempting by this deployment of the category to de-authorize certain forms of religious behavior, we might argue, as Smith does, that the category "demonic" serves a "locative function" in the most literal sense of "locating and establishing a place" (Smith 1978b: 427, 429–30, 437–39). In Smith's later work, of course, "locative" came to have a broader categorial meaning and was correlated with another term, "utopian."[1] Taken together, the two terms signify different "maps" or "worldviews" between which religious traditions oscillate, sometimes co-existing within the same tradition simultaneously.[2] I argue that 1 Corinthians is evidence for just such a co-existence of divergent religiosities within the Corinthian Christ association and that the tension this co-existence generates is absolutely basic for an "anthropological" understanding of this group.

---

1. For a roughly chronological development of Smith's thinking on these terms, see Smith 1971, 1974; 1978a: xi–xv, 67–207; 1990: 121–25. For a different, more developed proposal, see Smith 2004b.

2. Though a few words about the meaning of "locative" and "utopian" in Smith's thought are necessary, due to space considerations I include them in a footnote. In locative traditions, the soteriology tends to be based upon sanctification, and a chief concern of locative religionists is keeping things in place. Thus, resurrection language (for instance) is uncharacteristic of these traditions, as beings from the realm of the dead are out of place in the realm of the living. The soteriology of utopian traditions tends towards salvation, or escape from a place that is seen as oppressive. Resurrection language is quite common in these traditions: it does not matter if things keep their place or not if the cosmos is already perceived as being out of place or "out of joint."

The observation of this diversity has already defamiliarized our imagination of the Corinthian association. We are worlds removed from the naïve, apologetically influenced models used in some studies of 1 Corinthians, as this quote illustrates: "In apostolic times we have a full description of the services in Corinth, *and they remind you of a modern prayer meeting or an old-fashioned Methodist class meeting*" (Faulkner 1924: 395, emphasis added). Such a statement ignores a great deal of evidence from 1 Corinthians. If eating food sacrificed to idols (1 Cor 8–10), wildly speaking in tongues (1 Cor 14), and baptizing people on behalf of the dead (1 Cor 15:29)—not to mention overtly denying that there is a resurrection (1 Cor 15:12)—is characteristic of "old-fashioned Methodist class meetings," it is news to me. Such excision of historical differences in favor of abstract sameness is methodologically indefensible, not to mention unhelpful. For the purposes of this essay, it is difference and division—not continuity or identity—that will prove most useful.

I hope to further our understanding of the Corinthian Christ association by focusing upon the conflict surrounding the ritual meal known as the Lord's Dinner, which Paul discusses in 1 Cor 11. I will argue, on the basis of the diversity we have already observed within the Corinthian formation, that this ritual was taken up and divergently mythologized in conflicting ways intimately connected with group definition. I will also argue, on the basis of several cross-cultural analogies, that the conflicts, tensions, and contradictions this divergence generated both *structured* the history of the Corinthian formation and gave that structure its *historical dimension*. It is to the task of demonstrating this that we now turn.[3]

1. Demons and Divisions

The locative and utopian "maps" are both present within the Corinthian association. With Smith (1990: 138–43), I classify Paul as utopian. The centrality of resurrection to his thinking, and his explicit view of salvation as an escape from the "non-being" (*ta mē onta*) of death (1 Cor 1:29), place Paul squarely in a utopian stream. On the other hand, I classify many—but

---

3.   Given the context of this essay, it is appropriate that a few other methodological points be foregrounded and made explicit. In this essay, I am not approaching the text of 1 Corinthians as a Pauline specialist, nor as a scholar of Christian origins. Rather, my approach is that of a historian of religion who is interested in bringing the methods and theories of comparative religious studies sharply to bear upon one early Christian "site," 1 Corinthians. I will therefore approach this early Christian text as a generalist, and will avoid discussing thorny exegetical problems and "thick rehearsal" of the enormous dossier of New Testament scholarship in favor of a few secondary sources that I stipulate as exemplary.

not all—of the Corinthians to whom he is writing as locative, given their denial of the resurrection (1 Cor 15:12; see Parrish 2010: 25–45). Nonetheless, it cannot be denied that Paul is using the category of the "demonic" here in something like a locative—we might also say "situational," "border-lining," or *apotropaic*—manner. Like wild men at the edge of maps or dragons on the edge of nautical charts, "demons" for Paul constitute a boundary that should not be crossed—or, better, a threat that should not be allowed into the association—and Paul's adamant warnings represent his attempts to set up a bulwark against them. Smith notes that this usage of the category is common, and elaborates:

> [W]ith the demonic (as with analogous categories such as clean/unclean) we are not attempting to interpret substantive categories; but rather situational or relational categories, mobile boundaries *which shift according to the map being employed.* Demons serve as classificatory markers which signal what is *strong and weak,* controlled and exaggerated in a given society in a given moment. (1978b: 430, emphasis added)

In contrast to many other commentators on these passages, therefore, I will not take Paul at his word regarding the divisions between the "strong" and the "weak," the "cup of the Lord" and the "cup of demons." Smith's observation of the *relational* nature of such hierarchies, by contrast, allows us to explore the letter from a different angle. If Paul is operating with a different "map" of the social formation than some other Corinthians are operating with, then the "food fights" surrounding the Lord's Dinner might better be described as springing from the tension brought on by the "conjuncture" between Paul and the Corinthians than as a simple theological disagreement. In Smith's terms, this tension is a conflict between the locative and utopian ideologies which seem to be coexisting, however anxiously, at the time of writing 1 Corinthians.[4]

---

4.   A thorough review of the social setting of 1 Corinthians would be helpful at this point, but it would also bog down this essay excessively. See Adams and Horrell 2004: 2–13 for a concise review of the setting. More specialized studies can be found in Wiseman 1979 and Engels 1990. In addition to this, the work of the SBL Seminar on Ancient Myths and Modern Theories of Christian Origins, especially William Arnal (2011), Burton L. Mack (2011), and Stanley K. Stowers (2011), as well as Smith 2004c are valuable. Thanks primarily to these scholars, there is an emerging consensus "that the Corinthians were already in the practice of meeting together before Paul came along, that some kind of meal was part of the practice, and that Paul wanted to change that practice in order to align it with his gospel" (Mack 2011: 51). Jonathan Z. Smith's argument that the common interest that brought the Corinthians together both before and after Paul was "how to practice their traditional festivals for the dead away from their home districts" (Mack 2011: 51-52) is very plausible, given this context. This is probably how Paul gained a hearing from the Corinthians in the first place, and why he persuaded them to adopt *Christos* as their new patron deity. The Corinthians' reception of Paul might best

2. Four Winnebago Myths and Corinth

From the structure of Paul's own rhetoric—his use of the category "demonic" to regulate Corinthian practice, for example—as well as our knowledge of the social setting of 1 Corinthians, we can deduce something of the divisions existing within this social formation. But these examinations have only provided us with glimpses of the social formation. In order to fill in some of the blanks and color in the gray areas, it will be helpful to consider a famous ethnographic example that provides a good analogy for the kind of divisions we find at Corinth and the hierarchical nature of these divisions. This ethnographic example is found in Claude Lévi-Strauss's (1963) essay on the Winnebago, entitled "Do Dual Organizations Exist?"[5]

A few preliminary remarks on the Winnebago social structure will be helpful. They are divided into two moieties: "Those Who are Above" (*A*) and "Those Who are on Earth" (*B*). When Paul Radin was living among the Winnebago and learning about their society, he noticed a "curious discrepancy" in the Winnebago's accounts of their social organization. Though all recognized the dual organization between *A* and *B*, the way that they described this organizational "map" was quite different. Smith writes:

> The majority of [Radin's] informants described a circular village with equal areas belonging to the two moieties, divided from each other by an "imaginary diameter running northwest and southeast." The lodge of the Thunderbird clan,

be understood as "their reception of a traveling teacher/philosopher, with something of interest to say about 'wisdom,' 'spirits,' group identities, and meals in memory of ancestors" (Mack 2011: 52). And since a surprising number of the problems Paul addresses in 1 Corinthians revolve around food, this notion of a pre-existing association in the practice of meeting for meals is also quite plausible. This gives the Corinthians agency in their own group formation. They already had their way of carrying out their association's meal. This customary meal must have continued after Paul left Corinth, and this "vestigial" meal practice was not what Paul thought they should be doing in their capacity as a Christ association. Thus, I argue that the meal conflict is not best understood on the creation-and-fall model, as though Paul taught the Corinthians how to do things properly, only to see their practices "corrupted" once he left Corinth. Rather, it is more plausible to think that some of the Corinthians never stopped doing things in the fashion they did prior to meeting Paul, while others thought things should be done as Paul wanted. The meal practices were such a site of contestation because they symbolized different ideas of what the group should be.

5. This essay was a commentary on Paul Radin's monograph *The Winnebago Tribe* (1970), and was itself commented upon in Jonathan Z. Smith's *To Take Place* (1987), esp. 42–44. For what follows, I rely upon Smith's discussion of these other works. As interesting as the various Winnebago myths and social formations are, it is the theoretical implications of Radin's monograph and Lévi-Strauss's essay that are of the most interest here. Thus, the discussion of the Winnebago social organization is entirely a reiteration of, or extrapolation from, Smith's exemplary discussion.

the first of the four clans of the *A* moiety, stood at the southern extremity within the one half, with the other lodges belonging to *A* scattered throughout the moiety's "territory." The lodge of the Bear clan, the first of the eight clans of the *B* moiety, stood at the northern extremity within the other half, with the remaining lodges belonging to *B* scattered throughout the moiety's "territory." (Smith 1987: 42)

However, several of Radin's native informants insisted on a different model. In this second model,

there was no distinction between the two moieties. The ruling lodges (those of the Thunderbird and Bear clans) were in the center, with the other lodges clustered around them. The contrasts were between the village and the cleared land surrounding it and between the cleared land and the encompassing forest. The first model, which Lévi-Strauss terms a "diametric structure," and which is symmetrical and reciprocal (the one moiety's territory being the mirror image of the other), was "always given" by members of *A*. The second model, which Lévi-Strauss terms a "concentric structure," is hierarchical. It collects the ruling functions in the center in distinction to their lodges (regardless of moiety) and then distinguishes the human and inhabited realm from the cultivated land, and the cultivated land from the wild land. This latter diagram was described only by members of *B*. (Smith 1987: 42–43)

While both Smith and Lévi-Strauss make much of this "discrepancy," Smith relies upon Lévi-Strauss's "apt" critique of Radin to set the stage for his own interpretations of the data:

Radin did not stress the discrepancy; he merely regretted that insufficient information made it impossible for him to determine which was the true village organization. I should like to show here that the question is not necessarily one of alternatives. These forms, as described, do not necessarily relate to two different organizations. They may also correspond to two different ways of describing one organization too complex to be formalized by a single model, so that the members of each moiety would tend to conceptualize it one way rather than the other, depending upon their position in the social structure. For even in such an apparently symmetrical type of social structure as dual organization, the relationship between moieties is never as static, or as fully reciprocal, as one might tend to imagine. (Lévi-Strauss 1963: 134–35, quoted in Smith 1987: 43)

Lévi-Strauss also points out that the "diametric structure" of moiety *A* is more likely to be perceived as an inherently reciprocal and balanced structure, whereas in "concentric structures, the inequality may be taken for granted, since the two elements are, so to speak, arranged with respect to the same point of reference—the center—to which one of the circles is closer than the other." This leads Lévi-Strauss to a question that will prove helpful in our discussion of the Corinthian group: "How can moieties [or groups, or factions] involved in reciprocal obligations and exercising symmetrical rights be, at the same time, hierarchically related?" (Lévi-Strauss 1963: 139–40, quoted in Smith 1987: 43). While Lévi-Strauss goes on to provide a superior, if still problematic, solution to the "discrepancy" first noted by Radin,[6] it is Smith's own response to this question that I find most helpful.

While Radin maintained that the titles "Those Who are Above" and "Those Who are on Earth [Below]" have "no connotation of superior and inferior" (Radin 1970: 211, quoted in Smith 1987: 44), and Lévi-Strauss never fully grasped the import of his observation that "members of each moiety would tend to conceptualize [the social structure] one way rather than the other, depending upon their position in [that same] social structure" (Lévi-Strauss 1963: 134–35), Smith takes the question of hierarchy as central to the interpretation of the Winnebago data. He links together a catena of facts that clearly indicates hierarchy: the chief is selected from moiety *A*, never moiety *B* (Radin 1970: 272); moiety *A* as a whole is sometimes referred to as the "chiefs," while moiety *B* is sometimes called the "soldiers" (Radin 1970: 136); *A* has the power to determine the boundaries of the tribe, is responsible for declaring war, avoiding war in times of peace, and negotiating treaties with other tribes, while *B* is responsible for the internal order and discipline of the tribe; and so on.[7]

> Thus, it is from a perspective of power that *A* sees the village as symmetrical and reciprocal; it is from a position of subordination that *B* pictures the village as hierarchical. *A*'s position is one of relative clarity; hence, the mirror-image character of its picture of the tribal organization. *B*'s position is ambivalent; hence, its more highly valenced "concentric" diagram. (Smith 1987: 44)

Smith concludes: "These opposing positions give rise to two discordant ideological maps of geographical and social space" (1987: 45).

If we return to the Corinthian situation with this ethnographic example in mind, we find several analogous relations present within the social formation to which Paul is writing. Most obvious, at first glance, are the various "factions" or "parties" that seem to be present within the formation: for instance, 1 Cor 1:12, in which Paul reports that some Corinthians have sworn allegiance to different leaders: "I am of Paul! I am of Cephas! I am of Apollos! I am of Christ!" Furthermore, the implied distinction between the "strong" and the "weak" reveals an ideology of hierarchy, which Paul's epistle is not only evidence for, but also an instance of.

This is an important point to which Gerd Theissen, among others, has called our attention. While 1 Corinthians may be "mined" for "social facts" about the Corinthian Christ association, it is easy to forget that 1 Corinthians

---

6. See Smith 1987: 143–45 n. 100, for a long discussion and rectification of Lévi-Strauss's solution.

7. See Smith 1987: 44, for a fuller discussion and bibliography.

is itself a "social fact" (Theissen 1982: 137).[8] Yet, as Theissen demonstrates, the social fact of 1 Corinthians tells us a great deal about the social formation to which it was written.

We learn something about the position of Paul's "informants" in the social formation. We also learn something about Paul's critics and addressees. Theissen argues that the Corinthians' letter to Paul, to which 1 Corinthians is a response, "clearly is formulated from the standpoint of the strong" (1982: 137).[9] It appears that there was some kind of factional bias present in the letter, a bias that is reflected in the "slogans" that Paul quotes: other opinions on such things as *eidolothyton* "are not reflected, [since] the catch phrase 'all of us possess knowledge' (8:1) leave[s] little room for that" (1982: 137). The authors of this letter wrote as though they could represent the Corinthian formation as a whole, despite the obvious divisions among the group—the same divisions, in fact, that provided the occasion for the writing of the letter in the first place! Theissen proposes that the authors "comprise the leading circles" (1982: 137). This is possible. It is also possible that their act of textually representing the Corinthian group is a grab for power: by speaking out in the name of all the Corinthian Christ people, one can thereby silence any dissenting voices. In any case, the social fact of the Corinthians' letter is indicative of high status: the textual mode of representation would not have been available to all inhabitants of Roman Corinth. "Paul is thus informed on the basis of a perspective 'from above'" (1982: 137). It is telling, in light of this, that when Paul does receive conflicting information about the Corinthian group, it is in the form of face-to-face, oral communication (1 Cor 1:11; 11:18), and not from another letter. This oral report, as Theissen puts it, "sees things from below (1:26ff.; 11:20ff.)" (Theissen 1982: 137).

Yet, as in the Winnebago example, the divide between "those above" and "those below" is not healed by Paul's proposed solution. It is allowed to

---

8.   This is an important point. It is easy for those of us in the field of Christian origins, who are largely trained as textual exegetes, to take for granted the "transparency" of the early Christian writings, seeing them merely as "windows" to the "communities" behind them. The fact of the texts themselves is rarely noticed or questioned.

9.   *Pace* Theissen, I hesitate to impose "strong" and "weak" as substantive categories that are "native" to the Corinthian formation. Given the fact that the terminology of "strong" and "weak" also appears in the letter to the Romans—a group that Paul had not even met—this distinction may well be Paul's, and I see nothing in the various mentions of the "weak" that would require it to be a "native" term of Corinthian discourse. Rather, like the category "demonic," I hold that "strong and weak" are "situational or relational categories, mobile boundaries which shift according to the map being employed. [Categories such as 'demonic'] serve as classificatory markers which signal what is *strong and weak*, controlled and exaggerated in a given society in a given moment" (Smith 1978b: 340 emphasis added).

continue, with an ideological veneer that appears to suture the rift. When Paul writes his letter to the Corinthians, he is—almost by definition—addressing his reply to the "strong" who first represented themselves textually to him. By addressing the "strong" on their own terms, he reinforces their superordinate position. Note, for instance, that in almost every passage where he directly addresses the Corinthians using the second-person plural pronoun, he is discussing the concerns reported in the Corinthians' letter, sometimes going so far as to quote from their letter (1 Cor 7:1, 25; 8:1, 9–10, 11; 10:15, 31)—e.g., when he uses the well-known *peri de* formula (see similarly Theissen 1982: 137). Paul therefore reproduces the privilege of the "strong" party at Corinth.

Theissen in fact says as much when he discusses Paul's strategy of "love-patriarchalism," a strange term that he uses to describe the techniques by which Paul "allows social inequities to continue but transfuses them with a spirit of concern, of respect, and of personal solicitude" (Theissen 1982: 139). To put it another way,

> Paul's recommendation, based on love, that the higher classes accommodate their behavior to the lower classes, only mitigates the tension between the two but allows the differing customs to exist. The factual privileges of status enjoyed by the higher strata are preserved... Nor is participation in cultic meals [e.g., *eidolothyta*] excluded in principle. All that is prohibited [by Paul] is disturbing a weak person by doing so. In other words, everything must take place in a very "exclusive" circle. (Theissen 1982: 139)

This "exclusive circle" is the same circle that held more privileges than the other members of the group in the first place. Paul's solution is a "compromise" that in reality maintains the status quo, where "[t]he wishes (or prejudices) of the weak are upheld just as is the knowledge (and social privilege) of the strong. For that very reason," Theissen concludes, "it is realistic and practicable" (1982: 139), though he admits that this love-patriarchalism "cannot be considered the solution to contemporary social problems" (1982: 140).

Theissen's acknowledgment of the inadequacy of Paul's rhetorical strategy for solving contemporary problems is also a tacit acknowledgment of the profound asymmetry that it both sustained and made possible. In light of the Winnebago example, we can now use the asymmetrical positioning of these Corinthian parties as a useful ethnographic marker for the group. As with the conflicting "maps" of Moiety *A* and Moiety *B* among the Winnibago, it is from a position of power that Paul and the implied "strong" are able to view the solution provided in 1 Corinthians as symmetrical. I doubt that the implied "weak" would have viewed it in quite this way, although their position has been lost, partly due to the oral nature of their self-representations.

This excursus has gained for us a greater appreciation of the ideological concealment of asymmetry that can occur in small-scale social formations—even urban formations such as the Corinthian Christ association. The recognition of alternative maps of the Corinthian assembly, silenced by the nature of the historical record, allows us to rethink Paul. No longer does he need to be seen as the *sine qua non* of the Corinthian group. Rather, in a divided formation, Paul's voice appears as one among many, no matter what rhetorical spin he puts on his position when writing 1 Corinthians.

Thus, we can now appreciate the highly rhetorical nature of Paul's discussion of the Lord's Dinner in 1 Cor 11. Though the meal is called the "Lord's" Dinner, and is painted as a traditional meal, Mack has persuasively shown that the picture Paul presents, as well as the instructions he provides, are in fact his own sketches. The Lord's Dinner—a "tradition" Paul "received"—is, in its present form, a Pauline creation that has been subjected to instant-aging techniques in an effort to bolster his own authority.[10] Thus, Paul is able to present his version of the Lord's Dinner "as a contrast and correction to [the Corinthians] own meal and meeting practices" (Mack 2011: 52).[11]

10. This effort to bolster his authority is, in fact, the unifying theme of the four or five chapters surrounding the dinner text. In these chapters, Paul engages in a long series of arguments intended to make the Corinthians aware of their faults, while reminding them of his authority to point those faults out.

11. It is important, also, to note that the text does not present itself as a script for re-enactment. Nor is there any "sacramental" significance attached to the ritual; by contrast, it appears quite explicitly as a memorial meal in honor of the martyr—as in 1 Corinthians 11:24, where Jesus breaks the bread and says "Do this as my memorial" (Mack 2011: 53–54); cf. Stowers (1996: 69–70): "Against the instincts of Christian piety, Paul's story of the institution betrays the idea that these were sacred words repeated as part of the Lord's dinner celebration. If later Christianity had not appropriated this text into its liturgy, we would not suspect that it was part of the Lord's dinner celebration. The words of 11:23–26 remind the audience of a story that they should know, but there is no reason to think that Paul ever would have told the story in exactly the same words twice."

In addition to the non-sacramental nature of the meal, it is important to see Paul's use of the dinner tradition alongside the other tradition he claims to have received: the Christ myth of 1 Cor 15:3–5. The point of Paul's reference to the "dinner tradition" is not to remind the Corinthians that they have strayed from the proper liturgical script, but rather "to authorize his instructions to [them] about their own common meals in accordance with his notions of how an association should behave and think about itself if focused on the Christ myth" (Mack 2011: 53). This is "directly related to his own…gospel of the death and resurrection of Jesus Christ" in 1 Cor 15:3–5 (Mack 2011: 53). Note also that in Paul's rehearsal of the Christ myth at the end of the letter he adds himself to the end of the list of "appearances" Jesus had made, comparing himself to "one untimely born." Obviously, Paul did not "receive" a tradition that had his name on it; rather, he added himself to that tradition to underscore his own authority. It seems Paul has done the same thing with the dinner text. In both cases, the "received traditions" are rhetorical devices deployed according to Paul's own interests—mythmaking as social argumentation.

If, as many scholars have recently argued,[12] this Corinthian association pre-existed Paul's importation of Christ into Corinth, then, logically, this means it was a Corinthian association before it was a Corinthian *Christ* association. Paul "grafted" his *ekklēsia* form onto this association and tried to bring its pre-existing meal practices into conformity with his conception of a Lord's Dinner. This means that the text describing the Lord's Dinner is "a myth of origins that *grounds an association practice already in place*," and suggests that Paul "confiscated" the major markers of the Corinthians meal (breaking bread and drinking wine) and used them as "'reminders' for the martyr's death of Jesus" (Mack 2011: 5, emphasis added). The tensions and contradictions brought about by this confiscation of one socio-mythic structure by another, together with the ideological "smoothing over" that occurred to hide the seams, are, I think, what defines the Corinthian situation. The negotiation between these tensions and contradictions constitutes a clear instance of what Marshall Sahlins (1976) has termed a "structure of the conjuncture."[13]

3. Re-Placing Structure, Overcoming Event

Another excursion into a different distant ethnographic land will help us to understand the tensions inherent in the Corinthian conjuncture, and how these became mystified, mythologized, and symbolized by the ritual meal. This time, the distant land we will explore is Fiji, and since we are already using Marshall Sahlins's concept of the structure of the conjuncture to understand the Corinthian situation, he will be our guide.

In a long discussion of the complexities of Fijian kinship systems (Sahlins 1976: 19–54), Sahlins includes a brief reference to Lévi-Strauss's essay on dual organizations, applying it to a Moalan group that bears some situational analogy to the Corinthians, as we will see below. But first, a few words about Moalan social structure.

Most Moalan villages are divided into two groups: Land People and Sea People. The Sea People tend to be the Chiefs of these societies, as well as master-fishers who provide seafood to the Land People, who in turn serve as Warriors and provide pigs to the Sea People. In these small-scale social formations, "relations of production on sea and land are constituted in agreement with the structures of reciprocity among the categories so designated, and through this sea and land as natural elements are given cultural order" (Sahlins 1976: 37). The divisions of labor follow strictly along the lines of these cultural categories: "villages dominated by Land [People] do very little deep-sea fishing to this day, whatever the feasibility of access to fishing grounds." Nor will the Land people eat "pig in the presence of the

---

12. See n. 4 above.
13. See similarly Smith 2004c, who comes to similar, if less developed, conclusions.

Sea, [just] as the latter must not eat fish before Land—for fish and turtle are what the Sea People provide the Land," just as pig and taro are provided to the Sea (1976: 38). These reciprocal relations provide "the substance or nourishment which constitutes the other, and so must produce in the element of the other," as well as provide the models for "the domestic division of labor," which in turn constitutes the template for gender relations and patterns of marital exchange (1976: 38–39). But this dual relation of reciprocity is, in practice, permuted into "a typical [by Fijian standards] structure of four" (1976: 38). This structure is a social geography:

> [F]or ordinary labor, if (some) Moalan men do deep-sea fishing on occasion, it is the women's daily netting and collecting in the lagoon areas that yield the main supply of seafood...[W]omen weave mats and make bark cloth in the village, whereas all cultivation of crops in the interior "bush" is mans' work...women's activities are "inside," in the village and adjoining sea, flanked on either geographical extreme by the men's domains of deep sea and high forest... [In this way,] the land is socially bisected into village (*koro*) and bush (*veikau*), while the sea is likewise differentiated into the *wai tui* or "chiefly sea" of the men, beyond the reef, in contrast to the lagoon or inland side of the sea, place of women's activities, called by the same term (*dranu*) as inland fresh waters. In Marx's phrase, the nature known to man is a "humanized nature." (Sahlins 1976: 38–39)

After this general review of Moalan social structure, Sahlins brings out a very interesting "ethnographic example" (1976: 41) of how one Moalan village responded to the rupture of that social structure.

Noting first of all that the "symbolic coordinates of Moalan culture" are so resilient that they seem "to develop an immunity to changing circumstance" (Sahlins 1976: 41), Sahlins points to the village of Nuku, which he visited during his fieldwork, and which "has the usual dual organization of land and sea sections, although strictly speaking there has never been a single Land group in the community" (1976: 41). The village was founded in the latter half of the nineteenth century and populated entirely by master-fishers in the service of the Chiefs, "who had migrated from the capital village of Navucinimasi and ulteriorly from the islands of Gau and Bau. Yet by the local conception, certain Nuku groups were Land People" (1976: 41). Sahlins reports that he often suggested to the villagers that they were all Sea People, and that this fact was "readily admitted" (1976: 41). But, he writes, the Nuku villagers had created a sort of legal fiction, which prioritized the earliest immigrants to Nuku, who "*receive[d]* the fish from the sea and [were] warriors (*bati*) for the later groups; that is, they are 'Land' in relation to the true Sea People who arrived afterward" (1976: 41). In my language, I would call this a culturally patterned "re-emplacement strategy," which provides a solution to the historical experience of social displacement that was caused by the migration to Nuku.

Sahlins calls the Nuku example a "disclosure of the mechanism of cultural reproduction in the face of a historical disconformity" (1976: 41). His elaboration of this cultural reproduction is worth quoting at length:

> Mutilated by history, the moiety system is recreated by the transposition of symbolic correspondences from related domains to the population remaining. A dual division of groups into "Land" and "Sea" is restored by a congruent contrast between original and immigrant peoples. On the conceptual level, this particular procedure is especially facile, insofar as the temporal displacement remains unaffected—if needs be, the myth of settlement can be revised to conform to it—while the social distinction can always be thought one way or another. Yet such is merely the mechanics of the process. More fundamental is the fact that the moiety opposition is always present in village life, even in the absence of its historical existence, because the distinction between Land People and Sea People is continually *practiced* in a thousand details of rite and myth... The social duality is not only conceived; it is lived. (1976: 41–42)

Yet, as the saying goes, all is not well in Mudville—mighty Casey may strike out. As Sahlins puts it,

> the reconstruction of structure at the expense of event is not achieved without residue. If the symbolic scheme seems manipulable without error or failure, history subsists in a certain opacity of the real: there is no escaping the contradiction of a village at once composed of Land People and Sea People, and yet of Sea People alone... So in the Nuku case, the opposition of structure and event is overcome, but at the cost of a social complication which denies the structure even as it is confirmed. One dualism negates the other. (1976: 42)

In hectic social situations, cultural schemes may be re-emplaced, but without the social structures that made them possible and sustained them, they will not subsist without contradictions. Should the social economy remain tense or hectic, those contradictions may eventually be over-determined and bring about a reconfiguration of the structure. This is especially true when the structure contained contradictions even in most stable times, as is clearly the case with Moala: "Complementary yet unequal, symmetrical but asymmetrical, Fijian dualism contains an endemic contradiction: a conflict, as we have seen, of reciprocity and hierarchy" (Sahlins 1976: 43). For, as we have already learned from Lévi-Strauss, "even in such an apparently symmetrical type of social structure as dual organization, the relationship between moieties is never as static, or as fully reciprocal, as one might tend to imagine" (1963: 135; quoted in Sahlins 1976: 43).

Though I claim no simple parallels or isomorphism, there are analogies between the Nuku villagers and the Corinthian settlers. There is a situational analogy between the two groups in that both have experienced a relatively recent resettlement and/or displacement.[14] There is also an analogy in the

---

14. After being destroyed by Rome in 143 B.C.E., Corinth was refounded as a Roman colony in 44 B.C.E. and repopulated by military veterans and freed slaves. By Paul's time,

ideological schemes that structure the group. In the case of Nuku, it is the fictive perpetuation of a division (Sea People and Land People) that no longer exists in reality, and which eventually over-determines and reconstitutes the structure. In the case of the Corinthians, an analogous process is revealed to us in the historical record: the disconformity of the Corinthian association with the *ekklēsia* format which Paul brought to it, and his confiscation and redeployment of the Corinthians' own meal practices in service of his own already-formed notion of what a Christ association should be, led to contradictory notions of group identity and antagonistic relations between those invested in the "before" and the "after" of the Corinthian group. In the final pages of this essay I will elaborate on how the ritual meal became a semiotic "battleground" for this conjuncture.

4. Mapping the Corinthian Meal

In two separate papers,[15] Stanley K. Stowers (1996, 2001) has examined Paul's complicated and often contradictory statements in 1 Cor 8–11 and argued that the contradictions found in these chapters are not the result of Paul's lackluster mind or unawareness of the Corinthian situation, but are rather echoes of tensions and contradictions already found within the eating practices of the Corinthians themselves (1996: 78). Stowers contextualizes the Lord's Dinner within the larger arena of Hellenistic dining practices and shows how this ritual meal functioned both within and in opposition to this wider arena. When one considers the various meanings that the dinner ritual could have taken on—that is, what significance(s) the practices might have generated according to first-century Hellenistic codes of eating—it is not at all surprising that the Corinthians could have had a *very* different understanding of the ritual meal than Paul intended.

Stowers argues that the problems surrounding the Corinthian dinner could be explained, at least in part, by the tension between the meal's *form* and its *content*. The *form* of the meal is simple enough: it begins with broken bread and ends with the drinking of wine. Nor is the meal's *genre* especially mysterious: the etiological myth of the dinner's origins in 11:23–26 clearly

---

it had become a bustling seaport and center of commerce, with people coming from all across the empire to try and make a living there. With Arnal, Mack, Smith, and Stowers, I assume the Corinthians who made up the social formation addressed in 1 Corinthians were part of this "deracinated" class of relatively recent immigrants.

15.   One paper included in the second volume of the proceedings of the Ancient Myths and Modern Theories of Christian Origins seminar of the Society of Biblical Literature, entitled "On Construing Meals, Myths, and Power in the World of Paul" (2011), and another entitled "Elusive Coherence: Ritual and Rhetoric in 1 Corinthians 10–11" (1996).

identifies it as a memorial meal for the dead.[16] Yet by other standards, such as its lack of a ritual sacrifice and consumption of meat, the Lord's Dinner was closer to the everyday meal, which would have consisted primarily of bread and would have been prepared by women. The martyr myth that explains the significance of the bread—depicting it as the martyr's body, and thus potentially linking it to notions of sacrifice: "This is my body, which is broken *for you*"—shows that it holds pride of place in the meal, serving as its focus and centerpiece.[17] This is markedly different from what one would expect in the culture of context. While it is not unusual for the breaking of the bread and the consumption of wine to mark the beginning and end of the meal,[18] the fact that this was a *memorial meal for the dead* would have seemed strange, since such meals always featured sacrificial meat (see Stowers 1996: 76 n. 49). For bread, not meat, to be the focus of the memorial meal—a memorial meal that was self-consciously portrayed as a "sacrifice"—was a contradiction of form and content: "[w]here one expects filet mignon, there is white bread" (Stowers 2011: 136; cf. 1996: 76).

Within Hellenistic culture, the coagulation of such diverse eating codes in the form of the Lord's Dinner predictably, though not *necessarily*, would have led to contradictions that would have been both perceived and experienced or, in a word, lived (1996: 74). But, this seems to be Paul's intention. Everything about his description of the Lord's Dinner suggests that he both understood and developed the ritual in a way that distinguished it from ordinary meals and sacrificial meals (1996: 74). Why would Paul have done this?

Stowers brilliantly suggests that the answer lies in Paul's distinctive understanding of the Christ martyr myth, which "plays on a disjunction between the body and the self" and thus sets the ritual somewhat apart from other meals of the period. As Stowers demonstrates, commensality in the Greco-Roman world was intimately tied to community-formation as well as identity-formation (see also Garnsey 1999: 128–38). The meal codes fit together to provide someone with the truth of his or her identity, and this identity was a matter of flesh and blood. Body and self were *identical*, in

16. Which, interestingly, is a possible translation of the *eidolothyton* of 1 Cor 8–10. See Kennedy 1987, for a tantalizing, if not decisive, argument for this translation.

17. Intimately connected with dining practices was the structuring of gender relations: women cooked bread for the everyday meals, while the men sacrificed the animals and divided the portions for special meals or feasts (Stowers 1996: 74). It is tempting to think, as Stowers does, that perhaps some of the problems Paul was discussing with respect to the unruly women in the Corinthian association were caused, or at least occasioned, by the heightened importance of bread in the Lord's Dinner, which seemed to be taking the place of meat in the memorial meal and might possibly have been perceived as a loosening of the gender distinctions that structured ordinary meal practice.

18. A common feature of Hellenistic meals; see Stowers 1996: 75 n. 43.

both senses of the term (2011: 137). In this world, identity was pre-eminently a matter of belonging, and to eat in a community was to affirm that one belonged to that community. When a group sacrificed to the god, the deity in turn "provided signs about this truth [viz., the truth that one belonged to the group] during the skillful cooking, sharing and eating of meat in honor of the god. The medium for communicating this truth about flesh and blood was the flesh and blood of an animal from the best lineages that Greek animal husbandry could provide" (2011: 137).

Stowers notes that, generally, Greek anthropology made no distinction between the "body" and the "self." In other words, for the Greeks, one did not *have* a body so much as one *was* a body. In fact, the thing that distinguished a free male citizen from a woman, a child, or a slave was precisely how much control they had over their bodies/themselves. By contrast, Paul's exposition of the Lord's Dinner shows that he is operating with a different anthropology—a tripartite anthropology already present in his thought as early as 1 Thess 5:23—that relies upon the distinction between one's body and one's *self* or true identity. Though commensality is still constitutive of community identity and essential to group belonging,[19] the community is no longer tested, formed, or confirmed by the eating of meat. This is the dinner's most distinctive feature, and shows that the ritual is articulated both within and in opposition to the *doxa* of Hellenistic culture. Whereas, in the ordinary sacrificial meal, meat symbolizes the body and is the centerpiece of the meal, in the Lord's Dinner, the focus is on the bread, which is the symbol of an absent body, an absence that is structurally homologous to Paul's "utopian" understanding of the true self that may "inherit the kingdom of God" while "flesh and blood" cannot (1 Cor 15:50; cf. Stowers 2011: 137). This is why Paul holds that the members of the Corinthian association must not eat the bread or drink the cup without first "discerning the body" (11:29), since this discernment reveals the truth of the Lord's eating practice: "the true self consists in being beyond oneself just as the martyr [Christ] surpassed himself in giving up his body" (2011: 137).

This leads Stowers to note "a deep ambiguity" that is possible in the way this ritual meal was carried out. Though bread and wine are explicitly mentioned, "Paul…left the cuisine in the rest of the meal unspecified. What if someone brought meat or slaughtered a goat, piglet, or sheep?" (1996: 75). Stowers points to a number of mixed signals that could have arisen from such an eventuality. Since "Greeks traditionally did not distinguish between sacrificing an animal and butchering,"[20] this would have added "possible

19. Cf. 1 Cor 5:11, where Paul warns the Corinthians not to eat with those who call themselves "brothers" but live immoral, greedy, or idolatrous lives.

20. "To eat unsacrificed meat was an abomination that would surely be punished by the gods" (Stowers 1996: 75–76 and 82 n. 47).

'pagan' connotations to the feast" as well as introduced "an element, meat, that would normally be set above and in contrast to bread" (1996: 75–76). It is even possible that the *eidolothyta* that Paul is concerned about in chs. 8–10 were actually happening at the Lord's Dinner he discusses in ch. 11. If so, then we can understand the perplexity with which Paul tries to deal with these problems. Paul (and likely the Corinthians themselves) are so vexed because, from both an emic and an etic perspective, it would seem that the Lord's Dinner, perhaps more than any other practice of the Corinthian Christ people, was the ritual by which the Corinthian formation defined itself. The Lord's Dinner was so problematic because it was symbolically over-determined: it "was negotiating a new place in the larger code of eating" and not simply reproducing the old order of "gender and social relations" which had been naturalized in Greco-Roman ideology. Tensions also arose because the "new order of ritualized bread and wine, rather than meat, fit a new order of power in the city detached from the land" (1996: 78–79).

The cultural logic of the Lord's Dinner, at least as Paul conceives it, now seems obvious:

> If…meat is the natural product of men according to the patrilineal principle of the seed of the founding ancestor passed on as flesh, then bread is the fabrication of food by art, like spinning wool, the artifice of women and slaves. In Greek sacrifice, the body is present to be touched and eaten. But where is the body in the Lord's supper? It is present in its absence. The bread of human art is the reminder of a body that occupies no place. Christ who, by the art of his obedience and will triumphed through God's power, lives in a new plane of pneumatic existence where a body that one can touch seems superfluous. (2011: 138; cf. 1996: 78–79)

The ritual meal Paul describes in 1 Cor 11 thus perfectly exemplifies what Jonathan Z. Smith has termed a "utopian" religious practice. The problem is—as we saw at the beginning of this essay, and as I have argued extensively elsewhere (Parrish 2010)—that many of the members of the Corinthian Christ association were "locative" in their religious orientation. These were the Corinthian "spiritists" who were attempting to re-establish ties to their ancestors in the homeland, and who were engaging in oracular modes of contact with their recently dead, now buried in Corinth. These were the Corinthians who, by reason of those ancestral concerns, denied the resurrection—a notion that would appear both as a pollution and an abomination in a locative tradition.

In such a locative religious world, Paul, too, could appear as intrusive. His provision of *Christos* as a collective ancestor, analogous to Abraham, who could provide his devotees with an ethnic identity not based upon locale (so Arnal 2008), might have been very attractive to deracinated settlers interested in re-establishing their patterns of domestic religion in a diaspora setting. But the notion of resurrection likely would not have been attractive to them at all, especially in its vulgar (to locative sensibilities) formulation of 1 Cor 15:3–5, that "Christ was buried…and raised." Paul's "gospel" of the dead emerging from their tombs would not be "good news" to locative religionists.

Nor would the "spiritual" resurrection that Paul discusses in the later parts of 1 Cor 15 have been attractive to those with locative sensibilities. Though there is nothing inherently offensive in the notion of a spiritual resurrection, when it is wedded to the ritual meal, it becomes immediately problematic. As with the Moalan disconformity between a village comprised of Land and Sea People, yet really only of Land people, there is no escaping the contradiction between a memorial meal that is held in honor of a collective ancestor, but which does not feature the sacrificial meat of an animal raised and fed on the land where the meal takes place. The sacrificial meat, which secures the bond between the memorial meal and the structure of kinship, would be essential to those Corinthians who wanted to establish and maintain ties to their ancestral dead. The utopian logic of the bread of human artifice, which is featured as a sacrifice that denies the diners' citizenship in this world, is ultimately incompatible with the locative impulse to establish ties to the land and the ancestors via the eating of domestic meat. The Corinthians' ritual meal, which Paul co-opted in his effort to make the Corinthians into "Christ people," was based upon this locative ideology. Those who continued to feast upon the meat at the ritual meal, and those who followed Paul in focusing upon the bread, occupied different "maps," identified with different ideologies, performed a different ritual and, in the final analysis, were members of different social formations. The Corinthian conjuncture, which for a moment allowed two different social formations to appear as one, eventually over-determined its own contradictions through the ritual performance of the common meal, the Lord's Dinner. As in the Nuku case, the social actors invested in this formation overcame their historical dissolution for a time, but could not escape the complications generated by the structural denial of the event.

However, there is one important difference: in Nuku, *one* social formation was presented, ideologically, as *two*—a village of Land People lived as though they were both Land and Sea. At Corinth, the reverse was true: *two* social formations were made to appear, ideologically, as *one*. In 1 Corinthians, we see a dual social formation denying its structure even as it is affirmed—and, in the event, beginning to negate itself. So, while it is possible to say that 1 Corinthians outlines a "structure of the conjuncture," perhaps—with apologies to Sahlins—it is *also* possible to say that it shows us a conjuncture of structures, with an eventful history.

References

Adams, Edward and David G. Horrell. 2004. "The Scholarly Quest for Paul's Church at Corinth: A Critical Survey." In Edward Adams and David G. Horrell, eds, *Christianity at Corinth: The Quest for the Pauline Church*, 1–43. Louisville: Westminster John Knox.

Arnal, William E. 2008. "*Doxa*, Heresy, and Self-Construction: The Pauline *Ekklēsiai* and the Boundaries of Urban Identities." In Eduard Iricinschi and Holger M. Zellentin, eds., *Heresy and Identity in Late Antiquity*, 50–101. Tübingen: Mohr Siebeck.

———. 2011. "Bringing Paul and the Corinthians Together? A Rejoinder and Some Proposals on Redescription and Theory." In Ron Cameron and Merrill Miller, eds, *Redescribing Paul and the Corinthians*, 75–104. Atlanta, GA: Scholars Press.

Engels, Donald. 1990. *Roman Corinth: An Alternative Model for the Classical City*. Chicago: University of Chicago Press.

Farb, Peter and George Armelagos. 1980. *Consuming Passions: The Anthropology of Eating*. Boston: Houghton Mifflin.

Faulkner, John A. 1924. "Did Mystery Religions Influence Apostolic Christianity?" *The Methodist Quarterly Review* 73: 387–403.

Garnsey, Peter. 1999. *Food and Society in Classical Antiquity*. Cambridge: Cambridge University Press, 1999.

Kennedy, Charles A. 1987. "The Cult of the Dead in Corinth." In J. Marks and R. Good, eds, *Love and Death in the Ancient Near East: Essays in Honor of Marvin H. Pope*, 227–36 Guilford, CT: Four Quarters.

Lévi-Strauss, Claude. 1963. "Do Dual Organizations Exist?" *Structural Anthropology*, 132–63. New York: Basic Books.

Mack, Burton L. 2011. "Rereading the Christ Myth: Paul's Gospel and the Christ Cult Question." In Ron Cameron and Merrill Miller, eds, *Redescribing Paul and the Corinthians*, 35–74. Atlanta, GA: Scholars Press.

Parrish, John W. 2010. "Speaking in Tongues, Dancing with Ghosts: Redescription, Translation, and the Language of Resurrection." *Studies in Religion / Sciences religieuses* 39: 24–45.

Radin, Paul. 1970. *The Winnebago Tribe*. Lincoln: University of Nebraska Press.

Sahlins, Marshall. 1976. *Culture and Practical Reason*. Chicago: University of Chicago Press.

Shklovksy, Victor. 1965. "Art as Technique." In Lee T. Lemon and Marion J. Reis, eds and trans, *Russian Formalist Criticism: Four Essays*, 3–24. Lincoln: University of Nebraska Press.

Smith, Jonathan Z. 1971. "Native Cults in the Hellenistic Period." *History of Religions* 11: 236–49.

———. 1974. "Hellenistic Religions." *Encyclopedia Britannica*, 8:749–51. 15th ed. Chicago: Encyclopaedia Britannica Inc.

———. 1978a. *Map Is Not Territory: Studies in the History of Religions*. Studies in Judaism in Late Antiquity, 23. Leiden: Brill.

———. 1978b. "Towards Interpreting Demonic Powers in Hellenistic and Roman Antiquity." In *Aufstieg und Niedergang der römischen Welt*, II.16.1, 425–39. Berlin: W. de Gruyter.

———. 1987. *To Take Place: Toward Theory in Ritual*. Chicago: University of Chicago Press.

————. 1990. *Drudgery Divine: On the Comparison of Early Christianities and the Religions of Late Antiquity*. Chicago: University of Chicago Press.

————. 2004a. "*Dayyeinu*." In Ron Cameron and Merrill P. Miller, eds, *Redescribing Christian Origins*, 483–87. SBL Symposium Series 28. Atlanta: Scholars.

————. 2004b. "Here, There, and Anywhere." In *Relating Religion: Essays in the Study of Religion*, 322–39. Chicago: University of Chicago Press.

————. 2004c. "Re: Corinthians." In *Relating Religion: Essays in the Study of Religion*, 340–61. Chicago: University of Chicago Press.

Stowers, Stanley K. 1996. "Elusive Coherence: Ritual and Rhetoric in 1 Corinthians 10–11." In Elizabeth Castelli and Hal Taussig, eds, *Reimagining Christian Origins: A Colloquium Honoring Burton L. Mack*, 68–83. Valley Forge, PA: Trinity.

————. 2011. "Kinds of Myth, Meals, and Power: Paul and the Corinthians." In Ron Cameron and Merrill Miller, eds, *Redescribing Paul and the Corinthians*, 105–50. Atlanta, GA: Scholars Press.

Theissen, Gerd. 1982. "The Strong and the Weak in Corinth: A Sociological Analysis of a Theological Problem." In Gerd Theissen, *The Social Setting of Pauline Christianity: Essays on Corinth*, 121-43. Ed. and trans. John Schuetz. Edinburgh: T. & T. Clark.

Wiseman, J. 1979. "Corinth and Rome I: 228 B.C.-A.D. 267." In *Aufstieg und Niedergang der römischen Welt*, II.7.1, 438–548. Berlin: W. de Gruyter.

THE IDENTITY OF Q IN THE FIRST CENTURY: REPRODUCING A THEOLOGICAL NARRATIVE*

Sarah E. Rollens

Donald Wiebe's persistent demand for the academic study of religion to distinguish itself from the enterprise of theology has left an undeniable mark on religious studies. Because the study of religion emerged in a mostly Christian milieu, the study of Christianity (especially Christian origins) was particularly susceptible to the influence of theology. Even though scholars have reinvented the study of early Christianity in a number of important ways, many theological convictions and assumptions still implicitly inform biblical scholarship and its institutional activities; these persist often in the face of contradictory evidence which should prompt a reevaluation of the enterprise. Scholarly research on the Q document, which is a witness to a first-century Galilean movement, suffers from these implicit theological influences, because the identity that Q is seen to represent—an exclusively proto-Christian movement as opposed to a Second Temple Jewish movement—is often made to mirror the traditional, theological narrative of nascent Christianity.

The Q document's role in the study of early Christianity is subject to some debate. Its infancy in the field was tied to issues of the Synoptic Problem, and indeed its very existence depends on arguments about textual relationships among the Synoptic gospels. Although many of those issues are still contested today, the Two-Document Hypothesis, positing the Gospel of Matthew's and the Gospel of Luke's independent use of the Gospel of Mark and Q, has emerged as the most compelling Synoptic solution.[1] Recent decades have seen several scholars comment on Q's distinctive composition (Kloppenborg 1987; Jacobson 1992), its organizational motifs (Lührmann 1969), and its social-ethical critique (Arnal 2001; Horsley 1999; Vaage

*   I would like to thank Herb Berg for the many thought-provoking conversations that we shared which helped me clarify my ideas for this essay

1.   The Two-Document Hypothesis is not without noteworthy dissenters (e.g., Farrer 1957; Goulder 1989; Goodacre 2002; Powell 2006).

1994). Despite these significant developments in Q scholarship and *repeated* arguments for the close connection between early Christianity and Judaism,[2] the identity that Q represents in the first century has had little effect on the scholarly conception of nascent Christianity's relation to Second Temple Judaism, manifesting primarily in Q's repeated characterization as a proto-Christian text and contributing to an unsubstantiated and inaccurate portrayal of the relationship between Christianity and Judaism in the first century.[3] My argument here is that Q should have a place in scholarship on Second Temple Judaism in addition to its place in the study of early Christianity; indeed, it is indispensable to studying the relationship between Judaism and Christianity in the first century. Yet, the hitherto resistance to the conse-quences of the Q document and the lack of serious consideration given to its implications for the study of Judaism are directly related to implicit theo-logical positions and interests, which, as Wiebe pointed out throughout his scholarly career, hold great sway over the academic study of religion. And ultimately, the neglect of Q has contributed to a situation in which the study of Q is made to accomplish the same task as and reinforce the same narrative as theology (in this case, both Jewish and Christian theology), a situation that is argued by many to be a mutually beneficial relationship between the two, but deemed by Wiebe an unhappy failure.

1. Q and Identity

Almost all Q scholars identify themselves as New Testament scholars, scholars of Christian origins, scholars of early Christianity, or some variation thereof. At the very least, they are identified as such by the wider academic community. At the same time, the work that they produce about Q is unquestionably relevant to Second Temple Judaism. In other words, it seems that what the study of religion wants Q to be (i.e., a representative of nascent Christianity) sometimes overrides what it appears to represent (i.e., a variety of Second Temple Judaism). My argument begins by examining recent presentations of Q in modern scholarship and then speculates on theological and political factors that might determine this counter-intuitive characteriza-tion.

2.   For instance, William Arnal notes the "shrill reiteration of Jesus' having been Jewish" (2001: 9) in modern scholarship, even though, oddly, few scholars deny it.

3.   The terminology for these traditions in the first-century is admittedly problematic. "Judaism" and "Christianity" should both be understood to consist of a variety of forms, never distinct from social, political, and economic aspects of their environments. Here I use "late Judaism" interchangeably with "Second Temple Judaism." And although I use "early Christianity" and "Christian origins" throughout the essay, the identities of many of the earliest Christian communities were not as distinct from Judaism as the categories would suggest. Indeed, this latter point informs the argument of this essay.

The standard depiction of Q is as a proto-Christian document. Its Jewish elements are only secondarily discussed. Thus, Q is described as a "gospel" (e.g., Crum 1927; Funk et al. 1993; Kloppenborg 1994, 2009; Mack 1993; Piper 1994; Reed 1999; Robinson 1997) or as a "sayings source" (e.g., Kirk 1998; Lindemann 2001). For many, some of these sayings are wished, even willed, to stem from the historical Jesus. According to Leif Vaage, Q is "the earliest form of Christianity known to us" (1994: xi), and similarly for Christopher Tuckett, it represents a "Christian group" (1989: 356). Most often, Q is described simply as the literary source that complemented Mark in Matthew's and Luke's respective compositions. These labels seem harmless, if somewhat inconsistent. John S. Kloppenborg (Kloppenborg Verbin 2000: 398–408), at least, has questioned the nomenclature of "gospel" for Q, finding that the term is a useful designation to counter those who would not consider Q as theologically important as the "official" gospels. He argues that using the term "gospel" invites scholars to find the meaningful differences between Q and other texts that have traditionally been considered gospels. This is certainly a productive qualification, yet it reinforces Q's literary form as a uniquely Christian genre. In this way, the identity of Q— whether a gospel, a source of the gospels, a cache of Jesus' words, or the central text of a nascent Christian group—is reified as overtly "Christian." The description of its identity is dependent on a thoroughly Christian, if not canonical, framework.

Elements of Q's Jewishness have not gone unnoticed. Most scholars have approached the question of Q and Judaism relatively subtly. For instance, Adolf von Harnack (1908: 229–30) observed a century ago that Q was overtly Jewish, yet this identification did not stop him from importing Christian theological concepts into his interpretation. More recently, James Robinson (1971) and John Kloppenborg (1987) have demonstrated convincingly that Q has strong affinities with Jewish wisdom traditions. Furthermore, Richard Horsley (1999) views Q as derived from, and continuous with, Northern Israelite prophetic traditions. Likewise, although Migaku Sato's (1988) redactional analysis of Q has not been the most persuasive compositional theory of Q, Sato thinks that Q is best described as a prophetic text. And some scholars (e.g., Meyer 1970) have even found in Q evidence of a mission to the Gentiles, though this idea has been subsequently dismissed for lack of evidence (Arnal 2005: 140–43; Horsley 1999: 94–95). Thus, even though few studies have been concerned *systematically* to outline Q's Jewishness, a Jewish milieu is presupposed behind many of the most comprehensive studies on the document.

However, because of the noted tendency to describe Q's identity as overtly Christian (a category which itself reflects later social formation), studies that involve Q's Judaism tend to revolve around the *extent* to which Q was

Jewish or the *kind* of Judaism that it represents, the latter related to the recent emphasis on the diversity of Judaisms in the Second Temple period. The logic seems to be that although the Jesus movement retained many things that would rightly be called Jewish, it had evolved into something observably distinct, and so vestiges of Judaism that remain must be identified and explained. This has manifested itself in, among other things, studies constructing (and contesting) how Jewish was the provenance (first-century Galilee) from which Q was derived (Chancey 2002; Horsley 1996: 88–175; see also the excellent comments in Moxnes 2001a and 2001b). Horsley (1989, 1996, 1999) is perhaps the most vocal in his claims that the popular Israelite tradition preserved in Galilee would have been antithetical to the priestly elite form of Judaism in Judea. Many of these disagreements no doubt are also related to the quest for the historical Jesus, whose traditions are often thought to be preserved in Q (e.g., Lindemann 2001). Arnal (2001) has shown persuasively that depictions of the historical Jesus have been preoccupied with questions of Jewishness for a variety of reasons, and Q, as a potential representative of the historical Jesus, is therefore closely caught up in this debate of Jewish identity. So, while Q is still regarded as a significant Christian text, the degree of its Jewishness has become important to its profile.

Aside from these subtle affirmations of Q's relationship to or identification with Judaism, *explicit* efforts to outline Q's Jewishness are not wholly absent. Horsley's description of Q could be construed as an explicit attempt to engage with this issue, for he bases his project on the observation that Q is too often characterized as "in but not of Jewish society" (1999: 28). More overtly, Markus Cromhout (2007) aims to outline thoroughly Q's ethnic identity. He finds, somewhat uncontroversially, that Q's Jewishness is close to other contemporary forms of Judaism, with the exception that it lacks a strong notion of covenantal nomism. In a volume specifically devoted to reconsidering Jewish-Christianity, Arnal (2005) investigates Q's Jewish identity at each level of the text's redactions. Arnal demonstrates that the authors of Q take their Jewish identity for granted in the document's formative literary stratum, but become increasingly preoccupied with it in later redactions, as it becomes useful for their rhetorical goals. This is again uncontroversial, given that previous scholars had identified a Deutero-nomistic motif at the secondary redaction of Q (Lührmann 1969), with which the authors rebuked their real or imagined opposition. Thus, when scholars have explicitly examined Q for its sense of Jewishness, they have come up mostly with predictable results that locate Q soundly in a Jewish milieu, and, although Q contains some criticism of the tradition, it sees itself as continuous with that same tradition (Q 3:8; 7:31–35, esp. 11:39–44, 46–48, 52). It has not been seen as turning its back on it.

It seems, then, that scholars of early Christianity are increasingly comfortable noting Q's Jewishness, either by tacitly affirming it through their scholarship or explicitly seeking it out, though on the whole they still retain the text as representative of the field of Christian origins. This becomes especially clear when the presentation of Q in textbooks is examined. Although textbooks are admittedly aimed at less specialized audiences, they should not, I think, escape analysis. For Norman Perrin (1974), Q is again a "sayings source," representing apocalyptic Christianity (1974: 74–77) or more generally Palestinian Christianity (1974: 45–47). Other New Testament textbooks or introductions to early Christian writings (e.g., Ehrman 2000; Freed 1986; Harris 2002; Koester 2000; Mack 1995) reinforce Q's place alongside the canonical gospels. Most problematically, textbooks and introductions to late antique or Second Temple Judaism are totally silent on Q or simply perpetuate the idea that Christianity developed within Judaism, but quickly broke away from it. For Shaye Cohen (2006: 166–68), the early Jesus movement originated in Judaism but ceased to be such when it ceased Jewish practices. Lawrence Schiffman's *From Text to Tradition: A History of Second Temple and Rabbinic Judaism* (1991: 149) also classifies the Jesus movements among sectarian Judaism against some normative variety of Judaism. Whereas Schiffman at least indicates that early Christian literature—although not Q—might be relevant for studying late Judaism, Philip Alexander's *Textual Sources for the Study of Judaism* (1984), Alan Segal's *The Other Judaisms of Late Antiquity* (1987), and Jacob Neusner's *Judaism in the Beginning of Christianity* (1984) make no mention of Q. What these studies indicate is that, even though scholars of early Christianity repeatedly produce scholarship that demonstrates the centrality of Q's Jewish elements, the text is still not seen to be a legitimate representative of Jewishness in the first century.

Equally troubling is Q's absence in discussions of Jewish and Christian interaction in the first century. Scholarship on this topic abounds, and a number of models of Jewish–Christian interaction have been proposed, from the abrupt fracture or mutual "parting of ways" between the two traditions (Dunn 1991) to the more amorphous and slow development of distinct traditions from a hybrid unity (Boyarin 2004). But Q, despite its simultaneous Jewish and Christian characteristics, is mostly absent from these discussions. For instance, Daniel Boyarin (2004) focuses on Justin's writings, the Gospel of John, and rabbinic writings to illustrate his hybridity model.[4] Stephen Wilson (1995) uses some of the same texts as Boyarin, but focuses on the canonical texts as representative of nascent Christianity. Wilson's analysis finds a great variety among relations between Jews and Christians, but

---

4. I would like to thank T. Nicholas Schonhoffer for his suggestions about how Daniel Boyarin's work could contribute to my argument.

interestingly, despite his inclusion of Matthew's and Luke's views on Jews and things Jewish, Q is nowhere mentioned in his study.[5] For describing Jewish/Christian relations in the "early years," other texts such as the *Epistle of Barnabas*, Ignatius's letters, and the canonical gospels—the latter are especially important for their frequent stereotyping of Jews—tend to be more important. Most scholars seem to agree that the distinction between the two traditions, especially in the first century, is not always easily discernable. Regardless of how the separation between Judaism and Christianity is conceived, either as an abrupt rupture or a slow congealment of diverging identities, Q has been given no role in the discussion, as if its identity was firmly fixed in the Christian tradition from its inception.

Thus, Q emerges as a text from the first century that can be described as proto-Christian, because it predates and was incorporated into later Christian texts, but it is doubtless Jewish as well. Although scholars of Christian origins seem to struggle with how to characterize the identity of the text, I have shown that they appear to be increasingly comfortable correcting for the past over-emphasis on its Christianness. Yet scholars of Judaism have not found it useful to claim the text in any way, either as part of conceptual frameworks such as Second Temple Judaism or late antique Jewish thought. And Q has had no place in scholarly discussions about the relationship between the Judaism and Christianity in the first century. This counter-intuitive and counter-productive situation, I will show, is a natural outcome of implicit theological convictions in the study of both Christianity and Judaism.

2. Explaining the Characterization of Q

The preceding discussion should elicit one immediate question: in spite of all of the persuasive scholarship proving Q's dependence on and situation in Judaism, why has the characterization of Q as a predominantly Christian document remained so dominant, to the extent that Q cannot be seen as a legitimate representative of Second Temple Judaism? The answer lies in pervasive theological assumptions and convictions in the study of religion to which Wiebe (1984) alerts us. In this case, the characterization of Q is affected by (1) assumptions about the formative stages of Christianity and its relationship to Judaism in antiquity and (2) the desire of the discipline of religious studies to carve itself at the same "natural" joints which religious traditions do to demarcate themselves from each other. In other words, the study of religion (in this case, the study of early Christianity and the study of

---

5.   In part, Q's absence in Wilson's study can be explained by the period he examines: 70 C.E. to 135 C.E. This in itself is problematic because it reifies the year 70 C.E. as the turning point of identity formation for Jews and Christians. Because Q is prior to 70 C.E., it is seen to represent a time when Jewish Christianity was not yet contested.

Judaism) internalizes theological claims of its object of study. As Bruce Lincoln (1999) puts it, the study of these traditions permits those whose traditions are studied to define the terms in which they will be understood.

Initially it is important to note that some scholars have written Q off entirely as "just a hypothesis." It is here that we might find the easiest points of resistance to interrogating the identity that Q represents. If Q is only a hypothesis, it might be argued, then we are not obligated to give its identity (or its composition, redaction, ideological perspective, etc.) serious attention. Bart Ehrman (2000: 81), for instance, discourages definitive claims about Q's content and authors due to its hypothetical nature. However, the accusation that Q is merely hypothetical has been taken seriously and met with compelling arguments (Kloppenborg Verbin 2000: 1–3). Simply put, not only is Q (or something closely resembling it) the simplest solution to the complex literary relationship between Matthew and Luke, but also given the paucity of physical documents from antiquity, research on many other texts must work from the theory that later manuscripts resemble those from earlier periods—i.e., they too rely on educated hypotheses and textual reconstruction. To continue to ignore important questions about Q and its authors because of the text's hypothetical nature is "irresponsible" (Vaage 1994: 8). Therefore the failure of Q to affect our conceptions of Judaism and Christianity in the first century cannot be due to its hypothetical nature alone. At the very least, it only explains why Ehrman and those few scholars who share his view fail to employ Q in this manner.

Rather, the first set of influential factors that can help explain the characterization of Q as outlined above stem more from latent assumptions about the development and relationship of Judaism and Christianity in the first century. First, the fact that Q is often described as a source of Matthew and Luke greatly effects how Q is conceived. From the outset, this description situates Q in scholarly discussions that are almost wholly related to Christianity, because the Synoptic problem is, of course, a problem for Christians. This is unfortunately somewhat of a catch-22. On one hand, as noted at the beginning of this essay, the very existence of Q requires an argument that depends on the literary similarities between the Synoptic gospels. To talk about Q is to presuppose a discussion that involves three of the canonical gospels. However, at the same time, to repeat the relationship of Q to the canonical gospels makes it easier to see it in terms of its canonical ideas and whether it accords or deviates from them. Similarly, it is difficult to escape the idea that Q was on a trajectory of development toward something like the canonical gospels, a position probably fostered unintentionally by James M. Robinson and Helmut Koester (1971).[6] The nomenclature of "gospel"

---

6. Although Robinson and Koester's terminology of "trajectory" corrected previous descriptions of early Christianity that had privileged the tradition's unique elements, the

and "source", which I have shown to predominate in the descriptions of Q, act to reinforce the idea that Q was a formative stage of a more complete, canonical literary form. Thus, it remains difficult to extract Q from its Synoptic, and thus Christian, framework.

In addition to its role in the Synoptic problem, there is a second "marker" for Christianity in Q: the presence of the figure Jesus. If Jesus shows up in a text, then for many scholars, it is Christian by definition. However, it is becoming increasingly clear that arguing for a text's distinction or explaining a text's existence based on the presence of Jesus or his message is as problematic as it is unproductive (e.g., Mack 1988: 1–25). The Jesus in Q does not explain the production of the text or its authors' identities any more than it does in, for example, the Gospel of Luke or, more conspicuously, the Letter of James.[7] Furthermore, if we accept the authors' self-identification—something which must be done with great caution (Lincoln 1999)—then we see that Q does not even articulate a distinct Christian identity (Arnal 2005: 153), although it certainly contains elements that we would classify as belonging to a "Jesus movement" (Arnal 2005: 135–36). Arnal hints at an alternative when he suggests that the Q people attributed the various sayings to Jesus in their text because he was "a current local folk hero" (Arnal 2001: 203). This alternative, that Q is a Jewish document which utilizes Jesus lore, remains all but inconceivable to scholars of Judaism. The assumption that Q is *about* Jesus or that Jesus is the "main character" of Q is not easy to abandon. Moreover, Jonathan Z. Smith (1990) has convincingly argued that the fixation on origins, especially when Jesus is seen to be the ultimate origin of the Christian tradition, is greatly indebted to Protestant theological interests.

The theological interests expressed in the repeated depiction of Q as a canonical source and a gospel, as well as the presence of Jesus in the text— that is, its characterization as a Christian text—also explains Q's absence in Jewish studies. The persistent characterization of Q as an early Christian text would likely make it seem unacceptable to, or at least non-representative of, Second Temple Judaism. As noted, the majority of studies that purport to introduce varieties of Second Temple Judaism are silent on Q; and only a few give cursory attention to other early Christian writings. The repeated characterization of Q as a "gospel" or a "source" by scholars in the field of early Christianity contributes to this. The nomenclature of "sayings collection" would seemingly make Q more attractive to classification as a Jewish tradition, especially when viewed within the persuasive scholarship on

---

usage had the unfortunate consequence of suggesting a model of evolutionary development for Christian texts. See also Sanders 1977: 20–24.

7.   Indeed, several scholars have argued that the references to Jesus in the letter of James are later interpolations (Allison 2001; Kloppenborg 2007; Llewelyn 1997). I thank John S. Kloppenborg for drawing my attention to these studies.

wisdom literature by Robinson and Kloppenborg, among others, but thus far the comparison is only initiated from the study of early Christianity side. In addition, a text like Q would upset some dominant paradigms for thinking about varieties of late Judaism. For instance, the analysis of Q by Cromhout (2007), which found that Q shared much with contemporary Judaism except a strong notion of covenantal nomism, would contradict E. P. Sanders's (1977) conclusion about Palestinian Judaism, that covenantal nomism was the underlying *commonality* of all its diverse forms. And, of course, the presence of Jesus in Q would upset the traditional understanding of Judaism—unless we propose that Q represents the first manifestation of "Jews for Jesus." In short, there is no good reason for the Jewish tradition to claim (in my argument, *reclaim*) something that is repeatedly characterized as an early Christian gospel or source, especially when it disrupts traditional ways of characterizing the Jewish tradition in antiquity.

Here we can note, ironically, how the depiction of Q as a tradition that is continuous with "Northern Israelite" tradition, the argument advanced by Horsley (1999), also works to keep Q from being identified with late or Second Temple Judaism. Horsley claims that the Northern Israelite tradition represented in Q developed independently from the Judean tradition for almost 800 years. A prophetic renewal movement behind Q is perhaps the major counter-reconstruction of the Q people against that of the sage-like village philosophers (Mack 1993; Vaage 1994) or mid-level scribes (Kloppenborg 1994; Arnal 2001). Horsley's description of Q, however, has the odd effect of setting Q in opposition to other forms of Judaism contemporary with it. On one hand, Horsley is relatively successful at wresting Q free from a wholly Christian interpretation, but at the same time, because Q is deemed (ancient) "Israelite" over against (contemporary) "Judean", it does not become a meaningful representation of Judaism in the first century. It represents only a holdover of Israelite traditions past.

Finally, I suggest that the dominant description of the relationship of Q to Judaism is a microcosm of the traditional picture of the relationship of Christianity to Judaism, namely, that the origin of Christianity is a reform movement of Judaism. This notion acts to keep Q nominally separate from Judaism. This is essentially a theological position that not only accepts the biblical genealogy of the origin of Christianity—not to mention later super-cessionist and sometimes anti-Semitic accounts—but ignores external social and political factors, as well as cultural influences, that were external to Judaism but important for the development of Christianity. The idea of "reform" suggests that forms of Christianity both differentiated themselves from and transcended their Jewish context. The absence of Q in books about Second Temple Judaism or late Judaism also implicitly supports the picture that Judaism pre-dates and thus has nothing to learn from Christianity. It results, furthermore, in the odd situation that students of early Christianity are expected to be well versed in things Jewish from the first century but rarely vice versa. Again we have a model rooted in supercessionist theology, namely, that Christianity is still best explained as a reform movement of Judaism, and that to understand Christian origins one must understand Judaism.

Gerd Theissen (1978: 112–14) once suggested that the Palestinian Jesus movement—represented in large part by Q material—was a failure, because of its fundamental incongruence with its Jewish context. Although Theissen's study was marked by a number of theoretical and methodological issues (see Horsley 1996: 1–64), this point should give pause for thought, especially from the perspective of the academic study of Judaism. If we think of Q in terms of representing a legitimate form of Judaism in the first century, not a sectarian variety or a holdover from centuries prior, then we are allowed to see the movement it represents in terms of failure (see also, Arnal 2004). This permits us to ask real questions about the difference that Q makes for the origins of Christianity and the varieties of late Judaism. These questions involve such things as the production of the texts, the particular social, political, economic differences that the authors purport to address, the challenges of social formation, and the ways, successful or otherwise, of negotiating power structures and social forms in antiquity. In other words, these questions are not preoccupied with categories and essential identities. For as Jacob Neusner so eloquently writes regarding the concepts of "Judaism" and "Christianity" in antiquity,

> Not only have the available category-formations drastically distorted the character of the evidence, they also have predetermined that we ask the wrong questions to begin with. The documents attest to the world of their authors (in the case of the writings of individuals) or of their authorships (the textual communities that collective and anonymous writings represent)—that alone. (Neusner 1998: 237)

Because of the standard depiction of Q, for the reasons I have just outlined, scholars have not seen Q as a useful moment in mythmaking *with respect to Jewish and Christian relations*. Q is too often seen as a primitive gospel, produced prior to the heated debates seen in texts such as the *Epistle of Barnabas* or Ignatius's letters. It is regularly considered only an early Jesus movement—and it certainly represents such a movement—but it is also a "late" movement in Judaism. In *Border Lines* (2004) Daniel Boyarin argues persuasively that the social forms later called "Christianity" and "Judaism" underwent several centuries of disentanglement before settling into their current forms. Even if one does not agree with his precise dating—Boyarin argues this process was completed only in the third century—his larger point, that a clear-cut parting of ways is not an accurate description of the processes involved in social formation, seems to have taken hold in our field. Q fits nicely into this paradigm, witnessing to an early Jesus movement that did not see itself as independent of Judaism. Perhaps a more accurate description, given how its authors place themselves in relation to Israel's epic history, is that they saw themselves as bearer of the *correct* form of Judaism. In any case, the author's increasing claim on their Jewish identity shows that they were struggling to come to terms with their own identity. In other words, they nowhere designate themselves with one category of identity, suggesting that we should think twice before we do so. Yet scholars cannot discard the feeling that the presence of Jesus in the text and the utilization of material that later became central to Christian theology must somehow mean that Q is a proto-Christian text, must always be discussed in reference to the Synoptic gospels, and most dangerously, must be presented to future students as an unquestionable representative of early Christianity, not Second Temple Judaism or Palestinian Judaism.

Unless Q is allowed to make a difference in the study of early Christianity and Second Temple Judaism, the result is an academic enterprise that resembles the same enterprise as theology—both projects produce a mutually reinforcing narrative (Wiebe 1984: 416 **[20–21]**). This constitutes a second, institutional, and crypto-theological influence that keeps Q out of Jewish studies. The study of religion recapitulates in its curriculum and academic positions the very confessional claims made by (Western) religions.[8] Yet in carving itself up in this manner, it accepts the theological claims of exclusivity in Judaism and Christianity: that which is Christian is not Jewish, though that which is Jewish may also be Christian—the latter point, of course, reflects Christian theology and a Christian myth of origins. In other words, confessional theology interdicts Q's presence in Second Temple Judaism. Thus, despite evidence to the contrary, conclusions about Q do not disrupt traditional assumptions about the development of Christianity, either on its trajectory to the canon or in relation to Second Temple Judaism. If Q is wrested from these traditional frameworks, then it can contribute to a nuanced understanding of these topics.

3. Conclusion

The argument of this essay has centered on description, whether Q is more productively described as a Christian text or a Jewish text, and whether there might be room for both descriptions. Christopher Tuckett writes: "Most

---

8. One notable exception is the Centre for Jewish Studies at the University of Toronto. The Centre for Jewish Studies cross-appoints scholars from the Centre for the Study of Religion who research early Christianity, and accepts students who study early Christianity as well.

would agree that the Christian group which preserved Q was in some kind of relationship (however hostile) with Judaism" (1989: 356). This sort of description of the Q document, that the content represents something that is "with" or alongside the Jewish tradition, is problematic. One of the points of consensus among scholars of early Christianity is that Q is a variety of Judaism as much as it is a proto-Christian text. Objects are not fixed with one identity unless we essentialize them as such; rather their identities are constantly being constituted by the people asking questions about them and putting them to use for certain purposes. As long as the data in Q and its context are taken into account, the "object" that is Q can be multivalent: it is a Christian text, a Jewish text, a list of the grievances of frustrated intellectuals, a social critique, a (narratively challenged) memory of Jesus, a collection of sayings, or a cache of an early Judeao-Christian tradition (whether the core of a movement or not).

To reiterate, the issue is not that Q has not been made Jewish enough. Rather, it is that scholars have failed to use Q creatively as a *representative* text of both Christian origins and late Judaism. The problem is most troubling with the latter because of the enduring theological notion that Christianity emerged within, but broke away from, Judaism early on. This implies that knowing about first-century Judaism for understanding Christian origins is crucial, but not vice versa. On the contrary, I have suggested that Q is relevant to scholarship on Second Temple Judaism and on early Jewish–Christian relations. Its absence so far reflects theological presuppositions about essential differences in, origins of, and theological claims to exclusivity by these two traditions. These crypto-theological interests are not devious, by any means, but only the result of decades if not centuries of scholarship that have solidified the identities of first-century Judaism and Christianity in the minds of scholars and in the institutions in which they work. And because they are so pervasive in the academy, it is difficult to imagine alternative scenarios.

One of the major contributions of Wiebe's scholarship was the challenge to interrogate the political and theological implications involved in studying religion. As I have tried to suggest throughout, the identification of Q and the use to which it is put are not neutral; Q is simultaneously both Jewish and Christian, as most scholars seem to recognize. Evidently, there is both a theological and perhaps political need to keep Christianity and Judaism separate. As such an early text, Q suffers from this desire to classify and to make institutional distinctions. As a way forward, I modestly envision a perspective on Q that would be willing to admit that Q is not necessarily *about* Christianity and we are not always obliged to discuss it as such— although it certainly contains ideas that later became central to it. Just as Q is placed alongside the Gospels of Matthew, Mark, and Luke in courses on

Christian origins, so also it should be placed alongside texts such as *Ben Sira* and *1 Enoch* in courses on Second Temple Judaism. These practical actions would go a long way to ensure that biblical studies begins to reflect in actuality what these scholars of early Christianity claim Q to be.

References

Alexander, Philip S. 1990. *Textual Sources for the Study of Judaism*. Chicago: University of Chicago Press.

Allison, Dale C. 2001. "The Fiction of James and Its *Sitz im Leben*." *Revue Biblique* 118: 529–70.

Arnal, William E. 2001. *Jesus and the Village Scribes: Galilean Conflicts and the Setting of Q*. Minneapolis: Fortress Press.

———. 2004. "Why Q Failed." In Ron Cameron and Merrill P. Miller, eds, *Redescribing Christian Origins*, 67–87. SBL Symposium Series 18. Atlanta: Society of Biblical Literature.

———. 2005. "The Q Document." In Matt Jackson-McCabe, ed., *Jewish Christianity Reconsidered: Rethinking Ancient Groups and Texts*, 119–54. Minneapolis: Fortress Press.

Boyarin, Daniel. 2004. *Border Lines: The Partition of Judaeo-Christianity*. Philadelphia: University of Pennsylvania Press.

Chancey, Mark A. 2002. *The Myth of a Gentile Galilee*. Society for New Testament Studies Monograph Series 118. Cambridge: Cambridge University Press.

Cohen, Shaye J. D. 2006. *From the Maccabees to the Mishnah*. 2nd ed. Louisville: Westminster John Knox Press.

Cromhout, Markus. 2007. *Jesus and Identity: Reconstructing Judean Ethnicity in Q*. Matrix: The Bible in Mediterranean Context 2. Eugene: Cascade Books.

Crum, J. M. C. 1927. *The Original Jerusalem Gospel: Being Essays on the Document Q*. London: Constable & Company.

Dunn, James D. G. 1991. *The Partings of the Ways: Between Christianity and Judaism and Their Significance for the Character of Christianity*. Philadelphia: Trinity Press International.

Ehrman, Bart D. 2000. *The New Testament: A Historical Introduction to the Early Christian Writings*. New York: Oxford University Press.

Farrer, Austin M. 1957. "On Dispensing with Q." In D. E. Nineham, ed., *Studies in the Gospels: Essays in Memory of R. H. Lightfoot*, 55–88. Oxford: Blackwell.

Freed, Edwin D. 1986. *The New Testament: A Critical Introduction*. Belmont, CA: Wadsworth.

Funk, Robert W., Roy W. Hoover, and the Jesus Seminar, eds. 1993. *The Five Gospels: The Search for the Authentic Words of Jesus*. New York: Macmillan.

Goodacre, Mark. 2002. *The Case Against Q: Studies in Markan Priority and the Synoptic Problem*. Harrisburg: Trinity.

Goulder, Michael D. 1989. *Luke: A New Paradigm*. Journal for the Study of the New Testament Supplement Series 20. Sheffield: Sheffield Academic.

Harnack, Adolf von. 1908 [1907]. *The Sayings of Jesus*. New York: Putnam's Sons.

Harris, Stephen L. 2002. *The New Testament: A Student's Introduction*. Boston: MacGraw Hill.

Horsley, Richard A. 1989. *Sociology and the Jesus Movement*. New York: Crossroad.

———. 1996. *Archaeology, History, and Society in Galilee: The Social Context of Jesus and the Rabbis*. Valley Forge: Trinity Press International.

Horsley, Richard A. (with Jonathan A. Draper). 1999. *Whoever Hears You Hears Me: Prophets, Performance, and Tradition in Q*. Harrisburg: Trinity.

Jacobson, Arland D. 1992. *The First Gospel: An Introduction to Q*. Sonoma: Polebridge Press.

Kirk, Alan. 1998. *The Composition of the Sayings Source: Genre, Synchrony, and Wisdom Redaction in Q*. Supplements to Novum Testamentum 91. Leiden: Brill.

Kloppenborg, John S. 1987. *The Formation of Q: Trajectories in Ancient Wisdom Collections*. Studies in Antiquity and Christianity. Philadelphia: Fortress Press.

———. ed. 1994. *The Shape of Q: Signal Essays on the Sayings Gospel*. Minneapolis: Fortress Press.

———. 2007. "Judaeans or Judean Christians in James." In Phil Harland and Zeba A. Crook, eds, *Identity and Interaction in the Ancient Mediterranean: Jews, Christians and Others*, 113–35. New Testament Monographs 18. Sheffield: Sheffield Phoenix Press.

———. 2009. *Q: The Earliest Gospel: An Introduction to the Original Stories and Sayings of Jesus*. Louisville: Westminster John Knox Press.

Kloppenborg Verbin, John S. 2000. *Excavating Q: The History and Setting of the Sayings Gospel*. Minneapolis: Fortress Press.

Koester, Helmut. 1990. *Ancient Christian Gospels: Their History and Development*. Harrisburg: Trinity Press International.

———. 2000. *Introduction to the New Testament*. Vol 2, *History and Literature of Early Christianity*. 2nd ed. New York: W. de Gruyter.

Lincoln, Bruce. 1999. "Theses on Method." *Method & Theory in the Study of Religion* 8: 225–27.

Lindemann, Andreas, ed. 2001. *The Sayings Source Q and the Historical Jesus, Colloquium Biblicum Lovaniense XLIX*. BETL 158. Leuven: Leuven University Press and Uitgeverij Peeters.

Llewelyn, S. R. 1997. "The Prescript of James." *Novum Testamentum* 39: 385–93.

Lührmann, Dieter. 1969. *Die Redaktion der Logienquelle*. Wissenschaftliche Monographien zum Alten und Neuen Testament 33. Neukirchen–Vluyn: Neukirchener Verlag.

Mack, Burton L. 1988. *A Myth of Innocence: Mark and Christian Origins*. Philadelphia: Fortress Press.

———. 1993. *The Lost Gospel: The Book of Q & Christian Origins*. San Francisco: HarperCollins.

———. 1995. *Who Wrote the New Testament? The Making of the Christian Myth*. San Francisco: HarperSanFrancisco.

Meyer, Paul D. 1970. "The Gentile Mission in Q." *Journal of Biblical Literature* 89: 405–17.

Moxnes, Halvor. 2001a. "The Construction of Galilee as a Place for the Historical Jesus. Part I." *Biblical Theology Bulletin* 31: 26–37.

———. 2001b. "The Construction of Galilee as a Place for the Historical Jesus. Part II." *Biblical Theology Bulletin* 31: 64–77.

Neusner, Jacob. 1984. *Judaism in the Beginning of Christianity*. Philadelphia: Fortress Press.

————. 1998. "Judaism and Christianity in the Beginning: Time for a Category-Reformation?" *Bulletin for Biblical Research* 8: 229–37.

Perrin, Norman. 1974. *The New Testament: An Introduction—Proclamation and Parenesis, Myth and History*. New York: Harcourt Brace Jovanovich.

Piper, Ronald A., ed. 1994. *The Gospels Behind the Gospels: Current Studies on Q*. Supplements to Novum Testamentum 75. Leiden: Brill.

Powell, Evan. 2006. *The Myth of the Lost Gospel*. Las Vegas: Symposium.

Reed, Jonathan L. 1999. "Galileans, 'Israelite Village Communities,' and the Sayings Gospel Q." In Eric M. Meyers, ed., *Galilee Through the Centuries: Confluence of Cultures*, 87–108. Duke Judaic Studies 1. Winona Lake, IN: Eisenbrauns.

Robinson, James M. 1971. "LOGOI SOPHON: On the Gattung of Q." In James M. Robinson and Helmut Koester, eds, *Trajectories Through Early Christianity*, 103–13. Philadelphia: Fortress Press.

————. 1997. "The Real Jesus of the Saying Gospel Q." *Princeton Seminary Bulletin* 18: 135–51.

Robinson, James M. and Helmut Koester, eds. 1971. *Trajectories Through Early Christianity*. Philadelphia: Fortress Press.

Sanders, Ed P. 1977. *Paul and Palestinian Judaism: A Comparison of Patterns of Religion*. Philadelphia: Fortress Press.

Sato, Migaku. 1988. *Q und Prophetie: Studien zur Gattungs- und Traditionsgeschichte der Quelle Q*. Tübingen: J. C. B. Mohr.

Schiffman, Lawrence H. 1991. *From Text to Tradition: A History of Second Temple Rabbinic Judaism*. Hoboken, NY: Ktav.

Segal, Alan F. 1987. *The Other Judaisms of Late Antiquity*. Atlanta: Scholars Press.

Smith, Jonathan Z. 1990. *Drudgery Divine: On the Comparison of Early Christianities and the Religions of Late Antiquity*. Jordan Lectures in Comparative Religion 14, School of Oriental and African Studies. Chicago: University of Chicago Press.

Theissen, Gerd. 1978. *Sociology of Early Palestinian Christianity*. Trans. John Bowden. Philadelphia: Fortress Press.

Tuckett, Christopher. 1989. "A Cynic Q?" *Biblica* 70: 349–76.

Vaage, Leif E. 1994. *Galilean Upstarts: Jesus' First Followers According to Q*. Valley Forge: Trinity.

Wiebe, Donald. 1984. "The Failure of Nerve in the Academic Study of Religion." *Studies in Religion / Sciences religieuses* 13: 401–22.

Wilson, Stephen G. 1995. *Related Strangers: Jews and Christians, 70–170 C.E.* Minneapolis: Fortress Press.

THE FAILURE OF NERVE TO RECOGNIZE VIOLENCE IN EARLY CHRISTIANITY: THE CASE OF THE PARABLE OF THE ASSASSIN*

T. Nicholas Schonhoffer[†]

In an influential essay, Donald Wiebe (1984) argues that there has been a "failure of nerve in the academic study of religion." The discipline had been founded on the premise that it would pursue a scientific study of religion. Under the pressure of confessional interests, however, the theorization that is a necessary part of scientific study was forsaken in favor of theological speculation about an *a priori* accepted ultimate reality. Thus the *scientific* objectives that allowed the academic study of religion to gain legitimacy in the modern research university were abandoned for theological or crypto-theological work, which is incompatible with these core objectives.

In this article, I will take Wiebe's criticism as inspiration for analyzing scholarship on the "Parable of the Assassin" from the *Gospel of Thomas*. I will argue that (1) the scholarly treatments of the Parable of the Assassin represent a failure of nerve with respect to the role of violence in early Christianity; (2) this failure of nerve can be traced to contemporary political apologetic motives; (3) this failure of nerve can be corrected by turning to theories of violence in religion, which, in keeping with Wiebe's vision of a nomothetically oriented study of religion, can contribute to understanding this parable. In order to pursue this argument, I will first survey the literature on this remarkably under-researched parable. Particular attention will be given to the treatments of Charles Hedrick (2011) and the Jesus Seminar (Funk et al. 1988; Funk, Hoover, and the Jesus Seminar 1993), which, for different reasons, serve as the most important scholarly works on this parable. This survey will demonstrate that interpretations of this parable have often seen its violence as *strange* in the mouth of Jesus. Second, by

* I am indebted to John Kloppenborg, Aldea Mulhern, and Lana DeGasperis for their valuable comments on drafts of this essay.

† Ed. note: We regret to note our friend and colleague T. Nicholas Schonhoffer's sudden and untimely death, January 24, 2012.

examining examples of tolerated violence in the Eastern Roman Empire and in the language of the Jesus movement, I will demonstrate that this perception of strangeness is anachronistic.[1] Third, I will examine contemporary concerns that may motivate these anachronistic portrayals of violence. Finally, I will discuss theories of violence in religion in order to explain the Parable of the Assassin in such a way that the violence is not seen as exceptional, but as a natural part of the parable's religious expression.

1. Introduction to the Parable of the Assassin

The Parable of the Assassin is the third in a series of three short parables about the "Kingdom of the Father" that occur near the end of the apocryphal *Gospel of Thomas*. It is quite brief and can be reproduced here in full:

> Jesus said, "The Kingdom of the Father is like a man who wished to kill a powerful man. He drew his sword in his own house. He struck it into the wall in order that he would realize that his hand would be strong. Then he slew the powerful man." (*Thomas* 98)[2]

The parables are often considered one of the most distinctive forms of Jesus' speech, and only a handful of extra-canonical parables exist, which implies that the creative construction of parables must have been a rare activity among the early followers of Jesus (Scott 1990: 63–65; Stroker 1988: 95–97). Many scholars have taken the position that the *Gospel of Thomas* should be seen as early text and independent from the canonical gospels.[3] The Parable of the Assassin is a significant example of this rare literary form, but has attracted surprisingly little scholarly consideration.[4]

---

1. I use the term "Jesus movement" throughout this essay. While this term has occasionally been adapted in a more technical manner, I simply refer to followers of Jesus before "Christian" identity became solidified in any meaningful way.

2. All translations of the *Gospel of Thomas* are the author's.

3. John Dominic Crossan (1985: 37) is even willing to claim that this is now the position of the majority of scholars who study *Thomas*. One interesting aspect of the Parable of the Assassin is that, since it is unparalleled, even one who holds *Thomas* itself to be dependent on the canonical gospels would have to see this particular parable as independent. So, for example, a scholar like Craig Blomberg who holds that *Thomas* is dependent on the synoptic gospels can claim that "the two parables unique to *Thomas* (log. 97 and 98)…lay as much claim to authenticity as any of *Thomas*' logia, although they too have may have been retouched slightly by Gnostic redaction" (1985: 181).

4. For instance, in their main works on parables neither Scott (1990) nor Crossan (1973) discusses the Assassin. Scott mentions the parable in his introduction; as far as I can tell Crossan does not even mention it. Robert Doran writes that the series of parables in *Thomas* 96–98 "have attracted little attention and almost no effort has been made to read them in and of themselves" (1987: 347).

Relative to the attention paid to most parables attributed to Jesus, the neglect of the Parable of the Assassin is striking, and the arguments here advanced will endeavor both to explain and correct this oversight. The majority of efforts to understand this parable can be divided into five types, though, upon examination, none of these proposals is convincing: (i) The parable can be understood as an example of preparation before action, resembling Luke's stories of the Tower Builder and Warring King (Luke 14:28–33).[5] The Parable of the Assassin, however, differs from the stories of the Tower Builder and the Warring King, because the latter two explicitly stress that prudent preparation is taken, while striking a sword into a wall and thus knowing the strength of one's arm is not clearly adequate preparation for killing a powerful man (Hedrick 2011). (ii) The parable can be understood as an analogy for destroying something to which *Thomas* is perceived to be opposed.[6] However, such full allegorical interoperations are difficult to substantiate because, in the absence of any Thomasine (redactional) commentary, there is insufficient evidence for the association of the allegorical elements with their target domains.[7] (iii) The parable can be

---

5. William Stroker has clearly articulated this position, writing that "the point of the parable is determining the capacity to complete an intended action before actually beginning. There is general agreement that the dynamics are parallel to those of the Tower Builder and Warring King (Luke 14:28–32)" (1988: 102). Steven Davies has similarly stated that the parable "does have a superficially obvious meaning: one should prepare in advance." In elaborating on this position he compares the Assassin to the Tower Builder (2002: 120).

6. Gregory Riley suggests that "the sword is the (ascetic) will and power of the individual soul, which is tested against the 'house' of the body. Once it has shown that it can overcome the body, then the soul is able to overcome the 'strong man'" (1995: 153). Similarly, Robert Winterhalter claims that "the Christian warrior is to conquer error (*planē* in the New Testament) in two steps: (1) in her or his [*sic*] individual psyche and (2) in the collective belief system of the planet" (1988: 103). The house is the man's consciousness, and after conquering it he can conquer the outside world.

7. A particular problem with understanding this parable allegorically is that such understanding seems to presuppose understanding it within the *Gospel of Thomas's* symbolic system, but the imagery fits poorly within *Thomas's* symbolic system because of the use of killing as the parable's central act. Thomas tends to use death as the fate of those who have not found the Kingdom (*Thomas* 2, 18, 19, 59, 85, 111). The word "to slay" (*hōteb*) occurs in *Thomas* only in this parable. The verb "to kill" (*mout*) occurs elsewhere only in 60, 65, and 70. *Thomas* 65 is the Parable of the Tenants in the Vineyard, and the use of kill here is a natural part of the narrative. *Thomas* 70 seems to use being killed (*mout*) as the result of failing to obtain the Kingdom (here it is envisioned as being killed rather than tasting, seeing, or experiencing death [*mou*]). Only the enigmatic use of *mout* in *Thomas* 60 remains, and while the meaning of this saying is unclear, it does not obviously point to a variation in *Thomas's* use of dying as a metaphor. Since the metaphor of death is such an important concept for *Thomas*, it is curious that

understood as a combination of the first two models.[8] However, the combined approach is vulnerable to the criticisms advanced against the first two positions. (iv) The parable can be understood as a reference to Zealot activity.[9] Richard Horsley, however, has argued convincingly that the existence of the Zealots is to be restricted to the narrow time-frame of the Jewish War (1987: 62–145; Horsley and Hanson 1999: 190–259),[10] and there is no compelling reason to associate this parable with that period.[11] (v) The parable can be understood as part of a series of three parables which together comment on agency.[12] However, the readings that treat *Thomas* 96–98 together do not

Thomas would construct or use an allegory that expected killing to be understood in a manner outside of the symbolic system in which *Thomas* uses dying.

8. The first two possibilities for interpretation are combined by Richard Valantasis who proposes an interpretation of practice before performing an action, before suggesting that "the seekers, fighting the world and its ways to the end, must test their metal [*sic*], practice their swings, explore the limits of their ability to do battle, and then proceed to the killing of the world when they have shown their strength" (1997: 179). Similarly, Robert Grant writes, "it is more like the king going into battle who first makes an estimate concerning his prospects (Luke 14:31). He who would find the kingdom must count the cost. If he is strong enough, he can slay the 'great man' (probably the world; see Saying 78)" (1960: 188).

9. Joachim Jeremias holds that the parable "draws upon the stern reality of the Zealot movement" (1963: 196), concluding that "just as the political assassin first makes trial of his strength before he embarks on his dangerous venture, so should you test yourselves to see whether you have strength to carry the adventure through" (1963: 197). F. F. Bruce follows Jeremias, noting that the parable "may have come down from a period when Zealot activity gave it contemporary relevance" and concluding that "the point seems to be that any one [*sic*] who embarks on a costly or dangerous enterprise must first make sure that he has the necessary resources to carry it out" (1974: 148).

10. It is also worth noting that besides the bare act of killing there is little actual basis for making a connection between the Assassin and Zealots.

11. In fact, it is difficult to understand how a parable about Zealot activity would find its way into the Jesus tradition in the first place. It is worth noting, however, that Jeremias and Bruce are correct that the violence of the period would have given the parable context. In addition, the fact that the target of the assassination is called *ourōme emmegistanos* may indicate that he is a political figure, and thus that the assassination might have a political motivation.

12. The Parable of the Assassin is the last of three sequential parables that appear near the end of the *Gospel of Thomas*. Robert Doran argues that this complex contrasts the failure of the protagonist in 97 to the success of the protagonists in 96 and 98, so that "these three parables have been artfully arranged to stress that one must strive for the Kingdom but that the self is not enough. Self-enclosed existence can lead to a loss of one's substance. While 96 and 98 stress the action of an individual, 97 shows that an individual on her/his own cannot survive" (1987: 351–52). Richard Ford compares the "familiar and benign" action of the yeast to the totally "unidentifiable" breaking of the jar to the "well known and horrifying" action of the sword and proposes that the three

account for their individual origins, transmission, and meanings,[13] and contain various interpretive difficulties.[14]

The comments on the Parable of the Assassin here surveyed are hurried remarks in works dedicated to studying broader topics. There are two more substantial treatments, however, that need to be examined. This examination will help explain why so little attention has been paid to this parable. The first of these treatments is that of the Jesus Seminar, which is significant because it attempts to report the consensus position, established by voting, of a substantial number of scholars on the historicity of sayings and events attributed to Jesus.[15] The Seminar's concern with consensus extends to their final report on the sayings purporting to be co-written by "the Jesus Seminar" as a whole (along with Robert Funk and Roy Hoover), since the authors (or compilers) have "endeavored to let the Jesus seminar speak for itself" (Funk, Hoover, and the Jesus Seminar 1993: ix). While certainly not representing the consensus of all biblical scholars,[16] the results of the Jesus Seminar do represent a position on this parable with which a sizable sub-group of scholars agreed.

---

narratives, taken together, "explore dimensions of both control and limit" (2002: 296). Understanding the final container as a human being he suggests that the previous two might also relate to bodies (2002: 297). He concludes, "The Jar probes the pressures on trust that accompany debilitating catastrophe. The sword moves in the opposite direction, toward the potential for the breakdown of trust incumbent upon the achievement of successes" (2002: 304).

13.   While it is probable that *Thomas* does group parables together on thematic grounds, as the group in 63–65 seems to be a critique of wealth, each of these parables also contains independent meaning. In addition, it is certain that the Parable of the Leaven traveled alone because it is found in Matthew and Luke (Matt 13:13; Luke 13:20–21) and thus presumably also in Q. Since neither of the other two parables in this complex is obviously Thomasine, it is probable that they traveled independently prior to their current arrangement.

14.   Doran's arguments are vulnerable on three accounts: (i) the focus on "agency" is probably anachronistic in the collectivist societies of the ancient Mediterranean; (ii) two of the three solitary protagonists do succeed at their goals, which seems to undermine the moral about failing on one's own; and (iii) *Thomas* does presuppose that an individual seeker can succeed. Ford's arguments hold together better, though to some extent they share the focus on the individual, and, as the subsequent discussion of the portrayal of violence in this parable should show, it is not necessary to see the killing in this parable as a catastrophic destruction of civic order.

15.   This amounts to over one hundred scholars according to *The Parables of Jesus* (Funk et al. 1988: xii); 74 are listed in *The Five Gospels* (Funk, Hoover, and the Jesus Seminar 1993: 533–37).

16.   Critiques of the Seminar have been multiple, and have come from a variety of angles. One of the better known is probably that of Birger Pearson (1996).

According to the Jesus Seminar's initial report on the parables, their voting indicated that the Parable of the Assassin probably does not go back to the historical Jesus (Funk et al. 1988: 63).[17] Their main argument was that "this image contradicts the pacifistic image of the kingdom customarily associated with Jesus" (1988: 63).[18] Their final report on the sayings of Jesus, however, states that subsequent voting determined the Parable of the Assassin probably to go back to the historical Jesus (Funk, Hoover, and the Jesus Seminar 1993: 524).[19] Explaining this change, the Seminar notes their initial reluctance to attribute a story found only in a non-canonical source to Jesus, and praises their own willingness to overcome this reluctance: "attributing a parable of Jesus not attested in the canonical gospels and known only a few years was an act of courage that demanded careful consideration" (Funk, Hoover, and the Jesus Seminar 1993: 525).[20] Considering the amount of emphasis the Seminar places on critical scholarship[21] and that, other than adherence to the Christian canon, there is little reason to give any priority to canonical texts,[22] there would be room here to question whether this hesitation represents another failure of nerve on the part of the Seminar. This is not the failure of nerve under investigation, however, and so it is necessary to return to the issue of violence. In arguing for the parable's authenticity, the claim that the violence in the parable contradicts the peaceful images employed by Jesus is repeated, but now, according to the peculiarity of the criterion of dissimilarity, this argument is reversed, so as to imply that Jesus did employ this parable:

17.   It was placed in the grey category, meaning that "I would not include this item in the primary data base, but I might make use of some of the content in determining who Jesus was," or alternatively "Jesus did not say this but the ideas contained in it are close to his own" (1988: 21).

18.   They also argue that the parable reflects common wisdom, and hence is insufficiently distinct to associate confidently with the historical Jesus. The association of this parable with common wisdom probably does not hold up (Hedrick 2011: 3047–48).

19.   It was included in the pink category, meaning "I would include this item with reservations (or modifications) in the database" or "Jesus probably said something like this" (1993: 36).

20.   Similar things are also said about the other unique Thomasine parable, the "Empty Jar" (Funk, Hoover, and the Jesus Seminar 1993: 524), though the neglect of this parable has not been as total as that of the Assassin; for example, unlike the Assassin, a section is devoted to the empty jar by Scott (1990: 306–308).

21.   *The Parables of Jesus* contains, as an appendix, a manifesto on what it means to be a critical scholar (Funk et al. 1988: 93–94).

22.   Helmut Koester writes, "it is difficult to understand why the apocryphal gospels and acts are separated from their canonical counterparts. Neither the external attestation nor the internal evidence permits such a separation" (1980: 107).

> The sheer violence and scandal of the image of the assassin suggests that it might have originated with Jesus. It is unlikely that the early Christian community would have invented and have attributed such a story to Jesus since its imagery is so contrary to the irenic and honorific images, such as the good shepherd, they customarily used for him. In ancient society it was expected that kings and tyrants would act violently to enforce their will. Ordinary people were expected to refrain from violent behavior, unless, of course, they were brigands and revolutionaries. (Funk, Hoover, and the Jesus Seminar 1993: 524)

This is a problematic explanation. It claims that kings were expected to act violently, without considering that the Assassin is being used as simile for a kingdom. It similarly claims that the shepherd is an example of an irenic image, in opposition to the violent image of the Assassin, when, in fact, ancient Mediterranean society saw the shepherd as "both a marginal and dangerous figure" (Kloppenborg and Callon 2010: 227).[23] Additionally, as the next section will show, even a surface examination of the early Jesus traditions demonstrates that violent imagery is not especially uncommon.

In both of its treatments of the Parable of the Assassin, the Jesus Seminar focuses on the violence of this parable and the supposed contrast of this violence to the peaceful Jesus movement. Whether this violence is deployed to argue for or against the parable, its strangeness remains the center of the argument. Yet, the claim that the violence is exceptional is poorly supported, and so the question should be raised whether unsustainable preconceptions are showing through in the Jesus Seminar's examination of this understudied parable.

Such suspicions may be further supported by turning to Charles Hedrick's (2011) treatment of this parable, since he has produced the most extensive and thoughtful consideration of it. Hedrick immediately rejects the idea of denying this parable's authenticity on the basis of its violent imagery, noting that such imagery is used in other well-regarded parables (2011: 3031). He questions naming it "the Parable of the Assassin," since this already assumes a negative evaluation of the man's actions (2011: 3030–31). He also insightfully notes that the piercing of the house's wall probably implies that the house is constructed from "sun-dried mud-brick" (2011: 3041). This, in turn, implies that the protagonist is lower class and thus that a substantial social distance exists between him and the powerful man (2011: 3041). This social distance, combined with the fact that simply knowing the strength of one's hand is woefully insufficient planning, makes the parable shocking (2011: 3043–44). Success should not be expected, but occurs without explanation.

---

23.   Kloppenborg and Callon later write, "These structural features of pastoralism—the lack of supervision, transience, and the possession of weapons—help to account for the fact that shepherds in antiquity were stigmatized figures, often associated with bandits and agitators" (2010: 228).

To this point, Hedrick's interpretation of the parable is carefully considered, insightful, and avoids some of the Jesus Seminar's more problematic claims. Once he starts discussing the parable's violence, however, his arguments encounter problems similar to those of the Seminar. He argues that the parable "portrays, without qualification or censure, the breaking of one of the most sacred prohibitions of Hebrew and Samaritan Scripture: the apparent unjustifiable taking of human life (Exod 20:13, Deut 5:17 and Gen 9:5–6)" (2011: 3043). This parable, however, does not condemn its protagonist; instead, "in presenting the story without any criticism of the act or censure of the man, even the narrator is suspected of being without morals and conscience as well" (2011: 3044). Hedrick, therefore, determines that "In the absence of a stated motive, the story begs the question: is there ever a time when a deliberate homicide could be deemed justifiable even though prohibited legally and morally?" (2011: 3048). The parable ultimately serves as an extreme example leading to questions about morality in general and causing its hearer to ask "is there ever a time when I must challenge even the most sacrosanct laws, morals, taboos, and religious values of my community?" (2011: 3051). Yet when Hedrick attempts to understand how an ancient hearer would think through this dilemma, he lists a series of examples that could justify killing (2011: 3048–49). These cases, combined with some of the data about the ancient world that will shortly be surveyed, make the question of whether the act of killing could ever be justifiable a curious one—it clearly could be.[24]

While Hedrick and the Jesus Seminar treat the violence in the parable differently, they both treat it as something that renders the parable exceptional. For the Jesus Seminar, it is exceptional within the Jesus Tradition: so distinctive that either Jesus could not have said it, or so distinctive that early Christians could not have invented it. For Hedrick, the violence would have been so exceptional in relation to the moral codes of the hearers that the parable would need to be heard as a meditation on this issue.[25] For the Jesus Seminar, the strangeness of the violence is the central issue in determining the parable's authenticity. For Hedrick, the strangeness of the violence is the point to which Jesus is trying to draw attention. In both cases, thinking about this violence in Jesus' mouth is *strange*. Additionally, in both cases there appear to be stress points in their arguments where this exceptionality is not

24. Another objection to Hedrick's position is that the parables are not, in general, morality tales (cf. Crossan 1973: 57–66).

25. The discussion of the exceptionality of the violence of the parable is a comparative argument and comparison is always relative to a third term (Smith 1990). Thus, in arguing against the claims that violence in the parable is exceptional, I am arguing against the claim that it is exceptional with respect to the objects that Hedrick or the Jesus Seminar think it is. It may be exceptional in comparison to other objects (a certain normative definition of religion for example).

actually supported by their data, which raises the possibility that other concerns rest behind their desire to present the violence of this parable as being strange when associated with Jesus.

2. Violence in the Jesus Movement and the Roman Empire

The treatments of the Parable of the Assassin examined above focus on the exceptional nature of the parable's violence within the early Jesus movement.[26] In order to evaluate this claim, it is necessary to examine the evidence regarding attitudes towards violence from the literature of the Jesus movement, then to examine the more general ancient context. Since the goal of this examination is to criticize the contention that the violence of the Parable of the Assassin is strange in association with Jesus, it is necessary to evaluate some of the material from the Jesus tradition using the methods of historical Jesus scholarship. This should not be seen as an endorsement of these methods to access the historical Jesus, but only as an attempt to show that the methods of Historical Jesus scholarship, when employed consistently, should not lead to a *radically* pacifistic Jesus.[27]

Despite the peaceful image often associated with the Jesus movement, explicit discussion of "peace" is actually missing from the literature. In fact, as Richard Horsley notes, the only significant discussion of the word, in its conventional sense, denies that it has anything to do with Jesus' teaching:

> Only rarely in its relatively infrequent occurrences in the gospel tradition does the Greek term *eirene*, usually translated as "peace," mean the absence of conflict, violence, or war. In the most significant of these occurrences, Matthew 10:34 and Luke 12:51, Jesus declares that he came "not to bring peace but a sword." Otherwise *eirene* occurs primarily in Luke, where it means something like "salvation" in a comprehensive sense. (Horsley 1987: 150–51)[28]

The saying cited by Horsley is found not only in Matthew and Luke, and thus presumably Q, but also in the *Gospel of Thomas*:

> Jesus said, "Men think that perhaps I have come to cast peace unto the world, and they do not know that I have come to cast divisions onto the earth: a fire, a sword, and a war. For there will be five in a house, and there will be three against two, and two against thee, the father against the son and the son against the father." (*Thomas* 16)

26.   "Violence" is itself a difficult word to define, but I hope most of the ambiguity is avoided in this paper, in which it is used exclusively with reference to actions or depictions of agents doing physical harm to each other.

27.   For criticisms of the Historical Jesus studies, see Mack 2001: 25–40; Arnal 2005: 75–77.

28.   Michel Desjardins (1997: 16–18) provides a conflicting interpretation of the distribution of *eirēnē* (peace) in the gospels.

As a Q/Thomas saying, this pericope probably goes back to the very early stages of the Jesus tradition and clearly denies that "peace" is the essence of Jesus' message. There are several other sayings along the same lines, which can be found attested in only a single Gospel. For instance, in Matthew, Jesus claims that "From the days of John the Baptist until now, the kingdom of heaven has suffered violence, and the violent take it by force" (11:12, NRSV), or in Luke, Jesus warns that the time for traveling without purse and bag as he had earlier instructed (Luke 10:4) has passed: "now, the one who has purse must take it, and likewise a bag. And the one who has no sword must sell his cloak and buy one" (22:36, NRSV). Neither Matthew nor Luke has trouble including sayings portraying Jesus as actively associating violence with his mission.

Since the Assassin is a parable, it is worth paying closer attention to Jesus' other parables and similes to place the Assassin in its proper literary context. Although the saying about the binding of the strong man is technically an aphorism and not a parable, it has enough similarities with the Assassin to serve as a strong example of a comparable story within the Jesus tradition.[29] The version of this saying found in the *Gospel of Thomas* reads: "Jesus said, 'It is impossible for someone to enter the house of a strong man and take it by force, unless he binds the strong man's hands. Then he will rob the strong man's house'" (*Thomas* 35). This aphorism is also found in Matt 12:29, Mark 3:27, and Luke 11:21–22, and was probably in Q. It is one of the few sayings present in four extant early Christian gospels and three independent early Christian gospels. On the grounds of attestation, this aphorism has a high probability of belonging to a very early stage of the sayings tradition. Jesus' use of a metaphor that involves committing a violent act against a potent individual thus should not be regarded as exceptionally strange.

Turning to proper parables, violence is not foreign to this literary form either. In the Parable of the Good Samaritan, the man going down from Jerusalem "fell into the hands of robbers, who stripped him, beat him, and went away, leaving him half dead" (Luke 10:30, NRSV). While it might be objected that the robber's violence is negatively evaluated, they are not the main figures criticized by the parable—the Priest and Levite are. Robbers are simply a fact of life. In a stronger example, the Parable of the Tenants clearly features a central and positively evaluated character who performs acts of violence. The tenants kill the son of the owner of the vineyard, and if the version found in the *Gospel of Thomas* is the original, then the tenants are probably intended to be the heroes who defy their oppressive creditor (Kloppenborg 2006). On the other hand, if the synoptic version is preferred,

---

29. In their writings on the Assassin both Davies (2002: 120) and Bruce (1974: 148) compare it to the Binding of the Strong Man.

then the tenants are no longer the heroes, but now the owner is, and in revenge he "will come and destroy the tenants" (Mark 12:9, NRSV; cf. Matt 21:41; Luke 20:16). In either case, the positively evaluated protagonist of the parable kills. Images of violence and killing are not especially unusual among the parables.

The narratives tradition also portrays Jesus as implicated in violent activity. According to the synoptic gospels, Jesus was protected by the crowds against the authorities who wished to attack him. For example, after Jesus tells the Parable of the Tenants, the various authorities desire to move against him, but are afraid of the crowd: "when they realized that he had told this parable against them, they wanted to arrest him, but they feared the crowd. So they left him and went away" (Mark 12:12, NRSV; cf. Luke 20:19; Matt 22:46; see also Mark 11:32; 14:1–2; Matt 21:26–27; 26:2–5; Luke 19:47–48; 20:6–8; 22:1–2). In fact, according to Luke, what made Judas's betrayal significant was his ability "to betray him to them when no crowd was present" (Luke 22:6, NRSV), that is, when the threat of reciprocal violence from most of Jesus' followers would not be present. In addition, in a story found in all four canonical gospels, Jesus

> entered the temple and began to drive out those who were selling and those who were buying in the temple, and he overturned the tables of the money-changers and the seats of those who sold doves; and he would not allow anyone to carry anything through the temple. (Mark 11:15–16, NRSV; cf. Matt 21:12–13; Luke 19:45–48; John 2:13–17)

The narrative tradition also fails to describe a radically non-violent Jesus.

This discussion has not even touched on the more structurally violent parts of the Jesus tradition, such as the divinely sanctioned catastrophes associated with eschatological traditions or the inherent violence of the narratives of Jesus' arrest, torture, and death. There is simply no good reason to support the contention that violent imagery would have been out of place in the early Jesus movement. This argument should not be overstated. The intention is not to suggest that the Jesus movement was *excessively* violent, and a balanced examination of this topic would need, for example, to discuss the ethical injunctions from the Sermon on the Mount.[30] The argument here is simply that the Jesus movement was not so *excessively* pacifistic that they completely avoided the use of violent imagery, and even a cursory analysis of the tradition demonstrates this. The position of the Jesus Seminar cannot be sustained. This analysis, additionally, should begin to cast suspicion on whether the image of the Assassin would have seemed as strange to the parable's hearers as Hedrick thinks.

---

30. For attempts at more balanced approaches, see Desjardins 1997; Tite 2004.

An examination of broader ancient Mediterranean attitudes towards violence is necessary to develop these observations further. This analysis will show that the violent imagery found in the Jesus material should not be surprising. More importantly, such an analysis will show that an ancient audience hearing the Parable of the Assassin would not have asked whether homicide was ever acceptable, since everyone assumed that in some cases killing was necessary.

Depictions of violence in ancient literary sources were written in the context not only of culturally specific standards of what constitutes actual acceptable violence, but also of culturally specific rules about the portrayal of violence in literature.[31] The societies of the ancient Mediterranean were marked by a presence of violence in many locations that would seem unusual to people from a contemporary North Atlantic background. Bruce Malina vividly describes the situation in this way: "the Romans—like Mediterraneans in general, including Israel—were agonistic (fight-prone), hence willing to engage in physical conflict at the slightest provocation" (Malina 2001: 37).

To illustrate the toleration of violence in antiquity, Cicero is a useful example because of the *apparent* contrast of this violence with his generally humane reputation. Cicero, in *De Inventione*, shockingly places revenge as one of the positive qualities instilled in human beings by nature, together with duty, gratitude, reverence, and truth.[32] In this description, revenge is explicitly defined in terms of violence. The strangeness of this juxtaposition is significant for indicating that a categorical system quite distinct from the modern North Atlantic one is in play. In another striking passage about violence, Cicero warns that when dealing with bandits, violence is necessary and waiting for the intervention of law foolish:

31.   Martin Zimmermann writes, "Texts and images that transmit violence to posterity follow the rules and conventions of their own time and these may not be easily accessible to the modern observer. Those rules may be based, for example, on political ideologies, on criteria of who belongs to a society and who does not, on laws that govern life within the community, but they also depend on conventions of storytelling and literary representation" (2006: 344).

32.   The full passage reads "The law of nature is something which is implanted in us not by opinion, but by a kind of innate instinct; it includes religion, duty, gratitude, revenge (*vindicationem*), reverence, and truth. Religion is the term applied to the fear and worship of the gods. Duty warns us to keep our obligations to our country or parents or other kin. Gratitude has regard for remembering and returning services, honour, acts of friendship. *Revenge is the act through which by defending or avenging we repel violence and insult from ourselves and from those dear to us, and by which we punish offence.* Reverence is the act through which we show respect and cherish our superiors in age or wisdom or honour or any high position. Truth is the quality by which we endeavour to avoid any discrepancy between our statements and facts, past present and future" (Cicero, *De Inventione* 2.22.65–66; trans. Hubbell 1960: 231, emphasis added).

> Should our life have fallen into any snare, into the violence and the weapons
> of robbers or foes, every method of winning a way to safety would be morally
> justifiable. When arms speak, the laws are silent; they bid none to await their
> word, since he who chooses to await it must pay an underserved penalty ere
> he can exact a deserved one. (Cicero, *Pro Milo* 10–11; trans. Watts 1931: 17)

Direct violent action, outside of normal legal channels, is here argued to be
morally justifiable.

Writing on the issue of cruelty in Cicero, A. W. Lintott explains that: "I
am not trying to destroy his reputation for humanity, except perhaps for a
humanity which is idealized and anachronistic and which he himself would
have despised" (1968: 35). This goal is parallel to the aim here in discussing
Jesus. The intention is not to destroy his reputation for humanity, except for
an anachronistic humanity that he likely would not have understood, and
which may relate to contemporary political concerns that have their own
problematic implications.

What makes the references from Cicero significant is not only the
endorsement of violence from a generally ethical figure; it is that in neither
instance is Cicero's position unusual in his context. His praise of revenge
belongs in a long tradition, a tradition that, for instance, includes Aristotle,
who writes,

> to take vengeance on one's enemies in nobler than to come to terms with
> them; for to retaliate is just and that which is just is noble; and furthermore, a
> courageous man ought not to allow himself to be beaten. (Aristotle, *Rhetoric*
> 1.9; trans. Freese 1926: 97)[33]

---

33. While on the topic of Aristotle and violence, it might be worth noting that he
claims: "Generally speaking, all that is deliberately chosen is good. Now, men deliberately choose to do the things just mentioned, and those which are harmful to their
enemies, and advantageous to their friends and things that are possible" (Aristotle,
Rhetoric 1.6; trans. Freese 1926: 67). This statement is part of a long tradition of Greeks
praising the virtue of helping friends and harming enemies, a tradition that Mary Blundell
(1989) has collected an impressive amount of material about, demonstrating that the
fulfillment of either element of this virtue could be praised where the failure to fulfill
either element was reason for reproach. While most of Blundell's material comes from
before the period from which this parable emerged, she contends that in Greece "these
fundamental principles surface continually from Homer onwards and survive well into
the Roman period" (1989: 26). In fact, a version of this basic formulation can be found in
Matthew's Sermon on the Mount in which Jesus says, "You have heard that it was said,
'You shall love your neighbour and hate your enemy.' But I say to you, Love your
enemies and pray for those who persecute you" (Matt 5:43–44, NRSV). Matthew's Jesus
rejects this formulation but it is still prevalent enough that he has heard it and assumes
that others have as well. In addition the absoluteness of this rejection has been questioned
by Richard Horsley who notes that "there is no indication in the Gospels that loving one's
enemies had any reference to the Romans" (1987: 150).

More importantly, Cicero's attitude towards bandits is a reaction to a practical concern in the Roman Empire. Richard Shaw argues that banditry permeated the functioning of every level of Roman Society,[34] and John Kloppenborg notes that this includes Galilee,[35] from where, if it belonged to the historical Jesus, this parable would presumably have emerged. Moreover, as Shaw notes, "in the Roman Empire these instruments, in their modern form, of a deep and effective infrastructure of police power (local gendarmeries, solid networks of investigative agencies) simply did not exist" (Shaw 1984: 16). Instead, responses to banditry were, by necessity, often handled at a local level (1984: 16–17). This means that people were obligated to deal with the immediate threats of violence from bandits. Within this sort of practical situation, Cicero's statements seem simply to be sensible, and the claim that the hearers of the Parable of the Assassin might question whether killing was ever acceptable sounds very strange.

Violence was not limited to "illicit" sources either. The Roman Empire was built and maintained through the brutal exertion of military force. Zimmermann notes that "once a war had begun it was waged without restraint. In conquered towns, horrible massacres were purposely executed and the news thereof carefully spread to create fear and terror" (2006: 346). Not only conquest, but also maintenance of conquered territories was maintained by similar methods. As Horsley notes, "they also maintained the *pax Romana* by terror, i.e., by the threat and (when resisted) the use of further massive violence" (1987: 43). If the Parable of the Assassin originated from Galilee, then it came from a location that was involved in violent uprisings against Rome in 4 B.C.E., 66–70 C.E., and 132–135 C.E., and suffered significant violent reprisals from Rome in response.[36] The people of Galilee would have been familiar with the experience of Roman violence, and situated in a context where a radically pacifistic attitude appears difficult to maintain.

The discussion of attitudes towards violence in the Roman Empire could be extended to cover the rhetorical conventions—for example, those

34. Brent Shaw writes, "To judge from a number of 'barometric' readings this residual core of *latrocinium* was a common phenomenon in the societies that constituted the empire in any period one would care to investigate. Just as evidence of slavery can be found in every nook and cranny of Roman social structure and can be seen to affect almost every conceivable type of legal action that the state sanctioned, so too banditry appears as integral to the function of imperial society. Of course, one would not presume to claim that banditry is ubiquitous in the same way as the institution of slavery. Yet much the same resurfacing of the subject in the laws can be discovered" (1984: 8).

35. John Kloppenborg writes, "banditry was endemic to the empire and might reasonably be expected to be a permanent feature of mountainous regions such as Upper Galilee" (2000: 253).

36. A decent summary, particularly of the first two, is offered by Horsley 1987: 49–58.

described by the widely used rhetorical handbook *Ad Herennium*—that advocate the use of violent imagery.[37] It could also be extended to Roman law, which, for example, explicitly relates the possession of land to possession of the force to defend the claim (Kloppenborg 2006: 333–34).[38] Finally it could be extended to art, which often contained quite shocking images of violence.[39] However, this discussion should be sufficient to establish that the violence detected in the language of the Jesus movement should be expected given its broader cultural context, and that it is unlikely that the hearers of this parable would have questioned if killing were ever acceptable. Killing was something that people would have known sometimes needed to be done.

One possible objection to this position would be to claim that Judaism was radically distinct from the rest of Mediterranean culture, and provided the insulation from which the distinct anti-violence and anti-killing attitudes

37. *Ad Herennium* reads, "We ought…to set up images of the kind that can adhere the longest in memory. And we shall do so if we establish likenesses as striking as possible; …if we assign them exceptional beauty or singular ugliness…if we dress some of them with crowns or purple cloaks…or if we somehow disfigure them as, as by introducing one stained with blood or soiled with mud or smeared with red paint, so that its form is more striking" (3.22.37; trans. Caplan 1954: 221). We here return to the question of how the parable is remarkable. While the claims of Hedrick and the Jesus Seminar about the reasons for the remarkability of the parable cannot be sustained, the violence might be remarkable in its ability to attract attention or be particularly memorable.

38. Kloppenborg writes, "Ownership was not merely an abstract legal principle but involved having the *force* required to maintain possession and to repel hostile claims. Both Greek and Roman law observed a distinction between full ownership (*ktēsis, dominium*) and the right to exploit the land (*chrēsis, possessio*), the latter acquired by sale or by occupation and use (*usucapio*, normally over public lands). This distinction created room for contests over possession often involving the use of force" (2006: 333–34).

39. The phenomenon is well documented by Shelby Brown, who writes, "Gladiatorial and venatorial imagery was widespread and available to all social classes. It ranges from prefabricated, standardized representations in inexpensive media, intended for the lower levels of society, to individualized, carefully detailed, and expensive works commissioned by the very wealthy and powerful. Individual combatants as well as groups of gladiators, beast fighters, animals, and equipment were represented in figurines and illustrated on lamps, ceramics, gems, ivories, funerary reliefs, and—with more detail on—architectural reliefs, wall paintings (rarely preserved), and floor mosaics" (1992: 181). Brown has collected and evaluated a significant number of such images, many of which appear, by modern standards, to be quite grotesque. Lest one think that such images would be exclusive to the city of Rome, Brown notes that among the mosaics "some of the best preserved are in North Africa and Gaul" (1992: 182). To understand the significance of this in terms of perceptions of violence in antiquity, Brown suggests: "If one considers the likelihood that a rich patron today would choose attractively arranged scenes of the slaughterhouse or repeated images of public execution to decorate the borders or central panel of a living room or dining room rug, one can indeed see that social context is crucial" (1992: 197).

of this parable emerged. However, this does not seem to be the case. Even aside from ideological convictions, banditry and Roman Imperial violence were present in Galilee, and created material conditions where such ideology would be difficult to maintain. In addition, while Hedrick depends on the biblical prohibitions against homicide to illustrate how shocking the image of killing in this parable would have been (Gen 9:5; Exod 20:13; Deut 5:17), the frequent scriptural calls for outright genocide against the enemies of Israel show that the laws against homicide were not meant to apply to outsiders (Num 21:1–3; 31:13–18; 33:55; Deut 2:26–35; 7:1–6; 12:13–18; 20:1–18; Josh 7–8; Judg 11:31; 1 Sam 15:3).

In addition, there are several biblical cases in which individual homicides are positively evaluated. Hedrick (2011: 3048–49) proposes a number of possible comparisons that might occur to the mind of the parable's hearers when considering whether killing could ever be justified. He discusses Jael's killing of Sisera (Judg 4:17–31), Judith's killing of Holofernes (Jdt 13), Moses' killing of an Egyptian who was beating one of his kinfolk (Exod 2:11–14), and Abraham's willingness to sacrifice Isaac (Gen 22). Another story that should be considered here is that of Phinehas, who, seized by zeal, killed an Israelite man and a Midianite woman for having sex, and thus earned high praise from God and a perpetual priesthood for his family (Num 25:6–13). What makes the story of Phinehas significant is that, as John Collins (2003) has observed, it has often been used to legitimate violence, and Hellenistic Jewish authors are among those who have done so. For example, Philo considers that Phinehas's spontaneous actions should serve as an example to anyone who sees an insult to God's honour (*Special Laws* I, 54–57; trans. Colson 1937: 129–33).[40] Phinehas, therefore, serves as a

---

40.   The full passage from Philo reads: "but if any members of the nation betray the honour due to the One they should suffer the utmost penalties. They have abandoned their most vital duty, their service in the ranks of piety and religion, have chosen darkness in preference to the brightest light and blindfolded the mind which had the power of keen vision. And it is well that all who have a zeal for virtue should be permitted to exact the penalties offhand and with no delay, without bringing the offender before jury or council or any kind of magistrate at all, and full scope to the feelings which possess them, that hatred of evil and love of God which urges them to inflict punishment without mercy on the impious. They should think that the occasion has made them councilors, juryman, high sheriffs, members of the assembly, accusers, witnesses, laws, people, everything in fact, so that without fear or hindrance they may champion religion in full security. There is recorded in the Laws the example of one who acted with this admirable courage. He had seen some persons consorting with foreign women and through the attraction of their love-charms spurning their ancestral customs and seeking admission to the rites of a fabulous religion. In particular he saw, the chief ringleader of the backsliding, who had the audacity to exhibit his unholy conduct in public and was openly offering sacrifices, a travesty of the name, to images of wood and stone in the presence of the whole people.

clear example of a scriptural hero, who acts spontaneously to kill and whose actions Hellenistic Jewish authors take as an example that murder can sometimes be justified.

The Parable of the Assassin, despite its common name, does not necessarily refer to an assassin. It refers to a man who wants to kill a powerful man. No motive is given, making this a useless parable for posing questions of morality. Could the man have had a perfectly good reason? Perhaps the powerful man is a bandit, or a foreign enemy, or perhaps he has insulted the honor of God. To a first-century hearer, these would have been more practical than abstract concerns.[41] Moral justifications would have been easily imaginable. In addition, while the violence of the parable may have had some rhetorical impact, this violence would not have been heard as particularly distinctive given the significant amount of other violent imagery in the Jesus tradition and the level of violence that pervaded ancient Mediterranean society. In this respect, the arguments of Hedrick and the Jesus Seminar cannot be maintained. The violence of this parable is not special and an historically responsible interpretation of this parable should be one that treats the violence as unremarkable. Ultimately, I will attempt such an interpretation, but first, given the degree to which the treatments of this parable do not hold up under even a surface examination, the question should be raised of whether there are deeper motives underlying the scholarship that has drawn these conclusions.

3. Contemporary Motives for the Concern with Violence

Introducing a collection on violence in the New Testament, Shelly Matthews and E. Leigh Gibson remark that "Marcion's second-century distinction between the God of the Old Testament as responsible for violence and vengeance and the God of the New Testament as a God of mercy and love looms large in the consciousness of the West" (Matthews and Gibson 2005: 1). While an increasing awareness of the complexities of the Jewish tradition

So, seized with inspired fury, keeping back the throng of spectators on either side, he slew without qualm him and her, the man because he listened to lessons which it were a gain to unlearn, the woman because she had been the instructor in wickedness. This deed suddenly wrought in the heat of excitement acted as a warning to multitudes who were preparing to make the same apostasy. So then God, praising his high achievement, the result of zeal self-prompted and whole hatred, crowned him with a twofold award, the gifts of peace and priesthood, the first because He judged the champion who had battled for the honour of God worthy to claim a life free from war, the second because the guardian most suitable of piety is the priestly office."

41. In the present day, violence has not disappeared, but has been transformed, and appears less explicit. See Michel Foucault's *Discipline and Punish* (1995).

would prevent most scholars from *uncritically* holding the first part of the Marcionite logic, there seems to have been little critical reflection on violence in the New Testament. For instance, one of the biggest names in Historical Jesus studies can write, "it is not the violent but the nonviolent God who is revealed to Christian faith in Jesus of Nazareth" (Crossan 2007: 95), and that

> God's nonviolent justice confronts the normalcy of human civilization's violent injustice at a very specific time and place. The time is the 20s of the first common-era century, and the place is the twin territories ruled by Herod Antipas. (2007: 111)

Seeing Jesus' message as a breakthrough of peace into the world, even if the background of this world is more sophisticated than the popular under-standing of Marcionite logic, is still a norm both inside and outside of the academy.[42]

Richard Horsley (2005: 51) attributes this norm to a series of linked anachronistic assumptions. These include an individualistic perspective which understands Jesus as "an individual who taught other individuals," thereby focusing on images of Jesus as teacher. They also include a defini-tion of religion that opposes religion to politics, and thus, "with Jesus cate-gorized as religious, it was assumed that his teaching pertained to individual faith and religious ethics, not political and economic affairs" (2005: 51). Horsley argues that this position is linked to the foundation of modern biblical scholarship in Europe during the colonial period, and to Christian support for the maintenance of the Imperial project:

> the portrayal of Jesus as a sober advocate of nonresistance in opposition to revolutionary violence of "the Zealots" thus perpetuated the Western Christian appeal to Jesus' teaching of "love your enemy" as a device to suppress resistance to western domination. (Horsley 2005: 52)

The criticism of the non-violent vision of Jesus does not *need* to be seen as an attack on the ethics of the Christian tradition. From an ethical perspec-tive, this criticism *can* be understood as an attempt to recover the right for Christians to oppose injustice.

It is possible to expand on Horsley's claim that a particular definition of religion, one that excludes violent acts, is a contributing factor to the neglect of violence in studies of early Christianity. One might further

---

42. When I say the popular version of Marcion's logic, I refer to the version that Matthews and Gibson (2005: 1, 10) provide and which became common sense to many subsequent Christians. Marcion's own views towards Judaism should themselves proba-bly be seen as more sophisticated than the position here discussed.

suggest that maintaining a non-violent image of early Christianity is part of maintaining a certain definition of legitimate religion. Bruce Lincoln writes that:

> Confronted with the disquieting reality of religious conflict, popular wisdom typically comforts itself with the ironist's refrain: "how sad to see wars in the name of religion, when all religions preach peace." However well intentioned such sentiments may be, they manage to ignore the fact that virtually all religions allow for the righteous use of violence under certain circumstances. (Lincoln 1998: 65)[43]

As Lincoln notes, the idea that violence is a corruption of religion presupposes a particular, unsustainable, and normative view of religion. Since early Christianity is understood as the prototype for modern Christianity, which is in turn taken as the normative prototype for religion, early Christianity would, of course, *need* to be nonviolent in order to maintain the chain of prototypes that have established this idea of religion.[44] However, as Lincoln notes, this view of religion does not reflect most actual religious systems. Instead, it has the effect of restricting what sorts of "religious" discourses are legitimate. Since early Christianity is so closely linked to certain normative understandings of religion and since violence is excluded from these definitions, it makes sense that these definitional lenses might impair the observation of violence in early Christianity.

Of course, like all correlations of social effects with scholarly construction, it is necessary to be careful about identifying individual motives. It would be difficult, for example, to accuse Crossan of supporting the imperial project.[45] What is identified here are complexes of ideas that in various particulars can support the idea of a non-violent Jesus movement, and in other discursive contexts can support certain regimes of power. The contention that these complexes exist is strongly supported by the extent to which the denials of violence in early Christianity have misread the evidence; something other than dispassionate inquiry must be at work here.

---

43. Lincoln further suggests that scholarly analyses following this trend "rest on an understanding of what constitutes religion that is simultaneously idealized and impoverished: a 'Protestant' view that takes beliefs and moral injunctions (such as those that normally inhibit conflict) to be the essence of the religious, while ignoring most other aspects that might be included" (1998: 65).

44. On the role of religion as a prototype, see Smith 2004.

45. In fact, the quotations taken from him arguing for the peaceful nature of Jesus are drawn from a book, the stated aim of which is to oppose modern imperialism (Crossan 2007).

4. Why Violence Is Nothing Special but Is Central[46]

The violence of the Parable of the Assassin is not remarkable in the way that Hedrick or the Jesus Seminar have argued. It would not have been so shocking to a society utterly used to homicide that it would have triggered questions about whether killing was ever acceptable. Neither is it so out of place in the Jesus tradition that its distinctiveness becomes a powerful argument for, or against, its authenticity. The violence of the parable is not special, but the parable is still about violence. It is about a person, who, for motives that are never stated, wants to kill, strikes the walls of his house, and then slays a powerful man. The narrative of the parable is a series of violent desires and deeds.

The question, then, is how to understand the parable without relying on anachronistic understandings of violence. One promising interpretation emerges from Hedrick's reading of the parable as a violation of common sense, where the unprepared man succeeds against a stronger adversary without adequate preparation. Considering that stories of reversal which undermine conventional wisdom or social norms are characteristic of the parables,[47] the difference in social status should be seen as more significant than the victory's improbability. The parable uses a simple example to show how artificial the difference in conventional power ultimately is; status offers no protection against the strong blow of a sword. In fact, any initial assumptions about the improbability of success are ultimately called into question. What defense is eminence against a sword? As in the Parable of the Rich Fool, death evens out differences in social status (Luke 12:16–21; *Thomas* 63). The Assassin takes this image to an even further extreme, as does *Thomas*'s version of the Parable of the Tenants (*Thomas* 65): not only will the rich man eventually die and his riches then be meaningless, but even someone of lower class can potentially conquer a powerful man through a simple act of physical strength, which is the only qualification that the "assassin" apparently has. This serves as an illustration of the artificiality of conventional power positions. Importantly, this interpretation falls squarely within the expected range of themes associated with the parabolic genre.

In the spirit of Wiebe's project, it is worth trying to understand this parable's violence more thoroughly by turning to general theories of violence in religion. While the above interpretation suggests a reasonable literary interpretation, general theories allow for situating the parable in broader patterns

---

46. This title is a play on the title of an excellent essay by Maurice Bloch ("Why Religion Is Nothing Special but Is Central," 2008), who will be the subject of much of the discussion in this section. It is worth noting that I first read this essay and encountered Maurice Bloch in a class taught by Don Wiebe.

47. See, for example, Crossan 1973 and Scott 1990.

of religiosity. There have been several general theories that have tried to understand the role of violence in religion, not by seeing violence as deviant, but rather by claiming that "blood and violence lurk fascinatingly at the heart of religion" (Burkert 1983: 2). Such theories can serve as an important corrective to the idea that legitimate religion is opposed to violence. The two most famous such theories have probably been those of René Girard (1979) and Walter Burkert (1983, 1996). However, the theories of Maurice Bloch may provide more leverage here, because they do not require the contentious claim that there is an innate propensity towards aggressiveness in human beings that must be regulated through certain forms of ritual and myth. Instead, Bloch observes the function of violence in certain techniques of maintaining essentialised understandings of society (Bloch 1992: 6–7).

Bloch (1992: 2) has formulated a theory of religion primarily intended to describe ritual, but transposable onto a variety of myths and practices not traditionally understood as ritual. Bloch's model was originally derived from the fundamental structures that he observed in the Merina circumcision ritual, but he found that it could be generalized to describe certain "minimal religious structures" which appeared with a "startling quasi-universality" (1992: 3; 1986). In order to explain the presence of these minimal structures, Bloch observes that "the vast majority of societies represent human life as occurring within a permanent framework which transcends the natural trans-formative process of birth, growth, reproduction, ageing and death" (1992: 3). However, it is necessary to negotiate this imagined permanent reality with experiences of change and transformation. This is accomplished through a process that asserts the hierarchal superiority of the imagined permanent world over the transactional and changing world through a three-stage procedure (1992: 4).[48]

The first stage of Bloch's minimal structure is "initial violence" in which the religious actor is conquered by the transcendental and unchanging world. The changing vitality of life is surrendered for an unchanging transcendental world, often through ritual action that requires an attack on this native vitality. In the second stage, having relinquished the vitality and processes of life, one becomes "able to see oneself as being part of something permanent, therefore, life transcending" (Bloch 1992: 4). However, the actor can neither remain outside of life, nor return unchanged, since neither option would allow negotiation between the transcendental and the transactional to actually occur. Therefore, in the third and most important part of Bloch's model, the return to everyday life must be itself one of conquest. Bloch calls this conquest "rebounding violence." Within this rebounding violence, it is "not the home-grown native vitality which was discarded in the first part of

48. The word "transactional" is not original to Bloch's *Prey into Hunter* (1992), but adapted from "Why Religion is nothing Special but Central" (2008).

the rituals that is regained, but, instead, a conquered vitality obtained from other beings" (1992: 5). Via this substitution of vitality conquered by the returning transformed subject for the original native vitality, the hierarchical superiority of the transcendental world is asserted.[49]

This brief description should be inadequate to persuade most readers of the quasi-universal applicability of Bloch's model. Additionally, the Parable of the Assassin does not perfectly conform to this model. However, whether or not the full force of Bloch's model is accepted, it provides an opportunity for comparison. What is important is that the parable has significant points of correspondence with a pattern of depictions of violence that Bloch identifies in a wide variety of religious sources. This further implies that the violence of this parable should not be understood as something special, but instead as in continuity with a wide range of religious phenomena. If this comparison also provides suggestions about possible deeper structures underlying the parable, all the better.

Bloch's theory draws attention to the dual movement of conquest in the parable. The initial violence is directed at the protagonist's own house. The societies of the ancient Mediterranean tended to be focused on collectives rather than individuals, and employed the idea of the house as a particularly strong center for organizing human collectives (Moxnes 2003: 22–45). The man has thus attacked one of the focal points around which his identity would have been located. Despite the place of the house in ancient society, it was notably denigrated in the Jesus tradition and the *Gospel of Thomas* (Moxnes 2003).[50] Having attacked a central, but negatively evaluated, source of vitality, the man is transformed. Now he has knowledge of the strength of his hand and perhaps of the meaninglessness of his opponent's power in

---

49. Bloch writes that "an image is created in which humans can leave this life and join the transcendental, yet still not be alienated from the here and now. They become part of permanent institutions, and as superior beings they can incorporate the present life through the idiom of conquest and consumption" (1992: 5). It should be noted that while this process plays a role in the acceptance of the transcendental social, it does not need to be an acceptance of particular pieces of social information. In fact, religious activity often involves symbols that are vague in meaning. Bloch proposes a model that "instead of being embarrassed about this vagueness, makes it a central concern" (2004: 66). The very vagueness of the symbols functions in such a way that the participant defers to traditional concepts without fully understanding them. This deference serves as a preparation for the way life must actually be lived, since "people are almost conscious of the fact that they are constantly relying on the understanding of others and that they normally act in terms of beliefs they do not fully understand, but which they hold valid because of their trust in the understanding of others" (2004: 77). Thus ritual does not necessarily serve as a form of intellectual assent to particular points, but to a category of general possibilities, with details that can be filled in later.

50. See for example *Thomas* 16, quoted above.

relation to the strength of his hand. Given this knowledge he is able to project his power outward and conquer the powerful man. While the parable should probably not be read allegorically as referring to the violent conquering of one vision of the world by another, except perhaps at an explicitly structurally reductionist level,[51] it is important to note that it has correspondences to a pattern of depictions of violence that Bloch finds in a wide variety of myths and rituals.

Reading the parable by following Hedrick and expanding further on its socio-economic implications shows that the Assassin can be interpreted within the range of meanings normally associated with the parabolic genre. In this interpretation, the violence of the parable is used to make the point that the disparity between rich and poor can be easily bridged. All it takes is a single act of violence from a strong poor man, and he can conquer a "powerful man." The violence of the parable is central to its expression, but is not strange in terms of the attitudes towards violence in the Jesus movement.

Reading the parable by following Bloch and comparing its structure to his model shows that the Assassin's violence has notable similarities to general patterns of violence in a variety of religious traditions. This reading has consequences for the issue that I have argued underlies much of the failure of nerve to treat violence in early Christianity: the conflict with a normative definition that excludes violence from being conceivable as part of religion. The comparison with Bloch's patterns opposes the implications of this definition. The violence of the Parable of the Assassin is not strange as part of a religious expression; it displays a structure similar to a broad range of religious expressions.

References

Aristotle. 1926. *The "Art" of Rhetoric.* Loeb Classical Library, Aristotle. Trans. John Henry Freese. Cambridge, MA: Harvard University Press.

Arnal, William. 2005. *The Symbolic Jesus: Historical Scholarship, Judaism, and the Construction of Contemporary Identity.* London: Equinox.

Bloch, Maurice. 1986. *From Blessing to Violence: History and Ideology in the Circumcision Ritual of the Merina of Madagascar.* Cambridge: Cambridge University Press.

———. 1992. *Prey into Hunter: The Politics of Religious Experience.* Cambridge: Cambridge University Press.

———. 2004. "Ritual and Deference." In Harvey Whitehouse and James Laidlaw, eds, *Ritual and Memory: Toward a Comparative Anthropology of Religion*, 65–78. Walnut Creek: AltaMira.

———. 2008. "Why Religion Is Nothing Special but Is Central." *Philosophical Transactions of the Royal Society B.* 363: 2055–61.

51. This is what Bloch's model is pointing to. See n. 49.

Blundell, Mary. 1989. *Helping Friends and Harming Enemies: A Study in Sophocles and Greek Ethics*. Cambridge: Cambridge University Press.

Brown, Shelby. 1992. "Death as Decoration: Scenes from the Arena on Roman Domestic Mosaics." In Amy Richlin (ed.), *Pornography and Representation in Greece and Rome*, 180–211. Oxford: Oxford University Press.

Bruce, Frederick F. 1974. *Jesus and Christian Origins Outside the New Testament*. Grand Rapids: Eerdmans.

Burkert, Walter. 1983. *Homo Necans: The Anthropology of Ancient Greek Sacrificial Ritual*. Trans. Peter Bing. Berkley: University of California Press.

———. 1996. *Creation of the Sacred: Tracks of Biology in Early Religions*. Cambridge, MA: Harvard University Press.

Cicero. 1931. *Pro T. Annio Milone, In Calpurnium Pisonem, Pro M. Aemilio Scauro, Pro M. Fonteio, Pro C. Rabirio Postumo, Pro M. Marcello, Pro Q. Ligario, Pro Rege Deiotaro*. Loeb Classical Library, Cicero. Trans. N. H. Watts. Cambridge, MA: Harvard University Press.

———. 1960. *De inventione, De optimo genere oratorum, Topica*. Loeb Classical Library, Cicero. Trans. H. M. Hubbell. Cambridge, MA: Harvard University Press.

"Cicero." 1954. *Rhetorica ad Herennium*. Loeb Classical Library, Cicero. Trans. Harry Caplan. Cambridge, MA: Harvard University Press.

Collins, John. 2003. "The Zeal of Phinehas: The Bible and the Legitimating of Violence." *Journal of Biblical Literature* 122: 3–21.

Crossan, John Dominic. 1973. *In Parables: The Challenge of the Historical Jesus*. New York: Harper & Row.

———. 1985. *Four Other Gospels: Shadows on the Contours of Canon*. Minneapolis: Winston.

———. 2007. *God and Empire: Jesus Against Rome, Then and Now*. San Francisco: HarperSanFrancisco.

Davies, Steven. 2002. *Gospel of Thomas: Annotated and Explained*. Woodstock: SkyLight Paths.

Desjardins, Michel. 1997. *Peace, Violence and the New Testament*. Sheffield: Sheffield Academic.

Doran, Robert. 1987. "A Complex of Parables: GTh 96–98." *Novum Testamentum* 29: 347–52.

Ford, Richard. 2002. "Body Language: Jesus' Parables of the Yeast, Woman with the Jar, and the Man with the Sword." *Interpretation* 56: 295–306.

Foucault, Michel. 1995. *Discipline and Punish: The Birth of the Prison*. Trans. Alan Sheridan. New York: Vintage.

Funk, Robert, Bernard Brandon Scott, James Butz, and the Jesus Seminar. 1988. *The Parables of Jesus: Red Letter Edition*. Sonoma: Polebridge.

Funk, Robert, Roy Hoover, and the Jesus Seminar. 1993. *The Five Gospels: What did Jesus Really Say?* New York: HarperOne.

Girard, René. 1979. *Violence and the Sacred*. Trans. Patrick Gregory. Baltimore: Johns Hopkins University Press.

Grant, Robert. 1960. *The Secret Sayings of Jesus*. Garden City: Doubleday.

Hedrick, Charles. 2011. "Flawed Heroes and Stories Jesus Told: The One About a Killer." In Tom Holmén and Stanley Porter, eds, *Handbook for the Study of the Historical Jesus*, vol. 4, 3023–56. Leiden: E. J. Brill.

Horsley, Richard A. 1987. *Jesus and the Spiral of Violence: Popular Jewish Resistance in Roman Palestine*. San Francisco: Harper & Row.

———. 2005. "'By the Finger of God': Jesus and Imperial Violence." In Shelly Matthews and E. Leigh Gibson, eds, *Violence in the New Testament*, 51–80. New York: T&T Clark.

Horsley, Richard A. and John Hanson. 1999. *Bandits, Prophets, & Messiahs: Popular Movements in the Time of Jesus*. Harrisburg: Trinity Press.

Jeremias, Joachim. 1963. *The Parables of Jesus*. Trans. Samuel Henry Hook. London: SCM.

Kloppenborg, John. 2000. *Excavating Q: The History and Setting of the Sayings Gospel*. Minneapolis: Fortress Press.

———. 2006. *The Tenants in the Vineyard: Ideology, Economics, and Agrarian Conflict in Jewish Palestine*. Tübingen: Mohr Siebeck.

Kloppenborg, John and Callie Callon. 2010. "The Parable of the Shepherd and the Transformation of Pastoral Discourse." *Early Christianity* 1: 218–60.

Koester, Helmut. 1980. "Apocryphal and Canonical Gospels." *Harvard Theological Review* 73: 105–30.

Lincoln, Bruce. 1998. "Conflict." In Mark Taylor (ed.), *Critical Terms for Religious Studies*, 55–69. Chicago: University of Chicago Press.

Lintott, Andrew. 1968. *Violence in Republican Rome*. Oxford: Clarendon.

Mack, Burton. 2001. *The Christian Myth: Origins, Logic, and Legacy*. New York: Continuum.

Malina, Bruce. 2001. *The Social Gospel of Jesus: The Kingdom of God in Mediterranean Perspective*. Minneapolis: Fortress Press.

Matthews, Shelly and E. Leigh Gibson. 2005. "Introduction." In Shelly Matthews and E. Leigh Gibson, eds, *Violence in the New Testament*, 1–10. New York: T&T Clark.

Moxnes, Halvor. 2003. *Putting Jesus in His Place: A Radical Vision of Household and Kingdom*. Louisville: Westminster John Knox.

Pearson, Birger. 1996. "The Gospel According to the Jesus Seminar." *Occasional Papers of the Institute for Antiquity and Christianity* 35. Ed. Jon Ma. Asgeirsson. Claremont: Institute for Antiquity and Christianity.

Philo. 1937. *On the Decalogue, On the Special Laws 1–3*. Loeb Classical Library, Philo 7. Trans. F. H. Colson. Cambridge, MA: Harvard University Press.

Riley, Gregory. 1995. *Resurrection Reconsidered: Thomas and John in Controversy*. Minneapolis: Fortress Press.

Scott, Bernard Brandon. 1990. *Hear Then the Parable: A Commentary on the Parables of Jesus*. Minneapolis: Fortress Press.

Shaw, Brent. 1984. "Bandits in the Roman Empire." *Past and Present* 105: 3–52.

Smith, Jonathan Z. 1990. *Drudgery Divine: On the Comparison of Early Christianities and the Religions of Late Antiquity*. Chicago: University of Chicago Press.

———. 2004. "God Save this Honorable Court: Religion and Civic Discourse." In *Relating Religion: Essays in the Study of Religion*, 375–90. Chicago: University of Chicago Press.

Stroker, William. 1988. "Extracanonical Parables and the Historical Jesus." *Semeia* 44: 95–120.

Tite, Philip. 2004. *Conceiving Peace and Violence: A New Testament Legacy*. Dallas: University Press of America.

Valantasis, Richard. 1997. *The Gospel of Thomas.* London: Routledge.

Wiebe, Donald. 1984. "The Failure of Nerve in the Academic Study of Religion." *Studies in Religion / Sciences religieuses* 13: 401–22.

Winterhalter, Robert. 1988. *The Fifth Gospel: A Verse-by-Verse New Age Commentary on the Gospel of Thomas.* San Francisco: Harper & Row.

Zimmermann, Martin. 2006. "Conclusion: Violence in Late Antiquity Reconsidered." In Harold Allen Drake, *Violence in Late Antiquity: Perceptions and Practices*, 343–58. Trans. Claudia Rapp. Hempshire: Ashgate.

REDESCRIBING ICONOCLASM:
HOLEY FRESCOES AND IDENTITY FORMATION

Vaia Touna

> [T]he "critical insider" and "sympathetic outsider" converge, and ought to do so, only on the descriptive level but need not necessarily do so on the explanatory/theoretical level of that study. (Wiebe 1984: 421 **[26]**)

For the last several years I have been the local coordinator for a study abroad trip made by students from the University of Alabama to Thessaloniki, Greece. During the trips we visited many sites of archaeological interest; one such site was a Byzantine church dating to the fourteenth century C.E., located within the old city's walls in the upper part of Thessaloniki. When the students entered the church, the first things that attracted their amazed attention were the pitted frescoes that cover the interior of the church's walls. Their primary (and urgent) question was who damaged the frescoes, and why. For me, by contrast, the church's pitted iconography had become so familiar that I no longer even pondered the damage, and only when prompted by the students' curiosity did I realize that a whole discourse was up and running about the holes in that small church at the top of my city. And so I learned firsthand what Durkheim wrote in *The Elementary Forms of Religious Life* (1995: 54): "Habit easily puts curiosity to sleep and we no longer even imagine querying ourselves. To shake off that torpor, practical needs, or at least very pressing theoretical interest, must attract our attention and turn it in that direction." And if practical needs (i.e., to answer the students' questions) were what first returned the pitted frescoes to my attention, it was theoretical interests that prompted me most emphatically "to shake off that torpor."

1. On the Descriptive Level

For the people who attend this church there is no question that the icons painted onto the walls were damaged during the Ottoman occupation (begun in the fifteenth century C.E. and lasting four centuries, ending in the late nineteenth and early twentieth century), when the church had been turned into a mosque, with the addition of a minaret, and during which time the building had suffered considerable damage. It should be obvious that we have a case of iconoclasm here, i.e., the intentional act of destroying images, especially religious representations. But the characterization of the source of the damage done to the frescoes as iconoclasm is an interpretation and explanation derived entirely from insider descriptions and classifications. Too often, such description/classification is an easy fall-back for the scholar of religion, and comes to be absorbed into his/her theorizing as natural, self-evident and transhistorical. As Don Wiebe reminds us, however, it is precisely at the level of theorization that the outsider must be willing to diverge from the insider's characterization of the data (Wiebe 1984: 421 [26], as per the epigraph of this paper). To address the phenomenon of the pitted walls and the purported iconoclasm behind them, therefore, a critical approach must, as Russell McCutcheon insists, investigate the *uses* to which classificatory systems are put, who they authorize, and what kind of world they presuppose (McCutcheon 2003: 260).

As with every category, icon and iconoclasm have their own history, one that is seldom addressed by historians, who too often take both the entity and the act as natural and obvious. But the meanings of both icon and iconoclasm have changed over time, and in different periods have served different interests. It might be worth asking why the term "icon" and the ideas it represents are retrojected into the past with such ease, as if a linkage to something "sacred" were a consistent and timeless aspect of images and attitudes thereto.

The word "icon" has a definite and relatively recent history in the English language. It derives from the Greek word *eikōn*, and first appears in English in 1572 with the meaning of an image, figure or representation, found mainly in books of natural history (*Oxford English Dictionary* [OED] 1971: 12). By 1577 it can also refer to an image in the solid, a monumental figure or a statue, and as of 1579, a realistic representation or description in writing (OED 1971: 12). The use of the word to refer to a representation of some sacred personage in painting, bas-relief or mosaic is linked to the Eastern Church and is much more recent, first appearing in 1833. "Iconoclasm" (from the words *eikōn* and *klasma*, which means to break), by contrast, had "religious" connotations from the start. It first appears in English in 1797 describing "the breaking or destroying of images; esp. the destruction of images and pictures set up as objects of veneration (see iconoclast I); *transf.* and *fig.* the attacking or overthrow of venerated institutions and cherished beliefs, regarded as fallacious or superstitious" (OED 1971: 13). The doer of such deeds, the iconoclast, appears in English much earlier in 1596 and is specifically linked to ecclesiastical history: "one who took part in or supported the movement in the 8th and 9th centuries, to put down the use of images or pictures in religious worship in Christian churches of the East; hence, applied analogously to those Protestants of the 16th and 17th C. who practiced or countenanced a similar destruction of images in the churches" (OED 1971: 13).

In connection to icons we also have the terms "iconodule" (from *eikōn* and *doulos*, which means slave), someone who worships or venerates images; "iconophile" (from the words *eikōn* and *philos*, which means friend), a connoisseur of pictures, engravings, book illustrations and the like (in Greek the term has the meaning of someone who worships or venerates images); and the opposing "iconomach" (from the words *eikōn* and *machos*, which means fighting), one who is hostile to images. This last appears in English in 1552 (OED 1971: 13). Another term that is synonymous with iconoclasm is "iconomachy," defined as "a war against images; hostility or opposition to images, esp. to their use in connexion to worship," and which appears in English in 1581 (OED 1971: 13).

What this brief survey shows is that at least when it comes to icons, "sacredness" is not inherent in the term but was later imputed to it. It might be worth asking by whom and when such a quality was attributed to the cluster of ideas associated with "images." Was the attribution of "sacred" qualities associated with the defense or justification of specific historical activities? Attention should also be given to the terms iconomachos/iconoclast and iconodoulos/iconophilos—it should be noted that in Greek dictionaries the terms iconoclast and iconodoulos are defined as pejorative and ideologically charged terms used to characterize the iconomachos and iconophilos accordingly.

For many historians the terms are used so naturally—a naturalization that seems to transcend time and space—that the same conceptions are applied with ease to radically different historical periods. The iconoclastic controversies of the seventh and eighth centuries in the East are explained as being the result of theological debates: the *iconomachoi* or "iconoclasts" destroyed icons because according to their theology divinity should not be represented, and thus the veneration of these icons was deemed idolatrous; on the other hand, the *iconophiloi* or *iconodouloi* believe that they are not adoring the medium, but the idea it represents. A similarly theological reading is applied to controversies in the Muslim world (both internal and in conversation with Christianity), and again to the Reformation in sixteenth- and seventeenth-century Europe. In all three cases, the incidents are viewed and explained in terms of people's beliefs about and attitudes toward the icon as a symbol that represents some inner quality or concept. Iconoclasm emerges as a transhistorical essence that slowly unfolds over time. Consider, for example, Alain Besançon's approach to iconoclasm in *The Forbidden Image: An*

Intellectual History of Iconoclasm (2009). His history of iconoclasm begins in ancient Greece with the rise of philosophy, which, according to Bensançon, was intrinsically profane, and so exhibited an intrinsic iconoclastic tendency in tension with theology, which, of course, is intrinsically concerned with the "sacred" and so is iconophilic. In both "paganism" and Christianity these two opposed systems of thought—philosophy and theology—have been in constant conflict. Within Christianity, which was influenced by Greek philosophy, there were also iconoclastic inclinations, but the iconophiles' theology prevailed. It is clear that Besançon sees the concept of iconoclasm as transcending time and space, which thus allows him to draw lines all the way from the ancient Greeks to present forms of artistic iconoclasm. In all of the discussion, the focus of analysis is on the sacralization or desacralization of the object and the theological debates of those concerned.

As a result of focusing merely on ideological disagreement, both historical and theological approaches to iconoclasm are left unable to explain what is at stake in the active destruction of images even when the images in question are considered to be "sacred." The main object of study has been the attempt to retrieve the *meaning of the icon*, both for those who are supposed to be destroying images, and for those who adore, respect or venerate them. This approach is no different from the effort to retrieve the meaning of a text. Insufficient attention is given to the effects of the discourses that surround such activity, including the historical and/or theological discourse on iconoclasm itself, and the way that such a discourse impels a real or imaginative interest in *restorations*, including both the active renovation of the object to its "original" state and the process of creating a narrative to account for the loss of that "original" state.

Bruce Lincoln has rightly observed in *Discourse and the Construction of Society* that:

> no act of iconoclasm is ever carried out with the intent of destroying an icon's sacred power, for iconoclasts—who are regularly estranged from their adversaries on lines of class, politics, or national origin as well as those of religion—act with the assurance either that the specific image under attack has no such power or the more radical conviction that there is no such thing as sacred power. It is their intent to demonstrate dramatically and in public the *powerlessness* of the image and thereby to inflict a double disgrace on its champions, first by exposing the bankruptcy of their vaunted symbols and, second, their impotence in the face of attack. (1989: 120)

I contend, however, that the public display Lincoln refers to is useful for *both* parties to the conflict, and can be applied to myths at the core of *both* groups' identity—the communal identity that is so closely intertwined with the writing of history.

I return, then, to the holey frescoes found in the church (specifically the *Katholikon*, i.e., the central church) of the fourteenth-century Vlatadon Monastery in Thessaloniki. According to a book published by the monastery (*The Holy Royal Patriarchal and Stavropegic Monastery of Vlatadon*, 1999), there was a Christian church on this site from earliest times. Citing "unbroken oral tradition," the book asserts that it was here that the Apostle Paul preached to the Thessalonians during his second missionary journey in 51 C.E. (The Monastery of Vlatadon 1999: 8). It is said that the monastery owes its name to its founders, the brothers Dorotheos and Markos Vlattis (students of Saint Gregory Palamas, who is also known for defending the hesychasts), and was dedicated to the Transfiguration of the Savior. The Monastery is called "royal" because it was established by a grant from Empress Anna Palaiologina (Anna of Savoy), probably in 1354. Another name for the monastery, used during the period of Ottoman rule and still by many Thessalonians today, is *Tsaous Manastir*; this nomenclature likely dates back to the first Ottoman capture of Thessaloniki in 1387, at which time a guard-post must have been established at the monastery. The commander of the guard-post, a *tsaus* ("commander" in Turkish) was thus linked to the monastery's name (The Monastery of Vlatadon 1999: 18–19).[1]

The church building in which the pitted frescoes are found is a domed cruciform with peristyle, i.e., the shape of the cross is inscribed in a square, while the dome is supported on four columns. This architectural style belongs to the period when monasticism was flourishing in Thessaloniki, and the church is in fact the only one of the monastery's buildings that has survived (albeit with certain later alterations) from the Byzantine era and from the monastery's original structure, dating to around 1350. Alterations to the church first occurred at the time of the first capture of Thessaloniki by the Ottomans (1387), when it was, like many Christian churches in lands taken over by Muslims, converted into a mosque. It is worth quoting in full how the monastery's own history describes the alterations made to the church at this time:

> Two modifications were slight from a technical point of view: a) the hollow-ing out of a shallow recess in the center of the arch of the sanctuary to show the direction of Mecca (i.e., a *mihrab*); b) the creation of a pointed arch at the edge of the eastern vault, above the iconostas; c) one modification was signifi-cant: all the interior walls were covered with plaster which meant that the wall paintings were badly damaged with hammer blows which served to roughen the walls so the plaster would stick. (The Monastery of Vlatadon 1999: 28)

1. Other accounts exist of the origin of the monastery's name. According to one story, an individual named Tsaus destroyed the church. After doing so he became ill, but had a dream in which an old man promised to cure him if he would restore the damaged church. This Tsaus did as he was told and he got well.

Of these three alterations, the book draws special attention to the hammered frescoes and how they were badly damaged and covered with plaster. It is noteworthy that the icons, for some reason, were subsequently left covered with plaster despite the fact that in 1401 the Ottomans cancelled the sequestration of the monastery because it had been proclaimed Patriarchal (rather than exclusively royal),[2] and thus was returned to the Ecumenical Partriarchate of Constantinople. The monastery's church then remained under Patriarchal influence even when in 1430 Thessaloniki was captured for the second time, and to this day.

The book also records that over the years the church has been "renovated" three times. The first was in 1801, probably because parts of the exterior walls on the north and west sides collapsed; in this renovation, according to an inscription found inside the church, the building is characterized as "erected for a second time." A second renovation took place at the beginning of the twentieth century, as recorded by an inscription on a marble plaque located above the west door of the *Katholikon*. The third renovation, of particular interest for this chapter, took place in 1982, in response to the effects of a large earthquake that struck Thessaloniki in 1978. It was during this third renovation that the pitted frescoes were discovered (The Monastery of Vlatadon 1999: 19). According to the Byzantologist Chrysanthe Marvorpoulou Tsiume, who studied the wall paintings of the *Katholikon* after the removal of the Ottoman plaster, the paintings date to the end of the fourteenth and the beginning of the fifteenth centuries C.E., and thus had been covered for several centuries. According to the book:

> Apart from the purely technical measures which were taken and which were aimed at strengthening the walls of the church, the Department of Byzantine Antiquities of Thessaloniki attempted partially to restore it to its former state. Thus, the lime plaster on the outside surfaces of the interior north and west sides was removed, while the south wall was restored to its original form. The old elegance of the church is not yet evident, of course, but it is hinted at in a satisfactory manner by the wall-paintings. (The Monastery of Vlatadon 1999: 30)

Judging by the way local people talk about the church's damaged wall paintings today, there is no doubt that we have an act of iconoclasm, as iconoclasm is described by the *Encyclopedia of Religion*: "The intentional desecration or destruction of works of art, especially those containing human figuration, on religious principles or beliefs" (Apostolos-Cappadana 2005: 4279). According to such an understanding, the religious disputes/differences between "us" (Greeks, Orthodox Christians) and "them" (Turks,

2. According to the Ottoman law, whatever belonged to the former king after the capture of a city became the property of the Sultan.

Muslims or the heterodox) was the cause of this act of iconoclasm, and was what motivated the Ottoman iconoclast. Such an approach reasserts the status of the icons as sacred, explains the fact that they were only "partially" restored (in order to preserve their prior sacredness) and duplicates insiders' understanding of the icons as a link between their identity and that of past Greeks.

The trouble with such an approach, however, is that it does little more than reproduce the claims of the insiders: iconoclasm is the result of social conflict and an intentional act against religious symbols, evidence of conflicting religious beliefs, and aims to strip the icons of their sacred value. Such a perspective does not recognize that an act against a collective symbol might have no religious motivation/intention whatsoever. For example, if we carefully look at the two discourses on the holes that I have so far described—the common folk discourse on the holes, offered by the people who attend the church, and then also the more technical folk discourse, from the monastery's book—we will notice that there is a curious gap between the two, and that they contradict one another, at least partly. For the people who attend this church, the holes are clearly the product of the intentionality of the "infidels," while the monastery's book describes the act's origins in a very mundane way: "to roughen the walls so the plaster would stick" (The Monastery of Vlatadon 1999: 28). Could it be, then, that the holes were simply made for the purely pragmatic purpose of holding plaster more securely to the walls, and thus reflect *no* iconoclastic intentionality? Even if there was some specific motivation or symbolic intent behind the damage done to the pitted frescoes, it has long been lost to historical research. Therefore to try to explain the holes in terms of "origins" and "intentionality" would be in vain—especially considering how problematic the term "intentionality" is among scholars of literature.

Perhaps, however, trying to grasp the intention of the doer is not the only way to look at the issue: instead, we might shift our attention from the thing itself to its function and effect for those who use the pitted walls symbolically. The "origins" of the pitted icons and the theological disputes over orthodoxy vs. heterodoxy would not be under discussion if they did not serve some discursive interests today. Instead of asking about the motives behind iconoclasm's damage, my interest, rather, focuses on what restorations create. Do restorations try to restore the church to its "original form," as the book claims? And if so, then which is its original form: the state of the church in 1350, or in 1801 when it was "erected for the second time"? These questions of originality and authenticity, however, are best left to theologians or historians.

2. On the Explanatory Theoretical Level

The history of the icons on the interior walls of the church stopped abruptly sometime around fourteenth century C.E., when they were hammered and covered with plaster, and for more than six centuries the iconography literally did not exist. Thus the meaning the iconography might once have had, or what people's perception of the frescoes might once have been, has been equally lost. So in 1982, when the archaeologists and art restorers carefully removed the plaster, they discovered—or better, *created*—these holey icons. The restorers had to clean the plaster out of each hole, and thus manufactured a totally new symbol system around which, or upon which, a new discourse was made possible concerning the group's identity. For this was now a group of modern citizens of Greece, freed from Ottoman rule, and for whom this freedom had been purchased only a few generations before (i.e., in 1912 at the start of the 1912–1913 Balkan Wars). Furthermore the latest "restorations" of the church, according to the book, "partially restored" both its interior and exterior walls. It seems that restorations must work only up to a certain point, a point where it would still be allowable for members of a contemporary group, in this case Greek Christians, to claim continuity over time. The restorers, therefore, needed to leave enough traces (i.e. the holey icons/holes) in order to allow members of the group to develop a narrative that could, in the words of Mary Douglas, "impose system on an inherently untidy experience" (2002: 5). In this case, the systematization made possible by the holey icons serves a discourse on origins, authenticity, and identity for modern Greeks.

In particular, we should understand this new symbol system (i.e. the "restored" holey icons) as a part of a discourse on social "trauma"—an experience that puts a person or a group in a state of extreme confusion and prompts insecurity about identity, such as a foreign invasion or occupation. Long after the source of the confusion is gone, its traces are still on public display. The recurring trauma, made possible in part by the continually present discourse on the holey icons, becomes the occasion for members of a group to reunite and redefine themselves by sharing the same memories and seeing their group's identity as different from, and opposed by, some "other," and thus as distinctive. Moreover, according to Durkheim, it is a way for groups that are always on the brink of breaking up to experience collective agreement and social coherence, for the displayed "trauma" is a reminder of how things could be different.

Thus in contrast to the *Encyclopedia of Religion*'s approach to icons, the symbol in and of itself does not have a substance, or a meaning that transcends time. Instead, its meaning is historically conditioned, and it changes over time according to the way people understand themselves and engage with the symbol. Folk discourses about the holey icons portray for the group how "they" have suffered; in other words, the discourse on the damaged wall paintings is nothing other than the discourse on modern Greek identity, for which Christian Orthodoxy has played an important role. Though the Church does not have official political power, it can claim to understand and represent national interests in some cases even better than the state, and in this way to gain popular allegiance. The holey icons are therefore a useful tool, one that allows the Church to portray itself as the site where traces of Greek national identity can be found.

To press this point a little bit further, one might say that, seen in this light, the holey icons function just like any other tragic memorial, whether a war memorial or some other symbol that bears scars around which groups may construct a common sympathy. Take, for example, another of Thessaloniki's landmarks, the "White Tower," a cylindrical building 23 meters (75 feet) in diameter with a height of 27 meters (89 feet), on top of which is a turret 12 meters (39 feet) in diameter and 6 meters (20 feet) high. Originally constructed by the Ottomans to fortify the city's harbor, it became a notorious prison and scene of mass executions of Greeks during the period of Ottoman rule—understandably perhaps, it was known at the time by locals as the "Red Tower." Continuing the symbolism of color, when Greece gained control of the city in 1912, the structure was renamed the "White Tower." Although it may seem too tragic a symbol to serve as a landmark, today it is very much a visual synecdoche of the city, and provides an occasion to strengthen the collective sense of common identity by means of a present discourse on past traumas—just like the holey icons. And because meanings are constantly changing, overlapping previous meanings much like the plaster layers on top of the icons, the White Tower today has also become a symbol around which football (soccer) fans gather to celebrate their teams' victory against their adversaries! To conclude, we may now begin to understand the usefulness of iconoclasm as a way to study the hammered icons, for if we step back we will see in the holey icons a new symbol system being continually re-created, i.e. a social "trauma" comparable to other tragic memorials, and upon which a common memory is re-constructed strongly enough to unite the members of a group and allow them to make claims of authenticity, originality and identity, in order to create the impression of a linear link between their present and their imagined past.

References

Apostolos-Cappadona, Diane. 2005. "Iconoclasm: An Overview." In Lindsay Jones (editor-in-chief), *Encyclopedia of Religion*, 4279–89. 2d ed. Detroit: Thomas Gale.
Besançon, Alain. 2009. *The Forbidden Image: An Intellectual History of Iconoclasm.* Chicago: University of Chicago Press.

Douglas, Mary. 2002. *Purity and Danger: An Analysis of Concept of Pollution and Taboo*. London: Routledge.

Durkheim, Emile. 1995. *The Elementary Forms of Religious Life*. Trans. Karen E. Fields. New York: Free Press.

Lincoln, Bruce. 1989. *Discourse and the Construction of Society: Comparative Studies of Myth, Ritual, and Classification*. New York: Oxford University Press.

McCutcheon, Russell. 2003. *The Discipline of Religion: Structure, Meaning, Rhetoric*. London: Routledge.

The Monastery of Vlatadon. 1999. *The Holy Royal Patriarchal and Stavropegic Monastery of Vlatadon*. Thessaloniki: The Holy Royal Patriarchal and Stavropegic Monastery of Vlatadon.

The Oxford English Dictionary, vol. I–K. 1971. Oxford: Oxford University Press.

Wiebe, Donald. 1984. "The Failure of Nerve in the Academic Study of Religion. *Studies in Religion / Sciences religieuses* 13: 401–22.

IN LIEU OF CONCLUSION

THE IRONY OF RELIGION

William Arnal and Willi Braun

> Know then thyself, presume not God to scan;
> The proper study of mankind is Man. (Alexander Pope 1733–34)

The proper object of Religious Studies is *Religion*, ostensibly a set of human expressions and performances that merits a humanistic or social-scientific analysis in accord with our academic approach to other types of human behaviors. The distinction between Theology, which presumes and addresses supernatural or divine realities, and Religious Studies, which does not, is predicated on this identification of the subject-matter of a secular, or humanistic, or scientific approach to the study of Religion, one which is not required to bow to the dictates of Theology, confessional or otherwise, nor address Theology's subject-matter, nor be bound by Theology's methods.

Yet the contemporary practice and conceptualization of Religious Studies as a field not only distinct from Theology, but a worthy endeavor in its own right and on its own terms, is predicated on a further assumption: that "Religion" is a coherent category in humanistic, social-scientific, or generally non-theological academic terms, that is, an empirical category or a descriptively nominal one. Such a claim is critically necessary for any assertion of Religious Studies *as a discipline*. Disciplinary identity assumes a distinctive approach to a taxonomically coherent entity. The coherence of such entities as "literature," "society," "culture," and "psychology," for example, dictates a distinctive set of tools and approaches that respect the fundamental character of the phenomena that constitute the entity. These distinctive analytic methods ensure that literature is treated *as* literature, society *as* society, and so on, and that the rigorous techniques developed for studying these entities are learned and properly applied by the discipline's trained practitioners. Thus one would expect something similar if Religious Studies is conceived, as it normally and normatively is, as a discipline distinct from Theology.[1]

---

1. See, e.g., Tomoko Masuzawa: "[T]he disciplinary establishment of so-called religious studies, for whatever reason and with whatever justification, seems to hold fast

Here, however, we encounter the monumental *irony* of Religious Studies as a field and as a discipline.[2] "Religion" itself as a framework, a category, and thus as a demarcation for a non-theological discipline (Religious Studies) is defined precisely by its theological content.[3] And hence the futility of its perpetual efforts to distinguish itself from the very discipline—Theology— on which its existence is predicated. Various data that are grouped together by the concept or taxon "Religion" are linked, not by the analytic frameworks specified by humanistic or social-scientific interests, but by the assertions of various theologians and other religious practitioners that the objects in question have a claim to ultimacy or transcendence. The difference between Macbeth, which is a *literary* datum, and the Gospel of Matthew, which is a *religious* datum, is simply that the former is assumed to be *merely* literature, while the latter is taken by Christians to be somehow *more than* or *other than* literature. The creation of a field devoted to a set or class of sacred objects that are defined by their *extra* quality (*extra*-social, *extra*-anthropological, *extra*-empirical, *extra*-historical, *extra*-ordinary) is simply a restatement of their sacrality—i.e., their difference from other objects and their incommensurability with ordinary objects—and thus represents a religious or theological *practice*.[4] It does not matter whether we in Religious Studies orient ourselves to "scientific" *explanation* of religion, or to a more interpretative goal of *understanding* religion; it does not matter whether we accede to the specific dogmatic claims made for religious objects. In explaining or interpreting or describing religion, we are drawing a circle around a class of objects that devotees have identified as sacred, and we are asserting that they are indeed a distinct class, and, hence, that they *are*

---

to this bottom line: Religion is found everywhere; it is an essential and irreducible aspect of human life; it should be studied" (2005: 317).

2.   The emphasis on irony here is a (friendly) reorientation of the use of the term by Donald Wiebe (1991). Wiebe argues that Theology is an ironic discipline, applying the techniques of reason to the fundamentally irrational or "primitive" mental processes of Religion. Theology thus is a rational Trojan Horse in the walls of religion. With Wiebe, however, the irony is standing on its head. It must be turned right side up again.

3.   Leaving aside the historical *origins* of the concept, on which see especially Jonathan Z. Smith 2004. For the argument that Religion is a modern and Christian-derived category, see Asad 1993. For the claim that Religion as a taxon in its modern form is a fundamentally political category, see Arnal 2000, 2001. Recently, Daniel Boyarin has argued that "Religion," while a Christian construct, is not a product of the early modern period, but of late antiquity (2004: 11–17, 203–204).

4.   This is in fact Durkheim's definition of religion in *Les formes élémentaires de la vie religieuse* (1968 [1912]: 50–57): the practice of religion is the set of practices involved with this more or less arbitrary segregation of some objects as aspects of the realm of the sacred that is set apart from the realm of the profane.

sacred.[5] This is why the most robust effort to date to establish a *discipline* of Religious Studies—that of Mircea Eliade—is so justly accused of partici-pating in theological discourse in orienting our study to "the Sacred" (see McCutcheon 1997, 2003). Even the constitution of "religions" or "religious traditions" as our field's primary constituent data sets, and the comparison thereof in the mode of "world religions," has its roots in theology, as Tomoko Masuzawa has recently shown. And no wonder: "it seems obvious enough that the discourse of world religions takes for granted the idea of 'religion itself' as a 'unique sphere of life,' and that it presumes that this sphere is prevalent throughout the world and its history" (2005: 313).[6]

The irony is embedded in the very category of Religion itself. This is the problem. If we wish to study Religion, we are studying an object that is as theologically constituted as the gods themselves. Religion—and the study thereof—requires Theology for its cogency, just as the field or discipline of Religious Studies continues to require the existence of Theology as an amorphous Other against which to establish our otherwise indeterminate identity. This of course reinforces a deep intimacy between Theology and Religious Studies, an intimacy whose perpetuation has been the only real product of the fruitless "debate" over theological versus non-theological approaches to Religion,[7] a debate that takes place in various registers of key

5. This is precisely why we find in Religious Studies so much effort spent on the naively postulated and politically motivated "reductionism versus non-reductionism" debate, and why, more often than not, "reductionism" is regarded as a "dirty word" that is equated with an anti-religious "'holier-than-thou' self-righteousness" (Dawkins 1982: 113), even though "reductionism" is a scientific virtue (see Sperber 1996: 5–6; cf. Alton 1986).

6. Masuzawa adds: "What is at stake here is far more fundamental than the problem of border violations between historical science and theology; rather it is a question of whether the world religions discourse can be in any way enlisted, and trusted, on the side of historical scholarship" (2005: 326).

7. In the North American context this relationship is controversial and subject to some of the most heated "turf wars"—really a sibling rivalry for privilege on the same turf—in the academy, for which the famous older debate between Canadian scholars Charles Davis and Donald Wiebe continues to set the terms. See Davis 1975, 1981, 1984, 1986; Wiebe 1984, 1988, 1999; Bruce Alton's (1986), Lorne Dawson's (1986), and Hans Penner's (1986) meditations on this exchange and now the thoughtful reflection on the terms of the debate by the Belgian scholar, Lieve Orye (2005). In this debate, for which the Davis–Wiebe exchange is a synecdoche, the core controversy consists of arguments over demarcating or diminishing the line of difference between the study of Religion as a secular, humanistic, social-scientific, even scientific undertaking, and Theology as a confessional, hermeneutic, even ecstatic endeavor. At root it is a purity issue for people such as Donald Wiebe who regard Theology in Religious Studies departments as dirt, as "matter out of place," in Lord Chesterton's terms made famous by Mary Douglas (1984 [1966]: 35, 1975: 50). And it is an issue of tolerance, pluralism for those who argue that

terms.[8] Scholars of Religion fuel and justify their own institutional identity by constantly invoking and then exorcizing the specter of their very condition of possibility: Theology. It is as impossible to end or dismiss the "debate" as it is to resolve it. The issue here is no mere "postmodern" dismissal or dissolution of categories, nor is it, conversely, an effort to reify disciplinary boundaries, or to rule out interdisciplinary analysis of synthetic objects. Rather, the problem is that this *particular* category, this *particular* manner of classifying things, is intrinsically theological and therefore cannot provide any basis for a discussion or analysis of religious objects or data that is genuinely *non*-theological.[9] The question, therefore, of Religious Studies *versus* Theology or Theology *in* Religious Studies is moot. The objects of the classification "Religion"—this canonical text, that ritual, these gods—are, as we contend below, perfectly amenable to humanistic or social-scientific analysis outside the confines of Religion as such, i.e., as independent non-religious objects of various disciplinary investigations. But the *class* of objects so designated is not.[10]

So, let us then in all honesty hand over Religion to them that know what it is, to them that are sure which human productions, performances, affectations

theological inquiry is a sub-discipline of the study of Religion lest the study of Religion becomes an arid, even meaningless effort "wherein there is no ecstasy," as Davis argued (1984).

8. See, for example, Wilken (1989: 700) on how the choice of "prepositions 'of' and 'about' portend a profound redefinition of the subject matter [religion] that requires in turn a new relation between the scholar and the thing studied." Wilken suggests that the preposition "of" entails a relation where the scholar speaks "for" religion in the sense of "on behalf of" or "care for," while the preposition "about" implies an adversarial stance "care against religion," a phrase that Wilken approvingly takes from Wendy Doniger (Doniger O'Flaherty 1986) as semantic shorthand for Enlightenment-inspired critical distance, detachment that excludes love of the thing studied (Wilken 1989: 702). For a defense of "criticism" and criticism of the scholar as "caretaker" see Mack 2001; McCutcheon 2001; Lincoln 1996.

9. We take as axiomatic here that "religion" *eo ipso* is neither a substantive nor a taxonomic "unique beginner." Rather, the *summum genus* that comprises the *arts de faire* of human kind is "culture," i.e., all the data, bar none, that comprise humankind (see Smith 2000: 39). Insofar, and it is usually far indeed, as Religion has been classified as a genus or a species of culture, i.e., has been made an object *of* classification, it is a taxonomic deke, a move that has given disciplinary import to the fact that "Religions... are themselves powerful engines for the production and maintenance of classificatory systems" (Smith 2000: 38). In such cases, that is, the "religious" data themselves have imposed their own taxa onto a disciplinary system to which those taxa are not native.

10. So Asad 1993: 54: "The anthropological student of particular religions should therefore begin from this point, in a sense unpacking the comprehensive concept which he or she translates as 'religion' into heterogeneous elements according to its historical character."

and the like are religious and why "religious" must be *the* descriptive or classifying adjective for a given, or any, human datum. Let us transfer the deed of ownership of Religion to its legitimate disciplinary proprietors, to its epistemological and analytic virtuosi, the religiologists or theologians, be they confessional theologians, world religiologists, aficionados of the universal Sacred, or analysts of a natural *homo religiosus* or *religio eo ipso*. Let them, we say with utter seriousness and with an assist from Ernest Gellner and a sympathetic nod to Charles Davis, "succumb with ecstasy…[to] the difficulty of explicating the Other [Religion]…[and] let them content themselves with elaborating the theme of its inaccessibility, offering a kind of initiation into a Cloud of Unknowing, a Privileged Non-Access…a mystery on its own" (Gellner 1992: 56; cf. Davis 1984). Rudolf Otto and Mircea Eliade and their numerous descendants had and continue to have it right. They did and do in fact own Religion in substance, as a category, and as a discipline. That discipline is Theology. Pleas for the place of Theology in Religious Studies thus are redundant. Since Theology is probably best or at least most productively undertaken in a confessional context, it makes little sense to promote a generalized Theology (= Religion) in secular institutional settings. Dispensing with the study of Religion *qua* Religion in secular universities would block the covert inroads that confessional Theology has made into these secular institutions, most frequently in the form of Religious Studies departments and—for the greatest numbers of students—by means of the Religious Studies introductory course. In principle and in theory the entire designation "Religion" can be and should be left to theologians, obviating any need or justification for Religious Studies departments or courses that introduce students to Religion *qua* Religion in secular academies.

This, however, is not the end of the matter. There is another argument to be made, but it must be an argument that is altogether different from the familiar ones that, by virtue of enduring and regular repetition, have achieved the status of ritual incantations of a difference—of course, a spurious difference, hence no difference at all, as we have suggested—between Theology and Religious Studies.[11] The proposition to be argued, rather, is this: the data that are classified as religious *can* be, indeed *must* be, open to analysis from epistemological vantage points and theoretical commitments, and to disciplinary regimes *other* than those that constitute Religion as Religion and Religion's postulated data as religious, and the religio-theological epistemological and disciplinary practices that are defined by a religious constitution of Religion as an object of study. This *other than* is required by the general humanistic, social-scientific, critical *raison d'etre* of the secular and public

---

11. On "difference" as a politically charged rather than a theoretically justified term in the debates on theological versus non-theological or religious versus non-religious study of Religion, see Smith 1988 and 1997.

academy whose mandate is to generate and disseminate knowledge about and explanations of the material and social world. In other words, conceding Religion to the religio-theologian does not diminish, much less obviate, the general humanistic intellectual mandate to study the religio-theologian's religious objects in terms *other than* how they are classified and often represented, studied, and taught in Religious Studies departments. To theologians may belong the category, the demarcating circle of Religion, but such a concession does *not* imply their exclusive ownership of the stuff—the heterogeneous, quotidian human *arts de faire*[12]—that they may place *in* that circle.

Making intelligible, giving plausible and credible accounts of, the variety of human expressions and representations that, by applying one or another religious criterion, some people name "religious" or "religion" is, must be, part of the data that comprises humankind, data that are no less subject to the scrutiny of the secular academy than any other, putatively *non*-religious, expressions and representations.

Herein, however, lies a second problem that consists of a double neglect. One side of the neglect is that secular universities generally have not been resolutely committed to appropriating (confiscating?) the stuff inside the Religion circle as touchable data in their humanistic and social-scientific disciplines. That is, not only the Religion circle but the stuff inside the circle is systemically ceded to the Religion experts in the secular academy, even, we suspect, when a given university or college has no Religion experts or department. When, on the other hand, "religious" elements of human practice *are* taken up in disciplines such as sociology, anthropology, history, literature, archaeology, and so forth, it is usually done with a disciplinary "failure of nerve."[13] That is, the analysis of "religious" data is not usually done with unflinching adherence to the theoretical principles and methodologies that define these humanistic and social-scientific disciplines, but in *ad hoc* fashion and, more seriously neglectful, with tacit deference to, even reverence for, these elements as theologically pre-positioned elements that stand alone or apart precisely *as* religious. Hence the familiar "*of* Religion" courses— Anthropology *of* Religion, History *of* Religion, Philosophy *of* Religion, Sociology *of* Religion—or "*and* Religion" courses—Literature *and* Religion, Law *and* Religion, Art *and* Religion, Women *and* Religion. Here irony perches on irony, for apparently Theology (= Religion) is allowed comfortable, even if marginal, living space *on Religion's terms* in the secular academy's explicitly secular workshops. Religion is treated as Religion where in theory and disciplinary practice it is quite possible to give intelligible,

---

12. *Arts de faire* is taken from de Certeau 1974; see also Braun 2000: 11–15.

13. This opportunistically, and egregiously, redirects the "failure of nerve" argument made by Donald Wiebe in "The Failure of Nerve in the Academic Study of Religion" (1984; see repr. in this volume).

plausible, and relevant *non*-religious account of items of data contained in the Religion circle.

There remains, therefore, a contingent necessity for the continued existence of religion courses, even Religious Studies departments or programs, in secular academies as a necessarily interdisciplinary (and non-disciplinary) *corrective* to the unselfconsciously theological underpinnings of the concept of Religion in the non-theological disciplines and area studies of the public, secular academy. Indeed, this corrective orientation has been the hallmark of the most useful and theoretically sophisticated work being done by scholars of Religion today.[14] Our characterization of the genealogical and epistemic foundations of Religious Studies and its systematic constitution should not be taken as an indictment of the many scholars in the field using the rubric of Religious Studies as opportunities to work against the grain. Let it be clearly understood, however, that the necessity for work of this sort and for the programs and courses that sustain it is political and provisional, not principled and epistemological. As such, courses in Religion should then become a *contrepoint*, an enunciation that is deliberately set against the grain of the epistemological foundation and disciplinary logic that defines the object of interest and study as *extra* to anything else, as Religion or religious, whether in Religion departments or any other disciplinary precinct in the academy. This, we suggest, truly would be the "irony of Religious Studies"—with a wink at Don Wiebe (1991). In this ironical key, the aim of Religious Studies at the theoretical level is a fundamental deconstruction of its object, Religion. Religious Studies, as we posit its need, plays something like the role of the idiot, the unorthodox fool, to the serious "straight man" in the asymmetrical, uneven double act of Religious Studies in the academy. The introductory course, for example, thus is not a venue for introducing students to Religion or vice versa, but a forum for addressing issues of conceptualization and misconceptualization that have constituted Religion as a stand-alone object, for introducing classificatory thought and systems, for giving accounts of the historical and contemporary conditions that gave rise to and sustain Religious Studies in the secular academy, of the reasons why the academy in general is so resistant to lay hands on its mandate to study the stuff of Religion in non-religious terms.

This conception of the analytic vacuity of Religion as well as especially its consequences for scholarship have already been adumbrated in a celebrated passage from the work of Jonathan Z. Smith:

14. Offering a criticism of the category "religion" in many ways very similar to that suggested here, Timothy Fitzgerald (2000: esp. 12–15) likewise qualifies his criticism by noting that actual departments of Religious Studies and the scholars in these departments have been responsible for the application of non-phenomenological theoretical and disciplinary approaches to "religious" data.

[W]hile there is a staggering amount of data, of phenomena, of human experiences and expressions that might be characterized in one culture or another, by one criterion or another, as religious—*there is no data for religion.* Religion is solely the creation of the scholar's study. It is created for the scholar's analytic purposes by his imaginative acts of comparison and generalization. Religion has no independent existence apart from the academy. For this reason, *the student of religion, and most particularly the historian of religion, must be relentlessly self-conscious. Indeed, this self-consciousness constitutes his primary expertise, his foremost object of study.* (1982: xi, emphasis added)

The point may be pushed even further. As an idea, religion itself is the very embodiment of a failure or refusal to think seriously and rigorously about certain classes of human practice. The study of religion as religion, then, without the self-consciousness of which Smith speaks, is defined by the failure of nerve that Wiebe rightly laments.

References

Alton, Bruce. 1986. "Method and Reduction in the Study of Religions." *Studies in Religion / Sciences religieuses* 15: 153–64.

Arnal, William. 2000. "Definition." In Willi Braun and Russell T. McCutcheon, eds, *Guide to the Study of Religion*, 21–34. London and New York: Cassell.

———. 2001. "The Segregation of Social Desire: 'Religion' and Disney World." *Journal of the American Academy of Religion* 69: 1–19.

Asad, Talal. 1993. "The Construction of Religion as an Anthropological Category." In *Genealogies of Religion: Disciplines and Reasons of Power in Christianity and Islam*, 27–54. Baltimore: Johns Hopkins University Press.

Boyarin, Daniel. 2004. *Border Lines: The Partition of Judaeo-Christianity.* Philadelphia: University of Pennsylvania Press.

Braun, Willi. 2000. "Religion." In Willi Braun and Russell T. McCutcheon, eds, *Guide to the Study of Religion*, 3–18. London and New York: Cassell.

Davis, Charles. 1975. "The Reconvergence of Theology and Religious Studies." *Studies in Religion / Sciences religieuses* 4: 205–21.

———. 1981. "Theology and Religious Studies." *Scottish Journal of Theology* 2: 11–20.

———. 1984. "Wherein There is No Ecstasy." *Studies in Religion / Sciences religieuses* 13: 393–400.

———. 1986. "The Immanence of Knowledge and the Ecstasy of Faith." *Studies in Religion / Sciences religieuses* 15: 191–96.

Dawkins, Richard. 1982. *The Extended Phenotype: The Gene as the Unit of Selection.* San Francisco: Freeman.

Dawson, Lorne. 1986. "Neither Nerve nor Ecstasy: Comment on the Wiebe-Davis Exchange." *Studies in Religion / Sciences religieuses* 15: 145–51.

de Certeau, Michel. 1974. *L'Invention du quotidien.* Vol. 1, *Arts de faire.* Paris: Union générale d'éditions.

Doniger O'Flaherty, Wendy. 1986. "The Uses and Misuses of Other Peoples' Myths." *Journal of the American Academy of Religion* 54: 219–39.

Douglas, Mary. 1984 [1966]. *Purity and Danger: An Analysis of the Concepts of Pollution and Taboo.* London: Ark-Routledge & Kegan Paul.

———. 1975. "Pollution." In *Implicit Meanings*, 47–59. New York: Routledge & Kegan Paul.

Durkheim, Émile. 1968 [1912]. *Les formes élémentaires de la vie religieuse.* 5th edn. Paris: Presses Universitaires de France.

Fitzgerald, Timothy. 2000. *The Ideology of Religious Studies.* Oxford: Oxford University Press.

Gellner, Ernest. 1992. *Postmodernism, Reason and Religion.* London: Routledge.

Lincoln, Bruce. 1996. "Theses on Method." *Method & Theory in the Study of Religion* 8: 225–27.

Mack, Burton. 2001. "Caretakers and Critics: On the Social Role of Scholars Who Study Religion." *Council of Societies for the Study of Religion Bulletin* 30: 32–38.

Masuzawa, Tomoko. 2005. *The Invention of World Religions; Or, How European Universalism Was Preserved in the Language of Pluralism.* Chicago: University of Chicago Press.

McCutcheon, Russell T. 1997. *Manufacturing Religion: The Discourse on Sui Generis Religion and the Politics of Nostalgia.* New York: Oxford University Press.

———. 2001. *Critics Not Caretakers: Redescribing the Public Study of Religion.* Albany: State University of New York Press.

———. 2003. "Autonomy, Unity, and Crisis: Rhetoric and the Invention of a Discipline." In *The Discipline of Religion: Structure, Meaning, Rhetoric*, 54–82. London and New York: Routledge.

Orye, Lieve. 2005. "To Be or Not to Be Scientific is Not the Question: A Science Scholar's Challenge for the Study of Religion." *Council of Societies for the Study of Religion Bulletin* 34: 14–18.

Penner, Hans H. 1986. "Criticism and the Development of a Science of Religion." *Studies in Religion / Sciences religieuses* 15: 165–75.

Pope, Alexander. 1733–34. *An Essay on Man.* 4 vols. London. Facs. ed. Menston: Scholars Press, 1969.

Smith, Jonathan Z. 1982. *Imagining Religion: From Babylon to Jonestown.* Chicago: University of Chicago Press.

———. 1988. "'Religion' and 'Religious Studies': No Difference at All." *Soundings* 71: 231–44.

———. 1997. "Are Theological and Religious Studies Compatible?" *Bulletin of the Council of Societies for the Study of Religion* 26: 60–61.

———. 2000. "Classification." In Willi Braun and Russell T. McCutcheon, eds, *Guide to the Study of Religion*, 35–44. London: Cassell.

———. 2004. "Religion, Religions, Religious." In *Relating Religion: Essays in the Study of Religion*, 179–96. Chicago: University of Chicago Press.

Sperber, Dan. 1996. *Explaining Culture: A Naturalistic Approach.* London: Blackwell.

Wiebe, Donald. 1984. "The Failure of Nerve in the Academic Study of Religion." *Studies in Religion / Sciences religieuses* 13: 401–22.

———. 1988. "Why the Academic Study of Religion? Motive and Method in the Study of Religion." *Studies in Religion / Sciences religieuses* 17: 403–13.

———. 1991. *The Irony of Theology and the Nature of Religious Thought.* Montreal and Kingston: McGill-Queen's University Press.

———. 1999. *The Politics of Religious Studies.* New York: St. Martin's Press.

Wilken, Robert, L. 1989. "Who Will Speak *for* the Religious Traditions?" [American Academy of Religion 1989 Presidential Address]. *Journal of the American Academy of Religion* 57: 699–717.

INDEX OF AUTHORS

Abou El Fadl, K. 142, 144
Adams, E. 160, 175
Alexander, P. S. 181, 189
Allison, D. C. 184, 189
Allport, G. W. 70, 73
Althusser, L. 55, 60
Altizer, T. J. J. 23, 27
Alton, B. 232, 237
Anderson, C. P. 150, 156
Andresen, J. 80, 92
Ano, G. G. 71, 75
Apostolos-Cappadona, D. 216, 226
Armelagos, G. 157, 175
Armstrong, K. 119, 127
Arnal, W. E. 51, 60, 69, 72, 73, 123, 126,
    127, 153, 156, 160, 173, 175, 177–80,
    184–86, 189, 200, 214, 231, 237
Arnold, J. 45–47
Aron, R. 24, 27
Asad, T. 40, 42, 47, 69, 73, 121, 127, 231,
    233, 237

Baasten, M. F. J. 124, 127
Bal, M. 52, 60
Banerjee, P. 55, 60
Barrett, J. L. 63, 73, 80, 92
Barthes, R. 41, 47, 55, 60
Baum, G. 22, 27
Baumeister, R. F. 70, 74
Beinin, J. 136, 144
Beit-Hallahmi, B. 62, 73
Belavich, T. G. 71, 77
Bell, R. 115, 116, 127
Bellah, R. N. 23, 27
Belzen, J. A. 63, 67, 71, 73
Benedict, P. 98, 108
Berg, H. 112, 114, 127
Besançon, A. 216, 221
Bleeker, C. J. 13, 15, 27
Bloch, M. 92, 211–14
Bloor, D. 41, 47
Blumenthal, D. R. 16, 20, 27
Blundell, M. 204, 215
Boettcher, S. 96, 99, 108
Bolle, K. W. 18, 19, 27

Bossy, J. 102, 108
Bourdieu, P. 41, 47
Boyarin, D. 181, 186, 189, 231, 237
Boyer, P. 36, 47, 63, 73, 80, 92, 150, 156
Braun, W. 113, 127, 235, 237
Brenon, A. 45, 47
Bricmont, J. 41, 48
Brown, S. 206, 215
Bruce, F. F. 195, 201, 215
Bruner, J. 67, 73
Burke, T. 108
Burkert, W. 26, 27, 212, 215
Burkle, H. R. 20, 27
Burmeister, K. 106, 108
Burnett, A. N. 102, 108
Burrell, D. 17, 28
Butter, E. M. 71, 77

Callon, C. 198, 216
Campbell, M. 150, 156
Capps, W. H. 23, 28
Carrette, J. 64, 65, 67, 70–74
Chancey, M. A. 180, 189
Cherry, C. 101, 108
Chidester, D. 89, 92
Cho, F. 63, 74
Coe, G. A. 62, 69, 74
Cohen, S. J. D. 181, 189
Cole, B. 71, 77
Collins, J. 207, 215
Cook, M. 117, 118, 127
Cromhout, M. 180, 185, 189
Crone, P. 117, 118, 127
Crossan, J. D. 193, 199, 209–11, 215
Crum, J. M. C. 179, 189

Danziger, K. 65, 67, 68, 70, 74
Davies, S. 194, 201, 215
Davis, C. 8–10, 13, 22, 24, 28, 232–34, 237
Dawkins, R. 232, 237
Dawson, C. 11, 28
Dawson, L. 232, 237
Day, M. 35, 42, 47
de Blois, F. 124, 127
de Certeau, M. 235, 237

Desjardins, M. 200, 202, 215
de Vries, J. 11, 31
Dicker, H. I. 70, 74
Dixon, C. S. 102, 109
Doniger O'Flaherty, W. 233, 237
Donner, F. M. 120–22, 141, 145
Doran, R. 195, 215
Douglas, M. 217, 225, 232, 237
Draper, J. A. 190
Dreger, A. 35, 47
Drobin, K. U. 13, 28
Drummond, R. H. 6, 7, 19, 28
Duggan, L. 102, 109
Dunn, J. D. G. 181, 189
Durkheim, E. 36, 48, 217, 218, 231, 238

Edsman, C.-M. 6, 22, 28
Ehrman, B. D. 181, 183, 189
Eliade, M. 20, 28
Engels, D. 160, 175
Ernst, C. W. 140, 141, 145

Farb, P. 157, 175
Farrer, A. M. 177, 189
Faulkner, J. A. 159, 175
Fetzer, K. A. 103, 109
Fisher, A. J. 98, 109
Fitzgerald, T. 35, 48, 64, 74, 96, 100, 104,
    109, 236, 238
Flew, A. 10, 28
Ford, R. 195, 196, 215
Förstemann, E. G. 103, 109
Foucault, M. 41, 42, 48, 68, 74, 208, 215
Freed, E. D. 181, 189
Friedrichs, R. W. 11, 28
Fry, L. W. 72, 74
Funk, R. W. 179, 189, 192, 196–98, 215

Galloway, A. D. 22, 28
Garnsey, P. 171, 175
Gay, P. 7, 28
Geertz, A. W. 80, 88, 92, 134, 145
Geertz, C. 36, 48
Geiger, A. 115, 127
Gellner, E. 234, 238
Geyer, A. L. 70, 74
Giacolone, R. A. 72, 74
Gibson, E. L. 208, 209, 216
Ginzberg, C. 46, 48
Girard, R. 212, 215
Girardot, Norman J. 20, 28
Given, T. 45, 48
Goodacre, M. 177, 189

Goodenough, E. R. 11, 28
Görke, A. 122, 127
Gorusch, R. L. 70, 75
Goulder, M. D. 177, 189
Grant, R. 195, 215
Gregory, J. P. 80, 92
Greyerz, K. von 100, 109
Gaultieri, A. R. 6, 25, 28
Guthrie, S. 36, 48

Haag, N. 99, 109
Habermas, J. 41, 48
Hall, G. S. 62, 69, 74
Hanson, J. 195, 216
Harnack, A. von 179, 189
Harrington, J. 99, 109
Harris, M. 155, 156
Harris, S. L. 181, 189
Harrison, P. 35, 48,
Hart, D. G. 101, 109
Hawley, J. S. 57, 58, 60
Hawting, G. R. 125, 127, 141, 145
Headley, J. M. 98, 99, 109
Hebblethwaite, B. 6, 22, 28
Hedrick, C. 192, 194, 197–99, 207, 215
Heelas, P. 64, 72, 74
Henking, S. E. 66, 74
Hill, P. C. 70, 74
Hillerbrand, H. J. 98, 99, 109
Hipp, K. M. 71, 77
Hirschfeld, H. 115, 127
Holderage, B. 42, 48
Holley, R. 18, 28
Hook, S. 7, 28
Hoover, R. W. 179, 189, 192, 196–98, 215
Horowitz, D. 137, 145
Horrell, D. G. 160, 175
Horsley, R. A. 177, 179, 180, 185, 186, 190,
    195, 200, 204, 205, 209, 215
Horvath, T. 23, 31
Hsia, R. P.-C. 99, 109
Hudson, R. A. 90, 93
Hughes, A. W. 114, 127, 130, 136, 142,
    143, 145
Hume, D. 35, 48

Ingram, P. O. 23, 28
Institoris, H. 60

Jacobson, A. D. 177, 190
Jakubowsky-Tiessen, M. 100, 109
James, W. 62, 69, 70, 74
Jastrow Jr., M. 11, 13, 28

Jay, N. 52, 56, 61
Jeffner, A. 19, 28
Jeremias, J. 195, 216
Jurkewicz, C. L. 72, 74
Juschka, D. M. 56, 61

Kadar, J. L. 71, 77
Kahoe, R. D. 70, 74
Kauffmann, T. 100, 109
Kaufman, G. D. 16, 29
Kaufmann, T. 98, 109
Kegley, C. W. 16–18, 29
Kelley, B. S. 71, 75
Kennedy, C. A. 171, 175
Kershaw, S. 91, 93
Khan, L. A. 118, 119, 128
King, R. 35, 48, 64, 72, 74, 75
Kirk, A. 179, 190
Kitagawa, J. M. 7, 11, 13, 19, 20, 29
Kloppenborg (Verbin), J. S. 177, 179,
    183–85, 190, 198, 201, 205, 206,
    216
Klostermaier, K. K. 10, 11, 29
Klueting, H. 99, 109
Koerner, J. L. 96, 109
Koester, H. 181, 183, 190, 191, 197, 216
Kramer, M. S. 136, 145
Kristensen, W. B. 15, 29

Ladner, B. 17, 18, 29
Lang, P. T. 102, 110
Largier, N. 103, 109
Lawson, E. T. 63, 75, 79, 93
Leclerq, J. 29
Lederer, D. 99, 109
Lehmann, H. 100, 109
Leuba, J. 62, 69, 75
Lévi-Strauss, C. 59, 61, 161–63, 169, 175
Lincoln, B. 40, 48, 53, 59, 61, 119, 128,
    137, 145, 183, 184, 190, 210, 216,
    221, 238
Lindemann, A. 179, 180, 190
Lings, M. 119, 128
Lintott, A. 204, 216
Llewelyn, S. R. 184, 190
Lockman, Z. 137, 145
Lopez, D. S. 69, 75
Lott, T. 35, 48
Lotz-Heumann, U. 96–99, 109
Lührmann, D. 177, 180, 190
Luxenberg, C. 124, 128

Mack, B. 78, 93, 112, 128, 160, 161, 166,
    167, 175, 179, 181, 184, 185, 190, 200,
    216, 233, 238
Malina, B. 203, 216
Mani, L. 57, 58, 61
Manji, I. 131, 132, 145
Martin, J. A. 20, 29
Martin, L. H. 72, 75
Martin, R. C. 140, 141, 145
Marty, M. 17, 29
Marx, K. 43, 47, 48
Masuzawa, T. 64, 75, 107, 109, 150, 156,
    231, 232, 238
Matthews, S. 208, 209, 216
McCarthy Brown, K. 150, 156
McCauley, R. N. 63, 75, 79, 93
McClelland, J. C. 7, 24, 29
McCutcheon, R. T. 51, 52, 61, 64, 75, 78,
    84, 85, 87, 89, 93, 122, 128, 217, 218, 232,
    233, 238
McNamara, P. 80, 93
Meland, B. E. 18, 29
Melchert, C. 141, 145
Meyer, P. D. 179, 190
Michaelson, R. 24, 29
Miller, L. 71, 75
Monaghan, P. 89, 91, 93
Morgan, R. 10, 29
Mostert, J. P. 7, 17, 19, 29
Moxnes, H. 180, 190, 213, 216
Müller, F. M. 15, 29, 113, 114, 121, 128,
    149, 156
Murphy, T. 66, 67, 70, 75, 89, 93
Murray, G. 7, 29

Nelson, B. 8, 29
Neufeldt, R. W. 17, 30
Neusner, J. 11, 17, 23, 30, 113, 128, 181,
    186, 190, 191
Neuwirth, A. 119, 124, 128
Nicholls, W. 150, 156
Nietzsche, F. 41, 48
Nischan, B. 99, 110
Novak, M. 17, 30

O'Connell, L. J. 21, 30
Ogden, S. M. 11, 30
Oman, D. 71, 75
Omer, A. 78, 79, 91, 93
Orsi, R. 42, 48
Orye, L. 104, 110, 232, 238

Oxtoby, W. G. 13, 14, 16, 30
Ozment, S. E. 99, 110
Ozorak, E. W. 63, 75

Paloutzian, R. F. 62, 63, 75
Pannenberg, W. 6, 8, 21, 30
Papalas, A. J. 98, 99, 109
Pargament, K. I. 71, 75, 77
Park, C. L. 62, 63, 75
Parrish, J. W. 160, 173, 175
Pearson, B. 196, 216
Penner, H. H. 232, 238
Perrin, N. 181, 191
Peters, F. E. 119, 128
Peterson, D. C. 119, 128
Piper, R. A. 179, 191
Pipes, D. 133, 135, 145
Ponton, M. O. 70, 75
Pope, A. 230, 238
Powell, E. 177, 191
Powers, D. S. 141, 145
Preus, J. S. 105, 110
Puff, H. 99, 110
Pye, M. 10, 29

Radin, P. 161, 163, 175
Raschke, C. A. 7, 30
Reat, N. R. 20, 30
Reed, J. L. 179, 191
Rein, N. 101, 103, 110
Ricketts, M. L. 20, 28
Riley, G. 194, 216
Riley, P. B. 8, 24, 30
Rittgers, R. K. 102, 110
Robinson, J. M. 179, 183, 191
Rollens, S. E. 112, 114, 127
Roof, W. C. 64, 72, 75
Roper, L. 99, 110
Rose, N. 65, 68, 70–72, 76
Rubin, G. 59, 61
Rye, M. S. 71, 77

Safi, O. 131, 132, 141, 142, 145, 146
Sahlins, P. 167–69, 175
Said, E. 113, 128, 136, 150, 156
Sanders, E. P. 184, 185, 191
Sato, M. 179, 191
Saussure, F. de 54, 61
Schiffman, L. H. 181, 191
Schilling, H. 99, 110
Schimmel, A. M. 12, 30
Schoeler, G. 122, 123, 127, 128

Schopen, G. 35, 48, 104, 110
Schwartz, S. 131, 133, 134, 146
Scott, A. B. 71, 77
Scott, B. B. 193, 197, 211, 216
Sebeok, T. A. 54, 61
Seel, B. 74
Segal, A. F. 181, 191
Sen, M. 57, 61
Sered, S. S. 52, 61
Serjeant, R. B. 118, 119, 128
Sharpe, E. J. 6, 7, 11–13, 30
Shaw, B. 205, 216
Shklovsky, V. 157, 175
Shweder, R. A. 67, 76
Silberman, I. 70, 76
Simmons, G. Z. 142, 146
Slater, P. 23, 31
Slingerland, E. 63, 76
Sloan, J. 37, 48
Slone, D. J. 80, 93
Smart, N. 6, 8, 30
Smith, H. W. 99, 109
Smith, J. Z. 35, 48, 51, 61, 64, 76, 106,
　　110, 157, 158, 160–64, 167, 175, 176,
　　184, 191, 199, 210, 216, 231, 233,
　　234, 237, 238
Smith, W. B. 102, 110
Smith, W. C. 15, 22, 30, 150
Sokal, A. 41, 48
Sperber, D. 36, 49, 81, 93, 232, 238
Sprenger, J. 56, 60
Squier, R. K. 63, 74
Staden, H. 107, 110
Starbuck, E. D. 62, 69, 76
Stowers, S. K. 160, 166, 170–73, 176
Strauss, G. 99, 110
Streng, F. J. 10, 20, 30
Strenski, I. 101, 110
Stroker, W. 193, 194, 216
Szerszynski, B. 74

Taira, T. 88, 93
Taves, A. 69, 76, 79, 93
Theil, S. 124, 128
Theissen, G. 164, 165, 176, 186, 191
Thorensen, C. E. 71, 75
Tillich, P. 20, 30
Tite, P. 202, 216
Tuckett, C. 179, 188, 191
Turner, V. 56, 61
Tusting, K. 74
Tweed, T. 150, 156

Vaage, L. E. 178, 179, 183, 185, 191
Valantasis, R. 195, 217
Vernoff, C. 20, 31
Volavka, J. 90, 94

Waardenburg, J. 16, 31, 34, 49
Wach, J. 11, 20, 31
Wacholtz, A. B. 71, 75
Wansbrough, J. 117, 129
Warner, M. 152, 156
Watt, W. M. 115, 116, 129
Weedon, C. 53, 55, 61
Werblowsky, R. J. Z. 6, 12, 13, 31
Whitehouse, H. 36, 49, 63, 76, 87, 94
Widengren, G. 15, 31
Wiebe, D. 2, 3, 5, 6, 8, 13–15, 19, 23, 25,
   26, 31, 34, 37–39, 49, 62, 66, 76, 78, 83,
   92, 94, 95, 97, 102, 103, 110, 112, 113,

115–17, 119, 121, 125, 126, 129, 146, 150,
   156, 182, 187, 191, 192, 217, 218, 231,
   232, 235, 236, 238
Wiebe, P. G. 22, 31
Wilken, R. L. 233, 238
Williams, R. 50, 61
Wilson, S. G. 181, 191
Winterhalter, R. 194, 217
Wiredu, K. 86, 94
Wiseman, J. 160, 176
Wolfart, J. C. 102, 110
Woodhead, L. 64, 72, 74
Wulff, D. M. 62, 67, 69, 70, 76
Wundt, W. M. 62, 69, 77

Zeeden, E. W. 102, 110
Zimmermann, M. 203, 205, 217
Zinnbauer, B. J. 71, 77

CPSIA information can be obtained
at www.ICGtesting.com
Printed in the USA
LVHW101421171218
600747LV00009B/325/P

9 781138 110205